PROPHETS AND GRAVESTONES

WILLIAM TABBERNEE

PROPHETS AND GRAVESTONES

AN IMAGINATIVE HISTORY OF MONTANISTS AND OTHER EARLY CHRISTIANS

Prophets and Gravestones: An Imaginative History of Montanists and Other Early Christians

P. O. Box 3473
Peabody, Massachusetts 01961-3473

ISBN 978-1-56563-937-9

Printed in the United States of America

First Printing—May 2009

Cover Art: The cover reproduces the gravestone of Frankios, a young Montanist from Clusium, dating from about 412 C.E.; the remains of Roman aqueduct near the ruins of the ancient city of Pepouza in modern day Turkey; and a mosaic portrait from Ravenna of St. Perpetua, decorating the archiepiscopal chapel built ca. 500 C.E.

Photo Credits: William Tabbernee

Library of Congress Cataloging-in-Publication Data

Tabbernee, William, 1944–
Prophets and gravestones : an imaginative history of Montanists and other early Christians / William Tabbernee.
p. cm.
Includes bibliographical references (p.) and indexes.
ISBN 978-1-56563-937-9 (alk. paper)
1. Montanism. I. Title.
BT1435.T34 2009
273′.1—dc22

2008055319

To Ammamina, Maximilla, Priscilla, Perpetua, Quintilla, and Nanas:
Women whose courageous Christian faith, deep spirituality, and
prophetic vision transcend the vagaries of history.

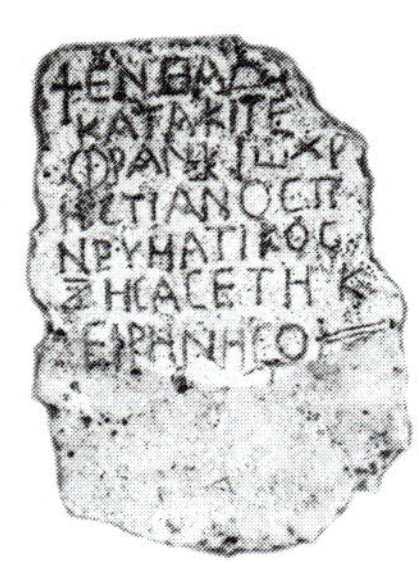

Contents

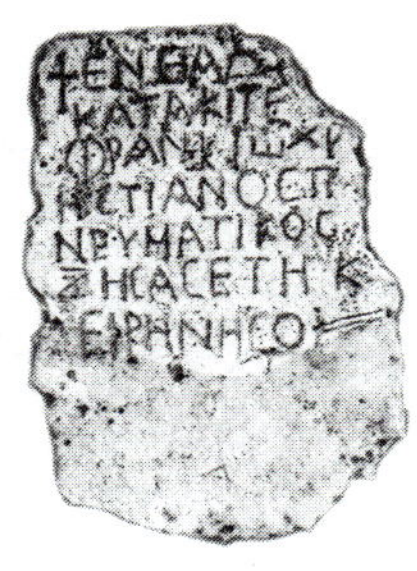

Maps and Figures

Maps

Photographs and Drawings

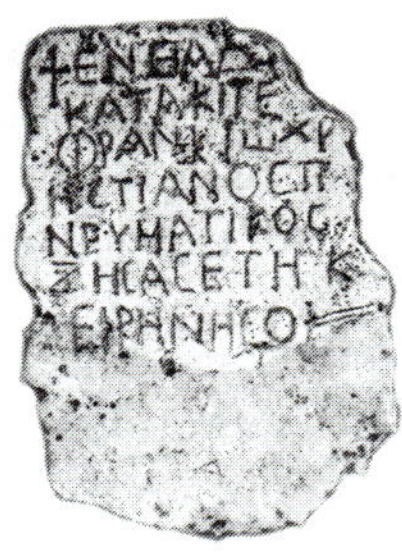

Preface

This book was begun in October 2001 during the first archaeological field campaign conducted at the site of ancient Pepouza in western Turkey. The previous year, in July 2000, an international team of scholars, which I led, had discovered the long-lost site. Having subsequently received official permission from the Turkish Directorate General of Monuments and Museums to conduct an archaeological surface survey of Pepouza and its vicinity, we were very excited and eager to see what, if anything, remained of Montanism's most holy city.

Not surprisingly, few of the archaeologists, land surveyors, geophysicists, geomorphologists, archaeological architects, and other experts who joined us in the field in 2001 knew very much, if anything, about Montanism, or the "New Prophecy" as it was originally called. As I began to tell my new colleagues about the fascinating stories of the Montanists who had lived and practiced their unique form of Christianity in the very places which we were now exploring archaeologically, they became more and more intrigued. Soon I began writing the chapters which comprise this narrative history and reading them aloud, a couple at a time, to small groups of the team. For the next five seasons, such reading became enjoyable after-dinner events, following a hard day's work in the field.

I am grateful for the feedback I received from my "Pepouza team" colleagues about the early drafts of many of the chapters in this book. Those who do indeed know at lot about Montanism, Peter Lampe, Vera Hirschmann, and Robert Jewett, provided an expert "sounding board" for my "judgment calls" about particular reconstructions of historical events. Their occasional peels of laughter at certain of my descriptions of people and events suggested that this narrative history of Montanism would, indeed, be a fun book for people to read—as well as be informative for those just learning about Montanism. The appreciative comments from the "*non-Montanist* experts" on the "Pepouza team," in particular Richard Petrovszky, Bärbel Hanemann, Reinhard Stupperich, Ayşe Çalık-Ross, Richard Engle, David and Donna Killen, and Hüsam Süleymangil, confirmed this assessment and encouraged me to complete the project by writing a comprehensive narrative history of Montanism throughout the whole Roman Empire, not just the history of Montanism in its homeland Phrygia.

The history of Montanism has been a passionate interest of mine for more than four decades. My knowledge about and understanding of the New Prophecy movement has been enriched over those many years by numerous teachers, colleagues, and friends. I especially wish to acknowledge a debt of gratitude to William Culican, Graeme Clarke, Jaroslav Pelikan, Rowan Greer, Timothy Barnes, Edwin Judge, William Frend, Greg Horsley, Turid Karlsen Seim, Susanna Elm, Maureen Tilley, Daniel Williams, Ronald Heine, Christine Trevett, Stephen Mitchell, Alistair Stewart-Sykes, and Andrew McGowan.

Kay Northcutt read the whole manuscript, and her constant reminders to allow the reader not only to see images but to employ all their senses as they imagine the people and events being narrated improved every chapter. As always, my other colleagues at Phillips Theological Seminary were extremely supportive of this writing project. I am especially grateful to the board of trustees of Phillips Theological Seminary and to Chester Cadieux, the chair of the board, for granting me sabbatical leave to complete this book.

Victoria Fischel was the research assistant for this project, and I am thankful to her and to Sandy Shapoval and Clair Powers, the director and reference librarian, respectively, of the Phillips Theological Seminary Library, for their help in obtaining all the relevant bibliographic material needed to make this book not only "fun to read," but useful to scholars and students.

Julia Chastain, my secretary, carefully typed and re-typed the various drafts of this narrative history—as she has typed the manuscripts of all my other work on Montanism for more than seventeen years. It is more than a coincidence that "Linus," one of the cats in Chapter 7, bears the name not only of one of the early bishops of Rome but also that of one of Julia's own beloved cats.

Richard Engle prepared the maps in this book, including the site maps of Pepouza and its vicinity. Kris Vculek produced the line-drawings of the various inscriptions. All the photographs which illustrate this book are my own.

I am grateful to James Ernest, formerly an editor with Hendrickson, for his encouragement throughout the conceptual stage of this project and to Shirley Decker-Lucke, editorial director at Hendrickson, for her expert editorial advice. Her work and that of Allan Emery, Sara Scott, and the production staff at Hendrickson have made this an exceptionally beautiful book.

William Tabbernee

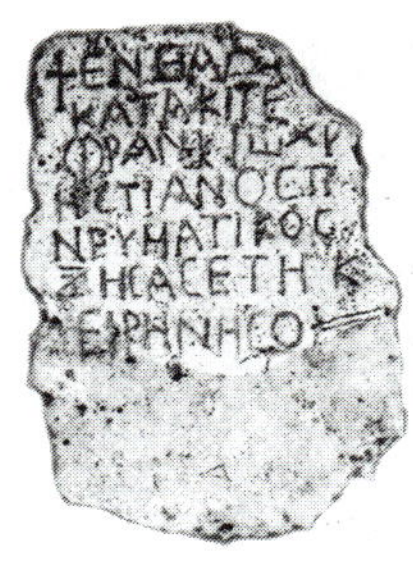

Timeline

Date	Emperor	Major Christian Personalities*
	Augustus (27 B.C.E.–14 C.E.)	
14	Tiberius (14–37 C.E.)	
37	Caligula (37–41)	
54	Nero (54–68)	
64		Peter and Paul (bishops of Rome?) (d. ca. 64)
		Linus of Rome (date uncertain)
81	Domitian (81–96)	
		Anonyma ("Jezebel") (*flor.* ca. 90)
98	Trajan (98–117)	
110		Ignatius of Antioch (*flor.* ca. 110)
117	Hadrian (117–138)	
120		Papias of Hierapolis (*flor.* ca. 120)
138	Antoninus Pius (138–161)	
		Ammia (prophetess at Philadelphia; *flor.* ca. 150)
		Quadratus (prophet; *flor.* ca. 150)
155		Anicetus of Rome (ca. 155–ca. 166)
		Quintus (apostate at Smyrna) (ca. 155/6)
		Polycarp of Smyrna (d. ca. 155/6)
160		Thraseas of Eumeneia (*flor.* ca. 160)
		Marcion (d. ca. 160)
		Philomena (*flor.* ca. 160)
		Apelles (*flor.* ca. 160)
161	Marcus Aurelius (161–180)	
		Justin Martyr (d. ca. 165)
		Montanus (*flor.* ca. 165)
		Maximilla (*flor.* ca. 165)
		Priscilla (*flor.* ca. 165)

*Montanists shown in bold type. The dates provided for the persons listed are the dates during which a given emperor ruled and the dates of known active ministry or work for Major Christian Personalities. The birth and death dates are provided, when significant, in the endnotes.

Date	Emperor	Major Christian Personalities
166		Sagaris of Laodikeia (d. ca. 166)
		Soter of Rome (ca. 166–ca. 174/5)
170		Ammia and Asklepios (Christians in Hierapolis; d. ca. 170)
		Aelius Publius Julius of Develtum (*flor.* ca. 170)
		Aurelius Quirinus [Phrygian bishop?] (*flor.* ca. 170)
		Melito of Sardis (*flor.* ca. 170)
		Papirius [Asian bishop?] (d. ca. 170)
		Sotas of Anchialos (*flor.* ca. 170)
		Apolinarius of Hierapolis (*flor.* ca. 170)
174		Eleutherus of Rome (ca. 174/5–ca. 189)
175		**Theodotus** (*flor.* ca. 175)
		Themiso (*flor.* ca. 175)
177		Potheinos of Lyons (d. ca. 177)
		The martyrs of Lyons (d. ca. 177)
		Irenaeus of Lyons (ca. 177–200)
178		Julian of Apameia (*flor.* ca. 178)
		Zotikos of Konana (*flor.* ca. 178)
180	Commodus (180–192)	
		Asterius Urbanus (*flor.* ca. 185)
189		Demetrius of Alexandria (ca. 189–ca. 231/2)
		Victor I of Rome (ca. 189–198/9)
190		Avircius Marcellus [bishop of Hieropolis] (*flor.* ca. 190)
		Miltiades (*flor.* ca. 190)
		Polycrates of Ephesus (*flor.* ca. 190)
		Praxeas (*flor.* ca. 190)
192		Anonymous [bishop of one of the cities of the Phrygian Pentapolis?] (*flor.* ca. 192)
		Zotikos of Otrous (*flor.* ca. 192)
193	Septimius Severus (193–211)	
198		Zephyrinus of Rome (ca. 198/9–217)
199		Serapion of Antioch (ca. 199–211)
200		**Alexander** (*flor.* ca. 200)
		Anonyma [Montanist prophetess at Pepouza] (*flor.* ca. 200)
		Gaius (*flor.* ca. 200)
		Proclus (*flor.* ca. 200)
		Aeschines (*flor.* ca. 200)

Date	Emperor	Major Christian Personalities
		Artemidoros [Montanist bishop at Temenothyrai] (*flor.* ca. 200)
		Clement of Alexandria (ca. 140/50–ca. 220)
203		Optatus of Carthage (*flor.* ca. 203)
		Perpetua and Felicitas (d. ca. 203)
205		**Diogas** [Montanist bishop at Temenothyrai] (*flor.* ca. 205)
		Ammion [Montanist woman presbyter at Temenothyrai] (d. ca. 205)
		Apollonius (*flor.* ca. 205)
208		**Tertullian** (ca. 160–ca. 220)
209		**Anonyma** (Montanist prophetess at Carthage) (*flor.* ca. 209)
		Anonyma (second Montanist prophetess at Carthage) (*flor.* ca. 209)
210		Agrippinus of Carthage (*flor.* ca. 210)
211	Geta (211) and Caracalla (211–217)	
216		Theoctistus of Caesarea [Syria Palaestina] (216–258)
217		Callistus of Rome (ca. 217–ca. 222)
		Atticus of Synnada (*flor.* pre-218)
		Celsus of Ikonion (*flor.* pre-218)
		Neon of Laranda (*flor.* pre-218)
222	Alexander Severus (222–235)	Alexander of Jerusalem (222–251)
223		Aurelius Gaius (*flor.* ca. 223) and Aurelia Stratoneikiane (d. ca. 223)
230		Firmilian of Caesarea [Cappadocia] (ca. 230–268)
235		**Anonyma** [Montanist? prophetess at Caesarea in Cappadocia] (*flor.* ca. 235/6)
238		Gregory Thaumaturgus [bishop of Neocaesarea in Pontus] (ca. 238–ca. 270/5)
240		Origen (ca. 185–ca. 253)
		Ambrose (Origen's patron) (*flor.* ca. 240)
244	Philip (244–249)	
248		Cyprian of Carthage (ca. 248/9–258)
249	Decius (249–251)	
250		Euctemon [bishop? of Smyrna] (*flor.* ca. 250)

Date	Emperor	Major Christian Personalities
		Karpos [Montanist? bishop of Julia Gordos in Lydia and martyr] (d. ca. 251)
		Agathonike and **Papylos** [Montanist? martyrs] (d. ca. 251)
		Novatian [Novatianist bishop of Rome] (ca. 251–ca. 257/8)
253	Gallienus (253–268)	**Moundane** and **Severos** (d. 253)
270	Aurelian (270–275)	
284	Diocletian (284–305)	
303		Agapius of Caesarea [Palaestina] (ca. 303–ca. 312/3)
304		**Thecla and her companions** (*flor.* 304)
305	Galerius (305–311)	**Quintilla** [Montanist prophetess at Pepouza] (*flor.* ca. 305?)
307	Constantine I (307–337)	
310	Maximin II Daia (310–313)	
312		**Theodotus** [Montanist? bishop? at Ankyra] (d. ca. 312)
		Severus [Novatianist bishop of Laodikeia Katakekaumene] (d. ca. 312/13)
313		Eusebius of Caesarea [Palaestina] (ca. 313–ca. 339/40)
		Marcus Julius Eugenius [Montanist/ Novatianist bishop of Laodikeia Katakekaumene] (ca. 313/5–ca. 340)
320		Pachomius (ca. 290–346)
328		Athanasius of Alexandria (328–373)
330		Eusebius of Nikomedia [archbishop of Constantinople from 339] (330–341/2)
337	Constantius II (337–361)	
348		Cyril of Jerusalem (ca. 348/9–386/7)
349		Paulinus of Trier [ancient Augusta Treverorum] (349–358)
350		**Hermogenes** (*flor.* ca. 350)
		Nanas [Montanist prophetess in Phrygian Highlands] (*flor.* ca. 350)
353		Hilary of Poitiers (ca. 353–367)
361		Aetius [Arian bishop of Antioch] (ca. 361/3–ca. 367)
362		Paulinus of Antioch (362–388)
366		Damasus I of Rome (ca. 366–384)

Date	Emperor	Major Christian Personalities
367		Epiphanius of Salamis (ca. 367–ca. 403/5)
370		Basil of Caesarea [Cappadocia] (370–379)
379	Theodosius I (379–395)	
		Didymus the Blind (ca. 310/13–ca. 398)
		Jerome (ca. 347–419)
		Marcella (*flor.* ca. 387)
385		**Anonymous** [Montanist teacher at Rome] (*flor.* ca. 385)
387		Paula (*flor.* ca. 387)
		Eustochium (*flor.* ca. 387)
395	Honorius (395–423) and Arcadius (395–402)	Augustine of Hippo (395–430)
398		John I Chrysostom [archbishop of Constantinople] (398–407)
400		**Alexander** [Montanist *pneumatikos*] (*flor.* ca. 400)
402		Innocent I of Rome (402–417)
407		**Frankios** [Montanist *pneumatikos*] (*flor.* ca. 407)
425		**Neikandros** [Montanist bishop of Kyzikos and *pneumatikos*] (*flor.* ca. 425)
450		**Eugenios** [Montanist? archdeacon at Hierapolis] (*flor.* ca. 450)
		Gennaios [Montanist? patriarch of Pepouza?] (*flor.* ca. 450)
500		**Paul** [Montanist *koinōnos*] (*flor.* ca. 500)
		Stephania (*flor.* ca. 500)
510		**Trophimos** [Montanist apostle from Pepouza] (d. 510)
515		**Praÿlios** [Montanist *koinōnos*] (d. 515)
518	Justin I (518–527)	
527	Justinian I (527–565)	
550		John of Amida/Asia [Monophysite bishop of Ephesus from 558] (*flor.* ca. 550)
717	Leo III (717–741)	
787		Euthymius [abbott of Byzantine monastery at Pepouza] (*flor.* 787)
		Theophylactus [senior monk at Pepouza] (*flor.* 787)

Map 1: The Roman Empire

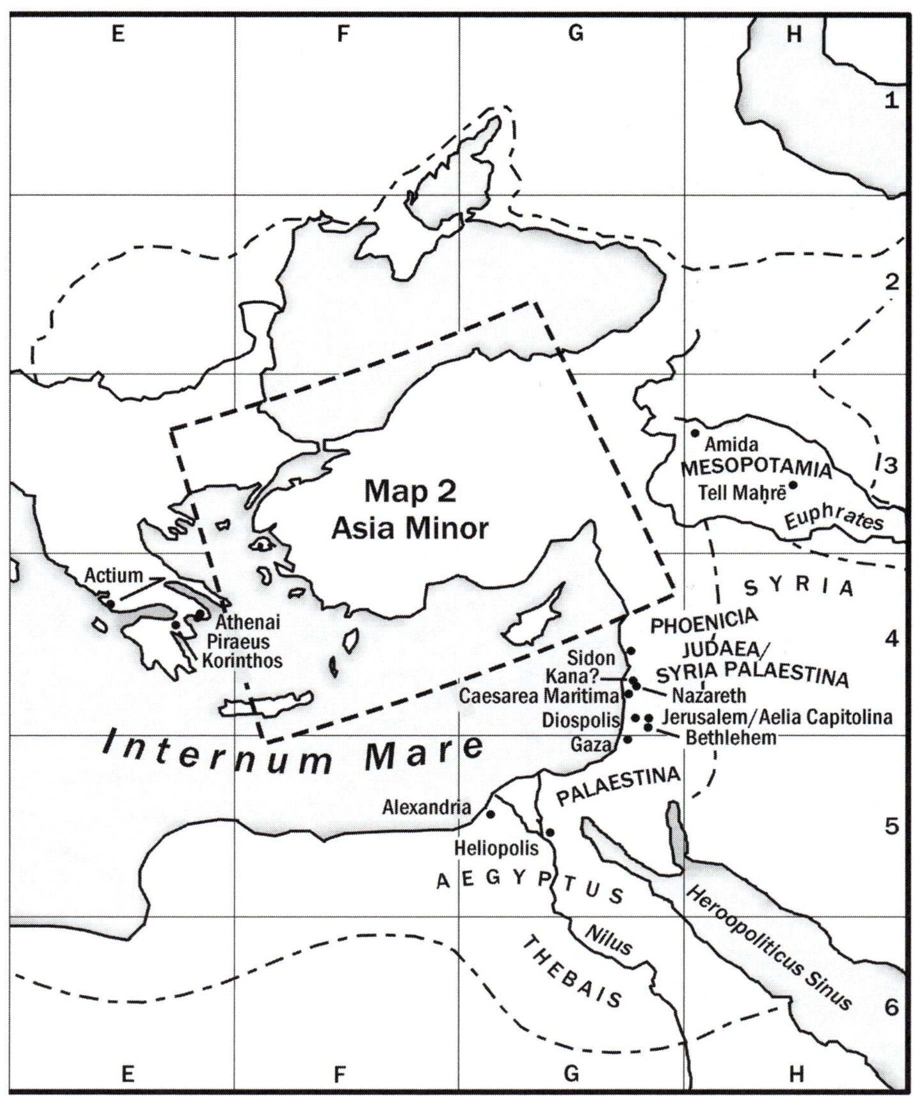
E
F
G
H
1
2
3
4
5
6
Map 2
Asia Minor
Amida
MESOPOTAMIA
Tell Maḥrē
Euphrates
SYRIA
PHOENICIA
JUDAEA/
SYRIA PALAESTINA
Actium
Athenai
Piraeus
Korinthos
Sidon
Kana?
Caesarea Maritima
Nazareth
Diospolis
Jerusalem/Aelia Capitolina
Gaza
Bethlehem
Internum Mare
PALAESTINA
Alexandria
Heliopolis
AEGYPTUS
Nilus
THEBAIS
Heroopoliticus Sinus
E
F
G
H

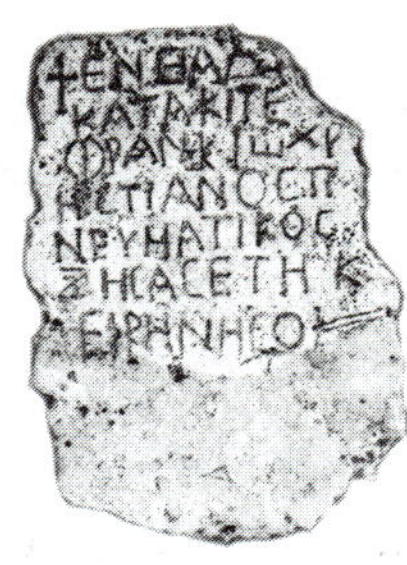

Note to the Reader

The book you hold in your hands is intended to be a history, not a story. More precisely, this work, as its subtitle states, is an imaginative history, not a fictional narrative, even though it is structured as a series of stories. The careful reader will discover that each vignette is based upon solid evidence. The whole of this work is intended to provide as exhaustive an account of the four centuries of Montanist activity and belief as is possible to do on the basis of all the extant primary textual and archaeological information of this group of Christians.

Every account of an event in the past is an exercise of imagination, no matter how well supported by direct or contextual data, because the full knowledge of a given event and the context that surrounds it, as though contained in some cosmic spreadsheet, lies outside human capacity to comprehend as raw data. Imaginative history is particularly suited to construction as a story or more often as a series of stories in a situation such as one confronts with the Montanists because, while there was once a vast amount of data to be mined, most of those data are no longer available to any historian simply because they no longer exist.

Because a history, as opposed to letters and journals, is written some time after the fact, the stories that portray the past are typically written by those whose culture and traditions have triumphed. Certainly the "history" of the "Montanists" has been written by the victors: those who labeled them heretics and drove them out of existence. Even the name, Montanists, by which they are most commonly known today, was first given them by those who opposed them, almost two centuries after the "New Prophecy" movement was established. As will be noted at greater length in the Introduction that begins the book proper, the victors also destroyed most of the evidence of the Montanists' existence. To our present knowledge, all of the original Montanists' writings have perished: only a very few monumental remains celebrating their lives have been discovered by archaeologists here and there throughout the extant ruins of the Roman Empire.

In the victors' presentation of their side of the story, they frequently give the historian significant testimony and evidence about the losing side. It is this evidence of the losers as preserved by the victors that I have sought to bring to light. For the reader who wishes for herself or himself to plumb the extant documents and ruins, the whereabouts of the bare evidence we still have is provided, in three places. Written texts are identified as sources at the end of each vignette. The architectural and monumental evidence, in part, is provided by photographs of places and drawings of monuments that exist to this day. The notes that are printed at the end of each chapter, but which are not needed to understand the narrative, explain to the reader my use of evidence we have and where I have used creative imagination to bring that evidence into the light for our understanding.

Every historian brings to the story told his, or her, convictions and assumptions. Impartiality may not be entirely possible for any human. But to the extent possible, it has been my intention to bring these ancient, so-called "heretics" into the light as the flesh-and-blood men and women they were, as the Christians they believed themselves to be, and as the courageous and loyal individuals they sought to be in the face of unremitting hostility.

While this book is primarily a history of the Montanists, it is also entirely suitable as a resource for the study of Christianity as a whole in the first six centuries of the Common Era. To that end, I have provided a study guide for use in a variety of settings, including book clubs, discussion groups, and formal undergraduate and master's level courses. This guide is found in *.pdf format on the Hendrickson Publishers web site at http://www.hendrickson.com/pdf/study_guides/9781565639379-sg.pdf. The reader may obtain these files without further cost simply by downloading them.

Abbreviations

General

ap.	*apud,* at, in
B.C.E.	before the Common Era
c.	century
ca.	circa
C.E.	Common Era
d.	died
esp.	especially
flor.	*floruit,* active, flourished
l(*l*).	line(s)
n.	note
Olymp.	*Olympias,* Olympiad
p(p).	page(s)
praef.	*praefatio,* preface
proem.	*proemium,* preamble
vol(s).	volume(s)

Biblical Texts

Old Testament

Gen	Genesis
Exod	Exodus
1–2 Kgs	1–2 Kings
Dan	Daniel

New Testament

Matt	Matthew
Rom	Romans
1–2 Cor	1–2 Corinthians
Gal	Galatians
1–2 Tim	1–2 Timothy
1–2 Pet	1–2 Peter
Rev	Revelation

Ancient Authors and Works

Act. Marcell.	*Acta Marcelli centurionis*
Act. Paul.	*Acta Pauli*
Act. Paul et Thecl.	*Acta Pauli et Theclae*
Aelius Publius Julius	
Sub.	*Subscriptio*
Anonyma (Carthaginian prophetess)	
Log.	*Logion/logia*
Anonyma (second Carthaginian prophetess)	
Log.	*Logion/logia*
Anonymous	
Fr.	*Fragmenta*
Anti-Phrygian	
Fr.	*Fragmenta*
Apolinarius of Hierapolis	
Ep.	*Epistula*
Apollonius	
Fr.	*Fragmenta*
Asterius Urbanus	
Fr.	*Fragmenta*
Augustine of Hippo	
Haer.	*De haeresibus*
Aurelius Quirinus	
Sub.	*Subscriptio*
Author of *On the Psalms*	
Fr. Ps.	*Fragmenta in Psalmos*
Author of the *Refutatio*	
Ref.	*Refutatio omnium haeresium (Philosophoumena)*
Basil of Caesarea	
Ep.	*Epistula*
Can. murat.	*Canon muratorianus*
Cod. justin.	*Codex justinianus*
Cod. theod.	*Codex theodosianus*
Council of Constantinople I [381]	
Ps.-can.	*Pseudo-canones*
Council of Laodikeia [between ca. 343–381]	
Can.	*Canones*
Cyprian of Carthage	
Ep.	*Epistula*
Cyril of Jerusalem	
Catech.	*Catecheses illuminandorum*
Dial.	*Dialogus Montanistae et Orthodoxi*
Did.	*Didache*
Didymus	
Trin.	*De Trinitate*

Dio Cassius
- *Epit.* — *Epitome*

Dionysius of Alexandria
- *Ep.* — *Epistula/ae*

Dionysius Barsalîbî
- *Apoc.* — *Commentarius in Apocalypsem*

Epiphanius of Salamis
- *Mens.* — *De mensuris et ponderibus*
- *Pan.* — *Panarion omnium haeresium*

Eusebius of Caesarea
- *Chron.* — *Chronicon*
- *Hist. eccl.* — *Historia ecclesiastica*
- *Mart. Pal.* — *De martyribus Palaestinae*
- (*L*) — (*Long recension*)
- (*S*) — (*Short recension*)
- *Vit. Const.* — *Vita Constantini*

Filaster of Brescia
- *Haer.* — *Diversarum haereseon liber*

Firmilian of Caesarea
- *Ep.* — *Epistula*

Gaius
- *Proc.* — *Adversus Proclum*

Gregory of Nyssa
- *Ep.* — *Epistula*
- *Vit. Greg. Thaum.* — *De vita Gregorii Thaumaturgi*

Hilary of Poitiers
- *In Constant.* — *In Constantium imperatorem*

Hippolytus
- *Antichr.* — *De antichristo*
- *Comm. Dan.* — *Commentarium in Danielem*
- *Haer.* — *Adversus omnes haereses*
- *Noet.* — *Contra haeresin Noeti*

Ignatius of Antioch
- *Eph.* — *Epistula ad Ephesios*
- *Magn.* — *Epistula ad Magnesios*
- *Phld.* — *Epistula ad Philadelphios*
- *Pol.* — *Epistula ad Polycarpum*
- *Rom.* — *Epistula ad Romanos*
- *Smyrn.* — *Epistula ad Smyrnaeos*
- *Trall.* — *Epistula ad Trallianos*

Irenaeus of Lyons
- *Ep.* — *Epistula*
- *Haer.* — *Adversus haereses*

Jerome
- *Comm. Gal.* — *Commentariorum in epistulam ad Galatas libri III*

Comm. Phlm.	*Commentariorum in Epistulam ad Philemonem liber*
Ep.	*Epistulae*
Vir. ill.	*De viris illustribus*
John of Ephesus	
Hist. eccl.	*Historia ecclesiastica*
Josephus	
Ant.	*Antiquitates judaicae*
Justin Martyr	
1 Apol.	*Apologia I*
Dial.	*Dialogus cum Tryphone*
Lactantius	
Mort.	*De morte persecutorum*
Lib. pont.	*Liber pontificalis*
Mart. Carp.	*Martyrium Carpi, Papyri, et Agathonicae*
(A)	*(Recensio A)*
(B)	*(Recensio B)*
Mart. Just.	*Martyrium Justini*
(A)	*(Recensio A)*
(B)	*(Recensio B)*
Mart. Lugd.	*Lugdunenses martyres*
Mart. Pol.	*Martyrium Polycarpi*
Maximilla	
Log.	*Logion/logia*
Montanus	
Log.	*Logion/logia*
Origen	
Cels.	*Contra Celsum*
Comm. Matt.	*Commentarium in evangelium Matthaei*
Fr. Tit.	*Fragmenta ex commentariis in epistulam ad Titum*
Princ.	*De principiis*
Pamphilus	
Prol. apol. Orig.	*Prologus in apologeticum Pamphili martyris pro Origene*
Pass. Mont. et Luc.	*Passio sanctorum Montani et Lucii*
Pass. Perp.	*Passio sanctarum Perpetuae et Felicitatis*
Pass. Pion.	*Passio Pionii*
Pass. Theod.	*Passio Theodoti Ancyrani*
Photius	
Cod.	*Bibliotheca. Codices*
Pliny the Elder	
Nat.	*Naturalis historia*
Pliny the Younger	
Ep.	*Epistulae*
Polycarp of Smyrna	
Phil.	*Epistula ad Philippenses*

Polycrates of Ephesus
- *Ep.* — *Epistula*

Praedestinatus
- *Haer.* — *Praedestinatus sive praedestinatorum haeresis et libri S. Augustino temere adscripti refutation*

Priscilla
- *Log.* — *Logion/logia*

Procopius
- *Hist. arc.* — *Historia arcane*

Protev. Jac. — *Protevangelium Jacobi*

Pseudo-Chrysostom
- *Serm. pasch.* — *Sermo in pascha*

Pseudo-Tertullian
- *Haer.* — *Adversus omnes haereses*

Quadratus
- *Apol.* — *Apologia*

Quintilla
- *Log.* — *Logion/logia*

Serapion of Antioch
- *Ep.* — *Epistula ad Caricum et Pontium*

Sozomen
- *Hist. eccl.* — *Historia ecclesiastica*

Tacitus
- *Ann.* — *Annales*
- *Hist.* — *Historiae*

Tertullian
- *An.* — *De anima*
- *Apol.* — *Apologeticum*
- *Apollon.* — *Adversus Apollonium*
- *Bapt.* — *De baptismo*
- *Carn. Chr.* — *De carne Christi*
- *Cor.* — *De corona militis*
- *Exh. cast.* — *De exhortatione castitatis*
- *Fr. ecst.* — *Fragmenta ex De ecstasi*
- *Fug.* — *De fuga in persecutione*
- *Jejun.* — *De jejunio adversus psychicos*
- *Marc.* — *Adversus Marcionem*
- *Mon.* — *De monogamia*
- *Paen.* — *De paenitentia*
- *Praescr.* — *De praescriptione haereticorum*
- *Prax.* — *Adversus Praxean*
- *Pud.* — *De pudicitia*
- *Res.* — *De resurrectione carnis*
- *Scap.* — *Ad Scapulam*
- *Ux.* — *Ad uxorem*

Val.	*Adversus Valentinianos*
Virg.	*De virginibus velandis*
Theodore of Heracleia	
Fr. Mt.	*Fragmenta ex commentariis evangelium Matthaei*
Theophanes	
Chron.	*Chronographia*
Trad. ap.	*Traditio apostolica*
Trajan	
Rescr.	*Rescriptum*
Vit. Pol.	*Vita Polycarpi*

Modern References

ANF	*Ante-Nicene Fathers*
ANRW	*Aufstieg und Niedergang der römischen Welt: Geschichte und Kultur Roms im Spiegel der neueren Forschung.* Edited by H. Temporini and W. Haase
AnSt	*Anatolian Studies*
CB	*The Cities and Bishoprics of Phrygia* [when cited by inscription number]. Edited by William M. Ramsay
CIG	*Corpus inscriptionum graecarum.* Edited by August Boeckh
CIL	*Corpus inscriptionum latinarum.* Edited by Friedrich Ritschl et al.
EG	*Epigrafia greca.* Edited by Margherita Guarducci
IMont	*Inscriptiones Montanistae* [= *Montanist Inscriptions and Testimonia* (when cited by inscription number)]. Edited by William Tabbernee
NewDocs	*New Documents Illustrating Early Christianity.* Edited by G. H. R. Horsley and S. R. Llewelyn
PG	Patrologiae cursus completus: Series graeca. Edited by Jacques-Paul Migne
SC	Sources chrétiennes

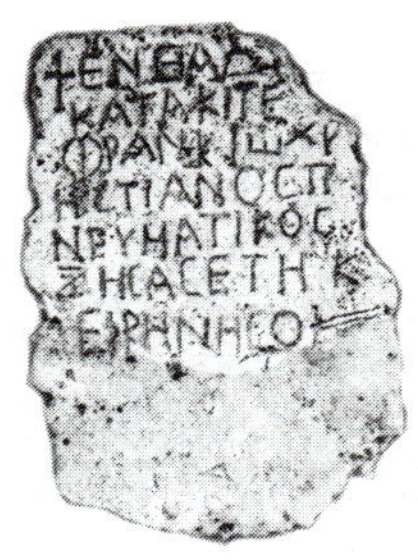

Introduction

The writing of history demands historical imagination. Despite claims to the contrary, "the facts" do not "speak for themselves." Reconstructing the past involves recognizing that not all of "the past" is recoverable and that not all that can be recovered is equally useful. The writing of history, especially ancient history such as a history of Montanism, demands creativity and imagination. It requires the ability to piece together what little extant evidence we may have, in order to present a picture and bring to life the story of "what actually happened" that is as accurate and authentic as possible. Even then, a particular historian's imaginative reconstruction is always provisional, subject both to the discovery of additional, as-yet-unknown, archaeological, epigraphic, or literary pieces from the past and to the creative imagination of other historians, who might use the same data more effectively. The writing of history is, therefore, a continuous process. The past is past, but what is known about the past and the history that can be reconstructed professionally and creatively from the known data is open-ended.

In the case of Montanism, the task of reconstructing the past is especially difficult, for the extant data are scarce and often indirect. Several reasons account for this scarcity. Almost from its inception Montanism was deemed by its opponents to be, at best, a deviant form of Christianity and, at worst, a heresy, thus a great deal of the original source material that historians would ordinarily employ no longer exists. The intentional destruction of such material by orthodox clergy, supported by imperial authorities from the time of Constantine onward, accelerated and intensified the natural processes by which historical data slowly disappear over the course of centuries.

The use of imperial power and authority against the Montanists was at times heavy-handed and uncompromising, and it could take a variety of forms. Constantine, fearful that the catholic God would deprive him of his empire if he did not enforce strict uniformity of catholic Christian beliefs and practices, ordered the burning of all Montanist books (as well as those of other so-called heretics). The loss of these books not only deprived fourth-century Montanists of their particular religious tradition but, lamentably, resulted in the loss of the very documents that would have supplied modern historians with a great deal of crucial primary source material. Later emperors enacted legislation that deprived Montanists of property and forced them to join "mainstream" Christianity, be exiled or, in some cases, be put to death. Justinian, in the sixth century, burned down

Montanist churches. One of Justinian's agents, John of Amida (also known as John of Ephesus), even burned the bones of Montanus, Maximilla, and Priscilla, the founders of Montanism. John not only destroyed the shrine that held the founders' bones but also confiscated the church building that contained the shrine as well as other Montanist buildings at Pepouza, the most holy city for those who chose to embrace and adhere to what they often referred to as the New Prophecy.

What then is left for us to use in reconstructing the history of this important movement that affected the lives of Christians and the development of Christian thought, theology, and practice from the middle of the second century on? The picture is more hopeful than might be apparent at first glance. The recent discovery of Pepouza, Montanism's most holy city for almost four hundred years (ca. 165–ca. 550 C.E.), and the archaeological surface survey work done at the site, and at other sites in the vicinity, provides crucial information about the geographic and physical context in which Montanism developed. The fieldwork also holds out the possibility that, when actual digging commences, new material evidence about Montanism will come to light.

In the meantime, the earliest extant primary source material relating to Montanism consists of around thirty inscriptions and an equal number of fragments of the *logia,* or "sayings" (including oracles) of Montanus, Maximilla, Priscilla, and a few later-generation Montanist prophets and prophetesses. Most of these *logia* have survived because they are quoted in extant *anti*-Montanist works and utilized for polemical purposes. The earliest opponents refer to the New Prophecy as "the sect of those named after the Phrygians," the Phrygians being the founders Montanus, Maximilla, and Priscilla. Later, this designation is frequently contracted into "the Phrygian heresy," or simply "the Cataphrygians." The term Montanist does not appear until the mid-fourth century.

Some *logia* of the original "New Prophets," as well as a few sayings uttered by early third-century Carthaginian Montanist prophetesses, are found in the writings of Tertullian. These *logia,* unlike those preserved by anti-Montanist authors, are used by Tertullian to defend the New Prophecy and its practices. Tertullian's somewhat more positive use of the *logia,* however, does not necessarily mean that he used them in a way absolutely consistent with their original context, purpose, or meaning. Tertullian, while always remaining a catholic, became involved with the New Prophecy movement around 208 C.E. The treatises he wrote after that date reflect an increasing influence of the New Prophecy, especially with respect to the practice of Christianity. Tertullian frequently promoted the New Prophecy's ascetic discipline, which adherents said was communicated by the Holy Spirit, the Paraclete, via Montanus, Maximilla, Priscilla, and the Paraclete's subsequent prophetic "mouthpieces."

Tertullian's writings after 208 C.E. are an indispensable extant source for Montanism, but care must be taken not to divide Tertullian artificially into a pre-Montanist and a Montanist. Much of what Tertullian believed and practiced before 208 C.E. he continued to believe and practice after that year. Moreover, Tertullian's understanding and portrayal of the New Prophecy movement may merely have been applicable to his own Carthaginian setting. The New Prophecy as it existed in Phrygia, the movement's place of origin in Asia Minor, may have differed considerably from the form it took in North Africa or, for that matter, in Rome or elsewhere.

A great deal of careful analysis is required to sort out fact from fiction in the allegations and charges brought against Montanism by the movement's catholic or orthodox detractors. The task of writing an accurate, albeit always provisional, history of Montanism on the basis of predominantly anti-Montanist (and, therefore biased) sources is made even more difficult by the anachronism inherent in terms such as catholic, orthodox, heresy, and heretics—at least for the period prior to the First Council of Nicaea in 325 C.E. Post-Nicene categories, devised by the theological and ecclesiastical "winners," do not easily apply to the "losers," especially when referring to the pre-Nicene period when there was still a great deal of fluidity in Christian thought and practice. For the first three centuries of Christianity, the lines between "orthodoxy" and "heresy," "mainstream" and "deviant" forms of the religion were very blurred. Thus in this book the use of words such as orthodox and catholic should not be taken as references to the institution of the Roman Catholic and Orthodox Churches that became more institutionally defined and developed after 325 C.E.

Issues relating to gender, access to ecclesiastical power, the influence of pagan cults on Montanism, conflicting attitudes toward the State, martyrdom, persecution, and the rich diversity of Christian thought in its formative stages all impacted the way Montanists and mainstream Christians viewed and related to one another. Consequently, such issues are dealt with extensively in the writing of this history of the New Prophecy movement.

This book intentionally uses a novelistic approach, but it is not a novel. Persons, places, and events are authentic. They are people who actually lived in the places mentioned and participated in the events described. All the actual quotations, whether in direct speech or extracts from ancient Latin or Greek writings, are the very words, in my translation (unless indicated otherwise), of the persons who said or wrote them. Biblical quotations are taken from the New Revised Standard Version. Historical imagination, however, has been used when reporting what people thought or felt and in developing the physical context in which specific events occurred. All dates given are based on the latest scholarly research. For the modern names, where known, of ancient cities, towns, or villages referred to in this book, see the General Index which also provides map numbers and coordinates for the ancient names. The Greek form of the names of cities, towns, or villages in ancient Asia Minor and Greece is normally utilized unless the Greek form could cause confusion, in which case either the Latin or English forms are used, such as for Ephesus and Constantinople. The Latin form is used for most other ancient places except, again, for very common English forms such as Rome (rather than Roma) and Carthage (rather than Carthago). The chapters and vignettes reflect both a linear (the chapters) and synchronic (the vignettes) approach to history, toward the goal of providing depth and fullness in understanding the lives and times of Montanists and other early Christians.

Map 2: Asia Minor

D
E
F
1
2
3
4
5
Sinope
PONTUS
BITHYNIA
Halys
Neocaesarea
Malos
Ankyra
GALATIA
PHRYGIA
Caesarea
Philomelion
Antiochia
CAPPADOCIA
Laodikeia Katakekaumene
Phrygian Galatia
PISIDIA
Ikonion
LYCAONIA
Lystra
Derbe
Laranda
CILICIA
PAMPHYLIA
Rhosos
Antiochia
Seleukeia Pieria
Daphne
Orontes
CYPRUS
Salamis/Constantia
D
E
F

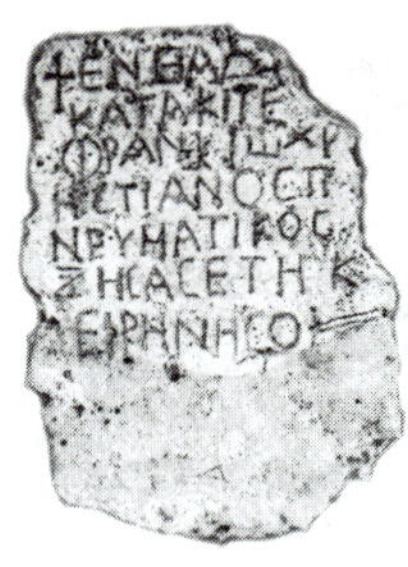

Prologue

Pepouza, Phrygia, ca. 178 C.E.

Zotikos and Julian undertake a crucial mission

The two middle-aged men are weary. It has been a long and tiring journey. One of the men, Zotikos of Konana, has been walking for five straight days. The first day had been relatively easy. Traveling on a well maintained arterial road, Zotikos had covered the twenty miles from his home to Apameia in a single day.

At Apameia, Zotikos had been joined by his friend and episcopal colleague, Julian of Apameia. Together, the two Christian bishops had traveled toward Pepouza in West-Central Phrygia. Now, fifty-five miles and three and a-half days later, they are almost there. Knowing that their destination is merely hours away gives the men renewed energy. They are determined to complete the final few miles before night fall.[1]

When they began their journey they walked on major Roman roads, but the road they are walking on now is narrow and in poor repair. Fortunately, for the past two hours the road has been more or less level, traversing the southern reaches of a vast plain. Most of the plain is part of an imperial estate where free tenant farmers grow crops that are taxed heavily by absentee Roman emperors.

Excited by—and yet somewhat anxious about—what they are to accomplish at the end of their journey, the two bishops quicken their pace as the road suddenly diverges to the left. There are more trees here, the fragrance of pines and oaks fills the air, and the slight breeze that cools their faces is a welcome relief from the scorching sun. In the distance directly ahead of them, they see a large mountain, rounded at the top like a huge dome. Light from the setting sun illuminates parts of the mountain, giving the domed top a surreal, celestial quality. At the same time, the clouds in the sky cast shadows over other parts of the mountain, sending shivers up the spines of both men and giving them a dark sense of foreboding.

The road the men are on descends steeply and, as they walk downhill, the mountain quickly disappears from view. Their new southern horizon becomes the rocky outcropping of the upper levels of the wall of a canyon. Suddenly, as the bishops round yet another bend, they have a magnificent view of a wide, fertile river valley far below them. Descending further, they pass through the city's necropolis, glad that the sun has not yet completely set. From the valley below, they hear the indistinct sounds of people finishing the day's chores. They pick up the

Figure P.1: Ömerçalı ("Montanus' Mountain")

faint blended aroma of hundreds of different meals being prepared all at the same time. It makes their mouths water. In the fading light they notice that the road forks again just ahead of them. The left fork passes along some tenement buildings nestled into the slopes of the canyon and then continues across the river, by means of a sturdy Roman bridge, to the southern quarters of the city.

Zotikos and Julian take the right fork of the road. This part of the road is totally on the north side of the river and leads to the main part of Pepouza, the city where they will attempt a crucial mission. Tomorrow Zotikos and Julian will attempt something that, if successful, should safeguard Christianity—as they know it—forever. But what if they fail? As the two men search out their lodging for the night, the possibility of failure is too horrendous to contemplate.[2]

Sources:

Anonymous, *Fr., ap.* Eusebius, *Hist. eccl.* 5.16.17; Apollonius, *Fr., ap.* Eusebius, *Hist. eccl.* 5.18.12.

Notes

1. The exact route which Zotikos and Julian took to reach Pepouza is unknown. The one described in this prologue is the most likely. Konana, cited by an anonymous author as Koumanē, was near the present-day Turkish village of Gönen. Eusebius of Caesarea (ca. 264/5–ca. 339/40) utilized the work of this anonymous author (from now on referred to as "the Anonymous") as his primary source about Montanism. Apameia was at Dinar (see Map 3). For details of all the anti-Montanist authors and other opponents of the New Prophecy referred to in this book, see Tabbernee 2007.

2. The topographical description of Pepouza, and of all other places in this book, is accurate. For Pepouza, see Tabbernee 2003 and Tabbernee and Lampe 2008. All references to miles are to Roman miles. One Roman mile, a thousand paces (*mille passuum*), equals 0.92 English miles or 1.48 kilometers.

Figure P.2: Roman aqueduct near Pepouza

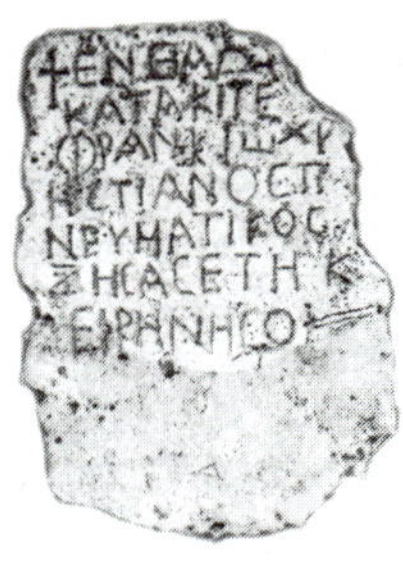

Chapter 1

Ardabau, Mysia, ca. 165 C.E.

Montanus has a vision

Never in their whole lives have the villagers seen anything like this. The man writhing in front of them has changed, within minutes, from the rational, well-respected, leading citizen of their village into a raving madman. Before their very eyes he has suddenly fallen into a trance, throwing his arms and legs around wildly. His body is twisting in contortions. Drool dribbles from his mouth.

Then, as quickly as the frenzied activity commenced, it stops. The man once again stands upright and almost rigid. Strange sounds are coming from his mouth. He begins to babble incomprehensibly. Simultaneously horrified and fascinated, they watch, not daring to move. What are they to make of all this?

Suddenly the man, whose name is Montanus, stops babbling. Still in a trance, he looks intently at the small crowd of people and says audibly and distinctly:

> Behold! A human being is like a lyre and I hover like a plectrum. The human being sleeps but I remain awake. Behold! The Lord is the one who stirs up the hearts of human beings and the one who strikes the heart in human beings.[1]

Those listening are stunned. Who is speaking? Is it Montanus or is it some supernatural spirit? What does it all mean? Is the voice coming out of Montanus giving them some explanation of what they are witnessing? Has Montanus just been "played" like some human instrument by God striking him the way a plectrum strikes the strings of a lyre? Is Montanus' trance really like a state of sleep when his own senses are inert so that the Lord, who never sleeps, can stir up Montanus' heart in order to reach his deepest emotions? If so, what is the purpose of it all?

As those who witness Montanus' first ecstatic experience one by one leave the village square to return to their own homes, more than a few of them have the same frightening thought: What if that which they have seen is not inspired by God but by the devil? That night the God who always remains awake has plenty of company.

The Christian community in the village is small but has recently gained some new converts, foremost among whom is Montanus. Stories that later circulate about Montanus claim that before his conversion to Christianity he was a priest of Apollo or even of Cybele, the Phrygian "Mother goddess."[2]

In the ensuing weeks Montanus periodically continues to exhibit strange behavior in Christian gatherings at the village. After each frenzied episode, he begins by uttering a formulaic statement in the first person, allegedly speaking as the mouthpiece of God. His puzzled and confused audience hears him say: "I, the Lord God Omnipotent am the One dwelling in a human being"[3] and "Neither angel nor emissary, but I, the Lord God the Father, have come."[4] The point of these statements seems to be to authenticate the source and legitimate the content of what Montanus will say next. Although many of his hearers remain skeptical, Montanus himself is convinced that he is a prophet inspired by God to communicate to the church what the church needs to hear in the new era that is dawning.[5]

The earliest self-commendatory formulae Montanus' listeners hear him recite are in the persona of "the Lord God, the Father." Before long, however, those listening to him hear utterances such as "I am the Word, the Bridegroom, the Paraclete, the Omnipotent One, I am All Things."[6] Later reports allege that Montanus even proclaimed "I am the Father and the Son and the Holy Spirit."[7]

Some of the leaders of the Christian congregation in the village where Montanus began his prophesying are convinced that it is *not* the Holy Spirit who inspires Montanus but a spurious, evil spirit. Concerned about the effect all this is having on the faithful members of their congregation, they rebuke Montanus, denouncing him as one of the false prophets Jesus warned would come. Their attempts to stop Montanus, however, fail miserably. Whereas they view the ecstatic phenomenon that accompanies Montanus' prophecies as an unwarranted break with genuine prophetic tradition, others see it as the very proof of the Holy Spirit's new prophetic gift to the church. Consequently, they support Montanus boldly so that he, and the prophetic spirit that "speaks" through him, can no longer be silenced.

  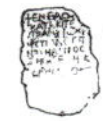

As Montanus' prophetic activity increases, Christians from neighboring settlements begin hearing and passing on rumors about what was happening in the village near them. Thirty years later, in places as far away as Ankyra, these stories are still being repeated. At that time, the period when the so-called New Prophecy had broken out was rumored to be the proconsulate of Gratus and the place a village named Ardabau, which, it was said, lay in Mysia somewhere near the border of Phrygia.[8]

Sources:

Anonymous, *Fr., ap.* Eusebius, *Hist. eccl.* 5.16.7–9; *Dial.* 4.4; Jerome, *Ep.* 41.4; Montanus, *Log., ap.* Anti-Phrygian, *Fr., ap.* Epiphanius, *Pan.* 48.4.1, 48.11.1, 48.11.9; Montanus, *Log., ap.* Theodore of Heracleia, *Fr. Mt.* 24.5; *Dial.* 3.1, 3.14, 4.5–6, 4.8; Didymus, *Trin.* 3.41.1.

West-Central Phrygia, ca. 167 C.E.
Montanus begins prophesying

"Why do you call the one who has been saved more than a human being?"[9] Before members of Montanus' latest group of disciples can attempt a faltering response to this puzzling question, the "voice" of the Holy Spirit, the Paraclete, speaks through Montanus:

> Because the righteous one shall shine a hundred times brighter than the sun and the little ones among you who have been saved shall shine a hundred times brighter than the moon.[10]

Montanus' followers are still somewhat puzzled but, by now, they know that the Paraclete has become Montanus' most frequent source of inspiration. They also know that Montanus' oracles are frequently based, if somewhat loosely, on the community's sacred writings.

To the more literate among them, it is apparent that this new oracle is a free-flowing interpretation of a saying of Jesus: "Then the righteous will shine like the sun in the kingdom of their Father."[11] One of the more astute disciples wonders whether the new oracle may also have been influenced by a passage in the book of Daniel: "Those who are wise shall shine like the brightness of the sky, and those who lead many to righteousness, like the stars forever and ever."[12] Another of them thinks the oracle is also reminiscent of Jesus' story about the farmer who sows his seed in good ground and is rewarded a hundredfold.[13] Yet another remembers that Jesus, at one time, called a child and put the child in the midst of his own disciples as an object lesson to teach them that the greatest in God's kingdom are those who have the humility and simplicity of little children,[14] warning them against putting stumbling blocks in the way of "little ones" who believe in him. Finally, someone else sees a connection with the allegorical story of the Son of Man at the end of time, separating people as a shepherd separates sheep from goats, on the basis of the service they have rendered to Christ himself by feeding, clothing, or visiting in prison the very least of humanity.[15]

That Montanus' *new* prophecies should be based on *old* scriptures is no surprise to the adherents of the New Prophecy. The Paraclete, they believe, has not come to Montanus to reveal new *content*. The Paraclete has come only to provide new and more complete understandings of what has already been revealed by the Israelite prophets, Christ, the apostles, and more recent prophets and prophetesses, such as the daughters of Philip, Ammia, and Quadratus. All of these preceded Montanus in an unbroken line of prophetic succession. The new and more complete understanding provided by the Paraclete in this new age is, for them, especially related to ethical behavior. Recently, Montanus' followers have heard him pronounce the Paraclete's prohibition *against* remarriage following divorce or the death of one's spouse. They have also heard instructions about keeping fasts strictly and even about the addition of new fasts. No wonder the Paraclete's latest insight communicated through Montanus should declare the brilliance of the righteous who rise above their normal human nature to live and act ethically.

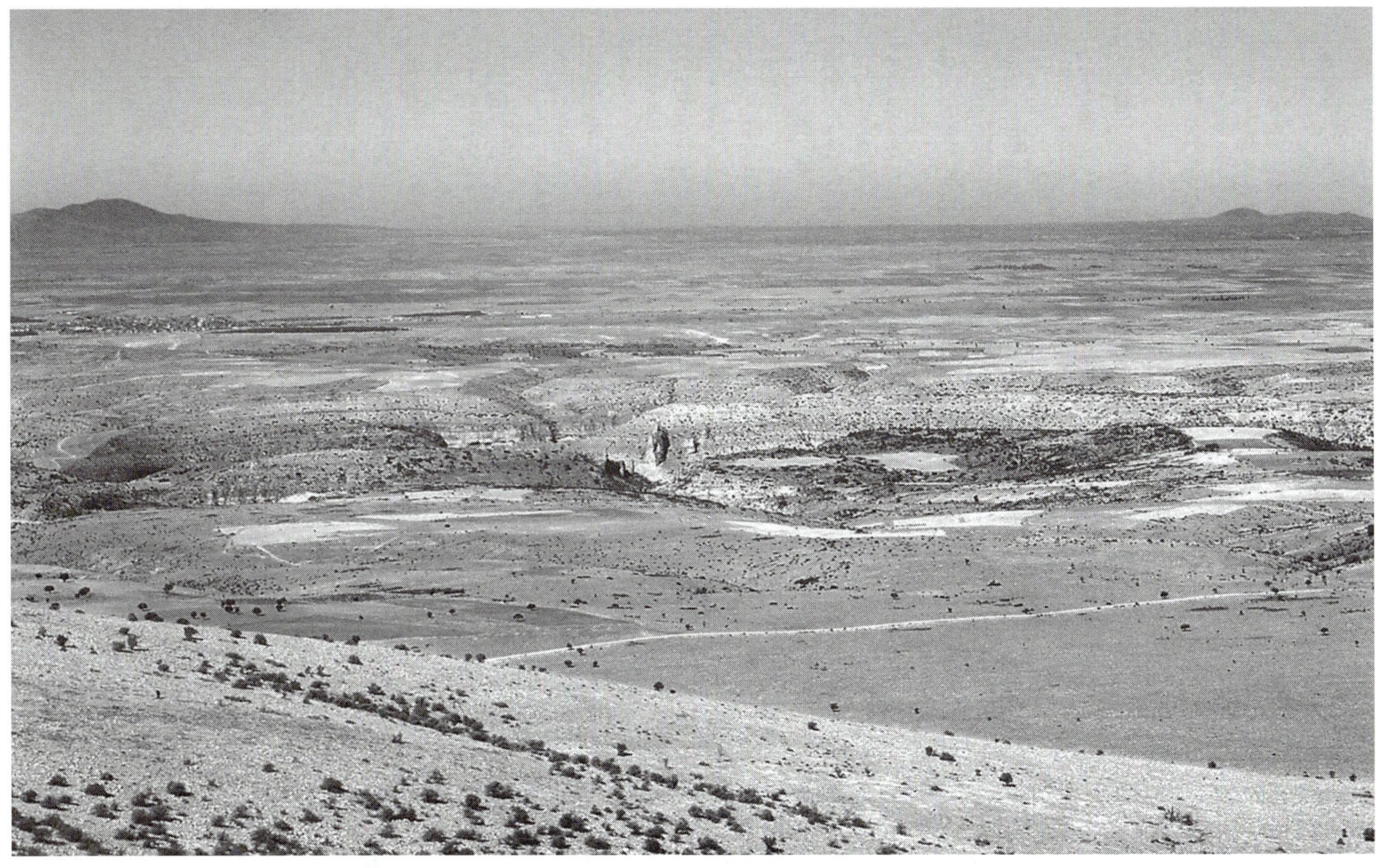

Figure 1.1: The view from Ömerçalı, looking north with the site of Pepouza in the foreground and the site of Tymion in the background

Among those who join Montanus' New Prophecy movement are some women. One day, perhaps to her own surprise as well as to that of those standing near her, one of these women, Maximilla, falls into an ecstatic trance, exhibits frenzied behavior and babbles strangely—just like Montanus had done. The spirit that speaks through Montanus, obviously, has found a second human instrument. Soon a third instrument, in the person of Priscilla, is added. Prophetic *charismata,* apparently, are contagious.

As curious villagers listen to the oracles uttered by the female prophets, they marvel at the consistency of the New Prophecy. Irrespective of whether the Paraclete speaks through Montanus, or Maximilla, or Priscilla, ethical rigorism and the virtues of ascetic practices are emphasized. "Bodily purity brings about spiritual harmony," proclaims the spirit through Priscilla. "The saintly servants (of God) should know how to manage sanctity."[16] "They see visions and, turning their faces downward, they also hear salutary sayings as clear as they are mysterious," people hear from Priscilla's lips.[17] They wonder if these are truly the new revelations of the Holy Spirit.

Maximilla proclaims her legitimacy as one of the New Prophecy's prophetesses by declaring:

> The Lord has sent me as adherent of this discipline, revealer of this covenant, interpreter of this promise; compelled, willing or not, to know God's knowledge.[18]

Soon this, at first reluctant, prophetess becomes so popular that she has to insist that her followers listen carefully to the true source of her oracles. "Hear not me, but hear Christ!" she complains.[19]

Perhaps taking her cue from Montanus who, on more than one occasion, warned of impending judgment, Maximilla also predicts that there will be "wars and a state of anarchy." "After me," she says, "a prophet shall no longer exist—only the end!"[20]

Sources:

Montanus, *Log., ap.* Anti-Phrygian, *Fr., ap.* Epiphanius, *Pan.* 48.10.3; Matt 13:43; Dan 12:3; Mark 4:16–20; Matt 18:1–5, 25:31–46; Tertullian, *Marc.* 1.29.4; *Fr. ecst., ap.* Praedestinatus, *Haer.* 1.26 (cf. Apollonius, *Fr., ap.* Eusebius, *Hist. eccl.* 5.18.2); *Jejun.* 1.3, 13.5, 15.1–2; Anonymous, *Fr., ap.* Eusebius, *Hist. eccl.* 5.16.9; Priscilla, *Log., ap.* Tertullian, *Exh. cast.* 10.5; Maximilla, *Log., ap.* Anti-Phrygian, *Fr., ap.* Epiphanius, *Pan.* 48.13.1, 48.12.4, 48.2.4 (cf. Eusebius, *Hist. eccl.* 5.16.18).

West-Central Phrygia, ca. 170 C.E.

Montanus finds the site of the New Jerusalem

The view from the mountain is spectacular. It is a crystal clear, sunny day without a cloud in the sky. The panorama before Montanus seems to stretch out

Figure 1.2: Site of ancient Pepouza

forever. Looking north, he can see the small mountain range, where he knows Temenothyrai lies at its foot. But being about thirty miles away, the city itself cannot be seen. A dozen or so miles closer, however, he can make out, though barely, the town of Tymion. Another much larger mountain range is visible to the east. From where he stands, those mountains appear to be blue in color. As he sweeps his eyes from right to left over the landscape, Montanus also sees blue mountains at the extreme western edge of the panorama. Because of the distance, those mountains seem very small.

What excites Montanus most of all is the magnificent view he has of the vast plain encompassed by the three mountain ranges. This huge expanse of flat land is, in fact, a plateau, its southern boundary clearly delineated by the northern rim of a long canyon. Although the river itself is hidden from his view by trees that grow on the land that lies between him and the southern rim of the canyon, when he looks more carefully Montanus can see the course of the Sindros River that flows from east to west through the canyon. Directly in front of him, however, perhaps no more than four miles due north, Montanus can see not only a large section of the rocky northern wall of the canyon and the edge of the plateau rising above it, but also parts of the city of Pepouza.

From where he is standing, Montanus sees that the normally narrow canyon suddenly opens up at the eastern end of the city into a large oval-shaped area, about three miles long. He can't quite tell how wide this river valley is but, judging from the expanse on the far side it must be at least a mile wide. Now that his eyes are focused on the site, he notices the road from Hierapolis that winds its way, far below him to his left, toward Pepouza. The road looks tiny from his vantage point, but he can make out the roof of a *villa rustica*, a Roman country farmhouse, and then a second one. Near the city, the road disappears from view as it winds down the slope leading to the place where the canyon opens up into the river flats. Montanus assumes correctly that, at that point, the road from the south leads to a bridge providing entry to the city.

Montanus can see that the main part of Pepouza lies a little farther to the west. He can even see where the road makes its way out of the canyon, its left fork leading to the commercial and residential sections of the city, past the necropolis. In the foreground on a raised terrace, well above the fertile river flats, Montanus notices some large buildings but, from where he is at this point he cannot determine exactly what they are. But he can tell that many of the city's private houses are also on that side of the valley, nestled into the lower slopes of the canyon's massive north wall. Half way up that wall is a large cave, which, he thinks, may at one time have had some cultic purpose such as housing the shrine of one of Phrygia's native religions.

Montanus' eyes travel up the far wall of the canyon, pausing briefly at the rim before once again focusing intently on the vast plateau all the way to Tymion and beyond. As he takes in the whole vista, he is absolutely sure that his search is over. He has found the place where the New Jerusalem will descend out of heaven as promised in the book of Revelation.[21]

Ever since he first had access to a rare copy of the book that records the revelation that, according to tradition, Christ himself granted to John of Patmos, Montanus has been fascinated by the apocalyptic images it contains. As the first part of the book is addressed to the seven major churches of Asia, Montanus feels that the whole apocalypse has special relevance to the Christians in his own area. Philadelphia and Laodikeia, after all, are almost neighboring communities and even Ephesus, the capital of the province of Asia, is not all that far away.

Given the fact that the emperor Hadrian destroyed the old Jerusalem in Syria Palaestina, replacing it with the Roman city of Aelia Capitolina, which Jews and Christians are not supposed to enter, Montanus had begun to speculate that the New Jerusalem might descend near a mountain in Phrygia instead of near the site of the old Jerusalem. Now, at last, he has topographical confirmation. The mountain on which he is standing is just like the mountain to which the prophetic author of the book of Revelation was taken by an angel so that the Spirit could show him "the holy city Jerusalem coming down out of heaven from God."[22] Most importantly, the plateau between Pepouza and Tymion is level enough and, to his mind large enough to accommodate both the physical descent and the cube-like dimensions of the celestial city. In his imagination, Montanus can already see the beauty of the city before him, with its twelve foundations inscribed with the names of the twelve apostles and adorned with separate jewels, its streets of gold, and its twelve gates of pearl. Theoretically situating this Jerusalem on the land between Pepouza to the south and Tymion to the north as he walks down the mountain, Montanus knows what he will do next. He will metaphorically name both Pepouza and Tymion "Jerusalem," he will make Pepouza, which is a larger city than he had first thought, the center of his movement, and he will encourage people from everywhere to gather there.

Sources:

Rev 1:4–3:22, 21:1–22:5; Epiphanius, *Mens.* 14; Dio Cassius, *Epit.* 69.12; Apollonius, *Fr., ap.* Eusebius, *Hist. eccl.* 5.18.2.

Notes

1. Montanus, *Log., ap.* Anti-Phrygian, *Fr., ap.* Epiphanius, *Pan.* 48.4.1. The first three sayings (*logia*) of Montanus quoted in this chapter are extant because they have been preserved by being utilized by Epiphanius (ca. 315–403/5), bishop of Salamis in Cyprus from ca. 367, in his *Medicine Chest Against All Heresies,* written ca. 374–377 C.E. Epiphanius' source for these *logia,* and for some of the *logia* of Montanist prophetesses, was an early third-century author helpfully designated the "Anti-Phrygian" by Nasrallah (2003, 4, 155–96). This, now unknown, author had written an anti-Montanist polemic, refuting the validity of the then called "New Prophecy" by attacking the content of the new prophets' *logia.* Epiphanius, *Pan.* 48.2.4–48.13.8 is an extensive segment of the Anti-Phrygian's polemic.

2. Whether or not Montanus had once been a priest of Apollo as claimed during the fourth-century by the author of the *Dialogue Between a Montanist and an Orthodox* (4.4) and (perhaps) by Jerome (*Ep.* 41.4) remains controversial, but a convincing case for this has been made recently by Hirschmann 2005, esp. 38–39, 50–53, 139–45; cf. Tabbernee 2006b, 537–38. Montanus' Latin name indicates that he was at least a free inhabitant of the Roman province where he lived.

3. Montanus, *Log., ap.* Anti-Phrygian, *Fr., ap.* Epiphanius, *Pan.* 48.11.1.

4. Montanus, *Log., ap.* Anti-Phrygian, *Fr., ap.* Epiphanius, *Pan.* 48.11.9.

5. The most recent monographs on Montanism, or on major aspects of Montanism, are Trevett 1996, Nasrallah 2003, Hirschman 2005, Tabbernee 2007, and Tabbernee and Lampe 2008. The main literary sources are conveniently made available to English readers in Heine 1989b. Heine's collection is dependent on de Labriolle 1913b, which contains 96 additional sources—all but one of which are from the fourth century or later. Tabbernee 1997b is the corpus of 95 Montanist and allegedly Montanist inscriptions (= *IMont*). Heine's collection of Montanist *oracles* (nos. 1–19; pp. 2–9) is based on, but not identical with, de Labriolle 1913a (nos. 1–19; pp. 34–105) which supersedes all earlier collections. The most useful published collection subsequent to de Labriolle's is Aland 1960 (nos. 1–25; pp. 143–48). Helpful synoptic tables of Heine's, de Labriolle's, and Aland's numbering systems are provided by Trevett 1996, 249 and McGinn 1997, 134–35. For a radically new classification system, see Tabbernee 2006a, 521–26. As not all the extant "sayings" (*logia*) of the prophets and prophetesses of the New Prophecy are "oracles," all their "sayings," including those which are "oracles," are cited in these notes as *logia* (abbreviated as "*Log.*"). On the Montanist sayings/oracles themselves, see also Groh, 1985, 73–95, Robeck 1992, 110–27; Elm 1994, 131–38; A. Jensen 1996, 128–35; Trevett 1996, 398–41; Tabbernee 2001a, 377–86; Nasrallah 2003, 140–48, 167–93. For a detailed discussion of Montanist pneumatology and the threat it posed to "orthodox" Christianity, see Tabbernee 2001b.

6. Montanus, *Log., ap.* Theodore of Heracleia, *Fr. Mt.* 24.5. This *logion* has not previously been included in published collections of Montanist oracles. On this *logion* and its Montanist authenticity, see Berruto Martone 1999, 98–99 and Tabbernee 2007, 281, 381.

7. *Dial.* 3.1; 3.14; 4.5–6; 4.8; Didymus, *Trin.* 3.41.1.

8. Anonymous, *Fr. ap.* Eusebius, *Hist. eccl.* 5.16.7. Neither a proconsul named Gratus nor a village named Ardabau has ever been identified. If Ardabau was, indeed, in Mysia, it must have bordered northwestern Phrygia; see Ramsay 1889, 398. Suggested locations further south for Ardabau have been unconvincing, as has the view that Ardabau was not a real place but rather a metaphorical appellation, perhaps for Pepouza and/or Tymion; see Tabbernee 1997b, 18. On the mid-160s being the date of the beginning of the New Prophecy, see Tabbernee 1978, 757–81 and Trevett 1996, 26–45. That each of the five *logia* quoted in this section of this chapter were uttered by Montanus *at Ardabau* (assuming Ardabau to have been a real place) and in the order given here (instead of later, elsewhere in Asia Minor, and in a different order) is probable rather than certain. For the later charge that Montanus equated himself with the Holy Spirit, see Chapter 28 below.

9. Montanus, *Log., ap.* Anti-Phrygian, *Fr., ap.* Epiphanius, *Pan.* 48.10.3a.

10. Montanus, *Log., ap.* Anti-Phrygian, *Fr., ap.* Epiphanius, *Pan.* 48.10.3. It appears that some of the followers of Montanus, Maximilla, and Priscilla wrote down verbatim the orally delivered *logia* of the founding prophets and prophetesses of the New Prophecy. These written versions of the *logia* were copied and circulated widely, being incorporated into both pro-Montanist and anti-Montanist books (Anonymous, *Fr., ap.* Eusebius, *Hist. eccl.* 5.16.10, 5.16.17, 5.17.1; Anti-Phrygian, *Fr., ap.* Epiphanius, *Pan.* 48.2.4–48.13.8; cf. Author of the *Refutatio, Ref.* 8.19.1). Tertullian (ca. 160–ca. 220) also owned, or at least,

had access to, one or more such books (*Fug.* 9.4), as did his contemporary Apollonius (see Eusebius, *Hist eccl.* 5.18.1). The collections of sayings available to Tertullian and Apollonius overlapped but need not have been identical. They certainly differed from the collection used by Epiphanius. No ancient collection of Montanist *logia* has survived. Those *logia* which are extant still exist because of their having been quoted by Tertullian or (frequently out of context and only partially) by an opponent of the New Prophecy.

11. Matt 13:43.

12. Dan 12:3.

13. Mark 4:16–20.

14. Matt 18:1–5.

15. Matt 25:31–46.

16. Priscilla, *Log., ap.* Tertullian, *Exh. cast.* 10.5a.

17. Priscilla, *Log., ap.* Tertullian, *Exh. cast.* 10.5b.

18. Maximilla, *Log., ap.* Anti-Phrygian, *Fr., ap.* Epiphanius, *Pan.* 48.13.1.

19. Maximilla, *Log., ap.* Anti-Phrygian, *Fr., ap.* Epiphanius, *Pan.* 48.12.4.

20. Maximilla, *Log., ap.* Anti-Phrygian, *Fr., ap.* Epiphanius, *Pan.* 48.2.4.

21. The mountain on which Montanus undoubtedly stood is accessible today via the village of Paşalar in the Turkish province of Uşak. Once known as Paşalar Dağ (Mount Paşalar) but now named Ömerçalı, it (at 1141 m above sea level) dominates the landscape and is visible from all directions in the general vicinity. For the significance of the mountain to Montanism, see Tabbernee 2003, 92–93 and Tabbernee and Lampe 2008, 101–102. On the influence of Johannine literature on early Montanism, see Aland 1955, 109–16; 1960, 111–43; Trevett 1996, 142–45. Heine argues that Johannine literature, especially the Gospel attributed to John, first influenced Montanism in Rome, rather than in Phrygia (see Heine 1987, 1–19 and 1989a, 95–100), but I am convinced otherwise and thus have assumed that Montanus himself was directly dependent at least upon the book of Revelation for his views—particularly those about the New Jerusalem in Phrygia.

22. Rev 21:10.

Chapter 2

Hierapolis, Phrygia, ca. 177 C.E.

Apolinarius ponders the New Prophecy

Apolinarius needs to go for a walk. He still hasn't made up his mind regarding what to do about the New Prophecy, which has become so disturbing in the whole region of Phrygia. He hopes the fresh air will clear his head before he has to chair what might be the most crucial meeting of his ecclesiastical career.

He begins his walk at the southern end of the colonnaded street that runs through the center of the city toward the necropolis. To the right he can see the magnificent Roman theater built through the generous patronage of the emperor Hadrian, who had visited Hierapolis half a century earlier. A little further on, also to the right but closer to the street, lies the Temple of Apollo and its adjacent Plutonium, whose pungent, deadly gases are a constant danger to unsuspecting visitors. Apolinarius gets an acrid whiff of sulphur. It burns his nostrils and almost makes him gag. He hurries away before the gas burns his lungs or makes him even sicker. Next to the Plutonium, Apolinarius can see the Oraculum, a small auditorium built over one of the fissures in the ground, where prophetesses of Phrygian cults pronounce their oracular responses to questions brought to them by countless seekers. Apolinarius pauses briefly to consider whether there might be similarities between the vapor-induced inspiration of pagan prophetesses and the utterances of Maximilla and Priscilla.

Passing first through the agora, the marketplace, and then through the Arch of Domitian, Apolinarius enters the necropolis that lies just outside the city. As always, he feels at peace among the hundreds of sarcophagi resting on their elevated platforms, some placed quite high above the ground. At one of these sarcophagi, he stops and gently touches the lettering on the lid: "For Ammia and Asklepios. The coffin is that of Christians."[1] Open declarations of Christian faith are still exceptions rather than the norm, and Apolinarius rejoices in the courage of this couple who had been members of the congregation he oversees as bishop.

Apolinarius is grateful for the shade provided by the colonnade as he walks back the way he had come. By now, the sun is high in the sky and it is hot. But before returning to his home Apolinarius cannot resist—if only for a brief moment—to leave the shade of the street and take the few steps to the edge of the plateau on which the city of Hierapolis is built. With the bright sun reflecting on the dozens

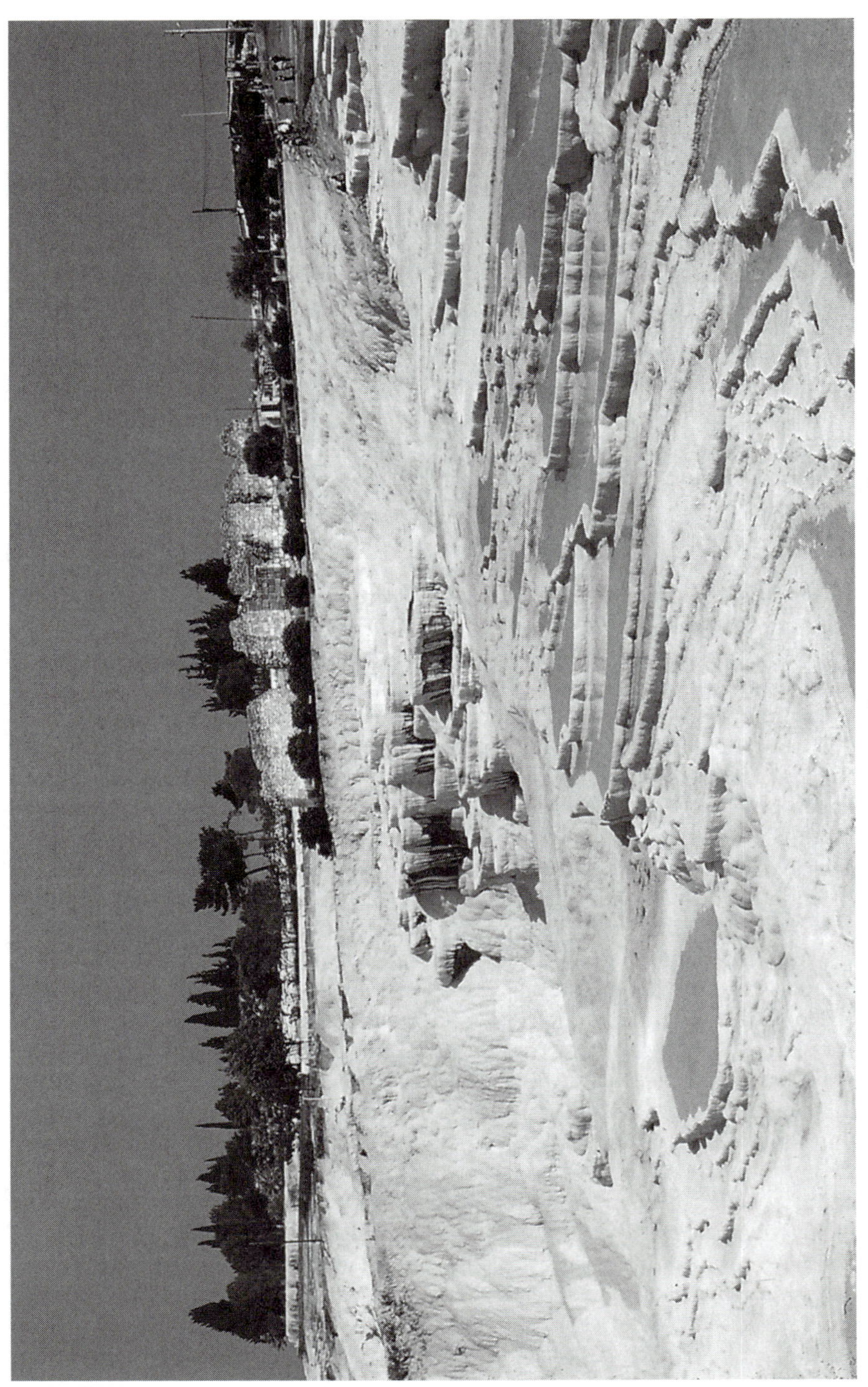

Figure 2.1: Travertine formations at Hierapolis

of large and small pools, he has a magnificent view of the spectacular semi-circular terraces that comprise the western slopes of the city. Centuries of calcium deposits from Hierapolis' natural springs have not only turned these terraced slopes pure white but have produced fascinating and beautiful stalactite formations. The overall effect is stunning.

Fortunately, a few clouds have appeared in the sky. As Apolinarius stands in his favorite spot overlooking the travertine formations, the shadows from the clouds play tricks with the scenery. At one moment Apolinarius seems to be looking at a seascape, with waves rolling in and breaking on the shore. The next moment the calcium-covered rocks with their stalactites look like the towers of a Roman fort. Another moment and the terraces look like long, broad steps leading up to a large white temple that somehow disappears in the clouds.

Having lingered longer than he had intended, Apolinarius turns on his heels, returns to the colonnaded street, and heads home. While staring across the travertine terraces, he had made up his mind. He will use whatever influence he has with his brother bishops to ensure that the so-called New Prophecy is denounced as blasphemous and declared a heresy.[2]

Sources:

Eusebius, *Hist. eccl.* 4.27, 5.16.1; Serapion, *Ep., ap.* Eusebius, *Hist. eccl.* 5.19.2; Eusebius, *Chron.* Olymp. 238.1; *IMont* 10.

Colonia Copia Claudia Augusta Lugdunum, Gaul, July-August, 177 C.E.

Potheinos considers the New Prophets
Christians are persecuted

Potheinos is an old man, more than ninety years of age. He breathes and walks with great difficulty, but he is not too frail to preside over yet another synod. As the bishop of Lugdunum, he oversees the Christians in that city as well as those who are members of the smaller Christian community in nearby Vienna.[3] Vienna, like Lugdunum, is also a Roman colony, named Colonia Julia Augusta Florentia Vienna.

It is the time of the Festival of the Three Gauls, and many residents from outlying districts have traveled to Lugdunum to participate in the celebrations. More than sixty cities and towns are expected to be represented at the festival this year, which begins on August 1st—Augustus' birthday. Just like every year for as long as he can remember, Potheinos has seen people arrive during the past few days from Belgica, Aquitania, and from other parts of Lugdunensis—the Tres Galliae. Some people come by horse or ox-drawn carts. Others come by boat along the Rhodanus and disembark at the quays that line both sides of the river. The more wealthy of the visitors stay in rented lodgings in Lugdunum itself, high above the Rhodanus at the point where, less than a mile to the east, the Arar runs parallel to the Rhodanus.

Potheinos stops to rest. The hill down from the terraces where Lugdunum is situated is steep, and even though he is headed down toward the river bank rather than up toward the theater, his lungs feel like they are on fire. He coughs noisily and sits down on a bench. From here he has a perfect view of both rivers and the canal that runs diagonally between them. He can also see the bridge that crosses the Rhodanus and the road that leads from the bridge to the Sanctuary of the Three Gauls. While Potheinos' lungs are not as good as they used to be, his eyesight is excellent for an old man, and from this vantage point he can see, in the distance, the Ara trium Galliarum, the Altar of the Three Gauls. That is, he can see part of the altar's enclosure—the rectangular walls that form the precinct within which the altar itself stands.

Potheinos has never been to Rome, but he has heard from others that the altar at Lugdunum is similar to its more famous counterpart, the Ara pacis Augustae, the Altar of Augustan Peace. The citizens of Lugdunum are proud that, although their altar's external walls are not decorated as beautifully as the Ara pacis in Rome, their altar is the earliest of its type dedicated by Augustus. It is also one of the few altars of its kind with an amphitheater attached to it. Double ramps, used especially during processions, lead from the altar into the arena of the amphitheater. As he thinks about the amphitheater, Potheinos shudders involuntarily. He doesn't know why, but it feels as if someone has just walked over his grave. With a strong sense of foreboding, Potheinos abandons his plan to go all the way down to the river. Having rested, feeling strong enough, he turns around and slowly walks back up the hill.

Given the urgency of the situation confronting the church in the Roman province of Gallia Lugdunensis, Potheinos has decided to call together the Christian presbyters and deacons of the region to discuss the matter. The issue at hand is what to make of the New Prophecy. The church in Lugdunum has a number of prominent members who had emigrated from Asia Minor. The highly respected presbyter Irenaeus, for example, grew up in Smyrna where, as a young man, he sat at the feet of Polycarp of blessed memory. It is rumored that Polycarp, the renowned and revered bishop and teacher, had himself been a disciple of the apostle John. Another in their midst, Alexander, a man who is not without his own share of apostolic charism, is a well known and respected physician originally from Phrygia. These men and others keep the lines of communication open between the churches of Gaul and the churches of Phrygia and other parts of the Roman province of Asia.

The new charismatic movement now sweeping Phrygia and the whole province of Asia disturbs and perplexes the members of the churches of Lugdunum and Vienna. On the one hand, as the reputation of Montanus, Maximilla, and Priscilla becomes more widespread because of their prophesying, many Christians in Gaul are ready to believe that these so-called "New Prophets" are truly inspired by the Holy Spirit and exercise an authentic prophetic ministry that should be heeded. On the other hand, the most recent reports by visitors from Asia, including Phrygia, brought disturbing new information. The leaders of the churches there apparently met officially on more than one occasion to test the genuineness of the New Prophecy. After examining carefully the oracles and other sayings of Montanus and the others, the bishops and presbyters in the homeland of the New Prophecy pronounced the sayings profane. They have formally rejected the sect and expelled its adherents from the church, thus excluding them from the fellowship of other Christians.

The excommunication of the New Prophets and their followers in Asia Minor presents a real pastoral problem for Potheinos and his fellow clergy in Gaul. What if the next time there are visitors (or especially if there are new immigrants) from Asia or, especially, from Phrygia these include adherents of the New Prophecy? Should these people be received warmly as Christian brothers and sisters and welcomed at the Eucharist or should they be excluded from fellowship as they would be in their home churches? How can one tell the difference between one who adheres to the New Prophecy and any other kind of Christian anyway? And, what is even more troublesome, have the bishops and presbyters in Asia Minor really made the right decision or have they prematurely rejected a genuine prophetic movement? Potheinos feels he has no other option than to do what his episcopal colleagues in Phrygia and elsewhere in Asia have done—convene a synod so that the clergy in Gaul may make their own responsible decisions about these matters.[4]

Maturus, a recent convert to the Christian faith; Sanctus, a deacon from Vienna; Blandina, a frail servant girl; and Attalus, a member of a prominent family from Pergamon, where he had been a pillar of the Christian community, are all taken into the amphitheater via one of the ceremonial ramps that run alongside the Altar of the Three Gauls. The arena, almost perfectly round, is smaller than many others of its kind. Certainly it is tiny in comparison to the famous Colosseum in Rome; no more than a dozen rows of tiered seats surround the arena. The small crowd, however, is rowdy, like the crowds in all the larger arenas elsewhere in the Empire, and they are thirsty for blood. The Festival of the Three Gauls is nearly over. There are only a few days left. For today's event the organizers have something special for the crowd, and those in the stands look forward, with anticipation, to what it might be.

As the four Christians enter the arena they, as is customary, have to run the gauntlet, being whipped as they run. Once in the center of the amphitheater, wild beasts are let loose upon them. The three men and one woman dare not run, wishing neither to turn their backs on the animals nor to appear cowards in the face of danger. Men with short swords, tritons, and nets prod the animals to attack and

Figure 2.2: Amphitheater at Lugdunum (Lyons)

maul their victims—all to the delight of the crowd. Blandina is tied to a stake—human bait to provoke even more ferocious attacks. Hanging there in the shape of a cross, she inspires courage in her fellow martyrs. Maturus and Sanctus are forced to sit in red-hot iron seats, the pungent stench of their roasting flesh filling the amphitheater. At sunset, Maturus and Sanctus are put to death with the sword in a mocking imitation of the dispatch of defeated gladiators, for whom they have substituted in the arena that day.

But then something unexpected happens. Inexplicably, the animals leave Blandina alone. She is taken down from the stake and, along with Attalus, returned to prison. During the day, Attalus had been paraded around the arena with a sign in Latin that read: "This is Attalus, the Christian."[5] Although the crowd is calling for his execution, Attalus is taken back to prison with Blandina.

The governor is awaiting a reply from the emperor, Marcus Aurelius, regarding what he should do with Christians, such as Attalus, who possess Roman citizenship. The governor and the prisoners do not have to wait long. The emperor's response decrees that those who recant and deny their Christian faith should be released and those who refuse to recant should be thrown to the beasts—unless they possess Roman citizenship, in which case they are to be beheaded. The governor, however, is so angry at Attalus that, instead of beheading him relatively painlessly, he has Attalus first tied to a chair made of brass which, like the iron chairs used to roast Maturus and Sanctus, is already red-hot. Blandina also has to endure the hot seat for a while before being thrown to a bull who tosses her relentlessly until, mercifully, she becomes unconscious. Neither Attalus nor Blandina recovers from the ordeal.

Altogether forty-eight Christians from Lugdunum, Vienna, and elsewhere in Gaul are arrested. Those who are still in prison—the Roman citizens and others not yet used as animal fodder—are not idle. They still have regular contact with relatives and members of the Christian community, who bring them food and care for them in other ways. The martyrs-to-be encourage one another and even help some who have apostatized renew their faith.

So much has happened in such a short time since some of them and their leaders had gathered formally to discuss the issues confronting them with respect to the New Prophecy. Potheinos, their beloved bishop, is dead, an early victim of the mob violence that had been unleashed against them. As he was dragged from the tribunal where he had boldly confessed his Christianity, he had been beaten viciously by bystanders. Barely breathing when he was thrown into jail, he had died there two days later. The others are glad the old man had been spared the more ingenious tortures their persecutors had inflicted on some of their other companions in the amphitheater.

They still cannot understand why the persecution began and accelerated so quickly. Didn't their former friends and neighbors know them well enough to recognize that the charges of infanticide, Thyestian banquets, and Oedipean incest were nothing but the false accusations of servants frightened out of their wits by the threat of torture? Couldn't they believe Blandina when she told the governor: "I am a Christian and nothing perverse takes place among us"?[6] Or why not believe

Biblis, who at first denied her faith but when put on the rack, instead of making up false accusations, declared that Christians could not be guilty of devouring children because they were not even permitted to partake of the blood of animals?

Some wonder whether the recently passed *senatus consultum*, the decree of the senate that allows convicted criminals to be used in gladiatorial shows, may have prompted the organizing officials to seize on a cheap way to supplement at least part of the heavy burden of putting on the games in Lugdunum. Perhaps—others speculate—the coinciding of a heightened sense of patriotism in the weeks leading up to the Festival of the Three Gauls and so many Christians from the countryside being in the city for the synod Potheinos had called to discuss the New Prophecy, ignited the spark that set off the pogrom against those already suspected of being disloyal to the Empire by not participating in the state cult.[7]

Whatever the actual reason or reasons behind the persecution, the Christians in prison feel that their leaders made the right decision about the New Prophecy. Some of them, believing that their status as martyrs-designate gives them special authority to do so, scribble out, with whatever writing implements they can lay their hands on in prison, letters denouncing the New Prophecy. These letters are attached to the formal notices setting forth the official decision of the synod at Lugdunum. The synodical notices and supporting letters from the martyrs are sent not only to the congregations in Asia and Phrygia but also to Eleutherus, the bishop of the Christian community in Rome. In doing this, the martyrs believe they are ambassadors for the sake of the unity of the churches. No matter how much some of the Christians at Lugdunum or Vienna may individually admire charismatic gifts such as prophecy, the ultimate good of the whole church, as they see it, depends on confirming, independently, the decision made about the New Prophecy by their sister churches in Asia, including Phrygia. To do otherwise would break the unity they share in faith and practice. As they write to Eleutherus, who is facing the same issues at Rome, they hope and pray that he will see things the way they do.

Sources:

Mart. Lugd. 1.1–2.8 (Eusebius, *Hist. eccl.* 5.1.4–2.8); Eusebius, *Hist. eccl.* 4.24.3–6, 5.3.1–4, 5.4.1, 5.5.8, 5.20.4–8; Irenaeus, *Haer.* 3.3.4; Anonymous, *Fr., ap.* Eusebius, *Hist. eccl.* 5.16.10; Oliver and Palmer 1955, 343 [*Senatus consultum, ll.*56–58].

Notes

1. *IMont* 10. Ammia and Asklepios' epitaph is not dated but is prior to 212, perhaps as early as 175 (Tabbernee 1997b, 91–93) and so may have existed in Apolinarius' time.

2. Whether or not Apolinarius (*flor.* ca. 170) actually presided over a synod of bishops rather than simply a local "church gathering" dealing with the New Prophecy remains a debated issue among scholars; see Tabbernee 2007, 15–20.

3. The Vienna referred to here (Map 1: B3–C3) is modern-day Vienne in France, not to be confused with Vienna (ancient Vindobona) in modern-day Austria.

4. As in the case of Hierapolis, it remains debatable whether there was an actual synod at Lugdunum which dealt with the New Prophecy or simply an informal gathering of church leaders—some of whom, as "confessors" (i.e., still-living witnesses for the faith) communicated the "prudent and most orthodox" decision they made to the Christian communities of Asia (including Phrygia) and to Eleutherus of Rome (ca. 174/5–ca. 189).

5. *Mart. Lugd.* 1.44. For the text and an English translation of the *Martyrs of Lyons* (i.e., ancient Lugdunum) and of many of the other *Acta martyrum* ("Acts of the Martyrs") referred to in this book, see Musurillo 1972.

6. *Mart. Lugd.* 1.19 (my translation).

7. On the Altar of the Three Gauls, see Fishwick 1972, 46–52; 1987–2005, 3.3: 105–27. The *senatus consultum* and its possible relevance to the Festival of the Three Gauls at Lugdunum is discussed by Oliver and Palmer (1955, 320–49, esp. 325). For the view that Montanism may have *indirectly* contributed to the outbreak of the persecution at Lugdunum, see Tabbernee 2007, 179–81.

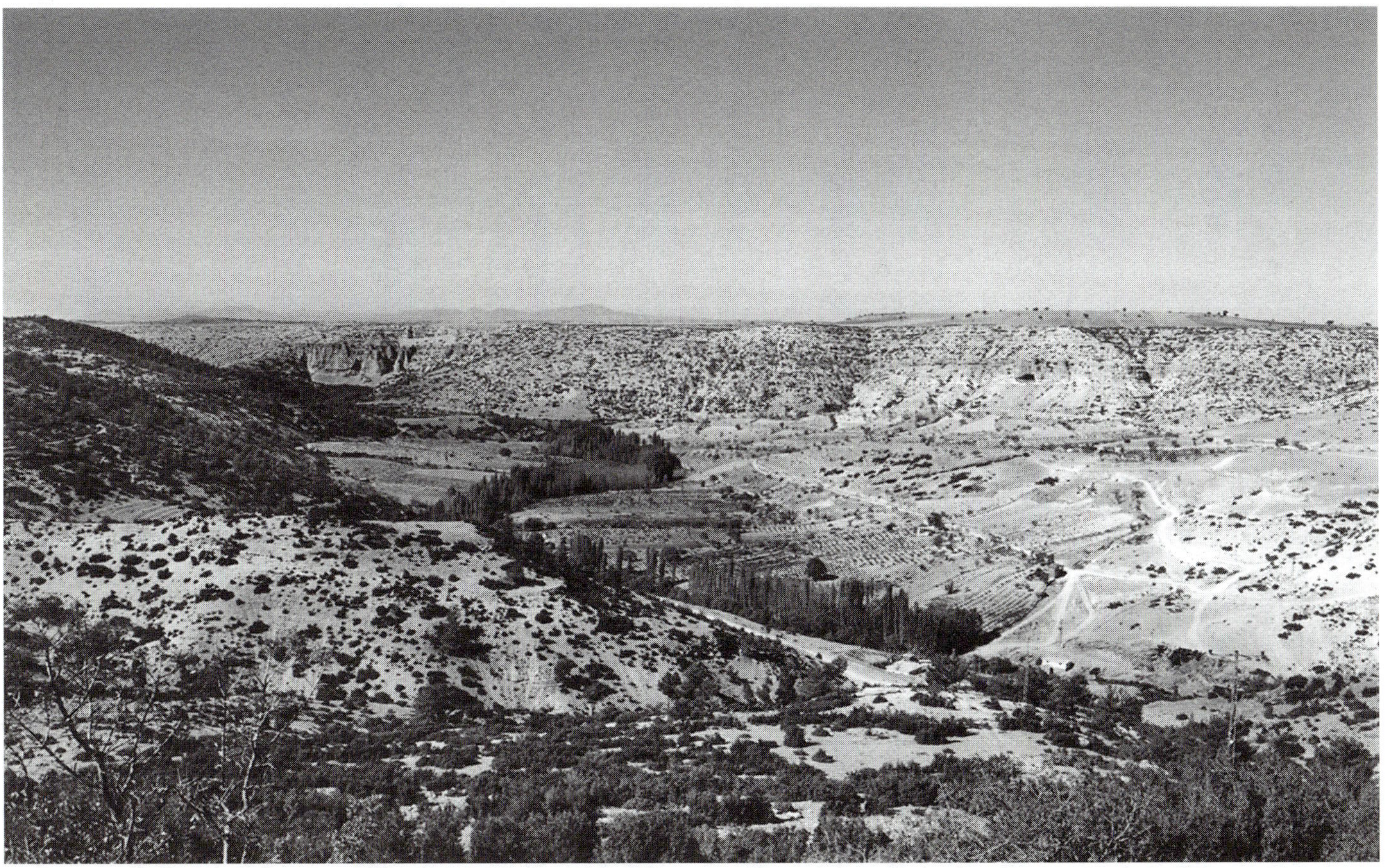

Figure 3.1: Site of ancient Pepouza. The course of the ancient Sindros River is shown by the row of poplar trees.

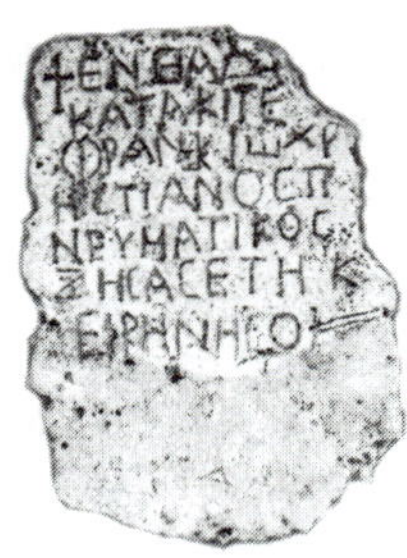

Chapter 3

Pepouza, Phrygia, ca. 178 C.E.

A failed exorcism

Zotikos is suddenly wide awake. He has slept fitfully, tossing and turning in the hard narrow bed provided for him by his host. He has not heard Julian get up from his borrowed bed in the same room, but Julian's firm hand on his shoulder rouses him immediately. Sitting boldly upright in bed, he looks at his fellow bishop conspiratorially. Without saying a word he gets up, puts on his tunic and his sandals, and follows Julian to the tiny kitchen where they hastily eat a breakfast consisting of chunks of freshly baked bread, goat cheese, and a drink made of yogurt, water, and salt.

What they are about to attempt will require opportunity, courage, and the power of God to accomplish. To prepare themselves for their task, they pray over the holy oil they have brought with them to consecrate it as the "oil of exorcism." The oil of exorcism is usually used during the rite of baptism, but it is not the baptism of a willing catechumen they are about to perform—it is the uninvited exorcism of someone already baptized.

Each man takes a vial of holy oil and tucks it into the folds of his tunic, ready for use. Bidding farewell to their Christian host, they leave the man's house and walk down the long narrow street that descends from the section of the city where they have spent the night toward the agora. As they walk downhill, they pass a number of insulae, blocks of two-, and in some cases, three-story tenement buildings, where countless families live out a crowded, noisy, and stenchy existence. They are glad their host owns a house, albeit a small one, built on the more desirable slopes of the northeast part of the city.

Closer to the commercial and civic center of Pepouza, Zotikos and Julian first turn left and then immediately right into the agora. Even at this early hour, the shops are bustling with life. A virtual cornucopia of aromas greet them as they pass by stall after stall. Having crossed the marketplace, the two bishops quickly descend some steps that lead past a fountain, to a path that goes to a burial chamber. As they enter the chamber through the narrow passageway, they see, in the center of the room, an unusual sarcophagus. It is made of iron plates, sealed with lead. The bishops are not superstitious, but their nerves are on edge as they stand before the large coffin that contains the bones of Montanus and Priscilla.[1]

Zotikos and Julian have heard rumors that Montanus hanged himself and that Theodotus, another early leader of the New Prophecy, also died horrifically—having crashed down from the sky as the just reward for ecstatic levitation. They are not sure whether to believe these rumors. Nor do they know how Priscilla died. But they do know that, some years before her death, an attempt was made by Sotas of Anchialos to exorcise the evil prophetic spirit from her.

It took a tremendous amount of courage for Zotikos and Julian to enter the chamber containing the bones of Montanus and Priscilla, a chamber that—undoubtedly—will one day also hold the bones of Maximilla and other prominent leaders of the New Prophecy. While it is a holy site for adherents of the movement and is already being visited by pilgrims, for the two orthodox bishops it is the foul grave of two demon-possessed false prophets. But they had to see for themselves that Montanus and Priscilla really are dead.

Taking no further chance that they themselves might become polluted, they quickly make the sign of the cross and hurry out of the chamber, the vials of oil still in the folds of their garments. Montanus and Priscilla are beyond exorcism, but Maximilla is still alive and they need walk only a few minutes to find her.

The sun is high in the sky as Zotikos of Konana and Julian of Apameia emerge from the dark tomb chamber; the brightness hurts their eyes. They turn left and follow the Sindros River for a hundred yards or so before turning left again into the residential part of Pepouza. The house they seek belongs to a man named Themiso. They know Themiso only by reputation. An early convert to the New Prophecy, Themiso became the leader of the movement at Pepouza after the deaths of Montanus and Priscilla.

After making a few wrong turns and stopping twice to ask for directions, Zotikos and Julian find the right house. They knock on the door. At first there is no answer. Then, after what seems like an eternity, the door opens with a creak. Standing there before them is not only a man who identifies himself as Themiso, but also a woman who can be none other than Maximilla herself!

The two bishops finger their vials of exorcism oil, but before they can speak Maximilla cries out in an ethereal voice: "I am being banished as a wolf from sheep. I am Utterance, and Spirit, and Power."[2] The bishops' fingers seem to freeze around their vials of oil. Neither one has time to pull out his vial and pronounce the liturgical formula for exorcising an evil spirit before Themiso slams the door shut, and Maximilla disappears from view.[3] The dumbstruck bishops stand there rigidly for a few moments, then regain their composure. Once more they pound heavily on the door, but this time there is no answer.

Sources:

Anonymous, *Fr., ap.* Eusebius, *Hist. eccl.* 5.16.13–17; Apollonius, *Fr., ap.* Eusebius, *Hist. eccl.* 5.18.12; *IMont* 1–2; Aelius Publius Julius, *Sub., ap.* Apolinarius, *Ep., ap.* Serapion, *Ep., ap.* Eusebius, *Hist. eccl.* 5.19.3; Maximilla, *Log., ap.* Asterius Urbanus, *Fr., ap.* Anonymous, *Fr., ap.* Eusebius, *Hist. eccl.* 5.16.17.

Notes

1. On the reliquary at Pepouza containing the bones of Montanus and other prominent Montanists, see Tabbernee 1997c, 206–17, esp. 213–17, and Chapters 34 and 38 below.

2. Maximilla, *Log.*, *ap.* Asterius Urbanus, *Fr.*, *ap.* Anonymous, *Fr.*, *ap.* Eusebius, *Hist. eccl.* 5.16.17.

3. The extant sources regarding the attempted but failed exorcism of Maximilla and Priscilla do not specifically mention the "oil of exorcism," but that the bishops intent on performing the exorcisms had such oil with them may be presumed. By about that time, the "oil of exorcism" was part of the liturgy of baptism (*Trad. ap.* 21) and soon thereafter, the Council of Ikonion (ca. 230–235) determined that Montanists wanting to become members of mainstream Christianity needed to be rebaptized; see Chapter 18 below.

Chapter 4

Apameia, Phrygia, ca. 190 C.E.

Division among the persecuted

The dungeon is dark and dank. A putrid odor, the result of seeping sewage, is so thick that Gaius and Alexander almost retch as they are pushed down the steep stone steps by the guards. It takes a while for their eyes to adjust to the darkness. When they do, they see that they are not alone. Indeed the small subterranean room is quite crowded.

One of the men who is already in the dark hole asks them if they are Christians also. For a moment Gaius and Alexander are taken aback. Open profession of Christianity among strangers is not common and could have disastrous consequences. Then they remember that here in this place there is nothing to be lost by admitting their allegiance to Christianity to those in the room. Indeed the reason they have just been thrown into jail is that they have already twice made public confession to being Christians. The first time was before local magistrates in their native city of Eumeneia. That was weeks ago. Since then they had been brought to Apameia to await the governor's visit to preside over the conventus juridicus, the court of justice, convened regularly at Apameia to deal with legal cases arising in the district. The journey itself had not been an unpleasant one, and under other circumstances Gaius and Alexander would have enjoyed the visit to the larger city.

Today on their way to the tribunal, they caught a glimpse of the beautiful waterfall that is the source of the Maiandros River. Earlier they had heard the rumor that the mountaintop from which the waterfall cascades into the large pool below is where Noah's ark came to rest after the flood, but they disregarded this rumor as legend, knowing that Mount Ararat lies much further to the east.[1] Along with others brought before the governor earlier that day, Gaius and Alexander had confessed their Christianity.

In fact, now that their eyes are accustomed to the dim light of the dungeon, Gaius and Alexander recognize some of the men and women who had preceded them in the trial procedure. They do not, however, recognize the man who has just asked whether they are Christians. He and some others are standing somewhat apart from the others in the room.

The man introduces himself and his companions as Christians who belong to the New Prophecy movement founded by Montanus, Maximilla, and Priscilla. As soon as he does so, a stern voice from the back of the dungeon warns Gaius and Alexander not to have anything to do with the adherents of the New Prophecy. "We don't want to appear to condone the spirit that speaks through Montanus and the women," the voice adds.[2] Gaius and Alexander concur heartily. They have had their own problems with followers of the New Prophecy. After all, Pepouza, the center of this movement that seems to be taking over Christianity throughout Phrygia, is situated only two days' walk from Eumeneia.

As Gaius and Alexander quickly make their way toward the person who issued the warning, they purposely shun the man who asked if they are Christians also. How dare he include them in his perverted definition of Christianity! Yes, Gaius and Alexander are Christians but they—unlike the followers of Montanus, Maximilla, and Priscilla—belong to the true faith. Tomorrow they will die as martyrs for that faith. The man who first spoke to them and his companions will also die—but for what and as what? Gaius and Alexander cannot imagine that a false prophecy is worth dying for. They certainly will not recognize the adherents of false prophets as fellow Christian martyrs! Physically they might all be put to death together, but they will definitely not be together in death.[3]

Source:

Anonymous, *Fr., ap.* Eusebius, *Hist. eccl.* 5.16.22.

Ankyra, Galatia, ca. 192/3 C.E.

A Phrygian bishop debates with adherents of the New Prophecy

The presbyters are at their wits' end. More and more of their parishioners are being persuaded that the New Prophecy is a genuine manifestation of the Holy Spirit. In fact, the debates raging between those for and those against the validity of the spirit who a quarter of a century ago had spoken through Montanus, Maximilla, and Priscilla, is enough to shatter one's eardrums. Try as they might, the presbyters cannot resolve the tension that threatens to split their church. They are reluctant, however, to state outright that the followers of the Phrygian prophets are deluded and in danger of falling into heresy. What if the Holy Spirit has, indeed, revealed some things through the Phrygians that the church needs to know?

On the other hand, what if the so-called New Prophecy is really a perversion of the true faith? Haven't some of their fellow presbyters and bishops in Phrygia already formally condemned the movement as blasphemous and heretical? The Ankyran presbyters are glad that soon they will be able to welcome a very important bishop to their church. This bishop has had great success in refuting the adherents of the New Prophecy elsewhere. Hopefully, he will achieve the same here.

The famous bishop arrives in the company of Zotikos of Otrous, whom he introduces as "our fellow presbyter," meaning by this, of course, that Zotikos is also a bishop.[4] It is soon apparent to the church leaders of Ankyra that they are indeed fortunate in having the experienced opponent of the New Prophecy and his fellow bishop visiting their congregation. The senior of the two bishops is not at all timid. He quickly attacks the adherents of the New Prophecy head-on. Day after day, he teaches all who will listen about the origins of the movement and he refutes every claim to legitimacy made by its proponents. Montanus, the bishop claims, was a recent convert to Christianity—not a person seasoned in the true faith. Montanus' downfall, the bishop explains, was that the immeasurable desire of his soul for preeminence gave the adversary—the devil—a way to enter into him. "Moved as by a wind or spirit, Montanus suddenly fell into possession of some sort," the bishop tells his audience. "In extraordinary ecstasy, Montanus became frenzied, began to babble and to utter strange noises. He pretended to be prophesying, but it was pseudo-prophecy, not real prophecy," says the bishop. "Montanus' manner of 'prophesying' was completely contrary to the manner of prophesying received by tradition and handed on by succession from the beginning of the church!"[5]

The bishop's statements spark a heated discussion about prophetic succession. The leading proponent of the New Prophecy at Ankyra argues passionately that the New Prophecy is legitimate. "Maximilla and Priscilla received the prophetic gift by succession from Quadratus and, in Philadelphia, from Ammia," he claims.[6] Everyone present has heard of Quadratus and, especially, of Ammia—both were famous prophetic figures from the region whose memory is still very much venerated. They also recognize the names of the other prophets and prophetesses referred to by the defender of the New Prophecy: Agabus, Judas, Silas,[7] and the daughters of Philip.[8] They know that some of the latter are buried at Hierapolis, along with their father, in a reliquary-shrine visited each year by hundreds of pilgrims. Most of those listening are convinced that if the prophets and prophetesses of the New Prophecy are part of this eminent line of prophetic succession, the New Prophecy must be a genuine movement of the Holy Spirit. It appears that the proponent of the New Prophecy has won the day. The visiting bishop, however, is not yet finished.

Adjusting the folds of his cloak, the bishop from Phrygia draws himself up to his tallest posture and speaks authoritatively:

> A *false* prophet, by definition, is a person in an extraordinary ecstasy in which he or she speaks without restraint and without fear—beginning with voluntary ignorance but ending up with involuntary madness of soul.[9]

To prove that this has, indeed, been said before, the bishop produces a small codex that he holds in his left hand. Pointing directly to the little book with the fingers of his right hand, he states:

> Having found some of their sayings in a certain book of theirs opposed to a book of Brother Miltiades in which they furnish proof concerning the impropriety of a prophet speaking in ecstasy, I have compiled an epitome.[10]

The people present can hardly believe what they are hearing and seeing. Right before their eyes was not the actual book written by one of the early leaders of the New Prophecy, but the next best thing: an abridgement of it made by the very bishop who holds the epitome in his left hand. They can't wait to hear him read aloud some of the *logia* of the founders of the prophetic movement that has them all so stirred up. Those in favor of the movement are certain the *logia* will vindicate the legitimacy of the New Prophecy. Those against it are equally certain the *logia* will demonstrate, as the bishop said, the falsity of the ecstatic speech of the so-called New Prophets. With a flair for the dramatic, the bishop hides the codex in the folds of his robe and tells his audience to come back the next day.

Early the next morning, all the people who had been present the previous day are back. They crowd into the house that serves as the meeting place of the largest house-church in Ankyra. They are joined by a number of others who, like their companions, have decided that their chores can wait a while. Sorting out the legitimacy of the New Prophecy must take priority while the learned bishop is in their midst.

As the bishop enters, there is a hushed silence. The bishop takes the precious little codex out of the folds of his cloak and begins to read a list of those whom he declares the church acknowledges as having prophesied according to the legitimate tradition handed down from the earliest Christian prophets. The adherents of the New Prophecy are on the edge of their seats as the bishop reads the same names they themselves had presented earlier, including Ammia and Quadratus! They wonder whether the bishop might be conceding defeat!

As he comes to the end of his list, the bishop, for the sake of those not present the day before, repeats what he had said about the definition of *pseudo*-prophecy: A *false* prophet speaks without restraint and without fear from voluntary ignorance to involuntary madness of soul in a state of extraordinary ecstasy. The bishop suddenly thrusts out his right arm and juts his bony fingers directly at the leading defenders of the New Prophecy. He shouts:

> They are able neither among the old nor the new covenant to point to a single prophet who was inspired by the Spirit in this manner: neither Agabus, nor Judas, nor Silas, nor the daughters of Philip, nor Ammia in Philadelphia, nor Quadratus—nor any others, not belonging to them at all, of whom they should now boast.[11]

The bishop slowly lowers his arm, but he keeps his gaze directly on the adherents of the New Prophecy before shifting his eyes to the others before him. He says tauntingly:

> If, as they say, the women around Montanus received the prophetic gift by succession from Quadratus and Ammia, let them show who among them received it from Montanus and the women![12]

The room is totally silent. The audience is stunned. The bishop has delivered two fatal blows against the legitimacy of the New Prophecy. The *manner* of prophesying by the New Prophets disqualifies them from claiming prophetic succession not only via those mentioned in the sacred texts of Christianity but also via more recent prophets and prophetesses such as Quadratus and Ammia or any others the New Prophecy might claim. Not one of these genuine prophets and prophetesses exhibited the strange phenomena that accompanied the prophesies of Montanus, Maximilla, and Priscilla. If Montanus, Maximilla, and Priscilla were legitimate prophets belonging to the genuine Christian prophetic succession, they should have prophesied in the same respectable manner as the prophets from Agabus onward prophesied: in full control of their senses.

The bishop not only deprives the New Prophets of their predecessors, he also denies them any legitimate successors. He continues his taunting. "The apostle deemed it necessary that the prophetic gift exist in the whole church until the final coming," he reminds his opponents.[13] He then pauses dramatically. When he has everyone's undivided attention again, he flings his right arm in the direction of the supporters of the New Prophecy once more, so that everyone present knows for sure to whom he is about to refer. "But they have not been able to point to anyone—this being already about the fourteenth year from the death of Maximilla!"[14]

The supporters of the New Prophecy are about to protest and point out that there *are* second-generation prophets and prophetesses that belong to the movement. One of these is Miltiades—not the Miltiades who wrote a book against them and was mentioned by the visiting bishop. The New Prophecy's Miltiades rose to prominence after Maximilla's death and now, at least in some circles, the adherents of the New Prophecy are popularly named after him.[15] But the defenders of the New Prophecy in Ankyra remain in their seats. They know that mentioning Miltiades is useless. Their opponent would merely dismiss Miltiades as a false prophet on the premise that he, like Montanus, Priscilla, and Maximilla, prophesied while in a state of abnormal and spurious ecstasy.

The next day there are even more people present at the lectures on the New Prophecy being conducted by the bishop visiting the Christian community at Ankyra. The previous evening the bishop had apologized for not having time to read aloud some of the *logia* of the New Prophets and show from their own words that the New Prophecy is illegitimate. But he promised to do so this morning.

At the back, there is standing room only and the few latecomers jostle one another as they try to get a better view of the bishop. By now his audience is used to the dramatic way he pulls out of the folds of his robe his own epitome of the New Prophecy's *logia,* written against the treatise by the "orthodox" Miltiades. They listen intently as the bishop reads aloud more of the oracles of Montanus,

Maximilla, and Priscilla—explaining in each case how the content as well as the manner of their prophesying proves they are fake rather than genuine prophets and prophetesses. The supporters of the New Prophecy in Ankyra, however, are far from persuaded by the bishop's explanations.

Source:

Anonymous, *Fr., ap.* Eusebius, *Hist. eccl.* 5.16.1–5.19.4.

Notes

1. The Apameia in West-Central Phrygia was distinguished from other cities of the same name, founded or refounded when the Seleucid dynasty controlled much of Asia Minor (ca. 281–188 B.C.E.), by means of the by-name *Kibotos,* derived from the Greek κιβωτός. A *kibōtos* was a wooden container or chest, the kind in which goods were transported on wagons which followed the trade routes of Asia Minor (including through Apameia) on their way to coastal seaports where the same chests were, without repacking, loaded onto ships. Various coins struck at Apameia Kibotos display wooden chests. As the word κιβωτός was used by the translators of the Septuagint (e.g., at Gen 6:14) for Noah's *ark,* a local Jewish (and, later, Christian) tradition developed linking the city with the resting place of Noah's ark. This tradition both influenced and was influenced by Jewish and early Christian artwork depicting Noah floating in a box-like ark (see R. Jensen 2000, 66). Some coins (e.g., Head 1887, 667 no. 313) struck during the time of Septimius Severus (193–211) and of subsequent emperors bear the legend ΝΩΕ (*Nōe,* i.e., Noah) on the obverse. The coins depict Noah and his wife twice: once within a floating *kibōtos,* and, secondly, safe on dry land. One of the best discussions of the Noah's ark tradition at Apameia remains Ramsay 1895–1897, 669–72.

2. See Anonymous, *Fr., ap.* Eusebius, *Hist. eccl.* 5.16.22.

3. The events described in this part of this chapter obviously took place prior to the writing of the Anonymous' work against the New Prophecy in ca. 193 (see next section). Assuming that the martyrdoms occurred during the latter part of the reign of Commodus (180–192), the date ca. 190 seems a reasonable conjecture.

4. Attempts to identify the unnamed bishop, referred to by scholars as "the Anonymous," have been unsuccessful. All that can be surmised from the paucity of personal information contained in the extant portions of his work is that he was the bishop of a city in Phrygia. This city was probably (but not certainly) Brouzos, Eukarpia, or Stektorion. His "fellow-presbyter" Zotikos of Otrous and Avircius of Hieropolis were, respectively, bishops of the two other cities which comprised the Phrygian Pentapolis. The view that Zotikos was a "bishop" is based on the fact that, at least until the end of the second century, it was common for bishops to refer to fellow-bishops as presbyters (e.g., cf. Irenaeus, *Ep., ap.* Eusebius, *Hist. eccl.* 5.24.14–17). For Avircius, see Chapter 5.

5. Anonymous, *Fr., ap.* Eusebius, *Hist. eccl.* 5.16.7.

6. See Anonymous, *Fr., ap.* Eusebius, *Hist. eccl.* 5.17.4a. According to both the adherents of the New Prophecy and opponents of the movement such as the Anonymous, a prophetess named Ammia from Philadelphia, and a prophet named Quadratus (perhaps from the same geographic region) were important links in the authentic chain of prophetic succession. There is no need to assume that the prophet Quadratus is the Quadratus who, in the time of Hadrian (117–138), wrote an *Apology* for Christianity (*ap.* Eusebius, *Hist. eccl.* 4.3.1–3). As Montanists claimed that Maximilla and Priscilla received their prophetic

charism as the immediate successors of Ammia and Quadratus (Anonymous, *Fr., ap.* Eusebius, *Hist. eccl.* 5.16.4), the latter must have been operative ca. 150–160.

7. Both the Montanists and their opponents appealed to a prophetic succession originating from Jerusalem. One branch of this succession came via Antioch in Syria, where, according to Acts 11:26, the followers of Jesus were first called Christians. Agabus was a prophet from Jerusalem who visited Antioch (11:27–28). Following the Council of Jerusalem, two other prophets from Jerusalem, Judas Barsabbas and Silas (15:22, 27, 31), were sent to accompany Paul and Barnabas to Antioch to report on the council. Silas, according to Acts, later accompanied Paul to Phrygian Galatia (15:40; 16:6), on his "second missionary journey" (15:36–19:20), thus providing the Christian tradition of prophetic succession in Asia Minor with a direct link between the first Christian prophets and those who succeeded them in Phrygia and Galatia.

8. The tradition of prophetic succession via Antioch in Syria was supplemented in the region by the tradition of the residence at Hierapolis of Philip's daughters (Polycrates, *Ep., ap.* Eusebius, *Hist. eccl.* 3.31.3 = 5.24.2; Proclus, *ap.* Gaius, *Proc., ap.* Eusebius, *Hist. eccl.* 3.31.4; Eusebius, *Hist. eccl.* 3.39.9 [on the testimony of Papias]). This prophetic tradition, however, was a fusing of separate traditions about Philip the *apostle* and about Philip the evangelist—who "had four daughters, virgins, who had the gift of prophecy" (Acts 21:9); see Eusebius, *Hist. eccl.* 3.31.5 and Tabbernee, 1997b, 504–8. Papias, the early second-century bishop of Hierapolis and (according to Eusebius) contemporary of Philip's daughters at Hierapolis (*Hist. eccl.* 3.39.9), tells a story, presumably on the authority of the daughters of Philip (3.39.9), about a Justus named Barsabbas who remained totally unharmed after drinking poison (3.39.9). Eusebius (*Hist. eccl.* 3.39.10) (and perhaps Papias himself) identifies this man with the Joseph Barsabbas surnamed Justus, who, along with Matthias, was one of the candidates to fill the vacancy, created by Judas Iscariot's betrayal, within the group of the twelve apostles (Acts 1:23–28). Trevett (1996, 33) wonders whether a confusion of traditions may have occurred regarding the prophet Judas Barsabbas, just as it had regarding the two Philips and their respective daughters. If so, such confusion would have provided an additional perceived (although not actual) link between prophets from Jerusalem and Asia Minor.

9. Anonymous, *Fr., ap.* Eusebius, *Hist. eccl.* 5.17.2.

10. Anonymous, *Fr., ap.* Eusebius, *Hist. eccl.* 5.17.1.

11. Anonymous, *Fr., ap.* Eusebius, *Hist. eccl.* 5.17.3.

12. Anonymous, *Fr., ap.* Eusebius, *Hist. eccl.* 5.17.4a.

13. Anonymous, *Fr., ap.* Eusebius, *Hist. eccl.* 5.17.4b.

14. Anonymous, *Fr., ap.* Eusebius, *Hist. eccl.* 5.17.4c. From his reference to thirteen peaceful years for Christians having been completed since the death of Maximilla (Anonymous, *Fr., ap.* Eusebius, *Hist. eccl.* 5.16.19; cf. 5.17.4), it appears that the Anonymous' visit to Ankyra occurred in ca. 192/3, that is, toward the very end of Commodus' reign or just after it and that the notes summarizing the content of his information about and arguments against the New Prophecy were written in 193; see Tabbernee 2007, 5–7.

15. The second-generation Montanist leader Miltiades is not to be confused with the non-Montanist "Brother Miltiades" who wrote an Anti-Montanist treatise (Anonymous, *Fr., ap.* Eusebius, *Hist. eccl.* 5.17.1). The Montanist Miltiades (Anonymous *Fr., ap.* Eusebius, *Hist. eccl.* 5.16.3), however, may also have written books (*Can. murat.* [*ll.*80–95]; see Tabbernee 2007, 107). Yet another author in the literary warfare which raged over the legitimacy of the New Prophecy during the late second century was the Montanist referred to by the Anonymous as having written a book countering "Brother Miltiades' book" (*ap.* Eusebius, *Hist. eccl.* 5.17.1). This Montanist author was, perhaps (but not necessarily) Asterius Urbanus (Anonymous, *Fr., ap.* Eusebius, *Hist. eccl.* 5.16.17); see Tabbernee 2007, 12–15.

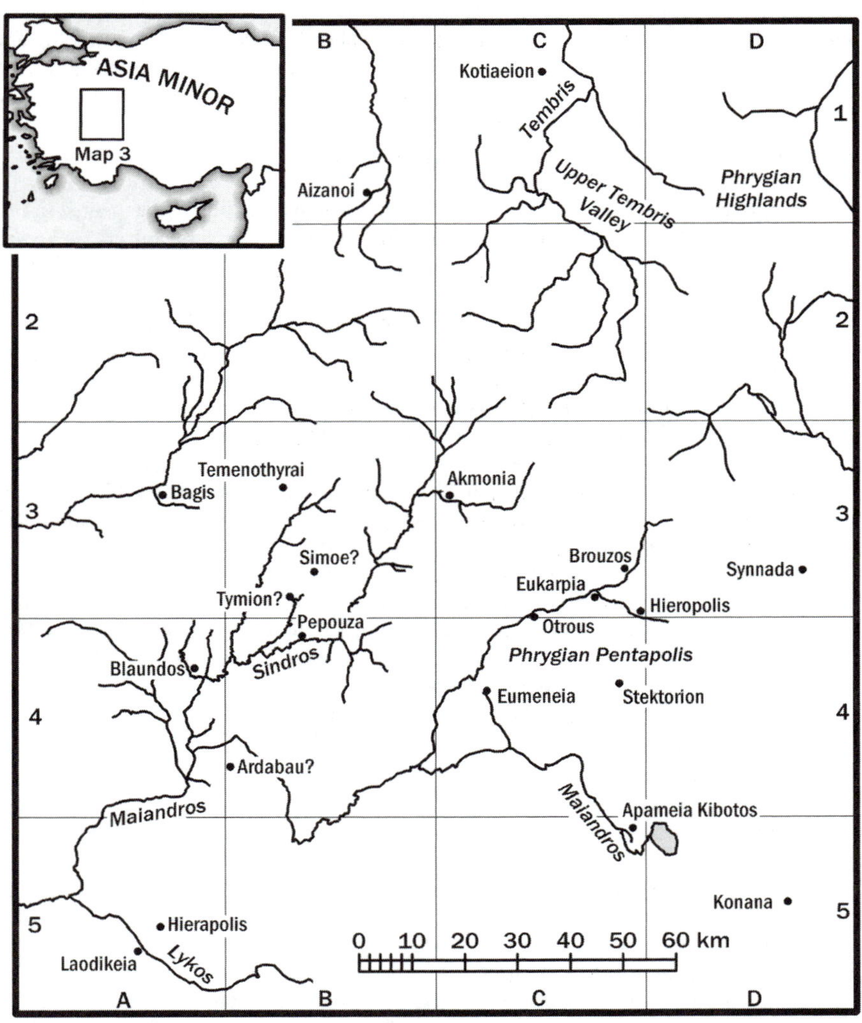

Map 3: West-Central Phrygia

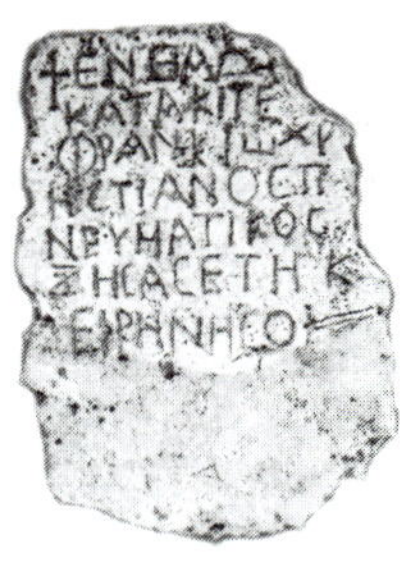

Chapter 5

Hieropolis, Phrygian Pentapolis, ca. 193 C.E.

Avircius buys a tombstone for himself

Avircius is very happy. Standing in the stonemason's workshop, he is looking at his own tombstone.[1] It is a bomos, a funerary altar, decorated with a small wreath on the back. Bomoi are common funerary monuments for those in the region who can afford them, so his own bomos should not attract special attention. An inscription covers the other three sides of the altar.[2] The letters have been carved very carefully. The master of the workshop proudly shows Avircius what he and his apprentices have done. Avircius checks the text of the inscription letter by letter. He is relieved; the apprentices are sometimes illiterate but they have not made any mistakes—or if they had, the master stonemason has corrected them without any evident traces of errors.

The text of the inscription is very important to Avircius. He worked on it for months before giving it to the stonecutters to carve. The text not only reveals that Avircius is seventy-two years old at the time he commissioned the tombstone and purchased the burial plot in which his body will ultimately rest, but it communicates only to those who "have eyes to see" that Avircius is a Christian. Nowhere in the text does Avircius use the word Christian, but he chose exactly the right phrases so that "those in the know" will catch their double meaning.

Avircius is rather proud of the opening statement, which says that he is the citizen of "an elect city."[3] Most people will assume he means Hieropolis—especially since he mentions Hieropolis at the end of the inscription as his native city, warning potential grave violators that if they are caught they will have to pay a heavy fine to the city treasury. But Avircius is really telling Christian readers who will, in the future, walk by his tombstone that the one buried there is a resident of the heavenly Jerusalem—the City of God. Avircius shudders. Not at the thought of himself lying in the grave—he has come to terms with his own mortality and is looking forward to claiming his citizenship in heaven—but at the thought of those ridiculous adherents of the New Prophecy teaching that the New Jerusalem will come out of heaven and be established near Pepouza, not far away on the other side of the mountain range he is now looking at. What trouble these followers of Montanus, Maximilla, and Priscilla have been causing among the members of his congregation! He hopes his friend and neighboring bishop keeps his promise to send him some specific information he can use to counter the arguments of these crazy followers of the so-called Phrygian prophets. As a resident of Phrygia himself, as well as a future resident of heaven, Avircius is annoyed that the Phrygian prophets have given Phrygia a bad name!

The master stonecutter coughs politely, and Avircius brings his thoughts back to the immediate task at hand. Yes, all the other significant phrases are there. The biographical section of his newly carved epitaph states that he is "a disciple of the holy shepherd" who sees everything;[4] that he, Avircius, has been taught by means of "faithful writings";[5] that he has traveled as far west as Rome and as far east as the land beyond the Euphrates River, meeting with like-minded people. As he reads, his thoughts go back to those journeys. One of his greatest joys was being able to open the pages of the codex containing the epistles of Saint Paul and read them while occasionally riding in an ox-drawn cart. Avircius touches the line on the bomos that reads "I had Paul with me in the carriage."[6] A broad smile crosses his face as he silently congratulates himself on that clever line.

Quickly, he looks again at the other clever lines. When mentioning that he has been to Rome, Avircius added "A people I saw there having a resplendent seal"[7]—a clear reference to baptized Christians (for those in the know!). Avircius is most proud of the two sentences that conclude the biographical section of his epitaph. They contain not only a cryptic reference to Jesus by means of the word "fish" (ΙΧΘΥΣ [*ichthus*]), the five letters standing for the phrase "Jesus Christ, God's Son, Savior," but also cryptic references to Christianity itself, to the Virgin Mary, and to the Eucharist. Double checking the sentences, carefully tracing each letter with his finger, he reads:

> Faith led the way everywhere and set before me as nourishment everywhere a fish from a spring, immense, spotless, which a holy virgin caught. And this she gave into the hands of her friends to eat always, and having good wine, giving mixed wine with bread.[8]

Avircius had not been able to resist the additional word play, describing the wine as "good" (ΧΡΗΣΤΟΝ [*chrēston*]), which, at least in the way the word is pronounced in the area where he lives, makes it sound like "Christ-wine." Avircius almost says the word Christ out loud but stops himself in time. It would not be a good idea to reveal inadvertently to the stonemason what the inscription really says.

Avircius is also pleased with the line that precedes the standard formula threatening grave violators with fines. He touches the inscription again and reads: "Let anyone who shares these sentiments pray for Avircius."[9] It will be good to be remembered and prayed for by orthodox Christians. Hopefully any non-orthodox Christians, such as the troublesome members of "the sect named after the Phrygians," will have the good sense not to pray for him—although Avircius wonders whether the prayers even of heretics might still be heard by God.

Avircius thanks the master stonemason and pays him. While Avircius looks forward to becoming an actual citizen of the elect city he mentions in the epitaph, he cannot help hoping that it may be quite a few years before the tombstone he has just prepared is needed.

Lost in thought on the way home, Avircius almost does not see the messenger waiting for him on the step of his house. Messengers often bring bad news, so Avircius is a little apprehensive as the messenger gives him a small packet.

Once inside the house, Avircius looks carefully at the packet in his hand. It consists of a cover letter and a small treatise in three parts. The letter addresses him formally as Avircius Marcellus. Avircius quickly glances at the opening sentence: "For the longest time, beloved Avircius, having been urged by you to compose some sort of treatise with reference to the sect of those named after Miltiades . . ."[10] He had almost forgotten that, following the deaths of Montanus, Maximilla, and Priscilla, a new leader of the New Prophecy named Miltiades emerged. He is a little surprised that the movement is already being named after this more recent leader, and he wonders whether this might be merely a local practice and adherents of the New Prophecy in other parts of the world might be named after other leaders. No doubt his friend, the expert on the movement, will know.

Avircius quickly scans the rest of the cover letter and learns that his friend, along with Zotikos of Otrous, has been in Ankyra where he spent many days debating with the leaders of the New Prophecy in that city. The presbyters of Ankyra, apparently, were so pleased with the results of the public debates that they asked Avircius' friend to leave them a written copy of his notes. Avircius' friend had not been able to do this but promised to write up something to send them after he returned home. Fortunately, to Avircius' relief, his friend had not forgotten his earlier promise to compose a treatise arguing against the New Prophecy for Avircius' use. Making the most of the opportunity, Avircius' friend had "killed two birds with one stone." Rather than merely sending notes to the presbyters in Ankyra, for their continued struggle against the adherents of the New Prophecy, the bishop had expanded his notes into a treatise—and sent Avircius a copy. As he holds the treatise in his hands, Avircius is overjoyed. Here, at last, is the material he needs to refute the New Prophecy at Hieropolis.[11]

Sources:

CB 657; Anonymous, *Fr., ap.* Eusebius, *Hist. eccl.* 5.16.3.

Notes

1. In 1883 William Ramsay discovered, 5 km south of Koçhisar (ancient Hieropolis), two fragments of a funerary altar containing substantial portions of a long metrical epitaph known already from the *Vita Abercii* (Ramsay 1883, 424–27; Nissen 1912, 1–55). The *Life of Abercius* is a fourth-century account of the ministry of a bishop named Ἀβέρκιος (*Aberkios*), Latinized as Abercius in the *vita*. The spelling Ἀβέρκιος instead of Avircius, is, presumably, due to local pronunciation. While much of the *vita* is legendary, dealing with fourth-century rather than second-century issues (Bundy 1989/90, 163–76), there is no reason to doubt the accuracy of the text of the epitaph contained within it.

2. The complete text of Avircius' epitaph has been able to be reconstructed on the basis of the extant fragments, the *vita,* and the epitaph of a man named Alexander (*CB* 656) which was modeled on that of Avircius. Numerous critical editions, translations, and scholarly discussions of the Avircius tombstone and inscription have appeared in print, some of the more recent ones being Kearsley 1992, 177–81; Merkelbach 1997, 125–39; Hirschmann 2000, 109–16; 2003, 133–39; and M. Mitchell 2008, 303–35. The translations of the various lines of the tombstone given in this chapter are my own.

3. *CB* 657, *l*.1.

4. *CB* 657, *ll*.3–5.

5. *CB* 657, *l*.6.

6. *CB* 657, *l*.12a (altered).

7. *CB* 657, *l*.9.

8. *CB* 657, *ll*.12b–16.

9. *CB* 657, *l*.19 (altered).

10. Anonymous, *Fr., ap.* Eusebius, *Hist. eccl.* 5.16.3. No one need doubt that the Aberkios of the epitaph is the Avircius Marcellus to whom the anonymous bishop (of one of the neighboring cities of the Phrygian Pentapolis) sent a copy of the treatise he had composed against the New Prophecy following his oral debate with adherents of the movement in Ankyra (see Chapter 4 and Frend 2003, 21–23, 86–87).

11. The name "Hieropolis," instead of the correct form "Hierapolis," is an error made in antiquity but does help to distinguish this city in the Phrygian Pentapolis from the more well-known Hierapolis (Pamukkale) in southwestern Phrygia.

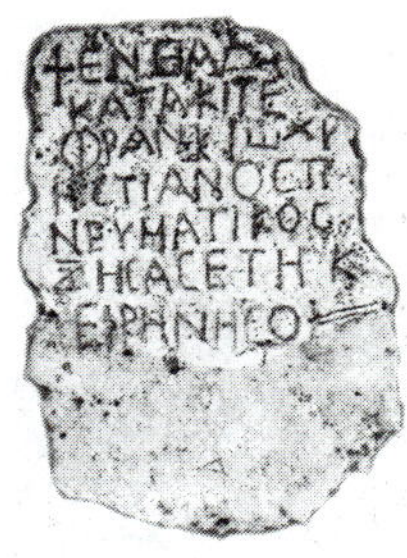

Chapter 6

Rome, Italia, ca. 193 C.E.
Victor writes letters of peace

Victor is stunned. He has just received a disturbing letter from Irenaeus, the bishop of Lugdunum. He has never met Irenaeus personally but knows that this famous bishop, while still a presbyter, had visited his predecessor, Eleutherus, and brought him a letter from the confessors of Lugdunum. That particular letter explained the position the churches in Gaul decided to take concerning the New Prophecy. It was a wise and prudent decision: prophetic gifts are not to be denied but need to be kept under ecclesiastical control.

Bringing matters under ecclesiastical control is exactly what Victor has been trying to do ever since he became bishop of Rome four years ago. The Christian community at Rome has grown so large that he himself is not sure exactly how many house-churches there are. There must be at least fifteen now, if not more. Some of them, however, carry out practices that differ radically from practices in other house-churches. This lack of uniformity troubles him. Victor likes to think of himself as a man of order, not chaos. In fact, Victor cannot stand chaos. The mere thought of it causes him to break out in a sweat. His palms become clammy and his heart rate soars.

Victor is furious at some of his presbyters, especially those in charge of the house-churches comprised mainly of immigrants from the Roman province of Asia, including that part of Asia known as Phrygia. These house-church communities insist on celebrating Easter as Christians still do in Asia. There, they conclude the Lenten fast on the fourteenth day of the Jewish month Nisan irrespective of the day of the week this happens to be. Victor can feel his blood boil at the stupidity of this practice. How ridiculous to finish the Lenten fast on a Monday and then to celebrate Easter three days later on a Wednesday! Everyone knows Jesus rose from the grave on a *Sunday,* not a Wednesday or any other day but a Sunday—the *first* day of the week, not just any day of the week. Victor cannot understand why some people want to finish the Lenten fast on the fourteenth exact anniversary of the day when Jesus died, the fourteenth day—the *quartus-decimus* of Nisan. The day Jesus rose from the dead is far more important and much easier to calculate. What makes the whole matter so problematic is that these Quartodecimans, as Victor calls them pejoratively, make a farce out of Christian unity and solidarity.

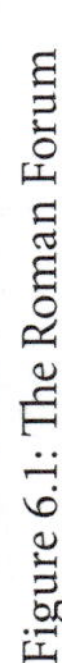

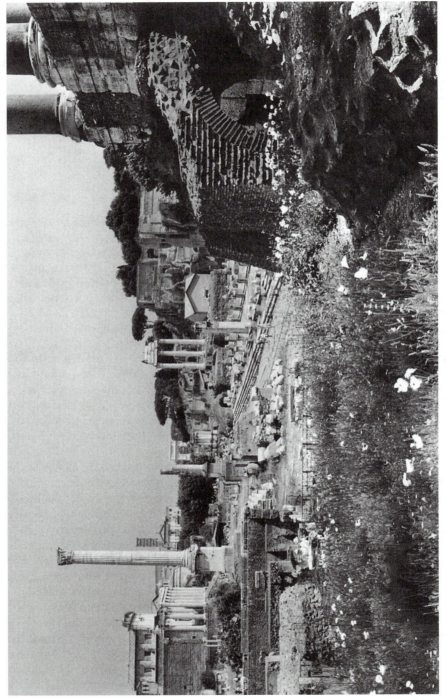

Figure 6.1: The Roman Forum

Two Easters in a single week by two different sets of house-churches in the same city is confusing, unmanageable, and disrespectful of Jesus himself. Do the Quartodecimans think Christ needs to be resurrected twice in one week? The chaos they are perpetuating for the church in Rome is unbearable.[1]

Some months earlier, Victor had decided to standardize the celebration of Easter for all the house-churches in Rome, including those comprised of immigrants from Asia and Phrygia. He informed each of the Roman parishes by letter to cease their divisive practice. If they did not do so, he would cut them off from communion. As a courtesy, Victor sent a copy of the letter to Polycrates, the bishop of Ephesus—the most senior bishop of the churches in the region of Asia and Phrygia, from which the Quartodecimans hailed. Not that Victor had any expectations that the churches in Asia and Phrygia would change their own practice of basing the date of Easter on the fourteenth of Nisan, and he certainly had no authority to tell the Asian bishops what to do. But he did (or thought he did) have that authority *in Rome*. Having exercised that authority, he simply wanted the Asian bishops to be informed about his decision before some of their former parishioners now living in Rome complained to them about the changes implemented in the capital. Because of the close connection between immigrants from Asia and Phrygia in Rome and those in Lugdunum, Victor had also informed Irenaeus of what he had done—thinking that Irenaeus would be pleased. In Lugdunum, as Victor knew from the information he received from Christians who had spent time in Gaul, Easter was now always celebrated on a Sunday. Victor, however, had totally miscalculated the response he would receive from Polycrates and Irenaeus. He expected the resistance from his own presbyters, with which he is now dealing, but he didn't realize that he would stir up such a hornet's nest among his fellow bishops.

Putting aside, for the moment, the letter that has just arrived by messenger from Irenaeus, Victor picks up the long letter he received from Polycrates a few days ago. The letter begins by telling Victor that Polycrates was so upset by Victor's action that he called together a number of the bishops in the province of Asia to discuss the matter. These bishops reaffirmed the validity of the tradition they inherited and continue to conclude the Lenten fast on the fourteenth of Nisan. Victor reads, for the third time in as many days, the relevant section of Polycrates' letter, quickly skipping over some of the details he knows already:

> We keep the exact day without tampering with it, neither adding nor subtracting. For in Asia great luminaries sleep who shall rise again at the Lord's coming . . . such as Philip, one of the twelve apostles, who sleeps in Hierapolis . . . and John, who leaned into the bosom of the Lord, . . . a witness and a teacher . . . who sleeps in Ephesus. Then in Smyrna there is Polycarp, bishop and martyr, and Thraseas, bishop and martyr from Eumeneia, who also sleeps in Smyrna. Need I mention Sagaris, bishop and martyr, who sleeps in Laodikeia, or the blessed Papirius, or Melito . . . who lies at Sardis awaiting the visitation from heaven when he shall rise from the dead?
>
> All these kept the fourteenth day of the month as the beginning of the Paschal festival, in accordance with the Gospel, not deviating in the least but following the Rule of Faith.

> And I, Polycrates, the least of you all, observe according to the tradition of my relatives, some of whom I have actually succeeded—for seven of them were bishops and I am the eighth. For my relatives always kept the day when the [Jewish] people put away the leaven.
>
> So I, therefore, my colleagues, having lived sixty-five years in the Lord, having conversed with Christian leaders from all parts of the world and having gone carefully through every sacred scripture, am not afraid of threats. Greater persons than I have said, "We must obey God rather than any human authority."[2]

Polycrates obviously took Victor's letter as a threat rather than the courtesy Victor intended it to be, and he sent copies of the response he wrote to Victor to other bishops elsewhere. Despite Polycrates' long list of "luminaries" from Asia who concluded the Lenten fast on the fourteenth day of the month of Nisan and began the three-day Paschal festival on that day, Victor is unconvinced. How can Polycrates say that he has gone carefully through every scripture when he has missed the main point that Jesus rose from the dead on a Sunday? The *only* day when Easter should be celebrated! Victor marvels at the way preconceived ideas and long-held traditions influence the way even careful exegetes read scripture. Let the luminaries turn over in their graves and let the Asian bishops do what they want about Easter, he is going to insist on uniformity of practice in Rome—for the sake of Christian unity. The Roman presbyters and their house-church communities will simply have to fall into line—even if some of those from Asia and Phrygia don't like it!

When Irenaeus' letter arrived, Victor had only glanced at it, stunned by the opening sentences. Before reading the rest, he first wanted to re-read Polycrates' letter. Now, hesitantly, still hurt by the rebuke he feels at reading Polycrates' letter and the early part of Irenaeus' letter, Victor returns to read the remainder of what Irenaeus had written to him. Victor is shocked that Irenaeus tells him to turn his mind to things that produce peace, unity, and love. Isn't that exactly what he is doing? Irenaeus obviously believes he is going about achieving peace, unity, and love in the wrong way. Irenaeus argues that he should not cut off whole Christian communities, such as the house-churches in Rome that have a different practice concerning Easter, simply because they observe the unbroken tradition of their predecessors. Victor reads the next part of Irenaeus' letter slowly.

> Such variation in observance did not originate in our own day, but very much further back, in the time of those who preceded us. They, according to their particular understanding, perhaps naively and inaccurately, established a tradition they have transmitted to posterity. In spite of such difference they lived in peace with one another and so must we. Divergent practice concerning the fast enhances the unanimity of the faith.[3]

Victor pauses to grasp the full meaning of what Irenaeus has written. Is Irenaeus saying that true Christian unity is not based on the uniformity that he, Victor, wants to enforce but on the extent of diversity he is willing to embrace? Victor finds himself deep in thought over that concept; it is not one he has come across before. Surely such diversity will bring about nothing but chaos, he thinks almost out loud.

Victor continues to read, being careful not to damage Irenaeus' letter by holding it too tightly in his clammy hands. Irenaeus reminds Victor that he is not the first Roman bishop to try to establish uniformity among the house-churches in Rome regarding the fourteenth of Nisan and the date of Easter. He tells Victor that, about thirty years ago, Anicetus also attempted to do this. Victor, of course, knows of Anicetus, but he hasn't heard the anecdote Irenaeus relates next in his letter. Polycarp, Irenaeus' own teacher and mentor while he was still in Smyrna, had, in response to a request for intervention by leading members of the Asiatic house-churches in Rome, come to visit Anicetus to discuss the same issue now confronting Victor. The matter had not been resolved by the two earlier bishops. Victor looks carefully at Irenaeus' account:

> Anicetus could not persuade Polycarp *not* to keep the day since Polycarp had observed it always with John the disciple of the Lord and with the other apostles with whom he had associated. Neither did Polycarp persuade Anicetus to *keep* the day as Anicetus said that he must stick to the tradition of the presbyters before him. But though there was this stalemate, they remained in communion with one another and in the Christian community Anicetus arranged for Polycarp to celebrate the Eucharist, manifestly out of respect. They parted company in peace, and the whole Christian community at Rome was at peace—those who kept the day and those who did not.[4]

Victor is taken aback. He is aware of the facts Irenaeus reminds him of, but not of their implication—at least not until now. What if he continues the long-standing tradition in Rome that copes with and even embraces the "clash of traditions" in the past? What if he changes his mind about forcing each of the house-churches to celebrate Easter on the same day? Would that really be such a catastrophe?

As Victor tries to resolve in his own mind whether or not to reverse his earlier decision and offer the troublesome house-church communities *litteras pacis,* "letters of peace," not just about Easter but also about other matters, such as the legitimacy of the New Prophecy, he walks to the window of his room and throws the shutters wide open. Suddenly, there is the distinct aroma of bread being baked. He has almost forgotten that today is Saturday. On Saturdays his wife bakes the *panis eucharisticus,* the eucharistic bread for the whole Christian community. Victor retraces his steps, through his tablinum, his study, into the atrium, and then into the culina, the kitchen.

His wife is so busy with her baking that she doesn't see him. He loves watching her, standing there with flour all over her apron. There is even some flour on her nose, where she has brushed it with the back of her hand. She is bent over slightly as she uses the bread-stamp to incise the sign of the cross on each new loaf she is preparing to place in the oven. She is making many loaves, for the many house-churches of Rome, all from the same dough. Finally she sees him and looks back at him with a smile that makes his heart skip a beat. How futile her labor of love would be if he ended up not sending to all the house-churches in Rome the eucharistic bread she is baking that he will consecrate tomorrow—bread that is not only the Body of Christ but the sign of visible Christian unity.[5]

Sources:

Irenaeus, *Ep., ap.* Eusebius, *Hist. eccl.* 5.24.12–17; Eusebius, *Hist. eccl.* 5.24.1, 9–11, 18; Polycrates, *Ep., ap.* Eusebius, *Hist. eccl.* 5.24.2–7.

Rome, Italia, still ca. 193 C.E.
Praxeas proposes one God in three modes

Praxeas lives up to the literal meaning of his name: he is a "Busy-Body." Just like a bee, he is always buzzing around sticking his nose into other people's business. First darting here, then flying off there; the man never rests. If only he'd produce some honey Praxeas' frenetic activity would be tolerable but, Victor suspects, Praxeas is merely stirring up the beehives.[6]

Praxeas, recently arrived in Rome from the province of Asia, is busily going from house-church to house-church among his fellow immigrants, teaching them something that seems strange to Victor—although Victor appreciates what Praxeas is trying to achieve. Praxeas, like Victor, strongly believes that there is only one God. The position of monotheism, however, is difficult to reconcile, at least in the minds of the non-sophisticated, with belief in the divinity of Christ—let alone also with belief in the deity of the Holy Spirit. Is there one God, or are there three? If there is *one* God, whom Jesus revealed as "the Father," then Jesus and the Holy Spirit cannot also be called "God." Or, if Jesus and the Holy Spirit are also "God," mathematically speaking, there cannot simply be *one* God. Busy-Body Praxeas, however, thinks he has the solution to this mathematical-theological puzzle. He probably came across the alleged solution while sticking his nose into some poisonous flowers in Asia, Victor assumes. He is not looking forward to his meeting with Praxeas later in the morning. What trouble these Asiatics are causing him! Victor almost regrets the decision he made a few weeks ago—when he saw his beautiful wife, with flour on her face, baking the bread of Christian unity—to issue letters of peace to the house-churches from Asia and Phrygia.

Praxeas, Victor knows, has been flitting from one house-church in the Asiatic sector to another, teaching that it was God the Father himself who came down into the Virgin Mary and was born a human being and was later crucified. This makes no sense to Victor. Can God the Father become the baby Jesus? Does this mean God and Jesus are identical? When Jesus died on the cross, did that mean God died too? Who was taking care of the universe during the three days when Jesus was in the grave? How could Jesus, after his resurrection and ascension, "return to the Father" if Jesus *was* the Father? Praxeas' "solution" raises more questions than it answers. This Busy-Body Busy-Bee should stay out of the theology business—he is causing more, not less, confusion about the being of God among the simple folk. What right Praxeas has, or thinks he has, to teach such nonsense is beyond Victor. The man has an over-inflated notion of his own importance. Just because, for a brief time in Asia, he suffered the discomfort of prison on behalf of the faith doesn't make him an authorized teacher of the faith!

A few hours later, Praxeas is shown into Victor's tablinum. The two men have met previously but haven't really come to know each other. Victor offers Praxeas some pears, pomegranates, figs, pieces of honeycomb, and bread—not eucharistic bread, of course, but other bread baked by his wife earlier that morning. The sight and aroma of the bread cause Victor to daydream. Before he knows what is happening, his mind recaptures the image of his wife standing in the kitchen, looking so beautiful and smiling at him with flour on her face—or was it her nose? He wishes he had kissed away the flour that day. Shocked at himself for having such a daydream during an important meeting, Victor forces his thoughts back to the present.

Victor is surprised that, having concluded their social pleasantries, Praxeas wants to talk not about the mathematical intricacies of the Godhead, but about the New Prophecy. Victor leans forward in his chair. He knows all about Montanus, Maximilla, and Priscilla—or thinks he does. He has, after all, just sent letters of peace to those house-churches in Rome that are comprised primarily of adherents of the New Prophecy—some of the very house-churches where Praxeas has been promoting his ideas about monotheism. However, as Praxeas comes from Asia, the birthplace of the New Prophecy, Victor is interested to learn more from a reliable source.[7]

Just as he was stunned when he received Irenaeus' letter about the Quartodecimans, Victor is stunned by what Praxeas tells him now. In Asia, all sorts of accusations have been made against Montanus, Maximilla, and Priscilla, ranging from demon possession to heresy. Praxeas is speaking rapidly and with a perceptibly higher pitch as he tells Victor that the New Prophets teach that the Holy Spirit did not come fully at Pentecost but came in the manifestation of the Paraclete only a few decades ago, to Montanus, Maximilla, and Priscilla—now if that isn't heresy, what is? Did these New Prophets and their followers want to add a fourth entity, the Paraclete, to the Godhead?

Victor wonders how the bishops in Asia in general and Phrygia in particular dealt with such heresy. Before he can open his mouth to ask the question, Busy-Body Busy-Bee, as Victor has come to think of Praxeas, rattles off the answer to the unspoken question. Lowering his voice for a moment, Praxeas informs Victor that bishops such as Apolinarius of Hierapolis excommunicated Montanus, Maximilla, and Priscilla, and that bishops such as Julian of Apameia and Zotikos of Konana even traveled to Pepouza to try to exorcise one of the prophetesses. Praxeas tells Victor that, in Phrygia, the New Prophecy movement is no longer a somewhat troublesome component of orthodox Christian communities but has become a network of schismatic churches, breaking the unity of the catholic church.

Praxeas' voice is now down to a whisper. Victor leans forward even further in his chair as Praxeas warns him conspiratorially that the New Prophecy is a threat not only to the unity of the church but to Victor's own authority as bishop. Victor can almost see his dreams of having a unified Christian community in Rome under his own episcopal control slipping away. Now Victor really regrets his earlier decision, or rather he regrets one part of the way he implemented that decision. He is still convinced that Irenaeus is right in emphasizing that Christian unity can embrace a certain amount of diversity, but he realizes now that that diversity has its limits. He, and the church, can tolerate diversity in *practice,* such as a difference in the date of celebrating Easter, but he and the church cannot tolerate diversity in *belief.* Heretical teachings such as those of Montanus and others concerning the Paraclete are intolerable. He is thankful to Praxeas for enlightening him about this dangerous aspect of the New Prophecy. He will withdraw his *litteras pacis* regarding the New Prophecy but still send the *panis eucharisticus* to those house-churches that differ solely in matters of practice rather than doctrine.[8]

The thought of "doctrine" reminds Victor that his own agenda for the meeting with Praxeas was not to talk about the New Prophecy but to discuss Praxeas' own strange ideas concerning what is beginning to be called "the Trinity." Praxeas' over-emphasis on monotheism may, in its own way Victor suspects, be as dangerous to orthodoxy as the New Prophecy's over-emphasis on the Paraclete. Praxeas' comments about the New Prophecy's views about the Holy Spirit give Victor the perfect opportunity to steer the conversation first to the divinity of the Holy Spirit and then to that of Jesus.

The men talk for a long time. Praxeas uses unfamiliar terms derived, Victor suspects, from Stoic philosophy, terms such as "modes of existence" to try to explain to Victor exactly what he means. Victor, though, finds it almost impossible to wrap his mind around the strange concepts. Praxeas says time and time again that he is not denying that Jesus is divine or that the Holy Spirit is divine. Praxeas admits, however, that he is not so much concerned with the Holy Spirit as with trying not to appear to be a polytheist while attempting to explain how Jesus can be God. There is only one God, Praxeas tells Victor for what seems like the tenth time—but that God exists in different "modes." Sometimes the mode is that of "Father," as when God created the world; sometimes it is that of "Son," as when God became a human being in the person of Jesus of Nazareth; and sometimes it is that of "Holy Spirit," as at Pentecost and in the activity of God in the church today. Victor still doesn't get it. To him, one God in "three modes of existence" or "three modes of being God" is incomprehensible. Victor, nonetheless, is prepared to give Praxeas the benefit of the doubt. Praxeas is obviously very intelligent and, with all his big words, sounds like he knows what he is talking about even though Victor is not sure exactly what it is that Praxeas is really saying. Whatever it is, it is certainly not like the teachings of the New Prophecy that Praxeas has demonstrated to be heretical.

As Praxeas leaves, Victor thanks him for enlightening him about the New Prophecy and tells him that, at least for the time being, he is allowing him to continue teaching people his solution to the problem of how Christians can reconcile monotheism with belief that Jesus is God. When the front door of Victor's house closes behind Praxeas, Victor admits to himself that he still doesn't understand what Praxeas tried to tell him. Modalism seems to Victor a silly idea. He hopes that other people have better luck understanding Busy-Body Busy-Bee than he has.

That night in bed, Victor has trouble sleeping. His tossing and turning keeps his wife awake also. She asks him what is wrong. Victor tells her about his conversation with Praxeas, first about the New Prophecy and then about Praxeas' strange theories. When he finishes telling her as best he can, in his own words, what he thinks Praxeas was trying to communicate, Victor's wife turns over and sits up. She lights the oil lamp next to the bed and then arranges the pillows comfortably behind her back. She asks Victor whether what Praxeas has been saying about God, Jesus, and the Holy Spirit might be a little like the different roles Victor himself plays at different times during his life—or even every day. He is, she reminds him, a father to their children, a son to his parents, and a husband to her. He is only one person, but the way he lives out his roles in relationship to those he loves can be viewed as different modes of being. He is one man who exists almost as three different men, all called Victor. Perhaps, she suggests, Praxeas is right; perhaps it is at least a little like that with the one God they worship.

Victor looks at his wife adoringly. How much smarter she is than he is, he marvels. She understands intuitively what Praxeas, the Busy-Body Busy-Bee, was trying to tell him this morning. Victor is still not absolutely sure that the concept of "modes of existence" or "modes of being" really solves all the theological issues involved in reconciling monotheism with the divinity of Jesus and of the Holy Spirit, but right now, he no longer cares. While his wife is telling him that the mode of existence she loves most in Victor is the mode of being called "husband," he notices, in the dim light, a trace of fine white flour dust on her nose. She snuffs out the lighted wick of the oil lamp, rearranges the pillows, and slips down under the covers. The aroma of baking bread becomes stronger as, ever so slowly, she moves toward him.

Sources:

Tertullian, *Prax.* 1.1–7; Pseudo-Tertullian, *Haer.* 8.4.

Notes

1. "Monarchical episcopacy" took a long time to replace "presbyterial governance" in Rome, but the process toward centralized episcopal control was accelerated, if not completed, by Victor I (ca. 189–ca. 198/9); see Lampe 2003, 397–408 and Brent 1995, 427–57, 537–40. On the sizeable "Asiatic" Christian population and the house-church communities in Rome, see La Piana 1925, 213–54; 1927, 213–20, 289–90; Lampe 2003, 359–80. It appears that prior to Victor, the diverse house-churches which comprised the "fractionized" Christian community in Rome were given a great deal of latitude in terms of liturgical practice and even of theological opinions; see Lampe 2003, 385–96, 403–8; Tabbernee 2007, 38–40.

2. Polycrates, *Ep., ap.* Eusebius, *Hist. eccl.* 5.24.2–7.

3. Irenaeus, *Ep., ap.* Eusebius, *Hist. eccl.* 5.24.13.

4. Irenaeus, *Ep., ap.* Eusebius, *Hist. eccl.* 5.24.16–17.

5. As in the pre-Constantinian period there was no enforced celibacy for clergy, one may assume that Victor was married. Whether Victor's wife baked bread, including eucharistic bread, is possible but by no means certain.

6. Most of what is known about Praxeas comes from Tertullian's treatise *Adversus Praxean* written ca. 210/11. In that treatise, Tertullian is dealing primarily with the impact on the Carthaginian church of one of the followers of Praxeas, not Praxeas himself; see Chapter 13.

7. Exactly when the New Prophecy spread to Rome is unknown, but it is reasonable to assume that it was brought to the capital of the Empire by immigrants from Asia Minor, including Phrygia. This may have happened as early as the latter part of the episcopate of Soter (ca. 166–ca. 174/5), but the late references to Soter having written against the "Cataphrygians" and having condemned the "Tertullianists" (Praedestinatus, *Haer.* 1.26–27) are anachronistic. By the time of Soter's successor Eleutherus, what to do about the New Prophecy in Rome appears to have been an issue and may explain why the confessors of Lugdunum sent Irenaeus to Rome to communicate their own decision about the matter (see Chapter 2).

8. As in the case of Victor's decisions about Quartodeciman practices, Victor's action of withdrawing "letters of peace," issued earlier, applied only to "the churches of Asia and Phrygia" *in Rome* (Tertullian, *Prax.* 1.5), not to churches *in* Asia and Phrygia; see Tabbernee 2007, 39–40.

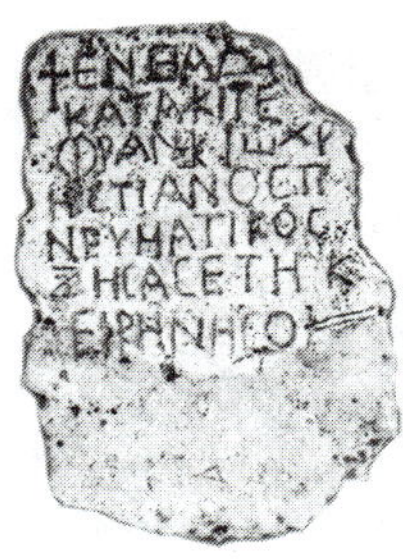

Chapter 7

Rome, Italia, ca. 200 C.E.

Proclus and Gaius debate the New Prophecy

Proclus has two problems. The first of these is Aeschines, who, like Proclus, is the leader of a group of Christians in Rome who are favorably disposed toward the New Prophecy. In fact, the group is known in some circles by Aeschines' name. Most of the members of the group, also like those in Proclus' group, are immigrants from Asia. In Rome, members of both groups live in the port district of Transtiber and most work in trades associated with the shipping industry.[1]

As Proclus contemplates his problems he is sitting on a big rock a few hundred yards up the hill from the west bank of the Tiber, near where he lives. The area is slightly wooded and the rock is large, flat at the top, and very comfortable. From this vantage point, Proclus can see Rome's huge amphitheater, commonly referred to by everyone as the Colosseum. He can also see the tops of some of the other large buildings in the main part of the city, on the other side of the river. What always captures his attention, however, is the hive of activity on the wharves just below him. The wharves are built on three levels, designed to accommodate the varying height of the Tiber at different times of the year. Today he can even recognize some of the doll-like figures in the distance as they are unloading the boats that have sailed up the Tiber from Ostia, Rome's seaport on the Internum Mare, the Mediterranean Sea. Proclus knows that some of the more wealthy members of his house-church buy and resell the goods that are transported to and unloaded on these docks. Others manage warehouses, such as the Porticus Aemilius, where the goods are stored until transported. Most adherents of the New Prophecy, however, are not wealthy and do the sweaty, back-breaking jobs on the wharves. It is a hard life in a smelly area of the city—a far cry from the hills, valleys, and plains of their native land, from which they brought their particular form of Christianity.

Proclus wishes that Aeschines had never become involved with Praxeas. In recent years, Praxeas has created quite a storm by teaching that God exists in three different modes of being—not in three different persons. Sometimes, as in the time of Israel's scriptures, God is God the Father who is the creator of all things. At other times, such as in the time described by the Gospels, God is God the Son, who through the cross redeemed humankind. At still other times, such as at Pentecost, God is God the Spirit who brought the church into being and

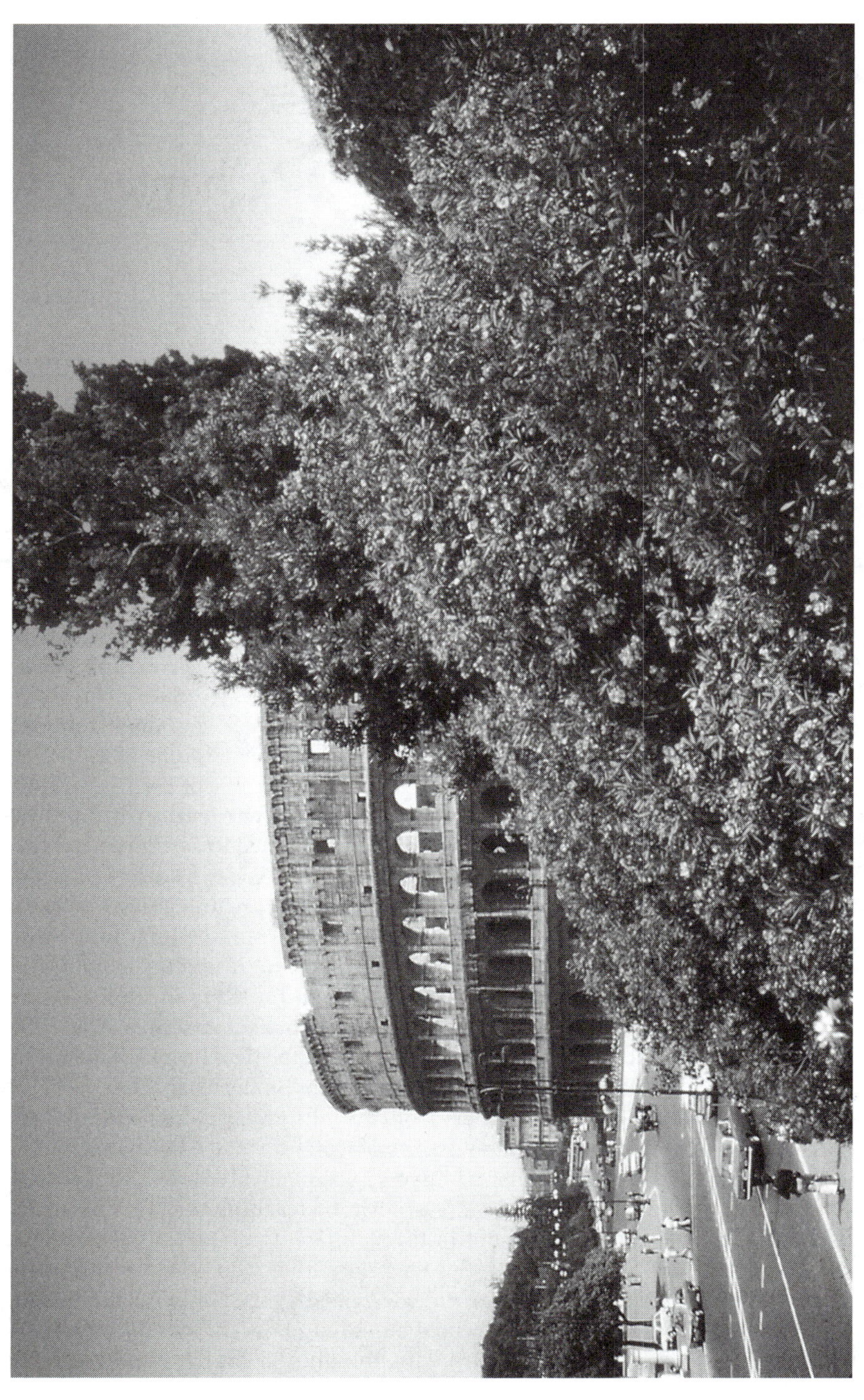

Figure 7.1: The Colosseum in Rome

empowers it even in the present age. Some of what Praxeas teaches resonates well with Proclus and other adherents of the New Prophecy. The differentiation of time into different phases when God acted in a particular way with respect to human beings makes a lot of sense. What does *not* make sense to Proclus is the view that God can only exist in one "mode" at any given time. There is a lot of discussion going on about referring to God as a Trinity—although no definitive formulation has yet been adopted. It is clear to Proclus, however, that it was not God the Father who was dying on the cross when Jesus was crucified, even though Proclus is prepared to call Jesus the Son of God or "God the Son." As one who accepts the teachings of Montanus, Proclus believes that the Paraclete or Holy Spirit, whose revelations about the way Christians are to act in the present age, communicated fully through the oracles of the New Prophets, is also fully divine. Proclus does *not* believe, however, that in this "Age of the Paraclete," God the Father and God the Son are nowhere to be found. Proclus believes that God is *always* Father, *always* Son, and *always* Holy Spirit. Praxeas and other "Modalists" are simply wrong. Why can Aeschines not see that! How can he talk some sense into Aeschines and prove to him, and to those who side with him, that the New Prophecy and the teachings of Praxeas are incompatible?[2]

Proclus' second problem is also a man—this one named Gaius. Gaius is a presbyter of the Roman Christian community, responsible for the house-churches made up of immigrants from the province of Asia, including Phrygia. The former bishop, Victor, decided that he needed a "superintendent" with quasi-episcopal authority to keep these house-churches in line, and he appointed Gaius to do this. Gaius, an orthodox churchman, did such a good job that the current bishop, Zephyrinus, even extended Gaius' responsibilities to include oversight of *all* the ethnic congregations.[3]

Proclus and Gaius have much in common. In fact, the two men like and respect one another. Unlike Aeschines, Gaius does not dabble in the troubling waters stirred up by Praxeas. Gaius and Proclus, however, disagree strongly about the teachings of Montanus, Maximilla, and Priscilla. Whereas Proclus considers these teachings true and proper for the church, Gaius does not.

Victor had tried to contain the New Prophecy by withdrawing his letters of peace, but in recent years the movement has grown rather than been eradicated in Rome. To settle the matter once and for all, Proclus and Gaius have agreed to have a formal debate about the New Prophecy. After all, many of the house-churches in Rome function not only as places of worship but also as schools of philosophy. Ever since Justin, the martyr of blessed memory, set up such a school in a rented apartment above the Baths of Myrtinus,[4] the Christians in Rome enjoy lively—and even sometimes public—discussions about theological issues.

With part of his mind still on the problems caused for the New Prophecy movement in Rome by Aeschines' adoption of the teachings of Praxeas, Proclus, a little reluctantly, makes his way down from the rock where he has been sitting. His legs have stiffened a little, so he stretches as well as he can. Now that he is older he is not as limber as he used to be and he forgets to stretch as he should. But, as his cramping legs remind him to do so now, he puts his hands on the top of the rock and pushes back, placing all his weight first on one leg then on the other. Proclus feels his calf muscles stretch until the cramps disappear. He stands up straight and, half-heartedly, tries to touch his toes—but he can only reach his shins. Proclus looks around self-consciously, hoping that no one has seen his failed attempt. As he walks up the hill to his home, his aching legs tell him that he needs to be in much better shape mentally than he is physically, if he is to have any chance of winning the debate.

While Proclus is on his way home to prepare for the debate with Gaius, Gaius himself is on the way to one of the two places he still wants to revisit as part of his own preparation. He has already been walking a long time from the city along the Via Ostiensis. If he were to go all the way, he would end up in Ostia itself, but the seaport is not his destination. His destination is a vineyard along the Ostian Way, about two miles south of the city. Although he enjoys an occasional glass of red wine and, as a presbyter, needs communion wine for the eucharistic celebrations in the house-churches he oversees, his purpose in going to the vineyard is not to purchase "the fruit of the vine" from the current owner—although, if he sees a bottle or two that take his fancy he might be persuaded to buy some wine. Gaius' reason for going to this particular vineyard on this particular day is to see again the grave where St. Paul is buried.

Last week Gaius made a similar excursion even further out of the city to a place where there are three springs. According to tradition, it was there that St. Paul was beheaded by a Roman soldier. Gaius saw the marble pillar upon which Paul placed his neck so that the executioner could chop it off cleanly, with one hefty stroke of his axe. The pillar is still there in the field. His guide, one of the local Christians, pointed it out to him. The guide also showed him the three springs, or fountains, very close to each other and to the pillar. Paul's head had bounced three times and miraculously created these much needed springs, Gaius was told, and Gaius doesn't doubt the story.

Now, close to the vineyard that is today's destination, Gaius thinks about another story from Christian tradition that he has heard repeatedly since his childhood. After St. Paul was beheaded, a wealthy Roman matron named Lucina had his body buried on part of her estate, the very vineyard he has nearly reached. The sun is quite fierce by this time of day and Gaius is perspiring. He stops for a moment, takes off his hat, and with his handkerchief wipes the sweat off his balding head. Thankful that he remembered to wear his hat today, he puts it back on and walks the remaining few yards to the gate of the vineyard.

Gaius opens the gate, enters, and closes it carefully behind him. As he walks between the rows of vines growing close to the ground into the cleared area that is now an extensive Christian cemetery, he wonders how Lucina was able to ensure that St. Paul's severed head was actually buried with the rest of his body. But by the time he reaches St. Paul's grave, Gaius has forgotten that such a strange thought ever entered his mind. Standing before the grave of the great apostle and martyr, with its simple but distinctive memorial monument, Gaius is glad that St. Paul is buried in his city and not in some obscure place in Asia. Gaius, as is his custom when visiting the tombs of the saints of the church, prays silently for the soul of the departed. He crosses himself, and then turns around to begin the long journey home.

The next morning Gaius rises early. He eats a hurried meal of bread, dates, and a little goat cheese, then sets off to visit the second memorial tomb on his list: the tomb of the greatest of all apostles. Gaius knows the quickest route to today's destination. From his house he makes his way to the Via Flaminia. He turns left onto that street near the Ara pacis Augustae, the altar the emperor Augustus dedicated to Pax, the goddess of peace, to symbolize the *Pax Romana:* the peace and stability brought to the whole world by Roman rule. Gaius heard that the first Roman emperor dedicated this altar on January 30th, the birthday of Augustus' wife, Livia, and he wonders if Augustus gave the huge monument to Livia as a birthday present. What a gift that would have been.

It's a pity, Gaius reflects, that Augustus was unaware that "peace on earth" can only come through the "prince of peace," whose own birthday isn't that far away from Livia's. Gaius looks past the Ara pacis to the enormous granite obelisk Augustus brought from Heliopolis in Egypt, to serve as the central mechanism of the Horologium Augusti, the huge sundial next to the Altar of Augustan Peace. Right now, the sun is too low in the sky to cast a shadow—by means of the pointer at the top of the obelisk—over the bronze grids of the sundial inlaid in the travertine slabs on the ground. The shadow wouldn't be much anyway, Gaius knows. Only a few decades after Augustus' death, the ground under the foundations of the obelisk shifted, causing the sundial to be grossly inaccurate. A just reward for constructing a monument to honor Helios, the sun god, Gaius muses—although he, paradoxically, regrets that the Horologium can no longer help him tell the time of day.

Fortunately, Gaius knows even without the help of the Horologium that, while it is still early in the morning, he has a lot to do. He sets off briskly again along the Via Flaminia. Gaius' destination, however, is not the Circus Flaminia, the area now used by the city's open-air markets, but the site of Nero's Circus. Gaius shudders as he thinks of that madman racing his chariot around the track of the circus. The circus was a small hippodrome used mainly for chariot racing. Work on building the circus had been initiated by Caligula when he inherited his mother's property, but the circus was named—naturally enough—after the emperor who finished the task, giving him his own private race course. Gaius visualizes Nero urging on his horses furiously, making his chariot almost tilt over as he takes the turn around the spina near yet another large obelisk stolen from Egypt by the Roman emperors. Nero need not have worried about pushing his horses so hard in order to win. None of his "competitors" would ever have thought of letting the emperor lose!

What is so horrible to Gaius is not that Nero held chariot races in his circus, the results of which were always predetermined, but that on one particular evening after the great fire, dressed like the charioteer he wasn't, Nero opened up the adjacent gardens to the populace. The daylight was fading as people, both rich and poor, arrived from the other side of the Tiber. Even the most hardened of the visitors gasped when they saw, among the garden trees, men and women nailed to crosses, the gardens themselves illuminated by the light of human torches—Christians set on fire, ostensibly as punishment for starting the fire that had raged through all but four of the fourteen districts of the city. Nero had set the fire to clear slum areas so he could build his "dream palace," and he was trying to shift suspicion from himself to the Christians, a group of people already suspected of abominable crimes. No one, however, other than his lackeys, really believed Nero's accusations against the Christians.

Sadly, while Nero's injustice toward Christians in Rome generated a measure of sympathy, no one stopped him. Christians were burned to death and crucified. They were put into animal skins and thrown to wild dogs to be torn to pieces, and, as in the case of St. Paul who was a Roman citizen, they were beheaded. St. Peter, though *not* a Roman citizen, was, like so many others, also crucified. Gaius marveled at the courage and humility of the Galilean fisherman who came to be known as "prince of the apostles." Considering himself unworthy to die in the same way Jesus did, Peter, according to tradition, had been granted his request to be crucified upside down.

Gaius turns right at the Aqua Virgo, the aqueduct that brings water from the Alban Hills to the Campus Martius, the Field of Mars. He rests for a while at the Pantheon, sitting on a stoop and admiring the façade of the beautiful building with its huge Corinthian columns. He looks for a long time at the large eagle, carved within a wreath, in the center of the triangular pediment above the columns. The eagle is the symbol of Roman power, power all too often directed at Christians—as in the time of Nero. Below the pediment Gaius sees the inscription the emperor Trajan commissioned, when he restored the temple after it had been destroyed by fire. Trajan honored the Pantheon's original builder, not himself—something the megalomaniac Nero would never have done. Gaius reads each letter carefully, knowing that some of the letters are abbreviations: M. AGRIPPA L. F. COS TERTIUM FECIT ("Marcus Agrippa, son of Lucius made this during his third consulship"). Feeling rested, Gaius can't resist going inside the rotunda for a few moments—despite the Pantheon's pagan character. He hopes no one sees him, it's just that Gaius loves seeing the shafts of light stream into the rotunda through the oculus, the eye-like circular hole in the rotunda's roof.

Still somewhat lost in thought about Nero and the martyrdoms that occurred during that evil emperor's reign, Gaius, out of habit, turns left upon leaving the Pantheon instead of walking toward the Tiber as he intended. He ends up at the Area sacra, where four temples from the period of the Roman Republic stand next to each other in a row. Gaius, stopping to get his bearings, notices the largest cat he has ever seen, lying in the sun. Gaius loves cats but cannot afford to keep one himself and so he stands very still, trying not to disturb the magnificent animal before him. If he owned that cat, he imagines, he'd call him Linus, after the bishop who succeeded Peter and Paul. As Gaius is not perceived as a threat, the enormous cat stays where he is and meows softly. A mother cat with four kittens appears out of nowhere and, before long, dozens of other felines come out from behind the pillars of the various temples, finding cozy places to bask in the sun. How can there be so many cats in one place? Gaius wonders. One very beautiful cat catches his eye. She has a sleek black coat and stunning, crystal-clear green eyes. The cat comes up to him and rubs her body against his leg, arching her back and purring loudly. She has obviously taken a shine to him and is putting her scent on him, claiming him for herself. The cat seems to want him to play with her, but Gaius has already stopped at the cat sanctuary too long. He puzzles over who feeds the cat rubbing against him and who cares for her, for Linus, and all the other cats. Gaius decides that he will come back here when he has more time. Perhaps he can bring some food and a brush to groom his newly found friend. In his mind he names her Lucy, after Lucina, the woman who buried St. Paul's body.

Gaius turns right and makes his way via some narrow side streets to the bridge known as the Pons Aelius. He uses it, rather than the bridge built by Nero a little further downstream, to cross the Tiber into the Ager Vaticanus, the "Vatican Field." As he crosses the Pons Aelius, the imposing mausoleum of Aelius Hadrianus, the emperor Hadrian, at the end of the bridge seems to be looking down on him ominously. He makes a sharp left onto the Via Cornelia. For a short distance the Via Cornelia follows the Tiber, which from where he is walking seems to be far below him. Ten minutes later he is at his destination.

Gaius is standing at the entrance to a narrow street. There are buildings on both sides, made with thin red bricks. The wall on the right looks like the façade of a long row of houses. Every few yards there is a doorway with a stone step in front of it. Above and beside each doorway is a series of windows; above the windows there are a few more rows of brick and then the roof. But these houses are not ordinary houses: they are "houses of the dead." Gaius is in the necropolis, the "city of the dead," built on the more-or-less, but not quite, level plain at the foot of the Vaticanus itself, one of Rome's famous seven hills—although Gaius is never quite sure exactly which hills should be numbered among the seven.

The necropolis is in the area still known as the Horti Neroniani, "Nero's Villa and Gardens," and not far from Nero's Circus, now never used. This is by no means the first time that Gaius has been in this necropolis, so he doesn't stop to look inside the doors of the mausoleums but quickly walks straight ahead in the eerie quietness of what is almost exclusively the pagan part of the cemetery. As he tries to hurry past the last mausoleum, he almost screams with fright as he suddenly bumps into somebody. But the "body," as frightened as Gaius, is merely another man visiting the necropolis—not a corpse or a ghost. Both men laugh with relief and Gaius continues on his way.

At what seems to be the end of the street, Gaius opens a door. The door is not the entrance to another mausoleum but a passageway. The left wall of the passageway has no doors or windows. Behind this blank wall, Gaius knows, are two mausoleums that are accessible only from the other side. The right wall of the passageway, however, does have a door. The door is open, and as he passes Gaius sees that the walls of that mausoleum are painted yellow and divided into large panels. Some of the panels are decorated with dainty leaves and twigs. Once past the mausoleum, Gaius turns right into a stairwell and climbs the ten steps that lead to a small patio at what, in an actual house, would be roof level.

From where he is standing, Gaius looks directly at the object he has come all this way to see: the Trophy of St. Peter. The large monument before him is an aediculum, a shrine in the shape of the façade of a small temple. Ever since the monument was constructed by the Christian community forty years earlier, it has been called the tropeion, the "trophy." Like the trophy given to a victorious athlete, St. Peter's trophy is a fitting symbol of his victorious martyrdom. Gaius descends the two steps at the far end of the patio. As the mausoleums have been cut into the slightly sloping part of the Ager Vaticanus, Gaius is now at natural ground level again, standing in a rectangular "field" that resembles a courtyard but is actually an open air graveyard. Even though there are, as Gaius knows, other tombs surrounding St. Peter's, the only monument that still marks a tomb is the aediculum.

Crossing the field, Gaius reassures himself that the trophy has suffered no damage since he was here last. The Christian community has done a good job of maintaining the aediculum and the courtyard-like field—and the area is so difficult to reach that no non-Christians are likely to stumble upon it. Even if they did, the aediculum itself would not draw particular attention since no inscription marks the grave as that of St. Peter. Only those who know, know.

The aediculum is built against a red wall that actually straddles the site of the original grave. The wall was built, Gaius has been told, during the time of the emperor Marcus Aurelius as a retaining wall during the construction of the clivus, a small street sloping uphill at the far end of the necropolis. It was at that time that the Christians of Rome decided that St. Peter's grave deserved a more ornate monument. They may have been able to persuade the workmen who built the red wall to construct the wall in such a way that it formed a semi-circular perpendicular niche over the grave or they may have cut the niche after the wall was completed. In either case, the edges of the front of St. Peter's original grave are now marked by long narrow marble slabs. Two tall columns have been erected, one at each end of the front base slab. These columns support a marble canopy that covers the whole visible part of the grave and fits into the wall niche. The canopy, in turn, is the base of the aediculum's "second-story." This consists of two pilasters supporting a horizontal fascia on top of which is a triangular pediment.

Standing very close to the aediculum and now looking up at it, Gaius feels not only a sense of awe but a strong connection to his Christian heritage. There before him, no longer in the ground but in a box in a small cube-shaped niche within the large semi-circular niche of the aediculum, are the bones of St. Peter. Gaius spends an extra long time in prayer, then crosses himself and, once again, heads back home. On the way, he thinks that Peter's bones and the bones of St. Paul, which he had venerated yesterday, are the real "trophies" of the apostles.

The big event for which Proclus and Gaius have been preparing is finally about to begin. For weeks, word about the debate has been spreading not only throughout the house-churches in the Asiatic sector of the city but throughout all the house-churches in Rome. So many Christians are expected to attend the debate that the original intention to hold it in one of the larger apartment house-churches in Transtiber was abandoned. Fortunately, Gaius' connections secured an invitation to use the villa of one of the wealthiest Christians in Rome.

The villa is outside the walls of the city, off the Via Appia. Built half a century ago, it consists of a number of separate buildings, some of them connected by colonnades. As Proclus approaches the villa from the private road that leads from the Via Appia, it almost seems like he is entering a small village. The first buildings he sees are tabernae, shops where the produce grown in the villa's gardens and the wine produced from the villa's vineyards are sold to the city's merchants and visitors. As he walks past the tabernae, he notices farm workers busily arranging fruits and vegetables and bottles of wine. The debate is going to be good for business once everyone arrives.

Proclus has never set foot on the property of one of the suburban villas, let alone been inside one, and he is astounded that the villa has its own aqueduct that brings water all the way from Rome to the property. The aqueduct, he notices, feeds two huge cisterns. The first one services the villa's bath complex with its frigidarium, or cold-water pool, and caldarium, or hot-water pool, as well as the nymphaeum, a multi-level building with a central fountain. The second cistern provides running water to the family's residential area. The residence is the largest private house Proclus has ever seen. Only the imperial palaces on the Palatium, another one of Rome's famous seven hills, are bigger. The entrance to the house is very imposing, with long marble steps flanked by Corinthian columns. The floor of the house is well above ground level. Below the floor is the cryptoporticus, a crypt-like porch that leads to the service area where servants are preparing delicacies for the guests who are about to arrive.

While Proclus is standing in front of the villa's main door, wondering whether to go inside since he is very early, Gaius, having arrived even earlier, is at the back of the house, amazed that the villa complex has its own circus—just like the one Nero constructed, or more accurately finished constructing, on the grounds of what was once the Horti Agrippinae, the gardens and villa of Agrippina, Augustus' granddaughter and the mother of Caligula. Unlike the circus he had seen a few days ago in Vatican Field, this particular circus is in excellent repair and, obviously, used frequently. Gaius notices the stables a short distance away among the other farm buildings, including the small but sufficiently comfortable rooms where the rustici, the peasants who till the land and do all the other agricultural tasks on the farm, live. He even hears one of the horses neigh.

The sound of footsteps on the gravel path makes him turn around. Proclus greets him politely, but awkwardly. How do two men who truly like and respect one another behave toward each other when they are about to do intellectual battle in a formal debate? Gaius and Proclus wish each other well. That seems to be the Christian thing to do, but each secretly hopes that his opponent will *not* do well. There is so much at stake.

After walking back to the main door of the house together, Gaius and Proclus walk up the steps and are greeted by their host. He takes them through the atrium to an enormous octagonal room that Gaius and Proclus immediately notice is heated. It was a little chilly outside, especially while standing still and looking at the circus, so the warmth feels good, but both men hope the room won't get too hot. They don't want the members of their audience to fall asleep while they are debating. Fortunately, the ceiling is very high and there are doors in three of the side walls that lead to the gardens. These doors can be opened later, if necessary, to let in some fresh air.

The floor of the room is made of square slabs of different colored marble, laid out in striking patterns. At the front of the room, parallel to one of the walls of the octagon, there is a long narrow table with three chairs behind it, facing two groups of wooden benches where those who have come to listen will sit. The benches have, no doubt, been built especially for the debate by the rustici. They probably used wood from the trees that grow on the property. There is a wide aisle in the center of the room, which greatly annoys Proclus. Why can't those who set up rooms understand that speakers, seated at the front of the room, don't want to address an empty space? It would have been much better if the room had been arranged into *three* groups of benches, with a central block right in front of the table. That way there would be two aisles, one to the left and one to the right of the central block, with side sections where benches could have been angled in line with the diagonal walls of the octagonally-shaped room, which would allow more people to be seated *and* to be seated *closer* to the table. This would also give Proclus and Gaius more eye contact with the members of their audience. But it would be impolite to say anything about the seating arrangement at this late stage, so Proclus merely, imperceptibly, shrugs his shoulders and swallows his frustration.

Their host, a very learned and eloquent man, has agreed to chair the debate as Zephyrinus, the bishop, is not able to be present. Seated in the middle chair behind the table, he looks out at the large group of people in the room. Every bench is filled and there are people standing against the diagonal walls at the back. The host clears his throat and the noisy hubbub of dozens of people speaking all at once dies down instantly. The owner of the villa introduces both Gaius and Proclus, extolling—a little too long and a little too pompously—their personal virtues and their erudition.

Gaius is the first of the debaters to address the hushed audience. This is right and proper. Gaius, after all, is one of the more senior presbyters of the Christian community in Rome and this gives him precedence over Proclus, a layperson. Gaius has done his homework and knows that the adherents of the New Prophecy rely heavily on both the Gospel and the Apocalypse ascribed to the apostle John. As this is a debate, he lays a trap for his opponent. Even though Gaius has the floor, he makes only a few preliminary remarks before asking Proclus to explain on what grounds he and those like him believe in the Paraclete and the future descent of the New Jerusalem at Pepouza.

Proclus, a little surprised at being given the opportunity to speak so quickly, takes the bait. He tells Gaius and the audience that members of the New Prophecy movement believe in the Paraclete because John's Gospel records that Jesus promised to send the Paraclete, the Holy Spirit. They also believe the testimony of the book of Revelation, the Apocalypse, in which John is said to have been taken by an angel to the top of a mountain where he could see the New Jerusalem descend out of heaven. This mountain, Proclus explains, was identified by Montanus as a mountain in Phrygia. Proclus notices Aeschines in the audience nodding in agreement and he is glad that Aeschines has come to support him, even though the two leaders of the New Prophecy movement in Rome disagree about Modalism. A slight pause in Proclus' speech gives Gaius the opportunity he needs in order to interrupt. "But neither the Gospel nor the Apocalypse was written by John," he shouts out. "They are the work of Cerinthus!"[5]

Proclus and the audience are shocked. Cerinthus is a notorious heretic who wreaked havoc among the churches of Asia. They all know the story that one day in Ephesus when the apostle John went to one of the public baths, he saw Cerinthus already there. Rushing out of the building without bathing, John had reportedly cried out, "Let us all flee, lest the bath-house fall down, for Cerinthus, the enemy of truth, is inside!"[6] How could Cerinthus, the enemy of truth, be the author of the Gospel and the Apocalypse that, according to tradition, were written by John himself? Gaius, however, is adamant that the apostle John could *not* have been the author of these books, and he quickly presents his evidence. The Gospel allegedly written by John differs markedly from the other Gospels. The other Gospels say that immediately after his baptism Jesus went into the desert for forty days, but the so-called Gospel of John says that Jesus went to Cana in Galilee and attended a wedding! The other Evangelists say that Jesus celebrated one Passover in Jerusalem; "John" says that he celebrated two. The Apocalypse says that non-believers will be tormented, whereas St. Paul says that it is the *believers* who will be persecuted.

The audience starts murmuring. What Gaius is saying makes some sense. If the writings attributed to John are so unlike the writings of Jesus' actual followers and those of St. Paul, perhaps they *are* the work of a heretic and nothing they say can be trusted: not about the wedding at Cana, not about the end times, and certainly not about the Paraclete and the New Jerusalem.

Proclus, who realizes that he is losing this part of the debate, tries to steer things in another direction. He calls on the authority of the *logia*, the "sayings," of the founders of the New Prophecy: Montanus, Maximilla, and Priscilla. These *logia*, he explains, contain the revelation of the Holy Spirit to the church in the present age. Fortunately, he has had the foresight to bring with him a codex in which the *logia*, to which he is referring, have been written down. The codex is his most prized possession. He shows the codex to the audience, but before he has a chance to quote from it, Gaius starts railing against the impudence of members of the New Prophecy movement in composing and promoting new scriptures. The implication is clear: those who write *new* scriptures are committing the same sin as Cerinthus and, like him, they are heretics.

Proclus has one more arrow in his theological quiver. Although it is customary to remain seated while teaching, he stands up and tells the audience that the real basis of authority for the New Prophecy movement is prophetic succession. He begins with the earliest Christian prophets in Jerusalem and Antioch and then mentions, in turn, Paul and Silas. Proclus places both hands on the table, leans forward, and says emphatically:

> And after him, four prophetesses, the daughters of Philip, prophesied in Hierapolis in the region of Phrygia. Their tomb is there, as is the tomb of their father.[7]

Proclus' reference to the tombs of Philip's daughters is an integral part of his argument. Appealing to tombs and reliquaries to validate the truth of one's claims is standard practice. Polycrates had done so, Proclus knows, by mentioning the great luminaries "sleeping" in Asia when he was writing to Victor, trying to convince him that the house-churches from Asia and Phrygia in Rome should be allowed to follow the Quartodeciman practice regarding Easter. Now Proclus is employing the same strategy. The tombs of Philip's daughters, genuine prophetesses in the line of genuine prophetic succession in which Ammia, Quadratus, Montanus, Maximilla, and Priscilla also stand, are in Asia, confirming, argues Proclus, that genuine prophecy, including the New Prophecy, can come and *does* come from Asia.

Proclus is about to go on to describe the large sarcophagus in Pepouza that holds the bones of Montanus, Maximilla, and Priscilla, when Gaius also stands up and interrupts him again:

> But I can point out the trophies of the apostles. For if you will go to the Vaticanus or to the Via Ostiensis, you will find the trophies of those who founded this church.[8]

Gaius' field research has paid off. He has just defeated Proclus with a final shot from his own bow: the bones and tombs of Saints Peter and Paul, the founders of the church in Rome, outweigh the bones and tombs of prophets and prophetesses from Asia. Gaius' reference to the physical remains of the mainstream church's apostolic succession, not Proclus' proof of the New Prophecy's prophetic succession, wins the debate.[9]

Sources:

Pseudo-Tertullian, *Haer.* 7.2; Tertullian, *Val.* 5.1; *Scap.* 4.5; Photius, *Cod.* 48; Eusebius, *Hist. eccl.* 2.25.5–6, 3.1.2, 6.20.3; Epiphanius, *Pan.* 51.4.5, 51.22.1, 51.34.1–2; Tacitus, *Ann.* 15.44.2–8; *Mart. Just.* (*A*) 3; Gaius, *Proc., ap.* Eusebius, *Hist. eccl.* 2.25.7, 3.28.2; Proclus, *ap.* Gaius, *Proc., ap.* Eusebius, *Hist. eccl.* 3.31.4; Dionysius Barsalîbî, *Apoc.* proem; Mark 1:9–12, 14:1–26; Matt 3:13–4:11, 26:1–30; Luke 3:21–22, 4:1–13, 22:1–39; John 1:29–2:11, 2:13, 6:4, 13:1–18:1; 2 Tim 3:12–13; Rev 9:3–5; Irenaeus, *Haer.* 3.3.2–4.

Notes

1. Other than that Proclus was the leader of the "non-Modalist" section of the adherents of the New Prophecy in Rome ca. 200, and that he engaged in a formal debate about the New Prophecy with Gaius, little is known definitively about Proclus. It is very likely (but not certain) that a comment by Tertullian about someone whom he describes as "*Proculus noster*" (*Val.* 5.1) is a reference of endearment ("Our dear Proclus") to the same Proclus. If so, the *noster* presumably indicates that Proclus was a "fellow adherent" of the New Prophecy rather than that Proclus came originally from (the New Prophecy group in) Carthage. The reference by Tertullian (*Scap.* 4.5) to a Proculus Torpacion who was a member of the household of the emperor Septimius Severus is tantalizing (cf. Lampe 2003, 337–38). Could it be that the leader of a "Montanist" group in Rome resided in the imperial palace (Carrington 1957, 2:396, 436)? As Proclus (or its diminutive Proculus) was a very common name, Proculus Torpacion was probably a different person; see Tabbernee 2007, 70; cf. Barnes 1985, 70, 316; Lampe 2003, 511. On Christians in Septimius' extended household (*familia*), see Lampe 2003, 330–39. Rather than living in the imperial palace on the Palatine above the Roman Forum, it is more likely that Proclus lived in the area known as Transtiber ("Across the Tiber"), today's Trastevere. A useful collection of the extant fragments of the published version of the debate between Gaius and Proclus (the *Adversus Proclum*) may be found in Grant 2003, 84–86.

2. On Praxeas and "Modalism," see Chapters 6 and 13.

3. According to a tradition preserved by Photius (ca. 810/20–ca. 891–893/4), patriarch of Constantinople from 858, Gaius was a presbyter in Rome during the episcopates of Victor (ca. 189–ca. 198/9) and Zephyrinus (ca. 198/9–217) and had been "appointed overseer (ἐπίσκοπον [*episkopon*]) of the ethnics" (ἐθνῶν [*ethnōn*]) (*Cod.* 48). This means that Gaius was the "superintendent" (not bishop!) of the house-churches comprised primarily of non-Romans, such as immigrants from "Asia and Phrygia." Although Gaius attributed 2 Timothy to St. Paul, 2 Timothy and the other Pastoral Epistles are "post-Pauline." Regarding prophetic succession, see Chapter 4.

4. The "Baths of Myrtinus" were, presumably, a privately run establishment with additional rooms, some of which, as in the case of Justin Martyr's residence, were utilized as apartments (*Mart. Just.* [*A*] 3). The precise location in Rome of the "Baths of Myrtinus" and Justin's residence, which also functioned as a Christian house-church-school from ca. 135 until Justin's martyrdom in ca. 165, is no longer able to be determined and was already unknown by the time Recension B of the *Martyrium Justini* was produced (Lampe 2003, 259 and n. 6). Undoubtedly, however, the baths and Justin's apartment were east of the Tiber somewhere near the center of the ancient city, not in Transtiber on the west side of the Tiber.

5. See Dionysius Barsalîbî, *Apoc.* proem.

6. Irenaeus, *Haer.* 3.3.4. For more about Cerinthus, see Klijn and Reinink 1973, 3–19.

7. Proclus, *ap.* Gaius, *Proc., ap.* Eusebius, *Hist. eccl.* 3.31.4.

8. Gaius, *Proc., ap.* Eusebius, *Hist. eccl.* 2.25.7.

9. For additional details concerning some of the Roman temples and other buildings and structures mentioned in this chapter, see Claridge 1998. A large section of the Aqua Virgo, the Virgo Aqueduct, was underground and still exists in part today supplying water, for example, to the famous Trevi Fountain (Claridge 1998, 58, 198). Remnants of the Villa of Agrippina were discovered in 1999 (Staccioli 2006, 25–26) during the construction of a parking lot in the Vatican. The pagan necropolis and tropeion of St. Peter were discovered underneath St. Peter's Basilica during excavations conducted in the 1930s and early 1940s; see Kirschbaum 1959 and Basso 1986. Whether or not the debate between Gaius and Proclus was conducted in a villa on the outskirts of Rome is likely but not certain. The ruins of a number of villas such as the one described in this chapter exist along the Via Appia and the Via Latina. On the appeal to tombs in the debate over the New Prophecy, see Tabbernee 1997c, 206–17.

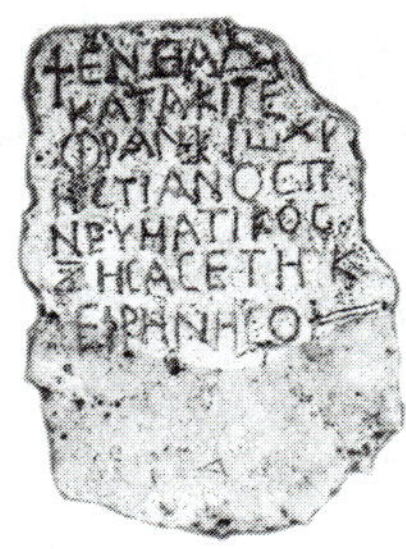

Chapter 8

Carthage, Africa Proconsularis, March 7, 203 C.E.

The blood of the martyrs

It is the emperor's birthday. Not the birthday of Septimius Severus, the senior emperor who bears the title "Augustus," nor that of his older son Marcus Antoninus Pius, known better by his nickname Caracalla, who also bears the title "Augustus." It is the birthday of Septimius Geta, Septimius Severus' younger son who five years earlier, at the age of only eight, had been given the title "Caesar." Today the boy emperor is fourteen years old. The imperial family is in Africa Proconsularis. They have spent most of their visit in Hadrumetum, Septimius Severus' birthplace. They honored the city with the *Jus Italicum,* giving it status equal to that of any city in Italia other than Rome itself. The citizens of Carthage, the capital of the province of Africa Proconsularis, are hopeful that their city may be honored similarly when the imperial family comes to visit them in a few weeks' time.

In order to show Septimius Severus how patriotic they are and the respect they have for the imperial family, the governor, a man named P. Aelius Hilarianus, has arranged special games in the amphitheater in honor of Geta's birthday. The games have been going on for several days now. They began with gladiatorial shows, but for Geta's actual birthday Hilarianus decided that a number of Christians, already condemned to death and in jail awaiting execution, will be the entertainment. Hilarianus has no doubt that seeing the condemned Christians, especially the women, fight to the death with wild beasts in the arena will please the people who are already crowding noisily into the stands of the amphitheater.

Hilarianus himself takes the most prominent seat in the amphitheater, after all the imperial family is not there personally to sit where he now sits. The governor thinks it is a great pity that Septimius Severus and his sons are not present to witness what he has arranged in Geta's honor. As three of the male prisoners are brought into the arena, Hilarianus smiles at the thought that the emperors will, nevertheless, be pleased when they hear reports of today's activities. But when he looks down at the Christians before him Hilarianus cannot believe the way they are behaving. They do not appear to be afraid. Instead, by their defiant bearing and impudent nodding in his direction with their heads, the men almost seem to be threatening him with divine retribution. The crowd, noticing the exchange of

Figure 8.1: Amphitheater at Carthage

ominous looks between the governor and the prisoners, demands that the men be made to run the gauntlet. The gladiators in the area form themselves into two parallel rows. Revocatus, Saturinus, and Saturus are scourged mercilessly as, one by one, they are forced to run through the human passageway, the gladiators taking great delight in cracking their short whips as hard as they can against the flesh of the prisoners.

When the running of the gauntlet is over, Revocatus and Saturinus are pitted against a fierce leopard. The leopard can smell the blood oozing from the torn flesh inflicted by the gladiators' whips. It rushes at the men, mauling them with its razor-sharp claws. Amazingly, the men survive the feline onslaught. The leopard retreats to its cage as Revocatus and Saturinus are put into wooden stocks in the center of the arena. With their hands and feet locked into the holes of the stocks, they are helpless to defend themselves as a ferocious bear is let loose to attack them.

Saturus is next. Dreading what he has just seen the bear do to his companions, Saturus secretly hopes that the leopard will not simply maul him but will kill him quickly with one huge bite. But the officer in charge of the spectacle changes the entertainment. Instead of allowing Saturus to be attacked by the leopard, Saturus is tied to a wild boar. The boar takes off across the arena at full speed, dragging Saturus painfully along the ground. The rope suddenly breaks, and the boar turns on the gladiator who had tied Saturus to the animal. The gladiator tries to escape but to no avail. The boar gores him, inflicting a fatal wound. Dazed but still conscious, Saturus, like Revocatus and Saturinus before him, is put into the stocks. But by now the bear has lost interest in "the game" and no amount of coaxing or prodding can get him to come out of his cage.

Immobile, locked in the stocks, Saturus watches with horror as the two young women he had instructed in the Christian faith are brought naked into the amphitheater. They are covered only in short gladiator nets that have been thrown over them—as if they were wild beasts captured in some forest. Felicitas, a slave who had only days before given birth to a baby girl, has milk visibly dripping from her breasts. Some of the women in the crowd notice the milk and suddenly there is a hushed silence. The slightly older woman is Perpetua, whom some of the people in the stands recognize as a member of the well-to-do Vibia family. Perpetua, twenty-two years old and the mother of an infant son, had also still been nursing her baby—until he was recently taken from her by force in prison. The poignant sight of the two young mothers, standing naked under the all-revealing nets, is too much even for this blood-thirsty crowd. The women are taken out of the arena while the spectators wait.

Suddenly a great roar goes up as the women, now dressed in simple, loose-fitting tunics, return. The roar is provoked by something the women cannot yet see: a mad heifer charging toward them at full speed. The heifer tosses Perpetua high into the air. Perpetua lands hard on her back with the wind completely knocked out of her. Moments later, still disoriented, Perpetua sees that Felicitas has also been thrown to the ground. Perpetua struggles painfully to her feet, walks slowly to Felicitas, and helps her up. Hand-in-hand, the Roman matrona and the slave

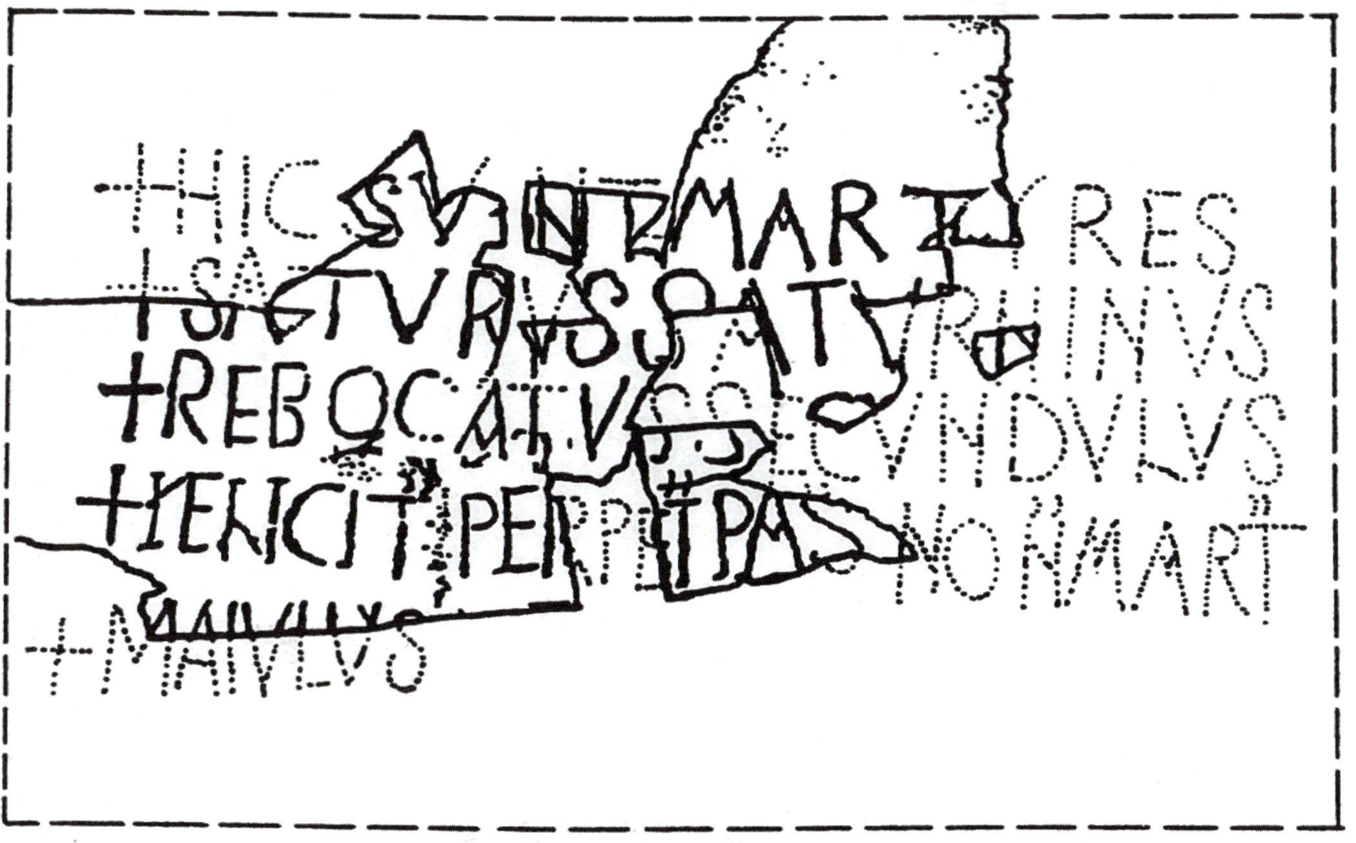

Figure 8.2: Memorial plaque honoring Perpetua, Felicitas, and their co-martyrs

girl stand side by side in the amphitheater for what appears to be a long time. Then, at least for the moment, they are led out of the arena via the Gate of Life.

The attention of the crowd is, once again, focused on Saturus who, having been released from the stocks, is attacked after all by the leopard. The amount of blood is so great that, to the other martyrs-to-be watching from where they have been rounded-up by the guards, it appears as though the man who had prepared them for baptism is himself undergoing a second baptism, a baptism of blood. The crowd roars again and demands even more blood. The remaining Christian prisoners, including Perpetua and Felicitas, walk quietly, on their own initiative, to the center of the amphitheater. They give one another the kiss of peace, their final act before martyrdom. One by one, they are dispatched by a gladiator. Perpetua is the last to die. Taking the trembling hand of the young, inexperienced gladiator who is to be her executioner, she gently guides his sword to her throat.[1]

Sources:

Pass. Perp.; IMont 14.

Carthage, Africa Proconsularis, ca. 204 C.E.

Preserving the memory of Perpetua and Felicitas

The man sitting at the small desk adjusts his oil lamp with great anticipation. As he has done almost every evening for over a year, he lovingly takes some papyrus sheets from their hiding place and thinks back to the night when they were placed in his hands.

The first bundle of sheets had come from Perpetua, of blessed memory. What a courageous young matron she was, even on her last night on earth. The man remembers how frightened he himself had been. He was one of the Christians who had been allowed into the jail to bring food for the prisoners' final meal. Characteristically, the martyrs-to-be had turned their "last supper" into a "Lord's Supper" by eating together an *agape* meal. During the meal, unnoticed by the guards, Perpetua had slipped into his hands the pages that now lie before him. At first he thought they must be letters. Perhaps Perpetua had composed a letter to her infant son to be read at a future date when the child would be old enough to understand—but how could anyone, of any age, really understand what it takes for a young mother to hold fast to the faith even if this means leaving her infant motherless? Or perhaps, he had assumed at the time, Perpetua decided to be reconciled to her father after all—her old father with the gray hairs, who had been beaten at the order of the governor because he could not convince his daughter to recant her faith.

A little later that same evening, Saturus, the catechist, had likewise given him some pages that he also took to be final letters from a soon-to-be dead Christian. At considerable risk to himself, the man smuggled the pages out of the jail. He did not dare look at them until he was safely home. He still remembers how, sitting at the very desk where he is sitting now, with the lamp adjusted just as it is now, he first read what had been entrusted to him. To his surprise, the pages were not letters but journals, written while Perpetua and Saturus were in prison.

The papyrus sheets are a little worse for wear after having been read so many times by the man. Still, he cannot help fingering the pages again. By touching them, it is almost as if he can still touch the martyrs themselves. He remembers how they held his hands and kissed his cheeks with the kiss of peace as they said their final goodbyes. He, as always, feels a little guilty that he is still alive whereas they died for the faith he too professes.

The man has been lost in thought for so long that one of the oil lamps sputters noisily and, after an extra burst of light, dies out. The noise of the lamp and the diminished light in the little room bring the man back to the present. He trims the wick, replenishes the oil, and makes a decision. It is time to write an account of the martyrdom of Perpetua, Felicitas, Revocatus, Saturninus, Saturus, and the others who died on Geta's birthday. Perpetua and Saturus, he has decided, must speak in their own voice. What he will do is write an introduction but then simply copy Perpetua's journal and Saturus' journal so as to have a continuous narrative. He will then append a conclusion.

The man has been influenced by the teachings of the New Prophecy whose adherents and writings have recently reached Carthage. The journals of Perpetua and Saturus include detailed accounts of the dreams and visions they had in prison, and the man is reminded of the prophecy of Joel that there would come a time when the people's sons and daughters would prophesy, old men would dream dreams, and young men would see visions. The man believes that this was fulfilled not only at Pentecost when the Holy Spirit came upon God's servants, both male and female. From what he knows about the New Prophecy, the man is convinced that the Holy Spirit, the Paraclete, continues to be active in the lives of contemporary prophets and prophetesses. Surely, the dreams and visions of Perpetua and Saturus are evidence that the Spirit is communicating matters of importance through them—just as the Spirit had done through the prophets and prophetesses in earlier times. He is not sure how to convey to others that the new prophecies are of equal, if not greater, worth than those of old.

The man puts down his writing implement for a moment and wonders whether Perpetua and the others had direct contact with any of the Carthaginian Christians who were promoting the New Prophecy. He himself had never spoken to the martyrs-to-be about the New Prophecy and he now regrets not having done so. He hopes that others had. Even if they had not, and even if Perpetua and her companions were totally unaware of the New Prophecy, their dreams, visions, and actions are still perfect examples and evidence of contemporary "new prophecy." At least in his own mind, the editor and distributor of their journal believes that the story of Perpetua and the others, while having lived and died simply as Christians, should be used to promote the cause of the New Prophecy. By reading his introduction to the story of these new prophets and prophetesses, others in Carthage and elsewhere will surely be persuaded of the legitimacy of the Phrygian "New Prophets" and of other contemporary "new prophets" in Carthage itself!

Three more times during the night the wicks of the man's oil lamps need to be trimmed and relit. He writes almost nonstop, pausing only briefly to stretch his legs that occasionally cramp. As the light of dawn gradually reduces the need for the oil lamps, the man composes the final paragraph of the *Passio sanctarum Perpetuae et Felicitatis.*[2] He looks out his window at the spectacular sunrise on this beautiful Carthaginian morning and is very pleased with what he has written.[3]

Sources:

Pass. Perp., esp. 1.1–3.1, 11.1, 14.1–21.11; *IMont* 14; Tertullian, *An.* 55.4; Joel 2:28–29; Acts 2:17–18.

Notes

1. Publius Septimius Geta (198–211) was born on March 7, 189. Both the *Pass. Perp.* (7.9; 16.2–3) and the sixth-century plaque, found in the Basilica majorum (the "Basilica of the Ancients") at Carthage (Tabbernee 1997b, 105–17) indicate that Perpetua and her companions died on March 7. The martyrs died in the amphitheater, most likely in 203. Despite opinions to the contrary (Frend 1965, 319–26; 1974, 333–51; Keresztes 1970, 565–78; 1989, 2:7–13), the long-held view that the persecution at Carthage was the direct result of an alleged anti-Jewish and anti-Christian edict issued by Septimius Severus should be abandoned (Barnes 1985, 331–32; Tabbernee 2007, 182–88).

2. The *Passio sanctarum Perpetuae et Felicitatis* was probably written within a year after the events it describes occurred but certainly before ca. 211/12 when Tertullian wrote his *De anima*. Tertullian refers to the *Pass. Perp.* at *An.* 55.4 but in a way which suggests that he himself was not the author. Given the "Montanist-like" tone of the introduction (1.1–6) and the conclusion (21.11) of the *Pass. Perp.*, it is likely, although not certain, that the author was an adherent of the New Prophecy movement at Carthage—just as Tertullian was after 208 (see Chapter 10). Later editions of the *Pass. Perp.* deleted or greatly modified the introduction and conclusion, in order to "tone down" the aspects which may have promoted (or have been seen to promote) the New Prophecy movement (Tabbernee 2005, 430–31). Significantly, only a single manuscript derived from the original edition has survived (Amat 1996, 85, 90).

3. Regardless of whether or not the original editor of the *Pass. Perp.* belonged to the New Prophecy movement, there is no conclusive evidence to prove that Perpetua and the others were *themselves* Montanists (Tabbernee 2005, 427–31; 2007, 62–65). For the view that the martyrs *were* Montanists, see, most recently, Butler 2006. In any case, the dichotomy between "Montanists" and "catholics" at Carthage is an artificial one. Even those who, like Tertullian, were adherents of the New Prophecy movement still saw themselves as "catholics." Irrespective of any "Montanist" or "pro-Montanist" leanings they may (or may not) have had, Perpetua, Felicitas, and their companions died as *catholic* martyrs and were always venerated as such; see also Tilley 1994, 829–58, esp. 832–36; A. Jensen 1996, 93–208; and Salisbury 1997.

Figure 9.1: Artemidoros' tombstone

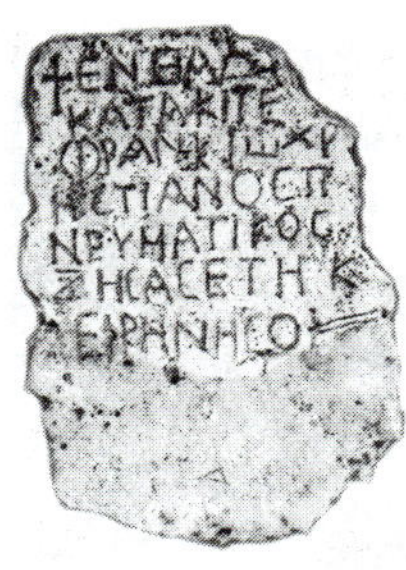

Chapter 9

Temenothyrai, Phrygia, ca. 205 C.E.
Ammion's epitaph

The grief is almost unbearable. Early this morning one of the women who went to check on Ammion found her dead in her bed. Now the Christian community at Temenothyrai is in shock. Their beloved Ammion cannot be dead. Despite the designation *presbytera,* she was not an "old woman" in the sense of being really "ancient." No one is sure exactly how old she was—as if her age really matters now that she is dead. Nevertheless, one of the women asks Diogas the bishop if he knows. Diogas explains that, as Ammion was an ordained woman presbyter, she must have been at least forty. But Ammion cannot have been much older than that—she had been a *presbytera* for only a few years.

All the women loved and respected Ammion. She had done so much for them. She encouraged them in their faith, visited them when they were ill, and, along with Diogas, administered the sacraments. But most of all, she prayed for them. Ammion was a woman of prayer—getting up well before anyone else and bringing the concerns of the community before God while others were still sleeping. Mostly she prayed privately with perfect attention to even the most minute detail. On the occasions when she prayed publicly in church, she astounded everyone. The images she evoked with her carefully chosen words captured the feelings of all who were present. Even the men are thankful that in the Christian community at Temenothyrai—a congregation influenced by the teachings of Montanus, Maximilla, and Priscilla—women, not just men, can be ordained elders, or presbyters, as they are called.

Diogas has not been a bishop for very long. It was only a few months ago that he had had the task of burying Artemidoros, his predecessor. The church has been in the habit of collecting money on a regular basis to help those in need and for other purposes. Still a presbyter at the time, Diogas convinced the other leading members of the congregation that some of the money should be used to commission a very special tombstone for Artemidoros and to pay for having an appropriate inscription carved on it. Fortunately, there is a stonemason's workshop in Temenothyrai itself. Diogas and some of the others had gone to the workshop and picked out a tombstone that was partially prefabricated. Diogas knew that the workshop specialized in "door-stones." But this was the first time he had

Figure 9.2: "Tymion Inscription"

looked closely at the beautiful funerary monuments. They all had doors carved on them, representing the entrance to one's "eternal house." The doors of some of the door-stones were decorated with simple geometric designs. Others had symbols indicating something about the deceased, such as ploughs and oxen for farmers or pruning hooks for those who worked or owned vineyards.

Diogas had chosen a door-stone for Artemidoros that has pilasters flanking its door. The pilasters are decorated with tendrils and leaves. The door itself consists of four panels and an arched transom. The door is divided into four panels creating the appearance of a large cross, which Diogas pointed out to the others. Even though the cross had been made unintentionally, this particular door-stone suited their purposes admirably. Each of the panels was already decorated with a low flat boss within a rhombus, which made the door look very realistic. The space within the arched transom, however, was still empty. Diogas had commissioned the stonemason to carve within the transom a communion paten with a round wreath-loaf decorated with a cross to represent the *panis quadratus*—bread that was scored so it could be divided easily into quadrants by the bishop during the eucharistic celebration. The epitaph commissioned read simply: "Diogas for Artemidoros, bishop, out of church funds. In remembrance."[1] The inscription was carved on the projecting fascia at the top of the stone. Seeing that the area around and above the transom was not needed for additional words, as a final decorative touch Diogas had asked the stonemason to fill it in with more tendrils and leaves.

Now Diogas has to do it all over again. He carefully writes down the text of the epitaph he will give to the stonecarver to carve on another door-stone. It reads: "Diogas, bishop, for Ammion, female presbyter. In remembrance."[2]

When Diogas arrives at the workshop, the master stonemason is already busy with another client. The client has in his hand not a small scrap of parchment like the one Diogas has, containing the text of Ammion's epitaph, but a much more official-looking document with seven seals attached to it. Diogas learns that the seals attest that the accuracy of the text the client wants inscribed has been verified independently by seven different literate persons. The seals remind Diogas of the seven seals in the book of Revelation, which Diogas, as the bishop of the New Prophecy-influenced Christian community in Temenothyrai, knows almost by heart.

The client who causes Diogas to wait explains excitedly that he is part of a delegation from Tymion and Simoe that had gone all the way to Rome to petition the emperor, Septimius Severus, to do something about the unjust taxes being imposed illegally on the tenant farmers of the region by unscrupulous and unauthorized persons. The client is careful not to name the perpetrators, but even Diogas knows who they are. He also knows that Tymion and Simoe are two settlements to the south of Temenothyrai on the imperial estate. He has even visited Tymion knowing that Montanus had taught that the New Jerusalem would descend out of heaven on the plateau between Pepouza and Tymion. In fact, the last time Diogas

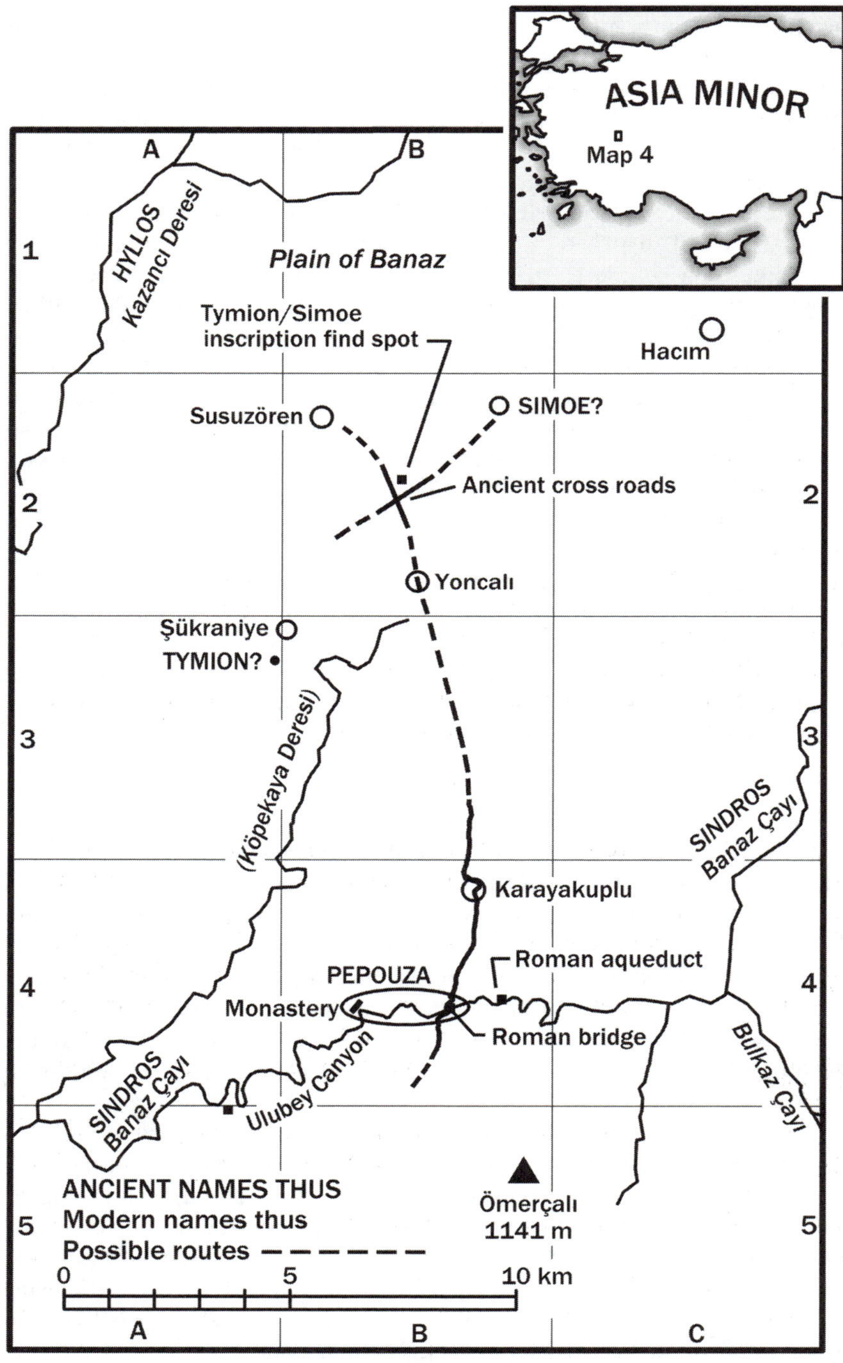

Map 4: Pepouza–Tymion area

was in Tymion, he walked to a hill just above the town. He was amazed at how clearly he could see from that hill all the way across the plain to the mountain where Montanus had first realized where the New Jerusalem would descend. As an adherent of the New Prophecy, Diogas was a little disappointed that the New Jerusalem has not come yet, but he is sure it will.

By now everyone in the workshop eagerly wants to know the text of the inscription to be carved on the beautiful marble block the client has chosen. The block has a pediment where it is decided that the Greek text, verifying the accuracy of the rescript, should be carved. The Latin text of the rescript is to be carved below the pediment on the rectangular field of the stone. After much heated debate, it is also decided that part of the bottom center of the stone will be cut away to form two "feet" for the stone. Holes will be drilled in the "feet," enabling the stone to be mounted on iron rods. This will place the text of the rescript at eye level for all to see. Even if those looking at the inscription cannot actually read, they will at least recognize the names of Septimius Severus and his sons and know that the inscription is an important one. It is decided that the marble block will be erected at the crossroads between Tymion and Simoe, as a warning to the perpetrators and a comfort to the tenant farmers.

The client moves the parchment slightly so that the sunlight streaming in through the workshop's solitary window falls on the text. He then reads out loud the date, the emperors' full name and titles, and the sentence stating that the rescript is addressed to "the tenant farmers among the Tymians and the Simoens."[3] Then, in his clearest voice, he reads out the exact words of the emperors:

> Our procurator will set himself against unlawful exactions and against those who continue to ask in a very demanding way for dues. If, however, the matter requires a higher authority he, in the manner of his office, will not hesitate to defend these persons before the governor of the province of Asia against those who in an unlawful way ask for dues.[4]

As soon as the client finishes reading everyone begins talking at once, commenting noisily about the rescript and whether it will have the desired effect. Finally, there is a concern whether, when the perpetrators see the stone standing in place at the crossroads between Tymion and Simoe, and when they are told by the procurator of the estate what it says, the unjust levying of taxes will stop. If not, they agree, the procurator should indeed take the plight of the tenant farmers to the governor in Ephesus and the proconsul should punish the perpetrators harshly.

When the client from Tymion leaves, it is time for Diogas to tell the stonemason what he needs. The text of Ammion's tombstone may not be as prestigious as the text of the rescript from Septimius Severus and his sons Caracalla and Geta, but for Diogas it is of much greater importance.

Sources:

IMont 3–4; Epiphanius, *Pan.* 49.2.5; Rev 1:1–22:21; Tabbernee and Lampe 2008, 57–58 [Tymion inscription].

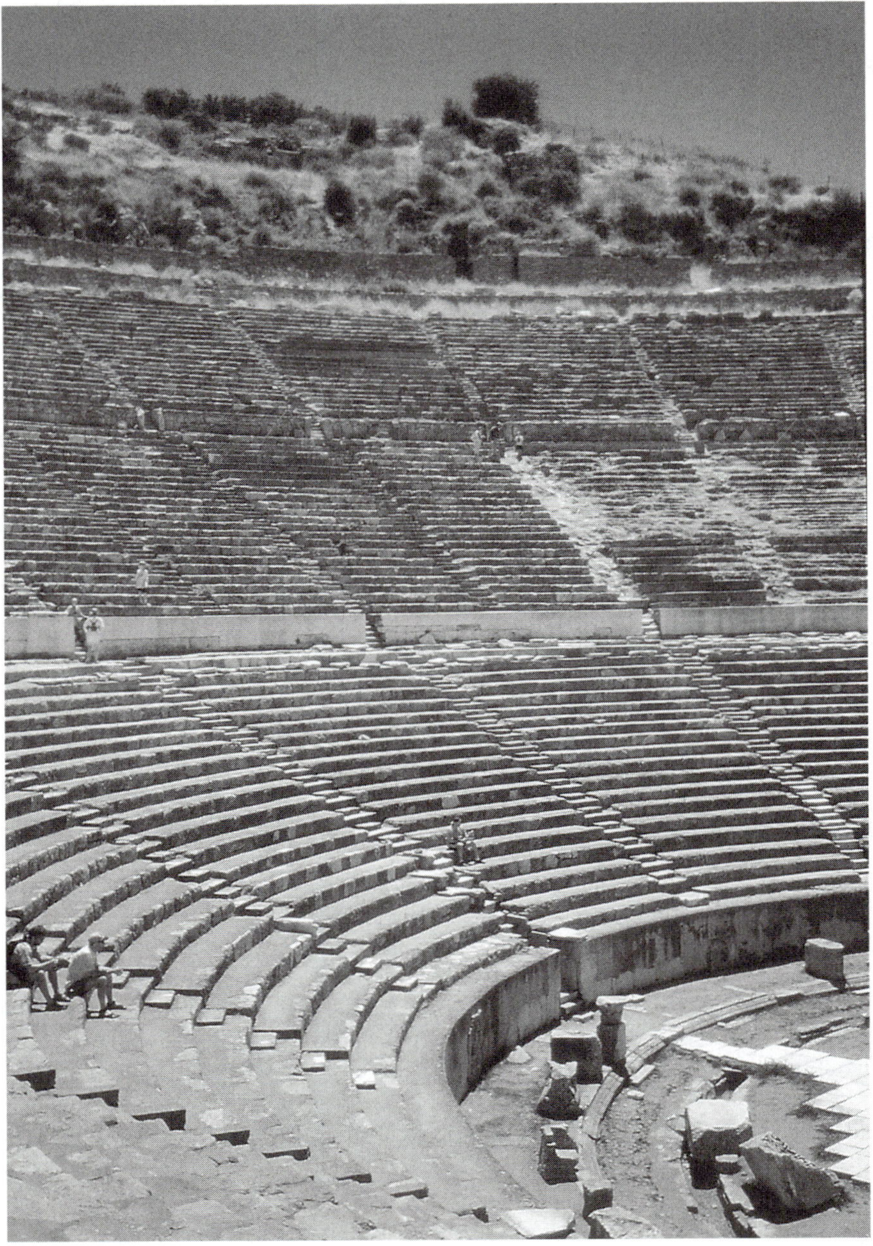

Figure 9.3: Theater at Ephesus

Somewhere in Asia, still ca. 205 C.E.

Apollonius "kills two birds with one stone"

At almost the same time that Diogas is commissioning Ammion's tombstone and the client from Tymion is commissioning the monument declaring the order of Septimius Severus that the tenant farmers of Simoe and Tymion are not to be taxed unjustly, a man named Apollonius is sitting at his desk writing against contemporary adherents of the New Prophecy. He cannot understand what they see in this movement, which has spread like wildfire from the Phrygian hinterland even to Ephesus, the foremost city in Asia.

Apollonius knows Ephesus well, although he doesn't live there. He loves the bustling metropolis. The first time he visited the capital he arrived by ship. Apollonius still remembers vividly the magnificent view of Ephesus' theater when he stepped off the boat onto the wharf and then onto Harbor Street. To him, the colonnaded street seemed like a funnel drawing his gaze directly ahead to the largest theater he had ever seen. He learned later that the theater, enlarged by the Romans to seat 24,000 people, had originally been built almost five hundred years earlier when Lysimachus, one of Alexander the Great's successors, ruled what is now the Roman province of Asia. The Greeks, as was their custom, had simply cut the seats and steps into the slope of Mount Pion. Apollonius remembers that, on that first day, he couldn't resist climbing all the way to the top row of seats. From there he had a magnificent view not only of the theater itself but also of the harbor. Then by walking along the row of seats all the way to his left, he could see most of the lower part of the city.

Apollonius also remembers that he could hardly believe his eyes when he saw there, below him, a street made completely of marble slabs. It ran parallel to the commercial agora, or marketplace, next to which was the most beautiful building he had ever seen. He ran down the theater steps so hurriedly that he almost slipped twice. Fortunately, he kept his footing. Walking at full speed along the marble street that had captured his attention, his goal was to reach the tall spectacular building as quickly as possible. Captivated by the genius of the architect who had used two sets of slender marble columns with Corinthian capitals to create the ethereal appearance of a two-story façade, Apollonius stood silently, almost reverently, in front of the building. On both sides of the entrance there were two pairs of female statues, each one identified by an inscription: ΣΟΦΙΑ (*Sophia:* "Wisdom"), ΕΠΙΣΤΗΜΗ (*Epistēmē:* "Knowledge"), ΕΝΝΟΙΑ (*Ennoia:* "Thought"), and ΑΡΕΤΗ (*Aretē:* "Virtue")—the characteristics of a man named in the inscriptions as Celsus.

Curious, Apollonius stopped a passerby to ask who Celsus was. The man, incredulous at the ignorance of Apollonius, explained that Celsus was Tiberius Julius Celsus Ptolemaeanus, who had been the Roman proconsul, or governor, of Asia many years earlier. The building was a library, the man told Apollonius, that had been built by Celsus' son Gaius Julius Aquila as a fitting memorial to his father. When the man continued on his way, Apollonius went into the building

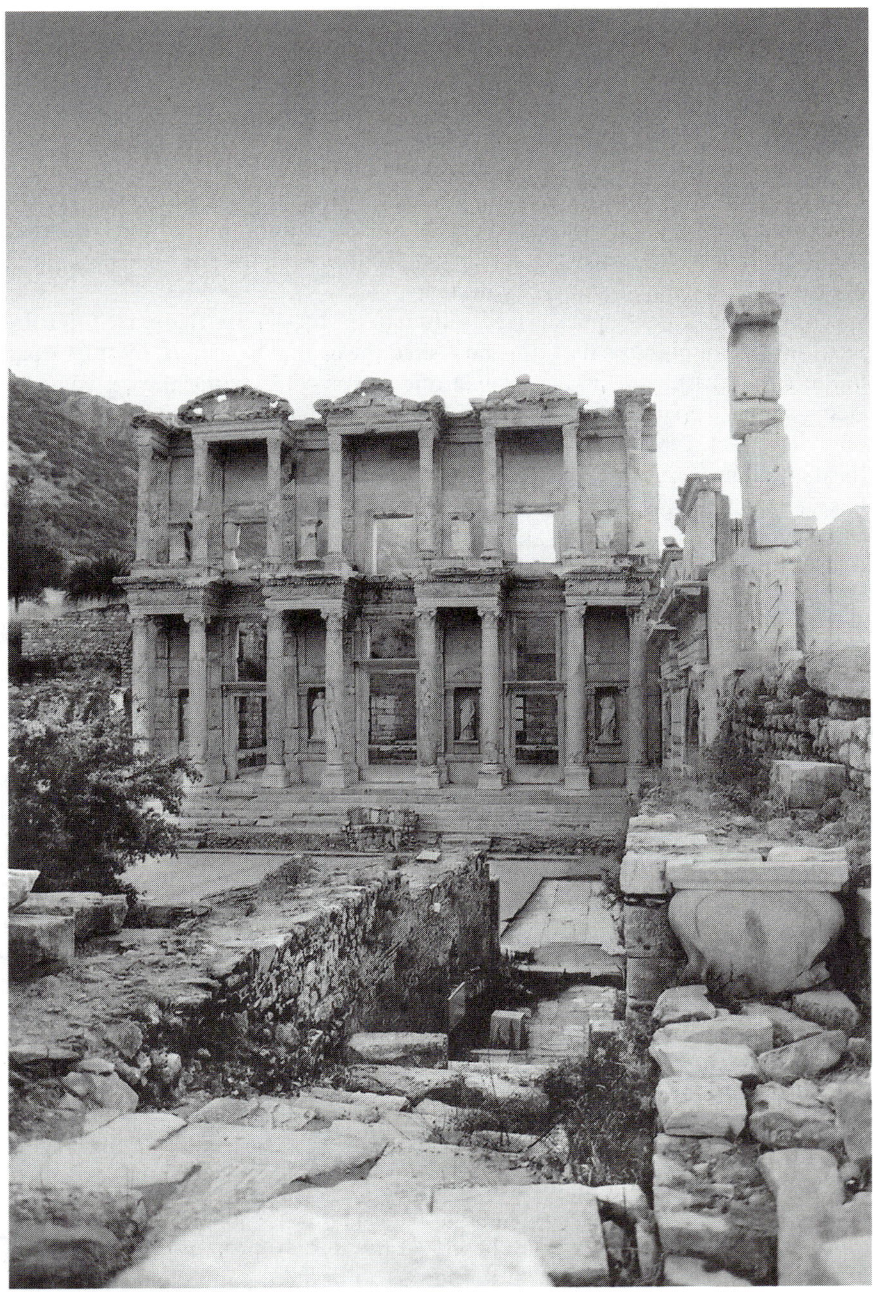

Figure 9.4: Library of Celsus at Ephesus

and even saw Celsus' sarcophagus; then he returned to the marble street that had first captured his attention.

But instead of retracing his steps, Apollonius turned right onto Kouretes Street. This street ran up the hill toward the older and more fashionable part of the city. Next to the Temple of Hadrian, Apollonius, fortunately, found the public latrine in time to freshen up before entering the complex of terrace houses directly opposite to meet his host. Apollonius had been amazed that his host's three-story home was fully heated, had running water, and even an inside toilet. He needn't have stopped at the public latrine after all. However, he was glad he had. It would not have been polite to request the use of the bathroom immediately upon being shown to his beautifully frescoed room in the terrace house. The terrace house, like one-story Roman houses built at ground level, included an atrium that was open to the sky. In the center of the atrium was a rectangular, slightly sunken pool, or impluvium, that collected much needed clean water whenever it rained. The columns of the peristyle surrounding the impluvium and the colorful exotic plants gave the atrium the feeling of a garden courtyard.

On his most recent visit to Ephesus, Apollonius had come across the story of a man named Alexander. Alexander was a Christian from another city who had been thrown into jail by the governor of Asia at the time, Aemilius Frontinus. When members of the Christian community in Ephesus heard about Alexander's plight they went to the jail and brought him food. Soon afterwards, when Alexander was freed, there were speculations that one of the Ephesian Christians, a highly placed official, had had a hand in securing Alexander's release. In any event, Alexander, claiming that he had been imprisoned simply for being a Christian, had been honored by the Ephesian Christian community as a martyr.

Not all who were witnesses ("martyrs") to the faith died for the faith. Sometimes called confessors rather than martyrs, those who had suffered physical punishment or been imprisoned in the name of Christianity were highly respected and honored by their fellow Christians. In some circles, Apollonius knew, confessors, as "living martyrs," were given quasi-clerical status and treated as if they were presbyters—even if they weren't really old enough to be elders in the church community.[5] Alexander had not been made a quasi-presbyter in Ephesus, but on the basis of calling himself a martyr, Apollonius had learned, Alexander had received all the rights and privileges of one bearing the designation "martyr."

When Alexander left Ephesus to go back to his home town, rumors about him began to trickle back to Ephesus. Apparently, Alexander was a charlatan, a common thief who committed robberies in the town he lived in before he came to Ephesus. The Christian community in Alexander's home town refused to accept him into their midst, not believing that the robber they knew could have become a Christian and "suffered for the Name." What a scandal!

Apollonius wondered whether the Christians in Ephesus could have been duped. To find out for sure, he had decided to do some research while he was in Ephesus. He went to the public archives and persuaded a clerk to let him look at some prison records. Sure enough, turning over the pages, he came across an entry recording the imprisonment of an Alexander for robbery. Alexander, of course,

Figure 9.5: Sophia at the Library of Celsus at Ephesus

was an extremely common name, but in Apollonius' mind there was little doubt. The Alexander supported and honored by the Ephesian Christian community was a fraud!

Now, sitting at his desk, Apollonius is sure that the same Alexander he believes had duped the Ephesian Christians, is, at this very time, deceiving the adherents of the New Prophecy in Pepouza. Apollonius has no sympathy for the leaders of the New Prophecy movement. Being fakes themselves, they deserve a taste of their own medicine. He does, however, feel sorry for the ordinary Christians being led astray by charlatans such as Alexander—at least, he thinks it must be the same Alexander! Setting aside the occasional troubling thoughts that the Alexander of the prison record he had seen may not be the same Alexander who had been helped by the Ephesian Christians and that the Alexander who had been helped by the Ephesian Christians may not be the same Alexander as the Alexander who now lives in Pepouza, Apollonius has convinced himself that it is the very same man. The more he thinks about it, the angrier he becomes. Can't those attracted to the prophecies of Montanus, Maximilla, Priscilla, and the more recent prophets and prophetesses of the New Prophecy movement see through an imposter like Alexander?

Apollonius calms down a little. He knows what to do next. If the people themselves cannot see through the charlatans, then he will show them—starting not with Alexander but with Montanus himself. He picks up his pen and writes:

> Who this recent teacher is, his works and teachings show. He is the one who taught you to dissolve marriages, the one who made fasts mandatory, who named Pepouza and Tymion (insignificant towns of Phrygia) "Jerusalem"—wanting everyone from everywhere to gather there—who appointed collectors of money, who devised schemes for receiving gifts under the pretence of "offerings," who provided salaries for those who publicly promote his "revelation" so that through gluttony the teaching of the "revelation" might prevail.[6]

Apollonius pauses. What a list of accusations against Montanus he has compiled! That should give those who want to follow Montanus second thoughts. But Montanus, even though he was the main founder of the movement, was not nearly as popular as his women co-founders. All three have been dead for more than a quarter of a century, but the memory of Maximilla and Priscilla is still alive and well for contemporary members of the New Prophecy. It is time to tarnish that memory a little.

Apollonius picks up his pen again and writes down what he knows about Maximilla and Priscilla. He stops, looks at what he has written, then adds: "We show, therefore, that these first prophetesses themselves, from the instant they were completely under the influence of the spirit, left their husbands."[7] What better proof that Montanus and the New Prophecy movement dissolves marriages could anyone need? Apollonius, however, also wants to attack the current leaders of the New Prophecy and he believes that, by focusing on the way they have idolized Priscilla, he has the perfect starting point.

"Were they not lying, therefore, when they called Priscilla virgin?"[8] Apollonius asks his future readers. He knows full well that, in the church at large, the term "virgin" is used not only for young women of marriageable age but also for women, including married women or widows, who have taken a vow to abstain from sexual activity. Some of these women, in fact, still live with their husbands in "spiritual marriages," practicing their asceticism at home. The opportunity to slur both Priscilla's reputation and to question the credibility of the contemporary leadership of the New Prophecy, however, is too great for Apollonius to resist.

Apollonius now turns his attention from the founders to the second generation of prophetesses and other leaders of the New Prophecy movement. He is eager to write down what he believes he knows about Alexander, but he restrains himself a little longer. He wants to introduce the story of Alexander with that of Themiso. Apollonius has read the account of the New Prophecy that the anonymous bishop who defended orthodoxy at Ankyra sent to Avircius Marcellus. He knows, therefore, of the attempted exorcism of Maximilla at Pepouza by Julian of Apameia and Zotikos of Konana. It is a pity, Apollonius laments, that the attempt had been stopped by Themiso and others. What he has heard about Themiso, however, means that Apollonius is not surprised at anything Themiso has allegedly done. Apollonius has picked up a rumor that Themiso, like Alexander, calls himself a martyr without having earned the right to do so. Indeed, according to the rumor, Themiso, unlike Alexander, hadn't even spent any time in jail. He had simply bribed the officials to avoid imprisonment. Then, instead of being ashamed of this he acted like he had a confessor's right to instruct those whose faith was better than his own. Themiso even composed a letter that, in imitation of apostolic letters, he sent to all the churches. Apollonius hadn't actually seen a copy of this letter nor did he really know whether the rumors about Themiso were true, but he feels it is his duty to pass on this piece of information. If Alexander could be a fraud, why not Themiso? Oblivious to the circularity of the argument, Apollonius reasons that Themiso's alleged illegitimate claim to being a martyr substantiates Alexander's similarly deceitful claim.

Being even more certain now than he was when he began writing his tract against the New Prophecy, that the Alexander who lives in Pepouza is the same Alexander who had briefly lived in Ephesus, Apollonius wants to "kill two birds with one stone." Not only does he want to expose Alexander as a fraud but he also wants to show that the prophetess who now resides at Pepouza as a successor to Maximilla and Priscilla is also a fraud because she hasn't seen through Alexander—something a person with the genuine gift of prophecy would surely have done.[9] Apollonius is proud that he has hit upon a double-edged sword with which to slay both "prophetess" and "martyr."

The next sentences Apollonius writes are provocative. "Who, therefore, pardons whose sins? Does the prophetess forgive the martyr's robberies or does the martyr forgive the covetousness of the prophetess?"[10] Apollonius has already accused the second-generation prophetess of receiving gold, silver, and expensive clothing, things genuine prophets and prophetesses are forbidden to receive according to a teaching which he believes goes all the way back to Jesus himself. The latest prophetess at Pepouza, therefore, has at least two strikes against her. She fails the test for genuine prophecy established by Jesus himself, and she fails to recognize Alexander as a fraud. Apollonius also knows of some other things that collectively, in his view, constitute a third strike against the prophetess: she dyes her hair, paints her eyelids, loves jewelry, and plays board games with dice. Is that any way for a Christian prophetess to behave?

Apollonius doesn't really believe that the prophetess actually forgave Alexander for the robberies he committed. Since she doesn't know about them, how can she forgive him? Nevertheless, posing the hypothetical question as to who would forgive whom is, for Apollonius, a clever rhetorical device—especially since he knows that, among the adherents of the New Prophecy and even among other Christians, there is the view that martyrs and confessors, because of their faithful suffering, have the power to forgive sins. Prophets and prophetesses, according to the teaching of the New Prophecy, also have this power. Apollonius totally disagrees with this inflated, alleged authority of prophets. It is God who forgives sins through bishops and presbyters, the legitimate, ecclesiastically appointed dispensers of grace: not uncontrollable prophets or—even worse—*prophetesses*! Perhaps martyrs *can* forgive sins, but only genuine martyrs recognized as such by the church.

Having introduced the concept of fraudulent martyrs to his readers, Apollonius turns to summarizing the main points of Alexander's story as he has construed it. People wanting more details about Alexander's robberies can go, as he did, to the public archives in Ephesus, he tells his readers—not that he believes any of them will do so, but at least it makes what he says about Alexander sound more convincing.

A troubling thought, one he had assumed would not reoccur, crosses Apollonius' mind as he puts the finishing touches to this part of his tract: What if the Alexander of the New Prophecy *isn't* the robber Alexander after all?

Sources:

Apollonius, *Fr., ap.* Eusebius, *Hist. eccl.* 5.18.2–14; Anonymous, *Fr., ap.* Eusebius, *Hist. eccl.* 5.16.3–17.4; *Did.* 1.1–16.7.

Notes

1. *IMont* 3. On Artemidoros' tombstone and the workshop at Temenothyrai which produced all the inscriptions mentioned in the first section of this chapter, as well as on other inscriptions including Diogas' own tombstone, see Tabbernee 1997b, 62–86, esp. 62–66, 72–76, 85–86.

2. *IMont* 4. That Montanists ordained women as presbyters (and as bishops) is clear from Epiphanius, *Pan.* 49.2.5. Although Ammion is considered by some recent scholars to have been a *presbytera* belonging to mainstream Christianity (Heine 1998, 824–27; Eisen 2000, 117–18; Madigan and Osiek 2005, 169–70), the provenance of her tombstone and

its early third-century date make it much more likely that she was a presbyter of the New Prophecy movement; see Tabbernee 1997b, 66–72; 2007, 374.

3. Tabbernee and Lampe 2008, 57–58 (*l.*10).

4. Tabbernee and Lampe 2008, 57–58 (*ll.*11–16). For additional details about the "Tymion inscription," see Tabbernee 2003; Lampe and Tabbernee 2004 (cf. Hauken, Tanriver, and Akbıyıkoğlu 2003, 33–43). The "Tymion inscription" was found at a spot 2.2 km southeast of Susuzören where, in the early third century, there was an intersection of a number of roads. The inscription, therefore, was set up in a prominently visible place between the two settlements named in the inscription. Tymion itself appears to have been 4.8 km to the southwest where the village of Şükraniye is now located. Simoe, the second settlement mentioned, is likely to have been 2.7 km northeast of the findspot, in an area which now is farmland; see Tabbernee and Lampe 2008, 49–74.

5. On the distinction between "confessors" and "martyrs" in the early church, see Delehaye 1921, 20–49 and Manson 1957, 463–84. An example of quasi-clerical status being given to a confessor is provided by Cyprian of Carthage (*Ep.* 38) in the case of a young man named Aurelius.

6. Apollonius, *Fr.*, *ap.* Eusebius, *Hist. eccl.* 5.18.2. Nothing is known about Apollonius himself other than his obvious familiarity with Ephesus and that he wrote for a non-Phrygian audience, probably somewhere in Asia ca. 205; see Tabbernee 2007, 45–49. For an evaluation of the reliability of Apollonius' information about Montanism, see Bauer 1971, 137–42 and Tabbernee 2007, 216–19.

7. Apollonius, *Fr.*, *ap.* Eusebius, *Hist. eccl.* 5.18.3a.

8. Apollonius, *Fr.*, *ap.* Eusebius, *Hist. eccl.* 5.18.3b.

9. Although frequently assumed to have been Priscilla (e.g., A. Jensen 1996, 142), it is much more likely, as taken for granted in this chapter, that the prophetess mentioned by Apollonius is a second-generation Montanist prophetess residing at Pepouza.

10. Apollonius, *Fr.*, *ap.* Eusebius, *Hist. eccl.* 5.18.7.

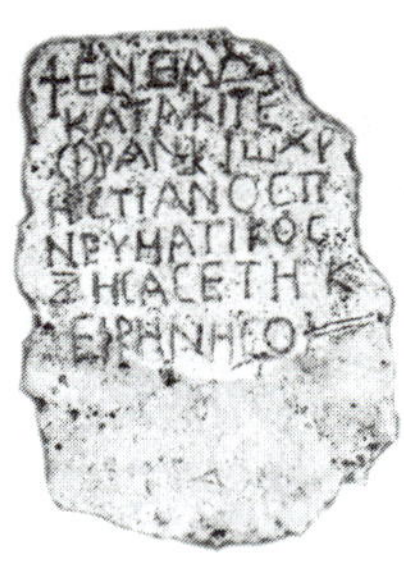

Chapter 10

Carthage, Africa Proconsularis, ca. 207/8 C.E.

Tertullian's treatise is pilfered

Quintus Septimius Florens Tertullianus is furious. An unscrupulous person whom he once considered a friend has made an unauthorized copy of the second, as-yet-uncompleted edition of his *Adversus Marcionem.* What is worse, the scoundrel has sold the copy to someone else who is making additional copies and selling them for profit. It is not so much the money that concerns Tertullian: he has plenty of money and has never written anything for the sole purpose of earning money. What is making Tertullian mad is that his reputation is at stake.

Tertullian wrote the first version of his treatise against the heretic Marcion some years earlier. As was his practice, he placed an authorized copy, the exemplar, in a small room that serves as a library and scriptorium in the house-church of which he is the patron. A number of people have legitimately copied the exemplar of the first edition, but Tertullian now considers that edition an inadequate, immature work. Years before Tertullian's time, Marcion, a wealthy ship owner and sea merchant from Pontus, taught that the God of Israel is inferior to the God revealed through Jesus. Marcion also produced his own emasculated version of the Gospels and St. Paul's writings. Arguing against the false teachings of Marcion required something more nuanced and sophisticated than the young Tertullian had been able to produce at the time.

Tertullian had removed the original exemplar from the scriptorium so that no further copies could be made. He also spent months producing a whole new version of the *Adversus Marcionem.* What a job that had been! Rewriting proved to be more difficult than writing the treatise in the first place. He was, however, able to finish a rough draft of his revisions, although the revised manuscript was still not ready to be an exemplar. It was not yet a final version. But Tertullian made the mistake of reading the draft aloud to a circle of his friends one evening. The next day both the manuscript and one of the so-called friends were gone—and now he has learned that not only are there people profiting from his many hours of literary labor but other people are reading his revised work in an incomplete and still inadequate form. It was his intention to make more revisions based on the feedback he received from his "public reading" and to add more content to the treatise. Now all that work has been for nothing! His only copy is gone forever. He is so angry that he could spit. But all he can do is to get over the loss of his rewritten treatise and begin to write it again for the third time. At least this will enable him to incorporate some of the new insights he gained from his recent involvement with the New Prophecy movement in Carthage.

Tertullian is amazed that so many of the teachings in the *logia* of the Phrygian prophets Montanus, Maximilla, and Priscilla resonate with his own thoughts on a variety of topics, especially those related to Christian life and practice. He came across a book of the *logia* and read it eagerly. He also spoke to other members of the various house-churches in Carthage and found that there are many who have already been influenced by the New Prophecy. Especially since the exemplar of the account of the *Passio sanctarum Perpetuae et Felicitatis* has been deposited in the church's scriptorium there is great speculation in Carthage that Carthage's recent and most famous martyrs were themselves adherents of the New Prophecy. Certainly, there are women in Carthage now who are prophesying and can definitely be deemed "new prophets." What a pity it is that some of the other members of the Carthaginian Christian community as a whole are opposed to the New Prophecy. Of what are they so afraid? Is not the Holy Spirit who inspires the prophets and prophetesses in this day and age the same one who inspired the prophets of old?

Tertullian cannot understand all the fuss. Being an adherent of the New Prophecy does not mean leaving the mainstream Christian community in Carthage. It simply means being open to the new revelations of the Paraclete, the Holy Spirit, communicated through the dreams, visions, oracles, and other sayings of Montanus, Maximilla, Priscilla, and their contemporary prophetic successors. Belonging to the New Prophecy movement within the church certainly does not mean leaving catholic Christianity to join a heretical sect such as the Marcionites.

At the thought of the Marcionites, a wave of anger again sweeps over Tertullian. He grits his teeth, clenches his pen, and goes back to work.[1]

Sources:

Tertullian, *Marc.*, esp. 1.1.1–3; *Pass. Perp.*

Antioch, Syria, ca. 207/8 C.E.
Serapion condemns the New Prophecy

Serapion is proud of being the Christian bishop of a city as important as Antioch. Antioch recently celebrated the founding of the city five hundred years earlier by Seleucus I Nicator, who also founded the Seleucid dynasty that ruled Syria for more than two centuries. The Romans are in charge now, but they spend most of their time at Daphne, a few miles away, in their beautiful villas surrounded by lush gardens and waterfalls.

Antioch, Serapion is delighted to tell anyone who is interested to know, is the city where the followers of Jesus first took the name *Christianoi.* Paul and Barnabas were among the early leaders of the Christian community at Antioch and they left from there to go on their missionary journeys. Serapion loves to go to Seleukeia Pieria, Antioch's port at the mouth of the Orontes, to look at the kind of boats on which the apostles sailed to unevangelized lands. The apostle Peter, of course, also spent time in Antioch. Serapion often shows visitors the grotto just outside the city where, according to tradition, Peter preached. On the way he tells them about the first Christian council, held right here in Antioch, where it was decided that gentiles as well as Jews could become *Christianoi*—though some people found that difficult to accept at the time and even the apostles, at first, disagreed about this matter.

Serapion is most enthusiastic when he tells visitors about Ignatius, Antioch's illustrious bishop martyr. Nearly one hundred years ago, Ignatius had been arrested for the faith in Antioch and taken under guard to Rome. On the way, Ignatius stayed at Smyrna where Polycarp, of blessed memory, was bishop. There he met with Christian leaders not only from Smyrna but from Ephesus, Magnesia on the Meander, and Tralles. While still in Smyrna, Ignatius wrote letters to the three Christian communities that had sent delegations to Smyrna. He also sent from Smyrna a letter to the church in Rome, begging the Christians there not to intervene in his impending martyrdom. "May I have the full pleasure of the wild beasts prepared for me,"[2] Ignatius had written.

> I pray that they will be found ready for me. Indeed, I will coax them to devour me quickly—not as happens with some whom they are afraid to touch. And even if they do not wish to do so willingly, I will force them to it.[3]

Serapion can almost recite the next part of Ignatius' letter by heart, he has read it so many times:

> Grant this to me; I know what benefits me. Now I am beginning to be a disciple. May nothing visible or invisible show any envy toward me, that I may attain to Jesus Christ. Fire and cross and packs of wild beasts, cuttings and being torn apart, the scattering of bones, the mangling of limbs, the grinding of the whole body, the evil torments of the devil—let them come upon me, only that I may attain to Jesus Christ.[4]

From Alexandria Troas, Ignatius had also written to the church at Philadelphia that had been hospitable to him and his companions, and similarly to the church at Smyrna, as well as to Polycarp. Polycarp himself has collected copies of all seven letters and forwarded them to the church at Antioch. Since then, dozens of additional copies of Ignatius' correspondence have been made, but Serapion is proud of yet another thing, namely that he possesses the original copies sent by Polycarp. Of course, these original copies are not his own personal possession, but as bishop of Antioch he has access to them at all times. He enjoys holding them in his hands and reading the wise ecclesiastical advice Ignatius had given regarding the role of the bishop, the presbyters, and the deacons in the church. Serapion is glad that the threefold ministerial structure Ignatius promoted is now being implemented in nearly all the churches. Ignatius had argued that nothing should be done liturgically in the church apart from the bishop's direct permission and authority—and Serapion is sure that this is the only way a Christian community can function effectively.

Serapion considers himself a second Ignatius. He would willingly die a martyr's death if called upon to do so. In the meantime, like Ignatius, he delights in corresponding with church leaders and hopes that he gives meaningful advice when called upon to do so. As is the practice, he has scribes make copies of all incoming and outgoing correspondence and he collects letters and documents written by other bishops. These are kept, locked away safely, in the scriptorium of the Antiochene Christian community. The scriptorium, which also functions as the church's library, is the tablinum, or study, in his own house.

Serapion, seated at the desk in his tablinum, is just finishing a letter to the church at Rhosos, a coastal town slightly northwest of Antioch, when he is interrupted by a servant who brings him another letter. Curious, Serapion stops what he is doing and quickly reads the new letter. It is from Pontius and Caricus, two churchmen whom he knows well for their impeccable faith. They are asking him about the New Prophecy. Fortunately, Serapion is well informed.

Deciding that the letter to Rhosos can wait, Serapion goes to the locked cupboards in the scriptorium and searches for a little while until he finds what he needs. It is a letter written more than twenty years ago by Apolinarius of Hierapolis in Phrygia, the leading opponent of the founders of the New Prophecy movement. It is not a private, nor even a mere episcopal, letter. It is a synodical letter, setting out the findings of a synod over which Apolinarius had presided dealing with the New Prophecy. Serapion is glad that one of his episcopal predecessors at Antioch received a copy of the letter and that it is being preserved so carefully.

In fact, now that Serapion has the correspondence in his hands again, he remembers that it consists not only of Apolinarius' own letter but also of some subscriptiones—brief appended statements and signatures of those present at the synod confirming that they concur with the synod's findings. Serapion knows that synods in those days were simple affairs, more like informal gatherings of autonomous bishops, and that the decisions of those bishops were not really binding on all those at the synod or anyone else. The decisions of synods such as the one at Hierapolis, however, provided useful precedents and gave local bishops excellent guidance for making their own decisions. Serapion, for the second time in as many minutes, rejoices in the wisdom of his predecessor who kept Apolinarius' letter and its appendices safe for posterity.

Serapion writes down everything he knows personally about the New Prophecy—which isn't a great deal since he himself has never met any adherents of the movement. The New Prophecy, as far as he knows, hasn't spread to Antioch—but it could! What he does know is that, in Syria as well as elsewhere in the world, orthodox bishops such as himself and other churchmen such as Pontius and Caricus need to be ever vigilant to ensure that the fake prophetic movement doesn't find a toe-hold in their churches. What a disaster that would be! Catholic bishops need to close ranks against the false prophets and practice episcopal solidarity if the New Prophecy is to be contained. Thank goodness Pontius and Caricus have written to him.

Having finished his own epistle, Serapion adds a final statement. He tells Pontius and Caricus:

> So that you also might know that the energizing influence of this false order of the New Prophecy, so named, has been an abomination to the whole episcopate throughout the entire world, I have sent you also a letter of the most blessed Claudius Apolinarius, bishop in Hierapolis of Asia.[5]

Serapion calls one of the scribes and asks him to make an additional copy of Apolinarius' letter. Serapion, like his predecessors, is very careful not to let the original copy of Apolinarius' correspondence leave its secure place in the church library.

As the scribe painstakingly copies the minuscule letters of Apolinarius' synodical letter, Serapion looks more carefully at the subscriptiones that are on separate pages. One of the subscriptiones reads: "I, Aurelius Quirinus, a martyr, pray that you will remain sound."[6] Serapion wonders who Quirinus was. He was obviously a confessor, a living martyr, but Serapion doesn't know anything about the circumstances of Quirinus' suffering for the faith. As Quirinus was present at the synod in Hierapolis, Serapion conjectures that he may have been a Phrygian bishop—but he is not really sure. What is certain, however, is that Quirinus' prayer, that all who read Apolinarius' summary of the synod's condemnation of the New Prophecy movement will remain sound in the faith, is as relevant today as it was when the sentiment was penned. Serapion imagines Quirinus, whether on earth or now—more likely—with the other martyrs in heaven, still praying for the spiritual and doctrinal health of all Christians. It will be good for Pontius and Caricus to know this.

Another of the subscriptiones catches Serapion's eye. It begins with an autograph—a signature statement providing name, place of origin, and title: "Aelius Publius Julius from Develtum, a colony of Thrace, bishop."[7] That is exactly the sort of autograph Serapion wants to send on to Pontius and Caricus because it proves that the New Prophecy is abominated by bishops throughout the entire world, not just in Hierapolis and Antioch. It also makes Serapion less certain that Quirinus was a *Phrygian* confessor/bishop. If Aelius Publius Julius could travel all the way from Develtum in Thrace to Hierapolis in Asia, perhaps Quirinus had also traveled to Hierapolis from somewhere outside of Phrygia.

Serapion looks back at Julius' autograph and continues to read: "As God lives in heaven, because the blessed Sotas, the one in Anchialos, wanted to cast out Priscilla's demon the interpreters did not give permission."[8] Serapion is amazed. He remembers vaguely hearing that Julian of Apameia and Zotikos of Konana attempted to exorcise Maximilla at Pepouza, but he did not realize that a similar attempt had been made by Sotas of Anchialos. When he had first looked at Apolinarius' synodical letter some years earlier, he did not examine the subscriptiones carefully and so had missed the detail about Sotas and Priscilla. For a moment he questions whether Priscilla might have traveled to Thrace and whether the attempted exorcism had occurred there, but he quickly rejects that possibility. Julius' double reference to Sotas as *makarios,* the blessed one, and the one in Anchialos, undoubtedly indicates that Sotas, the bishop of Anchialos, was already buried in Anchialos at the time Julius was writing—not that the attempted exorcism had taken place *in* Anchialos. Presumably, Serapion speculates, Sotas made the long journey to Pepouza and *there* attempted to cast the evil spirit out of Priscilla.

What fascinates Serapion even more than speculating about the location of the frustrated exorcism is the information supplied by Julius explaining why the exorcism was unsuccessful. Sotas, apparently, had been unable to hear any of Priscilla's so-called prophetic utterances because the people who interpreted her babbling into intelligible language refused to give Sotas access to her. Priscilla was so carefully protected by her henchmen that Sotas hadn't even seen her.

Serapion continues to read through the autographs and extended subscriptiones made by numerous other bishops attached to Apolinarius' letter. He wonders whether some of them could have been added well after the synod had taken place, by bishops not actually present but in full accord with the decisions made at Hierapolis, condemning Montanus, Maximilla, and Priscilla. Whatever the case, he has the evidence he needs to show Pontius and Caricus that there was (and is) a universal episcopal consensus that the New Prophecy is a dangerous deviation from genuine Christianity. Serapion gets up from his desk where he has been reading, and takes the subscriptiones to the second desk in the tablinum where the tabularius, the scribe, has just finished copying Apolinarius' letter. Serapion asks the scribe to copy the subscriptiones also.[9]

Sources:

Serapion, *Ep., ap.* Eusebius, *Hist. eccl.* 5.19.2–3, 6.12.3–4; Eusebius, *Hist. eccl.* 5.19.1, 4; Acts 11:19–26, 13:1–21:6; Gal 2:11–21; Ignatius of Antioch, *Eph.; Magn.; Trall.; Rom.,* esp. 5.2–3; *Phld.; Smyrn.,* esp. 8.1–2; *Pol.;* Polycarp, *Phil.* 13.1–2; Aurelius Quirinus, *Sub., ap.* Apolinarius, *Ep., ap.* Serapion, *Ep., ap.* Eusebius, *Hist. eccl.* 5.19.3; Aelius Publius Julius, *Sub., ap.* Apolinarius, *Ep., ap.* Serapion, *Ep., ap.* Eusebius, *Hist. eccl.* 5.19.3.

Notes

1. On Tertullian's pilfered manuscript and the production of the various editions of Tertullian's *Adversus Marcionem,* see Tabbernee 2000a. On Marcion himself, see Harnack 1999. Tertullian became influenced by the New Prophecy movement ca. 207/8. His treatises after that date show an increasing adherence to the movement. Despite earlier views to the contrary, there is now a scholarly consensus that neither Tertullian nor any other members of the "pro-Montanist" element within the Christian community at Carthage in Tertullian's time ever separated formally to form a separatist Montanist congregation; see Tabbernee 2007, 129–32.

2. Ignatius, *Rom.* 5.2a.

3. Ignatius, *Rom.* 5.2b.

4. Ignatius, *Rom.* 5.3. For Ignatius' letters and that of Polycarp, see Ehrman 2003, 1:201–353. The English translation of Ignatius, *Rom.* 5.2–3 is taken from Ehrman 2003, 1:277.

5. Serapion, *Ep., ap.* Eusebius, *Hist. eccl.* 5.19.2. Serapion was bishop of Antioch in Syria ca. 199–ca. 211. His letter to Caricus and Pontius could, theoretically, have been written at any time during the first decade of the third century C.E., but is more likely to have been composed later rather than earlier in his episcopate, namely, after he had established his reputation as someone from whom other clergy could receive wise counsel.

6. Aurelius Quirinus, *Sub., ap.* Apolinarius, *Ep., ap.* Serapion, *Ep., ap.* Eusebius, *Hist. eccl.* 5.19.3a.

7. Aelius Publius Julius, *Sub., ap.* Apolinarius, *Ep., ap.* Serapion, *Ep., ap.* Eusebius, *Hist. eccl.* 5.19.3b.

8. Aelius Publius Julius, *Sub., ap.* Apolinarius, *Ep., ap.* Serapion, *Ep., ap.* Eusebius, *Hist. eccl.* 5.19.3c.

9. The exact relationship between Serapion's own letter, Apolinarius' letter, which Serapion appended, and the subscriptiones also appended by Serapion, is difficult to determine conclusively, but the scenario described in this chapter seems the most likely (Tabbernee 2007, 16–24, 53–55).

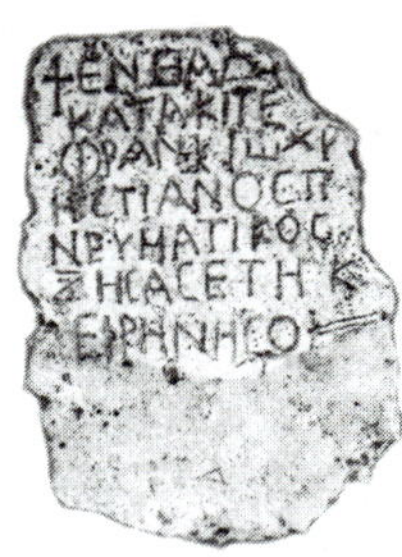

Chapter 11

Carthage, Africa Proconsularis, ca. 208/209 C.E.

Tertullian scores a few points for the New Prophecy

Tertullian is still not happy with his treatise against Marcion. Last year, after getting over the shock of having the manuscript of his first revised version stolen, he had started all over again and produced a totally new edition in three books. But there is so much more to say about Marcion and Marcion's pernicious undermining of true Christianity. After thinking about it for a long time, Tertullian has made up his mind: he is going to add at least one totally new book—probably two—to the *Adversus Marcionem.*

Never satisfied with anything he writes, Tertullian tinkers with the two passages about the New Prophecy he included in last year's revision of the *Adversus Marcionem.* By now Tertullian is fully involved in the New Prophecy movement in Carthage. He likes what Montanus, Maximilla, and Priscilla taught about the wide range of practical ways one can live out the Christian faith. What he likes even more is that many of these teachings agree with what he already believes. Only the other day, someone accused him of being a "rigorist," a person who takes a strong conservative stance on moral issues. The Carthaginian Christian who accused Tertullian of this used the term pejoratively. Tertullian took it as a compliment! After all, his tough line on ethical matters is being vindicated by the most recent revelations of the Holy Spirit. Tertullian cannot understand why everyone else can't recognize this. Perhaps they are confused because the strong rigoristic position on matters such as fasting and marriage appears to conflict with the greater laxity permitted in earlier times.

In revising his treatise, Tertullian wants to ensure that his readers come to understand that there is no inconsistency between the ethical revelations of the Paraclete via the oracles of the New Prophecy and what God has always intended—even in times past. Regarding marriage, which is an important topic for the treatise against Marcion because of Marcion's total rejection of marriage, Tertullian steers a careful course between rejecting *second* marriages and sounding too much like Marcion himself! In this context Tertullian knows he even has to defend God against the charge of lax standards in first allowing polygamy among Israel's patriarchs and then changing the rules. The dispensationalism inherent in the New Prophecy's way of understanding how God deals with humanity in different eras, however, gives Tertullian the perfect tool for explaining the situation. Any apparent inconsistency is due not to the God revealed by the Jewish scriptures having lax standards or to the God revealed by Jesus having a change of mind, but to a divine, but temporary, benevolence bestowed by God during previous eras. The Holy Spirit, knowing that in former times and under different circumstances the people of God who lived under either the old or the new covenant were capable of living out the full ethical dimensions of the faith, had graciously permitted greater laxity. This laxity, the *same* Holy Spirit has, in the new age, the "age of the Paraclete," rightly decided to amend. This is in total harmony with what, really, had always been God's highest standards.

In his revised treatise, Tertullian concedes that in previous eras the Spirit of God permitted various types of multiple marriages, such as polygamy among Israel's patriarchs and remarriage after the death of a person's spouse among early generations of Christians. He argues forcefully, however, that currently, in the changed circumstances of a Christianity "come of age," it is the prerogative of the Holy Spirit to reveal a more strict marital ethic for a people of God who are more mature. Tertullian crosses out some of the words he wrote previously and amends the text to read:

> Now, if at this present time a limit of marrying is being imposed, as for example among us a spiritual reckoning, decreed by the Paraclete, is defended, prescribing a single matrimony in the faith, it is the right of the One who had formerly loosened it to tighten the limit.[1]

The Paraclete has revealed a new way of calculating the number of permissible marriages. Whoever calculates using this spiritual reckoning discovers that the resulting sum is "one"!

Tertullian decides not to quote the specific prophetic oracle that contains the Paraclete's decree about monogamy; indicating that it exists is sufficient for the time being. Tertullian quickly turns to the third book of the *Adversus Marcionem* to remind himself of the way he had worded the only other passage in the treatise that refers to one of the sayings of the New Prophecy—a passage dealing with the New Jerusalem. He is satisfied with his earlier effort as he reads:

> This is the city with which Ezekiel was acquainted, the apostle John had seen, and for which the saying of the New Prophecy, which belong to our faith, provides evidence—having even predicted the appearance of an image of the city, as a portent, before it will actually be made manifest.[2]

Tertullian is glad he has available to him books that contain the oracles and other *logia,* or sayings, of Montanus and those of other prophets and prophetesses of the movement that so enthralls him. He wrongly assumes however that his future readers will also have access to similar books and can easily look up the oracles to which he alludes. He is even more mistaken when he assumes that, even if they could look up the sayings, his readers would draw the same conclusions from them as he does—or that they would be as impressed by the New Prophecy as he is.

For the next few weeks Tertullian works conscientiously at revising the other parts of the three original books of the *Adversus Marcionem*. He is a very busy man, with a very busy schedule, but he is also highly disciplined. Early each morning he works in his study, the tablinum, writing for several hours before granting audiences to his clients, receiving them in the atrium of his house, seated near the impluvium. As a man of wealth and position, his patronage is very important to those who depend on him. He dispenses not only money but also wise advice to people in need of either one. Nor does he restrict himself to helping fellow Christians, although over the years his clientele has included fewer and fewer pagans. His vitriolic attacks on the evils of the spectacles, or shows, performed in the theater and amphitheater at Carthage, have made him less than popular in non-Christian circles. After prandium, the late breakfast that functions also as lunch, followed by a brief nap, Tertullian is invariably back at his desk, writing till early evening or later if he doesn't have to host a banquet, attend a symposium, or convene a meeting of the council of elders.

By the beginning of the fifth week, he has made so much progress on the manuscript that he has written a substantial portion of an additional fourth book. In that book he accuses Marcion of being inconsistent in rejecting the Jewish scriptures and then not expunging the appearance of Moses and Elijah from the account of the Transfiguration, which he retained. Tertullian considers himself rather clever to have spotted such an inconsistency.

As he thinks further about the story of the Transfiguration, Tertullian's mind strays to the dispute he has been having with some of his fellow Carthaginian Christians about the significance of ecstasy for validating prophecy. The topic has come up because there is still no consensus in Carthage about the validity of the New Prophecy. Some argue that the way the original prophets and prophetesses of the movement fell into ecstatic trances indicates that they were false prophets. Others, such as Tertullian himself, claim that ecstasy is the very phenomenon that proves the prophecies are authentic revelations of the Paraclete. It is the same debate that raged in Phrygia decades ago, and Tertullian is tired of it. Contemplating the Transfiguration story, however, gives him an idea as to how to demonstrate the legitimacy of his own position on the matter of ecstasy. Although in the *Adversus Marcionem* Tertullian addresses Marcion in the first person, this is only a rhetorical device. Marcion is long dead and the intended audience for Tertullian's treatise is not Marcion or even contemporary Marcionites; the audience is catholic Christians, especially those in Carthage—some of whom are the very people who disagree with him about the New Prophecy. There is nothing, in Tertullian's opinion, wrong with scoring a few points on behalf of the New Prophecy in a treatise written against the heresy of Marcion. The story of the Transfiguration gives Tertullian the perfect opportunity to do this.

Tertullian goes to one of the cupboards in his tablinum and again picks up the codex containing the Gospel attributed to Luke, which he has been using. He finds the relevant passage, and copies it into his own manuscript:

> Peter said to Jesus, "Master it is good for us to be here; let us make three dwellings, one for you, one for Moses and one for Elijah"—not knowing what he said.[3]

"How was it that Peter did not know?" Tertullian asks his future readers.

> Was it an error? Or was it on the principle which we defend in the cause of the New Prophecy, that ecstasy, namely being out of one's senses, is a precondition of bestowed favor?[4]

Tertullian wants his readers to agree that Peter's "not knowing" was because of the latter. To persuade them further, he points out that Peter could not have known what Moses and Elijah looked like since the Jewish people were forbidden by law to have pictures or statues made of them or anyone else. Therefore, Peter must have recognized Moses and Elijah "in the Spirit" and not through his natural senses. He had, as the literal meaning of the word *ecstasis* implies, "stood outside of himself." In that ecstatic state, God bestowed on him the divine grace, or favor, of supernatural knowledge—a prophetic charism.

Just in case his future readers still haven't gotten the point, Tertullian spells out even more clearly the New Prophecy's operative principle regarding the legitimacy—or rather the essentiality—of ecstasy in prophecy. He writes:

> Whenever someone is in the Spirit, especially when that person sees God's glory or when God speaks through that person, the person concerned must necessarily be deprived of natural sense perceptions, being overshadowed by the power of the Divine.[5]

Tertullian admits, however, that on this particular point there is disagreement between the adherents of the New Prophecy and other Christians at Carthage whom, for the first time in writing, he pejoratively calls *psychici,* persons who think according to their physical nature, not according to their spiritual one.

Relationships between Tertullian and the *psychici* continue to be strained. Tertullian is more and more frustrated by the stupidity of those who are not prepared to acknowledge the Paraclete, and he finds himself periodically going for long walks from his villa to the seaside beneath Byrsa Hill to calm himself down. Fortunately, the scenery along the coast is always spectacular. The double harbor is his favorite spot. Built originally as ports in Punic times, the larger of the two harbors has colonnaded dry docks that can accommodate more than two hundred ships at any given time. Only a dozen or so vessels are in the harbors now, but the hustle and bustle of activity takes Tertullian's mind off the tensions between him and the *psychici*—at least temporarily.

Before he can stop himself, Tertullian is thinking again about the latest disagreement. Reports have come to Carthage about a Roman soldier who was also a Christian. When Septimius Severus decided to reward all the soldiers in the whole Roman army with both a monetary gift and a laurel wreath, this particular soldier had refused to wear the wreath during the ceremony when the emperor's gift was being distributed. Instead, the soldier simply stood in line with the garland in his hand rather than on his head.

When challenged by the tribune about his rude behavior, the soldier confessed that he was a Christian, for whom wearing a corona, a crown, was impossible. Tertullian, somewhat headstrong and impetuous himself, likes what he heard the soldier did next. Standing before the prefects while they considered what to do with him, the Christian soldier slowly and deliberately divested himself, item by item, of his military garb. His heavy purple cloak, his armor, his sword, even his sandals and the laurel crown, all lay before him on the ground as he was carted off to prison to await the granting of a different corona—the martyr's crown bestowed by Christ.

The Christian community in Carthage, as elsewhere, is divided over the question of whether the Christian soldier did the right thing. "Where does it say in scripture that we are not able to wear crowns?" some ask.[6] Others complain that the soldier, by his rash action, brought trouble on all the "bearers of the Name."[7] Tertullian and other members of the New Prophecy movement, on the other hand, strongly condone the soldier's action. To them, the soldier did what all Christians should do when faced with the choice of having to declare their allegiance publicly. Christians, even Christian soldiers, cannot serve two masters. They certainly cannot wear a crown bestowed by an emperor and in that way participate in a symbolic act that denies Christ as the only rightful king. If refusal to wear a laurel wreath leads to martyrdom, so be it. The soldier who refused to wear the wreath, among so many other Christian soldiers who did, was the only one who demonstrated his true colors—and his bravery.

Why the *psychici* cannot see that the Christian soldier was a hero—not a troublemaker—was at first beyond Tertullian's comprehension. Now, sitting at the edge of Admiralty Harbor, watching the boats sail out to sea, Tertullian has an insight. It is suddenly clear to him that the *psychici*'s rejection of the prophecies of the New Prophecy is related to their rejection of what appears to them to be voluntary martyrdom. Tertullian remembers that before he came to know those prophecies he, too, believed that one should avoid martyrdom at all costs. He had been taught by his bishop, Optatus, and some of the presbyters that Jesus told his disciples that when they encountered opposition they should shake the dust from their feet and flee to the next town.[8] There is, therefore, a precedent set by Jesus for flight during persecution. Tertullian is somewhat embarrassed as he recalls that he himself had once told his wife that it is better to "flee from town to town" than to stay and deny the faith under torture.[9] The *logia* of the prophets and prophetesses of the New Prophecy changed Tertullian's mind on the matter. Tertullian hurries home to consult his collection of the oracles of Montanus, Maximilla, Priscilla, and of later "New Prophets" in order to refresh his memory about their exact words on the subject.

Once inside his study, Tertullian quickly finds the relevant oracles. He is very well organized and has his own system of keeping track of items stored in the cupboards of his tablinum. The first oracle is in the form of the ipsissima verba, the very words, of the Spirit:

> Are you publicly exposed? That is good for you. For indeed, one who is not publicly exposed before people is being exposed publicly before the Lord. Do not be ashamed; right conduct brings you forward into the public arena. Why be ashamed when you are producing praise? Power is being generated while you are being stared at by humankind.[10]

Tertullian reflects on Perpetua and her co-martyrs in the arena of Carthage's amphitheater and thinks how applicable the oracle is to them and to all who, whether in an actual arena or not, stand up publicly for the faith—just as the Christian Roman soldier had done. The soldier made a conscious choice, a choice that led to his martyrdom—but it was the right choice.

The word "choice" triggers something in Tertullian's memory, and he searches through his collection of oracles until he finds the one he needs. Once again the exact words of the Paraclete confirm that those who choose to stand firm in the faith make the right choice, even though such a choice is tantamount to choosing martyrdom:

> Choose to die not in comfortable beds nor in miscarriages and susceptible fevers but in martyrdoms, so that the one who suffered for you may be rendered honor.[11]

Both the oracles he has found, Tertullian is sure, encourage martyrdom rather than flight. In rejecting the validity of the New Prophecy, the *psychici* are also rejecting what the Paraclete revealed about martyrdom and standing firm in times of danger.

Tertullian gets up from his desk and walks outside to the courtyard of his house. The house is at the top of a hill overlooking the Carthagiensis Sinus, the Bay of Carthage. It is a very clear day and Tertullian can see, in the far distance, some of the same boats he had watched leaving the harbor earlier that morning, sailing toward Sicilia on their way to Rome. What attracts his attention, however, is not the ships on the horizon but the stone lions that stand in his garden and the mosaic tiles that decorate the floor of his patio. Among the colorful images of flowers and birds are two beautiful mosaic deer with large docile eyes. They are perfect symbols of the *psychici* in Carthage, Tertullian thinks, especially the clergy: "lions in peace; deer in flight."[12] Because of their rejection of the New Prophecy they, like he himself used to be, he has to admit, have their bags always packed, ready to flee from town to town on the basis of the only text from the Gospels they care to remember. "Anyone recognizing the Spirit," Tertullian says aloud to no one in particular, "will hear the Spirit branding the runaways."[13]

Sources:

Tertullian, *Marc.*, esp. 1.29.4, 3.24.4, and 4.22.1–16, esp. 4–5; Rev 3:12, 21:1–22:5; Luke 9:33; Tertullian, *Cor.*, esp. 1.1–2.4; Matt 10:23; Tertullian, *Ux.* 1.3.4; *Fug.* 9.4 (cf. *An.* 55.5), 11.1–3.

Notes

1. Tertullian, *Marc.* 1.29.4.

2. Tertullian, *Marc.* 3.24.4.

3. Luke 9:33.

4. Tertullian, *Marc.* 4.22.4.

5. Tertullian, *Marc.* 4.22.5. The earliest clear references to Tertullian's involvement with the New Prophecy movement are the ones quoted from the *Adversus Marcionem* in this chapter. On Tertullian's view of remarriage, see Tabbernee 2000b and 2007, 151–53. On Tertullian's defense of ecstasy as part of the process of prophesying, see Nasrallah 2003, esp. 132–40 and Tabbernee 2007, 133–38.

6. See Tertullian, *Cor.* 1.6.

7. See Tertullian, *Cor.* 1.4.

8. Matt 10:23.

9. Tertullian, *Ux.* 1.3.4.

10. Tertullian, *Fug.* 9.4a.

11. Tertullian, *Fug.* 9.4b.

12. Tertullian, *Cor.* 1.5.

13. Tertullian, *Fug.* 11.3. In general, voluntary martyrdom was frowned on by mainstream Christians. Flight was preferable to apostasy. Any overt action, however, on the part of a Christian encouraging other Christians, who after their unprovoked arrest were in danger of apostatizing, to stand firm in the faith was deemed to be an acceptable exception to voluntary martyrdom. Similarly, any action by Christian soldiers which led to their own martyrdom was considered, in most Christian circles, to be a justifiable exception to the norm. Christian soldiers, like other soldiers but unlike civilians, did not have the possibility of flight. Christian tradition is full of "military martyrs" who drew attention to themselves by refusing to wear military dress (e.g., Eusebius, *Hist. eccl.* 6.5.5–7), take military oaths (e.g., Dionysius of Alexandria, *Ep., ap.* Eusebius, *Hist. eccl.* 6.41.22–23), or bear arms (e.g., *Act. Marcell.* 1.2, 2.1–2, 3.1, 5.1). Adherents of the New Prophecy, including Tertullian, therefore, did not differ from most Christians elsewhere in their condoning of the actions of soldiers such as the one described in the *De corona*. Paradoxically, the "non-Montanist" (i.e., the "non-Montanist-influenced") Christians within the Christian community in Carthage were out of step with their fellow "mainstream" Christians in other parts of the world; see Tabbernee 1985; 2007, 201–60, esp. 208–10.

Figure 12.1: Tombstone of a sacrificed child in Carthage

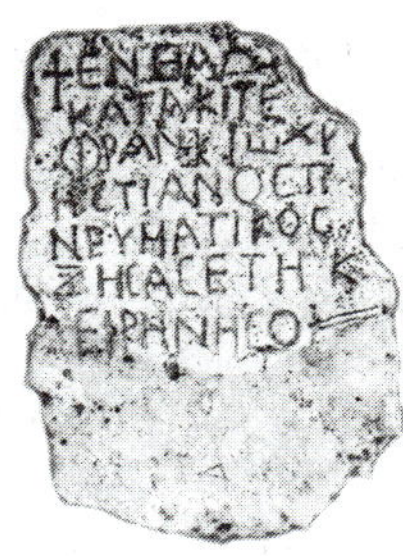

Chapter 12

Carthage, Africa Proconsularis, ca. 209/10 C.E.
Protecting the sanctity of human life

Tertullian has to force himself physically to stay where is he, seated on a wooden bench in a wooded grove. The trees are ancient, with long narrow limbs that cast dark shadows on the uneven ground. Beneath the trees, where there were once beautiful gardens, there are now overgrown beds of plants—most of them weeds. In the center of the grove is a sunken pit. It is the tophet, the Punic crematorium. Scattered all around are other pits where grave robbers have uncovered countless ceramic urns. Some of the urns are broken open, displaying the ashes of children—so many children!

A bird screeches just behind Tertullian and Tertullian nearly jumps out of his skin. The bird sets off a cacophony of noise as other birds join in. The birds sound just like children—frightened children—Tertullian thinks, screaming as they are being sacrificed to Baal Hammon and his consort Tanit, blood-thirsty Phoenician gods brought by the traders who founded the Punic settlement at Carthage. Tertullian can see the remains of the temples of the two gods at the edge of the grove, and shudders.

How even primitive people like those comprising the Punic population living in Carthage before the Romans conquered them could sacrifice their own children, their own flesh and blood, is beyond Tertullian's comprehension. But he wants to understand how people can have such disregard for human life, for the body. That's why he is here now, forcing himself to listen to the cries of all those butchered children. Not that he wants to write a treatise on child sacrifice, even though some people have accused Christians of infanticide. He has already dealt with that accusation and others, such as alleged incest by Christians, in his *Apologeticum* ("Defense"). Tertullian allows himself a wry smile as he remembers his immature attempt at humor by telling the emperors and anyone else reading his defense of Christianity how carefully Christian men must note where their mothers and sisters are sitting during one of the Christians' "secret meetings" late at night, so that when the oil lamps go out and it is dark, they don't inadvertently have sex with someone who *isn't* their mother or sister—otherwise it wouldn't be incest! It was Tertullian's hope that the *ludicrous* example would enable those who gave credence to the *ludicrous* charge of incest realize that it was exactly that: a *ludicrous* charge. He is not sure he will try such rhetoric again.

What Tertullian has come to ponder in the tophet sanctuary today is not how to counter the charges of infanticide, incest, or even cannibalism, but how to make a case for the resurrection of the human body and how to counter the challenges made to this orthodox Christian belief by the Carthaginian followers of Philomena. Philomena, a Roman-based prophetess, is now dead, but there are still people alive who were taught by her personally, and in Carthage some of these people are denying the bodily resurrection of the dead. "Modern Sadducees," Tertullian calls them, "enemies of the flesh."[1]

Despite himself, Tertullian is somewhat impressed by Philomena. Like Maximilla and Priscilla, she was a prophetess/virgin whose *logia* were written down, copied, and circulated by her followers. Tertullian, ever the collector of such *logia*, has a book containing the *logia* of Philomena, just as he has in his possession a book of Priscilla's *logia*. As far as he can tell, Philomena's teachings were more sensible than those of some of the other heretics such as Marcion, Apelles, or Valentinus, against whom he has already written treatises—but she was a heretic nevertheless. Her greatest accomplishment was having modified and toned down the heresy of Marcion. When Apelles separated himself from Marcion, his former teacher, Tertullian learned, Apelles went to Philomena and *she* became his teacher. The Apellian system of understanding God, the world, human nature, and the body is, therefore, really the Philomenian system, Tertullian realizes—even though it was popularized by Apelles and carries his name.[2]

The Apellians, like other groups that have a dualistic understanding of the relationship between God and the world, spirit and matter, divinity and humanity, "despise the body" and "call the body bad."[3] To them only the spirit is important; the body or "flesh" is irrelevant. The Apellians are at the opposite end of the theological spectrum from the *psychici*, the mainstream Christians in Carthage who are so critical of Tertullian, but they also differ greatly from the adherents of the New Prophecy movement. Those who follow Montanus, Maximilla, and Priscilla, to distinguish themselves from the *psychici*, "carnal, natural people," call themselves *spiritales*, "spiritual people," but they *do not*, Tertullian wants to point out, deny the flesh altogether, like the Apellians and other "modern Sadducees" who, because they despise the body, reject the concept of bodily resurrection. In fact, Tertullian believes that it was precisely against these "enemies of the flesh" that the Paraclete had spoken astutely through the prophetess Priscilla, an oracle Tertullian has read countless times: "They are bodies, yet they hate the body."[4]

Sitting in the grove near the tophet hasn't given Tertullian any new insight into how people can have so little regard for human life—but it has reaffirmed for him its sanctity and importance. The body, while it may need to be kept under control, is to be honored and celebrated—not just in this life but throughout eternity. Hatred of the body is heresy, not something engaged in by adherents of the New Prophecy. The body is so sacred and so important to what it means to be human that, even in the resurrection, Christians will not be bodiless spiritual entities.[5]

Having clarified his thoughts about the body, Tertullian feels that he can now escape the tophet sanctuary and leave behind its perverted and tragic misuse of tiny human bodies. He gets up from his bench and walks out of the grove into a field where he sees hundreds of headstones, set up by grieving parents to mark the buried urns containing the ashes of the infants they voluntarily or involuntarily handed over as sacrificial victims for their gods. Tertullian is grateful that he, unlike those sad parents, believes in a bodily resurrection, and he hurries home to keep the promise he once made to write a book on the subject.

Sources:

Tertullian, *Carn. Chr.* 1.1, 8.2; *Res.*, esp. 2.2–4.1, 5.2, 11.1; *Praescr.* 30.6; *Mon.* 1.2; Priscilla, *Log.*, *ap.* Tertullian, *Res.* 11.2; *Marc.*, esp. 3.11.2; *Val.*

Carthage, Africa Proconsularis, July 210 C.E.
Tertullian defends the New Prophecy's ascetic discipline

It will soon be August 1, the anniversary of Augustus' birthday and the first day of the Roman New Year. This has been a productive year for Tertullian. He has written and published half a dozen treatises. What pleases him most about his successful literary endeavor is not the magnitude of its output but the extent to which he has been able to explain and promote the New Prophecy in the context of writing on a wide range of topics. In the *De resurrectione carnis* ("On the Resurrection of the Body"), which he began to write after leaving the tophet sanctuary, he not only quoted Priscilla's *logion* pointing out the inconsistency of those who hate the body while being bodies of flesh themselves, but explained that the Paraclete's coming through the New Prophets cleared up all former ambiguities in scripture. Such ambiguities included the exact meaning of the parables, the favorite texts of heretics since they could interpret them in all sorts of perverted ways. "Anyone drawing water overflowing from the Paraclete's fountains," Tertullian had declared, "will no longer be consumed by burning questions or thirst for any new doctrine: the mystery of the gospel is plainly and clearly proclaimed by the New Prophecy."[6]

After completing the *De resurrectione carnis,* Tertullian decided to concentrate on writing books on practical topics, taking up themes arising from the claim made in *De resurrectione carnis* that the Paraclete made everything crystal clear. In quick succession, he had written about chastity, monogamy, fasting, and flight during persecution. In his *De exhortatione castitatis* ("On Exhortation to Chastity"), he quoted two of Priscilla's *logia* to support the New Prophecy's emphasis on an ascetic lifestyle that includes a call to periodic, but limited sexual abstinence and rigorous fasting. These *logia,* conveying the oracles of the Paraclete, are the same sayings the earliest audiences of the New Prophecy in Phrygia had heard: "Bodily purity brings about spiritual harmony. . . . The saintly servants (of God) should know how to manage sanctity."[7]

Thinking back now on what he wrote, Tertullian is glad he stressed the importance of *purificantia* ("purity") as the key element in an ascetic lifestyle for Christians who take seriously the discipline of the Paraclete, whether through fasting, abstinence from sex within marriage, or refraining from entering into another marriage after divorce or the death of one's spouse. Tertullian knows that not every Christian is willing or humanly capable of meeting the discipline mandated by the Paraclete, but it is an ideal to which he aspires and one he hopes others will aspire to, too.

The *De exhortatione castitatis* had been occasioned by a request for advice by a Christian friend in Carthage. The man's wife had died some time ago and the man wasn't sure whether he should remarry. If he had asked Tertullian that question some years earlier, Tertullian would have advised him that, as long as he married a Christian rather than a non-Christian woman, all would be well. The influence of the New Prophecy on Tertullian, however, meant that he gave the inquirer advice that was quite different: he exhorted chastity by urging his friend to remain "once-married." As part of his argument, Tertullian presented a new hierarchy of values by classifying virginity into three kinds, or *species*. The first kind is virginity from *birth*. The second kind is virginity from *rebirth*, namely from baptism, including permanent or periodic voluntary virginity, through sexual abstinence by mutual consent within marriage. The third kind is virginity from the time of the *death* of one's spouse. By voluntarily not remarrying, even though St. Paul had allowed this "in the Lord," his friend, the widower, could be a virgin.

Never short of a provocative phrase, Tertullian had denounced second marriages as nothing but "a species of fornication."[8] He wonders now how the man for whom the treatise was written reacted to that particular statement—and then he remembers that he used an even more graphic description of remarriage as "adultery-in-series"[9] in his *De monogamia* ("On Monogamy"). Using the spiritual calculator provided by the Paraclete, Tertullian's strict arithmetic had argued that one plus one equals *two*. Irrespective of whether a person has two spouses concurrently (bigamy) or sequentially (digamy), the number two is one too many for those who heed the Paraclete.

While he is reflecting on the books he has written during the past twelve months, Tertullian is perched on a wall at the top of Byrsa Hill, the highest landmark in Carthage. Immediately below him he can see the Roman hippodrome, and in the distance to his left is the Bay of Carthage. The view out to sea is, once again, spectacular on yet another clear day with brilliant sunshine. At the edge of the shore, looking very small but clearly defined, is the double harbor very near the tophet sanctuary. How things can change radically over time, Tertullian thinks to himself. The Punic murderers of so many children are no longer here, murdered in turn by the Romans who, at the very spot where he is sitting, literally decapitated both the Punic rulers and the whole of Byrsa Hill. The Romans not only tore down all the buildings, including the temples situated on the Punic acropolis, but also leveled the top of the hill, plowing everything under and salting the earth. In light of such evidence of dramatic historic change, right before their very eyes every time they come to Byrsa Hill, why the *psychici* cannot understand that the Paraclete, so much more than the Romans, had the right to initiate some changes in moral discipline is incomprehensible to Tertullian.

The *psychici* consider the Paraclete to be the instigator of a *new* discipline, a discipline too harsh for them to keep. But had not Jesus himself promised that the Holy Spirit would lead them into the fullness of truth that of necessity could, like the rule against remarriage, be considered new and burdensome? Tertullian feels himself getting worked up again. Of course, the new discipline can be considered burdensome—its very "burdensomeness" is the reason why it wasn't imposed earlier when Christians were not yet ready to bear the full burden of the will of Christ. The Paraclete is really the restorer, not the originator, of practice. The Paraclete does not *innovate;* the Paraclete *renovates,* by ensuring that people return to the principles underlying the message of Christ and the apostles, as they are set out in the Rule of Faith. How many more times does he have to explain this to the *psychici*? Tertullian wonders. He is pleased, though, that his *De monogamia* is published and in circulation so that more and more people can understand what the New Prophecy really teaches.

It is now in the middle of the afternoon, a long time after prandium. The slight hunger pains in his stomach remind him that fasting is a discipline that, like all the disciplines revealed by the Paraclete, can certainly be considered burdensome. Tertullian loves to eat. In fact, he finds himself thinking about his favorite food: soup. He is not sure why he loves soup so much. Perhaps it is because of the way it feels when it goes down, smooth like a drink—but far more substantial than a drink. Maybe, he considers, he likes soup because it is hot. He was once served a bowl of soup that was cold. He was in his pre-Christian days then, and he threw the bowl full of cold soup against the wall, barely missing the slave who dared to serve the soup without first testing its temperature. But the real reason he likes soup, Tertullian reflects, is because of the many layers of flavors he can taste in it—whenever he has the patience to eat the soup slowly, which of course he rarely has.

Tertullian starts daydreaming about his favorite soup. It is a soup made from the wild mushrooms that grow in the fields up the hill from his house. Tertullian has often been drawn to the kitchen by the delicate aroma of the ingredients when his wife is cooking this particular soup. Where soup is concerned, Tertullian's wife no longer leaves it to the servants to prepare. She does it herself. First, she chops up lots of vegetables to make the stock. Tertullian is always amazed at his wife's knife skills. Holding the edge of the carrots, potatoes, onions, and celery with her left hand to keep the vegetables from slipping away on the smooth wooden cutting board, she moves the sharp knife in her right hand at a speed so fast it is almost imperceptible. She has the knack of keeping the bottom edge of the knife, the part close to the handle, on the board itself while the rest of the blade flies up and down like a machine, slicing each vegetable evenly. When she has finished chopping the vegetables, his wife cuts up some garlic cloves, puts a little olive oil into a large pot, and throws in the chopped vegetables and the garlic. She puts the pot on the wood stove in the corner of the culina, the kitchen, covers the pot, and lets the vegetables and garlic cook gently for ten minutes. When the ten minutes are up, she removes the lid, adds some water, replaces the lid only partially, and adds some wood to increase the heat so that the mixture boils hard.

While the vegetable stock is cooking, Tertullian's wife slices the wild mushrooms she gathered less than an hour beforehand and cuts up some leeks and a few more onions. She heats some olive oil in a pan, mixes in butter until the whole mixture is frothing, and then adds the onions, leeks, and, finally, the sliced mushrooms. She simmers them gently on the stove, making sure she doesn't overcook them. It is at this point that the aroma from the kitchen usually draws Tertullian out of his tablinum into the culina, his mouth watering—as it is now, just thinking about it. He then watches expectantly as his wife adds the contents of the pan into the pot, knowing that the soup will soon be ready, garnished with thyme and other condiments.

Fasting, Tertullian is the first to admit, *is* a hardship. He would like to eat soup every day of his life, but the Paraclete teaches discipline over all one's appetites—including food. Didn't fasting originate with God's command to Adam to abstain from the tree of the knowledge of good and evil? Hasn't fasting been practiced by all true believers from Adam's day until now? Didn't all Christians in Carthage engage in a total fast from Good Friday till Easter Sunday morning? Why, then, do the *psychici* accuse the members of the New Prophecy movement of "novelty" when they insist on the importance of fasting? Not that Tertullian minded writing a treatise on the topic. He enjoys writing, but writing the *De jejunio adversus psychicos* ("On Fasting Against the *Psychici*") should have been unnecessary—except perhaps, Tertullian admits to himself, with respect of one matter.

Adherents of the New Prophecy, unlike the *psychici,* during Lent engage in a xerophagy, that is, a *dry* diet. No meat, fruit, or juicy vegetables were eaten—and, to Tertullian's regret, *no soup*! But, although he craves soup terribly during this period of time, he is prepared to bear this hardship for the sake of the Paraclete's revealed discipline. After all, isn't there a resemblance between their dry diet and the manna of old? Couldn't the manna the Hebrews ate in the wilderness be described as "the angelic bread of xerophagy"?

No wine is permitted during the time of xerophagy, only water—but only water for drinking, not for bathing. The *psychici* condemn the xerophagies, saying that they resemble pagan practices. Tertullian has to admit that these apparent resemblances exist, but he has an answer that he derived from reading the *Apology* by Justin, the martyr of blessed memory: the pagan resemblances are a point in their favor because the devil often initiates divinely initiated practices. In any case, thinks Tertullian, sitting on the wall atop Byrsa Hill reflecting on this year's publications, why all the fuss? As he had pointed out to the *psychici* in the *De jejunio,* the Paraclete's demands with respect to xerophagies are very modest:

> For how little is the banishment of food among us? Two weeks in the year (not even complete ones—exclusive of course, of Saturdays and Sundays) of eating dry foods only, offered to God, abstaining from what we are not rejecting but postponing.[10]

Another of the *psychici*'s complaints Tertullian addressed in his defense of the New Prophecy's practice of fasting is that the followers of Montanus, Maximilla, and Priscilla extended the *stationes,* the half days of fasting practiced by all Christians in Carthage on Wednesdays and Fridays. The *psychici* break their fast at the ninth hour, that is, three hours after the noon hour. Members of the New Prophecy however continue their fast until the early evening. Tertullian remembers vividly the heated debates he had with the *psychici* over this issue. *They* argued that because Peter entered the temple at the ninth hour, the hour of prayer, his period of fasting must have been over. *He* argued that because the ninth hour was the hour of the Lord's death, it is wrong to *stop* fasting at the ninth hour.

Exegetical hairsplitting and semantics were not enough to make either side give in, and Tertullian finally decided that the real reason the *psychici* will not accept the New Prophecy's modest "additional" and "novel" fasts is the *psychici*'s own gluttonous nature. In the latter part of his *De jejunio,* Tertullian confronted this issue head on:

> For to you your belly is your god, and your lungs a temple, and your paunch a sacrificial altar, and your cook the priest, and your fragrant smell the Holy Spirit, and your condiment spiritual gifts and your belching prophecy.[11]

That particular sentence had not won Tertullian any friends or influenced people among the *psychici,* but Tertullian no longer cared. He was sick of the stubbornness of his detractors. He wrote the *De jejunio* more for his fellow adherents of the New Prophecy, to support them by providing reasons for maintaining their so-called "new fasts" in the face of opposition from the *psychici,* than for the *psychici* themselves. He had little hope of persuading the *psychici* anyway.

Tertullian had explained to the members of the New Prophecy that their opponents, the *psychici:*

> Reject the New Prophecy not because Montanus and Priscilla and Maximilla proclaim another God, nor because they evade Jesus Christ, nor because in some aspect of faith or hope they pervert the Rule of Faith, but simply because they teach to fast more frequently than to marry.[12]

Tertullian gets up from his perch on the wall on Byrsa Hill for a little while to stretch his legs. He walks a few hundred yards to his left. From his new position, he can now see the tophet sanctuary even more clearly and he thinks about the way everything is related. Blatant disregard for the human body leads to child sacrifice and indifference to the sacred pleasures of the body within marriage and through well prepared food—especially soup. But lack of discipline toward the body leads to the overindulgence of all the appetites, to gluttony, and to an unwillingness to die an honorable martyr's death. In this *De jejunio,* Tertullian couldn't resist referring to Apicius' dishonorable end. Apicius, one of the members of the *psychici*'s house-churches in Carthage, had been arrested for the faith and, like Perpetua and her honorable co-martyrs, had been condemned "to the beasts." But instead of having a modest *agape,* or "love feast," as his last meal—as Perpetua and the others had done—Apicius allowed the *psychici* to stuff him so full of food and wine that he died drunk and belching.

The noise of heavy boots marching on the pavement startles Tertullian for a moment until, looking around to the other side of the top of Byrsa Hill, he sees the changing of the guard at the proconsul's residence. The guards do look magnificent in their bronze breastplates, distinctive helmets, and red cloaks, Tertullian can't help observing. By fasting, Christians are keeping their own *stationes,* periods of "guard duty," being ready at all times for whatever might happen given the ambiguous legal status in which Christianity finds itself. Christianity is not a *religio illicita,* an outlawed or illegal religion, but neither is it a *religio licita,* a religion recognized by the State as legitimate and, therefore, protected.

Tertullian has read a copy of a *rescript* by the emperor Trajan to Pliny the Younger, governor of Bithynia-Pontus. In that rescript, Trajan laid out the principle that governors and other Roman officials should not seek out Christians. They should, however, try Christians who are brought before them by *delatores,* that is, personal accusers. On the other hand, they should take no notice of anonymously written accusations against Christians, as people who are unwilling personally to accuse Christians in a formal legal hearing may have unworthy motives. The rescript was issued almost one hundred years ago now, but it is still the main legal principle underlying the way Christians are treated. When all is quiet politically, governors are content to leave the Christians alone. Whenever there is trouble, however, the Christians are blamed and local persecution erupts, compelling the governor to deal with the situation.

As the Roman soldiers on Byrsa Hill complete the changing of the guard with military precision, Tertullian remembers how, in his *Apologeticum,* he had pointed out to the provincial governors the injustice of the haphazard way they deal with Christians:

> If the Tiber rises as high as the city walls, if the Nile does not send its waters over the fields, if the heavens give no rain, if there is an earthquake, if there is a famine or pestilence, straightway the cry is "Away with the Christians to the lion!" What! Shall you give such a multitude to a single beast?[13]

Tertullian can't help smiling at the grim humor he had used, but—sadly—the reality was too many lions and too many Christians thrown to those lions for there to be anything funny about the situation. He cannot help thinking, though, that in the context of the debate between him and the *psychici* regarding fasting, an overfed Christian is of far more benefit to lions than to God. Christians who practice rigorous fasting, on the other hand, not only potentially deprive the lions of a big meal but, unlike Apicius, are strong enough and disciplined enough to endure their martyrdom courageously. They are also strong enough to stand firm and not flee in times of persecution.

After having completed the *De corona,* in which he primarily dealt with the issue of alleged voluntary martyrdom, Tertullian gave a lot of thought to the related topic of flight during times of persecution. Earlier this year he had written a whole treatise on the subject. He had been asked to do so by a man named Fabius, whose request enabled Tertullian to clarify his own thoughts about persecution, flight during persecution, and about martyrdom itself. The *logia* of the prophets and prophetesses of the New Prophecy had caused Tertullian to change some of his earlier opinions. Whereas he had once argued that martyrdom is the will of God and persecution is not, he had come to realize that his earlier view meant subscribing either to a God who is not all powerful or to a God who is not all good. How immature that view was, Tertullian concludes as he goes over in his mind the arguments he had employed in the *De fuga in persecutione* ("On Flight During Persecution"). Nothing—whether good or evil—he had told his readers, happens without the express will or consent of God. The devil can only do Christians harm if God allows it. God allows the devil, or the devil's human agents, to persecute Christians not because God is not all good, but because persecution is the way God allows the faith of Christians to be tested. Through the testing of Christians and their victorious martyrdoms, the church is both strengthened by the steadfastness of the martyrs and purified through the departure of apostates.

Persecution, therefore, originates *with* God although it is not carried out *by* God, and flight during persecution is flight from God's will. Flight avoids the opportunity to show that one can stand firm and it dishonors God through its lack of trust in the power of God to sustain one in times of trial. The *psychici* argued that "The one who turns and runs away lives to fight again another day." Tertullian had countered by saying, "You mean, to *flee again* another day!"[14]

The afternoon is slipping by quickly. Tertullian has stayed longer on Byrsa Hill than he intended. He is even more hungry now than he was an hour ago, but it has been good to reflect on all the issues he had written about this past year. He just wishes the *psychici* had been persuaded by his arguments or, better still, that they would accept the teachings of the Paraclete. Tertullian is certain that it is only through the power of the Paraclete that Christians can discipline the body with respect to martyrdom, chastity, monogamy, and fasting.[15]

Tertullian's stomach growls unexpectedly and as he heads home to his beautiful, desirable wife, he secretly hopes that she has spent her afternoon cooking his favorite mushroom soup.[16]

Sources:

Priscilla, *Log.*, *ap.* Tertullian, *Res.* 11.2; Priscilla, *Log.*, *ap.* Tertullian, *Exh. cast.* 10.5; Tertullian, *Res.* 63.9; *Ux.* 2.2.3–5; *Exh. cast.*, esp. 1.3–2.1, 4.1–6, 9.1; 1 Cor 7:39–40; Tertullian, *Mon.*, esp. 2.1, 2.4, 3.10, 4.1, 4.3, 14.5–7, 15.1–3; *Marc.* 1.29.4; John 16:12–13; Tertullian, *Jejun.*, esp. 1.3–4, 2.3, 5.4, 9.1–6, 10.1–13, 12.3–4, 14.2, 15.2, 16.8, 17.9; Gen 2:17; Exod 16:14–35; Justin Martyr, *1 Apol.* 5–6, 62–64; Acts 3:1; *Pass. Perp.* 17.1; Trajan, *Rescr.*, *ap.* Pliny the Younger, *Ep.* 10.97.1–2; cf. Pliny the Younger, *Ep.* 10.96.1–10; Tertullian, *Apol.* 5.5–8, 40.2; *Fug.*, esp. 1.1–6, 2.2, 3.1, 4.1–3, 5.1, 8.1, 10.1; *Cor.*

Notes

1. Tertullian, *Carn. Chr.* 1.1; *Res.* 11.1. The *De resurrectione carnis* fulfills a promise which Tertullian made in his *De carne Christi* ("On the Flesh of Christ") that he would deal with the resurrection of "our own body" in a subsequent treatise (*Carn. Chr.* 25.2). A draft of the *Carn. Chr.* may have been written as early as ca. 200–203 but appears not to have been published, with appropriate revisions to the preface and conclusion, until shortly before *Res.* was published (Braun 1962, 268, 573; 1974, 271–81). In some manuscripts *Res.* is titled *De resurrectione mortuorum* ("On the Resurrection of the Dead"). The main issue at stake, however, was not whether the *dead* would be resurrected but whether the resurrected dead would be resurrected *with a body* (*of "flesh"*) rather than, merely with a soul (or "spiritual body"). Consequently, *De resurrectione carnis* ("On the Resurrection of the Flesh") is the

more accurate title. Both treatises were written to counter what, until recently, were called "Gnostic" challenges to mainstream Christianity by "Gnostics" such as Marcion, Apelles, and Valentinus. Terms such as "Gnostic" and (even) "Montanism," however, are anachronistic constructs created by later opponents and later-still scholars in an attempt to confine, caricature, and control two second-century movements, each of which was far more diverse than the generic terms "Gnosticism" and "Montanism" convey. Regarding "Gnosticism," Williams (1996) and King (2003), among others, have recently proposed that the category needs to be rethought and probably abandoned. It is certainly better to refer simply to "Marcionites," "Apellians," "Valentinians," and so forth and to speak of "Marcionite exegesis," the "Apellian *symbolon,*" or "Valentinian cosmology," rather than lumping everything together under the "dubious category" (Williams' term) of "Gnosticism."

2. On Philomena, Apelles, and the "Philomenian-Apellian system," see A. Jensen 1996, 194–222. Regrettably, one of Tertullian's lost works is a treatise written against the "Apellians" (*Carn. Chr.* 8.2–3). Whether or not the oracle by Priscilla quoted by Tertullian at *Res.* 11.2 was originally uttered in an anti-Philomenian/Apellian (or at least an "anti-[so-called] Gnostic") context, as Tertullian assumed, is possible but not certain. Tertullian frequently (e.g., *Res.* 11.2), but not invariably (e.g., *Jejun.* 1.3), cites Priscilla as "Prisca," which was probably her actual name, the diminutive form being an endearment and the name by which she was more commonly known.

3. Tertullian, *Carn. Chr.* 8.2; *Res.* 5.2.

4. Priscilla, *Log., ap.* Tertullian, *Res.* 11.2.

5. "Montanism" has sometimes been characterized as either a "Gnostic" (e.g., Froehlich 1973, 91–111) or an "anti-Gnostic" movement (e.g., J. Davies 1955, 90–94). It was neither of these—although, with regard to the body, the "Montanists" about whom some evidence still exists had both "anti-Gnostic" and "Gnostic-like" attitudes and practices—but, even so, "Montanists" in different parts of the world and/or at different times appear to have had varying attitudes and practices. For example, whereas the Carthaginian adherents of the New Prophecy were against bodily adornment and frowned on women wearing jewelry or being without a veil either in public or "in church," even a prophetess in Pepouza itself was accused of loving to wear make-up and jewelry (see Chapter 9). Unlike the Philomenians/Apellians, adherents of the New Prophecy did not "hate the body" or consider it evil. The body, sex, and procreation were, for them, the gifts of a good God. Such gifts, however, were to be used responsibly and with the discipline revealed by the Paraclete.

6. Tertullian, *Res.* 63.9.

7. Priscilla, *Log., ap.* Tertullian, *Exh. cast.* 10.5. See also Chapter 1.

8. Tertullian, *Exh. cast.* 9.1.

9. Tertullian, *Mon.* 4.3.

10. Tertullian, *Jejun.* 15.2.

11. Tertullian, *Jejun.* 16.8.

12. Tertullian, *Jejun.* 1.3.

13. Tertullian, *Apol.* 40.2.

14. Tertullian, *Fug.* 10.1.

15. For additional information about Tertullian's New Prophecy-influenced understanding of martyrdom, chastity, monogamy, fasting, and flight during persecution, see Tabbernee 2007, 147–53, 249–53. The translations of *Apol.* 40.2 and *Jejun.* 16.8 quoted in this chapter are taken from *ANF* 3:47, 4:113 respectively.

16. Regrettably, the name of Tertullian's wife is not known. Despite a painting of a proconsular palace on Byrsa Hill on display in the National Museum of Carthage (also situated on Byrsa Hill), archaeologists are divided over the existence of such a palace at the site.

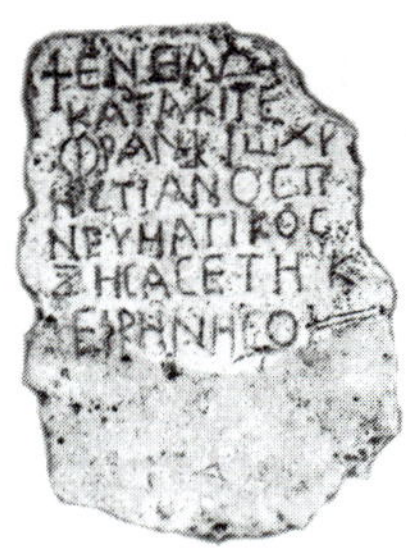

Chapter 13

Carthage, Africa Proconsularis, ca. 210/11 C.E.

Separating the tares from the wheat in the church

Tertullian is sure that, next to Rome, Carthage must be the city that attracts the greatest number of theological misfits within Christianity. Some years ago, there was a woman who turned up in Carthage from the Cainite sect who taught waterless baptism of all things.[1] If ever there was a ridiculous concept, waterless baptism must be it! Even ridiculous practices or beliefs, however, can be a blessing in disguise. While at first Tertullian thought the woman's activity was a curse, it ended up being a blessing in that it caused him to write a treatise on baptism. No one had ever done that before. Justin, the martyr of blessed memory, to be fair had given a brief description and explanation of Christian baptism in his *Apology* to the emperors. Church manuals such as the *Didache* provided details regarding the "Two Ways" to be taught to catechumens—those who were preparing themselves for baptism—and instructions to bishops, presbyters, and deacons on how to perform baptisms. No one had written a whole treatise about baptism. It was one of Tertullian's early works. He is sure he would do a better job now of writing such a treatise, but, unlike the way he felt about his earlier attempt to write a treatise against Marcion, he sees no need to revise the *De baptismo* ("On Baptism"). It is good enough.

Tertullian has no doubt that his time is better spent writing a totally new treatise about another Christian misfit: Praxeas. What a lot of trouble that so-called teacher from Asia caused in Rome and everywhere else! "Double-Trouble" could be another nick-name for Praxeas. This Busy-Body Busy-Bee not only persuaded Victor, the bishop of Rome, to withdraw the *litteras pacis* he had already issued to the Roman house-churches that were supportive of the New Prophecy but he also talked Victor into tolerating Praxeas' strange teachings. Tertullian fumes as he thinks about this double travesty. By now Tertullian's pen is already racing across the page: "In this way," Tertullian writes, "Praxeas managed two pieces of the devil's business: he drove out prophecy and brought in heresy; he routed the Paraclete and crucified the Father."[2]

Satisfied that his rhetorical skills have not deserted him, Tertullian is pleased with this double sentence. It sums up exactly what he wants to say about "Mr. Double-Trouble." Praxeas caused Victor to let the devil have a double success. By *not endorsing* the legitimacy of the New Prophecy within the Christian community, Victor forced the Paraclete to "take flight" from the official house-churches in Rome to non-official ones. On the other hand, *by endorsing* Praxeas' right to teach his theories about God's "modes of being," Victor condoned the heretical view that it was really God the Father who had died on the cross![3]

What is so tragic, Tertullian points out as he continues to write, is that after having persuaded Victor to do what he did, Praxeas himself changed his mind—at least about Modalism. Tertullian even knows about the existence of a handwritten document Praxeas produced, renouncing his former theological errors. But the seeds a person sows continue to grow even when the sower no longer wants them to grow. They take on a life of their own. Like the tares in Jesus' parables, the evil seeds Praxeas sowed grow so fast that they overtake and choke the plants trying to grow from good seed. Praxeas the Busy-Body Busy-Bee may no longer be pollinating his tares personally but other people are—not only in Rome but also here in Carthage.

Tertullian sighs as he remembers how only a few years ago, when Praxeas' tares were first being sown in Carthage among the unsuspecting, doctrinally asleep, simple-minded *psychici,* God chose him to pluck up the young tares as they grew and throw them away. At that time his arguments against Praxeas' views and his own, still immature, teaching about the Trinity won the day. Praxeas' heresy was eradicated before it could truly take hold. But since then, two things have occurred.

Tertullian is simultaneously sad and frustrated about the first of these occurrences. It is amazing how one moment one can be a hero and the next moment a villain. After being held in high regard and praised by the *psychici* for the way he spoke out against Praxeas' Modalism, these very same carnal-minded people at Carthage, who reason only according to their physical nature and not their spiritual one, now refuse to accept Tertullian's views about the New Prophecy. They look down on him for acknowledging that the Paraclete revealed new ethical implications of the gospel via Montanus, Maximilla, and Priscilla. Try as he might to defend the New Prophecy's understanding, the *psychici,* including the bishop of Carthage, refuse to be persuaded. Fortunately, many other Christians in Carthage *have* come to see the light, and there are now numerous adherents of the New Prophecy in Carthage. There hasn't been a formal split in the Christian community at Carthage, but tensions are running high. The worst aspect about all this, Tertullian laments, is that, while he is still greatly respected by the majority of "ordinary" Christians in Carthage, his influence with the official leadership of the Carthaginian church is greatly reduced.

His own diminished theological influence with those in powerful ecclesiastical positions in Carthage bears directly on the way Tertullian sees his own effectiveness with respect to the second thing that has happened. While the *psychici* have been arguing with Tertullian over the New Prophecy, they haven't noticed that Praxeas' tares have started to grow again. Tertullian sighs once more as he knows he has to counter Praxeas' strange ideas all over again. Even though Praxeas himself has repudiated those ideas, a follower of Praxeas who refused to accept the fact that Praxeas himself recanted is in Carthage—watering the Praxean tares that have been growing while the *psychici* have been sleeping! And now, Tertullian fears, the *psychici,* and those, who like them no longer see him as their theological champion, may not take much notice of him. But he has to try. If the Lord wills it, Tertullian believes, the Praxean tares that have sprouted again will once more, through his efforts, be eradicated. If the *psychici* don't want to take any notice of him, so be it. Then the Lord, in the Lord's own good time, perhaps at the *end* of time, will gather up the Praxean tares with other evil crops, and burn them all together in the unquenchable fire. But he himself must still do what he can now to combat the Modalist heresy started by Praxeas. If nothing else, the treatise he is now writing against Praxeas' ridiculous ideas will give him yet another opportunity also to defend and promote the New Prophecy's understanding of the Holy Spirit, the Paraclete.

Having finished the introduction to his new treatise, Tertullian immediately gets to the heart of the matter. Picking up his pen again, he counters Praxeas' idea of the one God who as Father is born and suffered as Jesus Christ by writing:

> We, on the other hand, as always *but even more so now as better informed by the Paraclete who indeed leads into all truth,* also believe in one God but subject to this "dispensation," or *oikonomia,* that there is also a Son of this one God, who has proceeded out of that one God, by whom all things were made and without whom nothing was made. We believe that this Son was sent by the Father into the Virgin and was born of her: man and God, Son of Man *and* Son of God, called Jesus the Christ. We believe that he suffered, died, and was buried "according to the scriptures," having been raised to life by the Father and taken back into heaven, sits at the right hand of the Father and will come to judge both the living and the dead. We believe that in accordance with his promise, the Son, out of heaven, sent from the Father the Holy Spirit, the Paraclete, the sanctifier of the faith of those who believe in Father, Son, and Holy Spirit.[4]

Tertullian tells his readers that this is the *regula,* the "measuring stick," by which all doctrine is to be judged: it is the Rule of Faith. It is as old as the gospel but is reemphasized and clarified by the Paraclete—as taught by those who adhere to the New Prophecy. Whatever theories one might have about the one God, one needs to take into account that the Rule of Faith declares that "unity" has been distributed into "Trinity":

> Three "degrees of divinity," but one "condition"; three "forms of divinity," but one "substance"; three "aspects of divinity," but one "power." In short, three "Persons," but one "God."[5]

Tertullian knows that the concept of "unity distributed into Trinity" may be as difficult for people to grasp as Praxeas' Modalism. Fortunately, he has a simple illustration to share. It is an illustration revealed by the Paraclete through one of the prophets or prophetesses of the New Prophecy. Tertullian is not sure which prophet or prophetess it was through whom the Paraclete communicated so aptly how the Persons of the Godhead can be different and yet the same, but for Tertullian the human instrument is irrelevant: it is the oracle that matters. Tertullian quotes from memory what the Paraclete taught:

> God brought forth the Word as a root brings forth a shoot, and a spring brings forth a stream, and the sun brings forth a beam.[6]

Tertullian is sure his readers understand that the "Word" is the Son and that "God" is God the Father. The Father brought forth the Son, as well as the Holy Spirit, in a way that is mirrored every day in nature. A root brings forth a shoot that in one sense did not exist before, but in another sense has always existed. In light of his earlier comments about Praxeas' teachings being like tares, Tertullian wishes the Paraclete had begun his illustration with a different analogy, but hopefully his readers won't be distracted by thinking about tares, as he has just done. Tertullian really likes the next two analogies. A spring brings into being a stream with the same water, but it is a different entity—even though it is really the same. Sunbeams derive from the sun, are not identical with the sun, yet are substantially the same. This really is true in each of the pairs in the triple analogy. As with the Trinity, there is only one entity but there are different degrees, forms, and aspects of that entity. How wise the Paraclete is to communicate with such clarity the mysteries of faith!

Tertullian is ranting, not to anyone in particular but out loud to himself. He has been doing a lot of that lately. Usually his wife simply ignores his private outbursts. She has lived with him for almost twenty years now and knows his temperament. At heart he is a kind man. He is certainly a loving husband. He is also very good with their servants and with his clients. But he has a temper that, before he became a Christian, used to get him into lots of trouble. Now his temper is mostly under control, but whenever he notices anything unfair or unjust his old nature reasserts itself in the form of righteous anger.

Tertullian's wife has learned that, left alone, Tertullian will get over whatever is upsetting him now. He prides himself on being able to discern the nature of his problems, deciding promptly what to do about it, doing exactly that, and then getting over it—quickly. Today, however, Tertullian's wife cannot help asking what the bishop has done that is so upsetting to him.

Tertullian stops his private rant in mid-sentence. How does his wife know that Agrippinus is the cause of his anger? The answer to this unspoken question is obvious: lately the bishop of Carthage has become the bane of Tertullian's existence. The man's pastoral stupidity knows no bounds.

Instead of continuing to rant to himself Tertullian, now that he has an audience, shares with his wife (she did ask, after all) Agrippinus' latest folly. "Pontifex Maximus has issued an edict,"[7] Tertullian tells her, using an ironic epithet that indicates his contempt for the man who is acting as if he possesses supreme powers like the Roman emperors who have ultimate religious as well as political authority. Who does Agrippinus think he is: the "bishop of bishops"?[8] Tertullian's wife is astounded as Tertullian explains that "Pontifex Maximus" has just published a written statement declaring that the church (by which Pontifex Maximus means himself) has the right to forgive sins—even the most serious of sins. Doesn't the self-styled "bishop of bishops" realize that to advertise forgiveness is to encourage licentiousness?

Not that Tertullian has anything against the forgiveness of sins. God knows that he was and is still a sinner in constant need of God's forgiveness. Didn't he conclude his treatise *De baptismo* by encouraging all neophytes when they pray in church for the first time after their baptism not only to ask God for grace for themselves but to pray likewise for "Tertullian the sinner?"[9] Tertullian explains to his wife that he doesn't even really have a problem with the concept that the *church* has the power to forgive sins—as long as the bishop doesn't advertise this or think that he, in his own person, is the one who forgives.

In better days for the Christian community at Carthage, when Optatus was still bishop rather than Pontifex Maximus, Tertullian wrote a treatise called *De paenitentia* ("On Repentance"). In that book, Tertullian set out the penitential system practiced by the Carthaginian Christian community. Carthage's penitential rite is a carefully crafted system that demonstrates both the seriousness with which the church views post-baptismal sin by its members and the steps needed to be taken by those who, regrettably, commit such sin in order to be reconciled to the church: reconciliation being the formal expression of *divine,* not human, pardon. Divine grace and justice are held in balance by the possibility of the *paenitentia secunda,* a second repentance after one's original repentance prior to baptism. A person's "second *forgiveness,*" however, can only come after appropriate penance—penance that includes spending a period of time, the exact length of time determined by the council of elders, being excluded from receiving the Eucharist.

Pontifex Maximus' edict will undermine the whole traditional penitential system, Tertullian confides to his wife, as he shows her the codex in which he has been recording the oracles of the Paraclete communicated via the *logia* of the prophets and prophetesses of the New Prophecy movement. He points to one of the sayings: "The church has power to forgive sins, but I shall not, lest they should commit others also."[10] Just in case his wife may be a little confused about who the "I" and the "they" are in this statement, Tertullian explains that, because it is the Paraclete who is speaking through one of the prophets or prophetesses, the "I" can refer both to the Paraclete and to the Paraclete's human instrument. The New Prophecy, Tertullian elaborates, teaches that only prophets and apostles—not ordinary bishops like Pontifex Maximus—have been given special authority by God to forgive sins. The Paraclete in this oracle, however, teaches that not even the prophets or prophetesses of the New Prophecy movement, such as the one who here speaks in the first person so that others may hear the voice of the Spirit, should exercise this authority—lest those who have committed the sin so forgiven take for granted that it is all right to commit other sins. Tertullian's wife, of course, already assumed that is what the oracle meant but she lets Tertullian make the unnecessary explanation anyway.[11]

Tertullian has settled down a little but is still somewhat disturbed about Agrippinus' foolish edict, so his wife suggests that they go to the baths. She knows very well that Tertullian likes taking a bath and that this relaxes him. Fortunately, Carthage's best public baths, the Imperial Baths commenced by the emperor Hadrian and completed by Antoninus Pius, Hadrian's successor, are only a short distance from their house. In fact, the impressive two-story building is situated on the beach less than a mile downhill from where they live. Tertullian's wife is glad the road back to the house has only a gradual slope so she will not get too hot again right after bathing.

When they reach the baths, Tertullian and his wife are amazed, as usual, by the immense size of the building. It covers nine acres of land. At ground level there are huge furnaces and storage areas for the tons of wood used to stoke the furnaces. The baths themselves, one for men and a separate one for women, are on the second level surrounded by twelve gray granite columns, each one fluted and capped off with a Corinthian capital. As they go to their respective sections of the baths, Tertullian watches his wife walk down the long corridor and, for a brief moment, wishes he could go with her. In his mind's eye he envisages her beauty, a beauty so intense that it always melts his heart and makes him hungry with desire. Turning toward his own end of the baths, Tertullian thinks he had better spend an extra long time in the frigidarium.

Sources:

Tertullian, *Bapt.* 1.1–20.5; *Did.* 1.1–16.7; Tertullian, *Prax.*, esp. 1.1–2.1, 2.4, and 8.5; Matt 13:25–26, 30, 41–42; John 1:1, 3, 16:7, 13; 1 Cor 15:3–4; Tertullian, *Pud.*, esp. 1.6, 21.7a, 21.16–17; *Paen.*, esp. 7.1–14, 8.1–8, 10.1–12.9; Anonyma, *Log.*, *ap.* Tertullian, *Pud.* 21.7b.

Notes

1. On the unnamed woman teacher at Carthage who promoted "waterless baptism," see A. Jensen 1996, 193–94 and R. Jensen (forthcoming) who argues that the woman was offering an alternate initiatory rite involving holy oil rather than water. Elsewhere Tertullian (*Praescr.* 33.10) describes the "Cainites" as a contemporary form of Nicolaitans (cf. Rev. 2:6). Most of what is reported by early heresiologists such as Irenaeus (*Haer.* 1.31.1–2), Pseudo-Tertullian (*Haer.* 2.5), and Epiphanius (*Pan.* 58.3.1–5) about the Cainites, however, is almost totally fictitious; see Pearson 1990, 107 and Williams 1996, 170–72.

2. Tertullian, *Prax.* 1.5.

3. See Chapter 6 for Praxeas and Victor. On Modalism, see also Chapter 28. For a discussion of Tertullian's New Prophecy-influenced understanding of the Trinity, as set out in his *Adversus Praxean*, see McGowan 2006 and Tabbernee 2007, 158–61.

4. Tertullian, *Prax.* 2.1.

5. Tertullian, *Prax.* 2.4.

6. Tertullian, *Prax.* 8.5. It is possible that this oracle may have been uttered by a contemporary prophet or prophetess at Carthage (see Chapter 14), but, as the theology of the oracle reflects that of the second century, it may also have derived from one of the founders of Montanism or from one of their immediate successors.

7. Tertullian, *Pud.* 1.6.

8. Tertullian, *Pud.* 1.6.

9. Tertullian, *Bapt.* 20.5.

10. Anonyma, *Log., ap.* Tertullian, *Pud.* 21.7b. This particular *logion* is not attributed by Tertullian to Montanus, Maximilla, or Priscilla and, therefore, is likely to have been uttered by one of the anonymous second-generation Montanist prophetesses at Carthage—on whom, see Chapter 14. There may also have been (male) prophets at Carthage at the time belonging to the New Prophecy movement there but, if so, no specific reference to them has survived.

11. Regrettably, Tertullian never mentions "Pontifex Maximus" by his real name. In *Pud.* 1.6 Tertullian calls him facetiously "Apostolic Sir" and in *Pud.* 21.16 calls him, even more pejoratively, "O *Psychicus.*" From Cyprian *Ep.* 71.4 it appears that the bishop of Carthage at this time was Agrippinus. Despite even recent views to the contrary (Brent 1995, 503–35; Merdinger 1997, 32–33; Osborn 1997, 175 n. 31), Barnes (1985, 30–31, 141, 247) has shown convincingly that "Pontifex Maximus" was not Callistus, bishop of Rome (ca. 217–ca. 222), but the local Carthaginian bishop. On Tertullian's understanding of repentance and penitence both before and after his involvement with the New Prophecy, see Tabbernee 2001a.

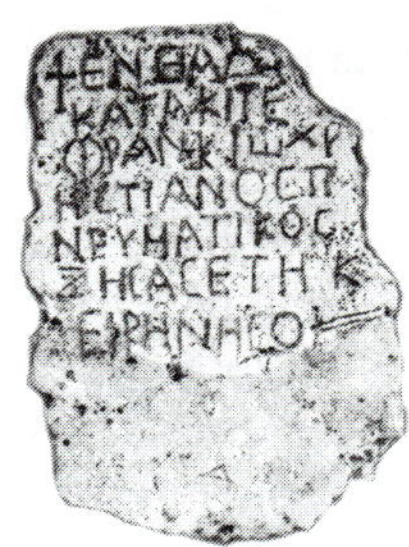

Chapter 14

Carthage, Africa Proconsularis, ca. 211/12 C.E.

Genuine revelation in the new era of the Paraclete

The house-church where Tertullian is both a member and a patron is filled to capacity. The house, a Roman-style villa, is big enough to accommodate the fifty to sixty people, including children, who gather together on Sundays and sometimes during the week. In fact the congregation meets in Tertullian's own house. The villa has an atrium at the front of the house and a second courtyard with a summer triclinium, or dining room, at the back of the house. The design of the house provides two large meeting spaces, which makes it perfect for a house-church, since it provides enough space for the catechumens and the faithful to meet separately for the latter part of the liturgy when the Eucharist is celebrated. Only the faithful are allowed to be present when the bread and wine are consecrated. The catechumens, those who are still being instructed in the faith, must wait until they are baptized before they can partake of the sacred bread and wine. At the end of the first part of the worship service, the catechumens and other non-baptized persons, including most of the children, go to the summer triclinium for instruction while those who have already been baptized stay in the atrium to participate in the "Liturgy of the Faithful."

Today, during the Eucharist, Tertullian notices that one of the women, a prophetess, seems particularly lost in thought. He hopes that she is actually having one of her visions, as is frequently the case. The woman is amazing; she has the gift of conversing with angels and, so she claims, even with the Lord. Her visions appear to be triggered by various parts of the liturgy: a reading, a prayer, or the sacraments themselves. Tertullian is sure that it is the Holy Spirit, the Paraclete, who gives the prophetess revelations while she is in an ecstatic state. The Carthaginian prophetess is a contemporary version of Maximilla and Priscilla—and even of Ammia and Philip's daughters.

The prophetess Tertullian is watching closely right now is not the only new-generation prophetess of the New Prophecy movement in Carthage. Out of the corner of his eye, Tertullian can see one of the others. That particular prophetess recently had an incredible dream, which she related to Tertullian and other church leaders. She told them that during the night while she was in bed sleeping, she felt the gentle touch of an angel's wing on her neck. She thought she had awakened because the presence of the angel was so real that she was sure that if she reached out with her right hand she could touch the angel, just as the angel had touched her neck. The angel's touch felt just like a kiss.

In recounting her dream, the prophetess hesitated, seemingly embarrassed to continue. It had taken quite a bit of coaxing to convince her to repeat what the angel had told her: "An elegant neck," the angel had said, "and fittingly bare! It is good that you are uncovered from your head to your privates, lest you not benefit from the neck's freedom."[1] What a strange thing for an angel to say! The prophetess wanted to keep the dream to herself, but because she is accustomed to submitting her revelations to Tertullian and the other elders, so they can test their validity and authority, she had told them the dream. She had blushed profusely under her veil, as she had repeated verbatim the angel's exact words.

In the Carthaginian Christian community there are two kinds of elders: presbyters and seniores. The presbyters are ordained clergy who rank immediately below the bishop and perform important liturgical functions authorized by the bishop. The presbyters are the priests of the church, assisting the bishop in performing baptisms, celebrating the Eucharist, and being the spiritual and pastoral leaders of the various house-churches scattered around the city. The seniores are lay persons who perform only minor liturgical functions such a leading a prayer during a worship service or reading from the sacred writings. They are, as their full title—*seniores laici*—indicates, "*lay* elders." Like village elders in every country hamlet in Africa Proconsularis and elsewhere in North Africa, the seniores laici in the Carthaginian church are older men who, because of their wisdom, experience, influence, and status, are entrusted with the overall well-being of the Christian community. Because Carthage has multiple house-church communities, the various seniores laici associated with those house-churches comprise a Carthage-wide council of elders. Over the years this council has become a powerful entity. It selects and appoints the bishop of Carthage whenever there is a vacancy, it advises the bishop during his episcopacy, and it deals with issues of discipline. Part of the council's disciplinary function is to ensure that prophecy, which in Carthage is deemed a legitimate charism, is kept under control. Not all that is alleged to be revelation is indeed revelation. The collective spiritual discernment of the council of elders is needed to test all reported dreams, visions, and oracles, in order to determine whether these contain genuine revelation.[2]

Tertullian enjoys being at the sessions of the council that test the validity and authenticity of prophecy. Ever since he became influenced by the New Prophecy movement, which has won many adherents in Carthage, he has been fascinated with prophecy. He has in his possession a book that is mainly a collection of the oracles of Montanus and Priscilla, and he has also begun his own compilation of the more recent revelations of the Paraclete, such as those mediated by the prophetesses who are now present in the worship service in his own house-church.

Being one of the few highly literate people among the seniores laici in Carthage, Tertullian, after volunteering, was appointed the secretary of the council for the sessions that test the validity of contemporary prophecy. This allows Tertullian to write down the content of a new prophecy as soon as it is related, ensuring its accuracy. It always amazes him how people's minds play tricks on them. Only a few days after the initial recounting of a particular vision or dream, the way it is told can change considerably. He is glad he has a written record.

When the revelation contained in a particular vision or dream, or better still in the ipsissima verba, the very words, of a prophetic oracle, is deemed authentic, he can then quote this revelation in his own writings as proof that the Paraclete continues to operate in the current era. In fact, Tertullian believes that the current era, inaugurated by the Paraclete's revelations through Montanus, Maximilla, and Priscilla, is the best and final era for people of faith. It supersedes, in his view, the era of God the Father, when God was operative in creation and with humankind primarily through the various covenants with the Jews. The new era, the era of the Paraclete, or Holy Spirit, also supersedes the age of Christ and the apostles, because the earliest Christians were too immature spiritually to receive or understand the full implications of what it means to live the Christian life with all of its ascetic demands. It is not that the new revelations of the Paraclete provide new doctrinal content concerning what Christians are to *believe*—Christ and the apostles did that. The Paraclete merely provides new, although stringent, ethical guidelines for how mature Christians are to *conduct themselves*!

Sometimes the Paraclete's directives are extremely specific. This was the case with the prophetess' dream about the angel and the neck. It took a while, but it was Tertullian who figured out what the Paraclete was trying to communicate. It was a prescription concerning the exact length of a modest woman's veil! The Paraclete was mandating that a woman's veil should be at least as long as the equivalent of her unbound hair. Just as a woman's neck is completely covered naturally by her long hair, a veil should be as long as her hair if not longer. That way no part of her neck will be uncovered in public or even in church. The angel's comment about the prophetess' total nakedness in bed was an ironic way of pointing out that nakedness—even if only the neck—is inappropriate in public or in church.

At Carthage there is an ongoing debate over whether or not virgins should be veiled in church. Some are of the opinion that, regardless of whether virgins are veiled in public, they need not be veiled in church. After all, pubescent teenage virgins do not wear a veil in church, so why should older unmarried women do so? The veil is a symbol of being married, either to a husband or to Christ. In every house-church in Carthage there is special seating for "dedicated virgins," that is, women who have taken a vow of chastity and dedicated themselves to the service of God. They belong to the Order of Virgins, which is akin but not identical to, the Order of Widows that also exists in Carthage. The widows have special reserved seating as a sign of respect for them as "altars of God."[3] Both groups wear veils in church. The opponents of veiling all women in church argue that veiling virgins prematurely confuses the distinction between dedicated virgins and those who have not yet decided whether to marry or to join the Order of Virgins.

Not that the decision to join an order is really an unmarried woman's to make. A young woman's father normally arranges a marriage for her rather than allowing her to be a dedicated virgin, even if she wants to be one. Finding an economically prudent or socially advantageous match for one's daughter has priority over life-long virginity, and this is true for even the most devout Christian fathers. Dedication to Christ has its practical limits. Only the most determined and persistent young women can persuade their fathers to permit them to "take the veil" and to continue to live at home as dedicated virgins, rather than be married off to some man.

Partly because of the small percentage of young women who actually become dedicated virgins, but mainly because of an insistence on total modesty, Tertullian and those in agreement with him argue that *all* virgins, even teenaged young women, should be veiled in church. Responding to his opponents' claim that St. Paul in his First Letter to the Corinthian community only stipulated that *women,* not *virgins,* be veiled in church, Tertullian invariably counters that this is a meaningless distinction—splitting hairs unnecessarily. The category "women" obviously encompasses virgins!

Given that the relevant passage in First Corinthians speaks about the veiling of women in the context of prophesying,[4] Tertullian argues that for all women, including virgins, being veiled in church means not only being dressed modestly but also being dressed appropriately for potential prophesying. The Spirit is like a wind and one never knows when or upon whom the Spirit will descend, so all women, especially virgins, should always be prepared to be the vehicle for the Paraclete's revelations. How tragic it would be if when the Spirit comes, the women on whom the Spirit descends cannot, for lack of a veil, utter publicly in church the words communicated to them. Not that prophecy always works that way; often a revelation is simply communicated to the council of seniores first. But it is better to be prepared for a spontaneous public revelation of the Spirit's message than to prevent it for lack of a veil.

Tertullian, when he realized the meaning of the prophetess' dream about the angel touching her neck, knew that the Paraclete was clarifying Christ's will on the matter. He decided to write a treatise on the veiling of virgins, the crucial component being the Paraclete's most recent revelation on the matter through the prophetess' dream. At the beginning of the treatise Tertullian wrote: "They who have heard the Paraclete prophesying even to the present time bid virgins be wholly covered."[5]

Now, sitting among the members of his own house-church and seeing all the women veiled, even though in other house-churches meeting concurrently in Carthage this is not yet the case, Tertullian can hardly wait for the worship service to be over. He eagerly looks forward to the moment when, after most of the members of the congregation have gone to their respective homes, the council of seniores will meet in his tablinum to hear the latest revelations of the Paraclete via the prophetess who converses with angels.[6]

Sources:

Tertullian, *An.* 9.4; Anonyma, *Log., ap.* Tertullian, *Virg.* 1.7, 17.3; *Apol.* 39.1–5; *Pud.* 14.16; Polycarp, *Phil.* 4.3; 1 Cor 11:1–16.

Notes

1. Anonyma, *Log., ap.* Tertullian, *Virg.* 17.3. On the Montanist prophetesses in Carthage, see Tabbernee 2001a; 2006a, 523–25; 2007, 135–38.

2. On the seniores laici, see Frend 1961, Shaw 1982, and Tabbernee 2005, 435–38.

3. See Polycarp, *Phil.* 4.3. On the Order of Widows, see Thurston 1989; Tabbernee 1997b, 521–22; Eisen 2000, 143–57.

4. 1 Cor 11:1–16.

5. Tertullian, *Virg.* 1.7. For additional information about the conflict in Carthage over the veiling of virgins, see Dunn 2004, 135–42; Tabbernee 2007, 114–15, 153–54.

6. For another example of a Montanist prophetess who "converses with angels," see Chapter 27.

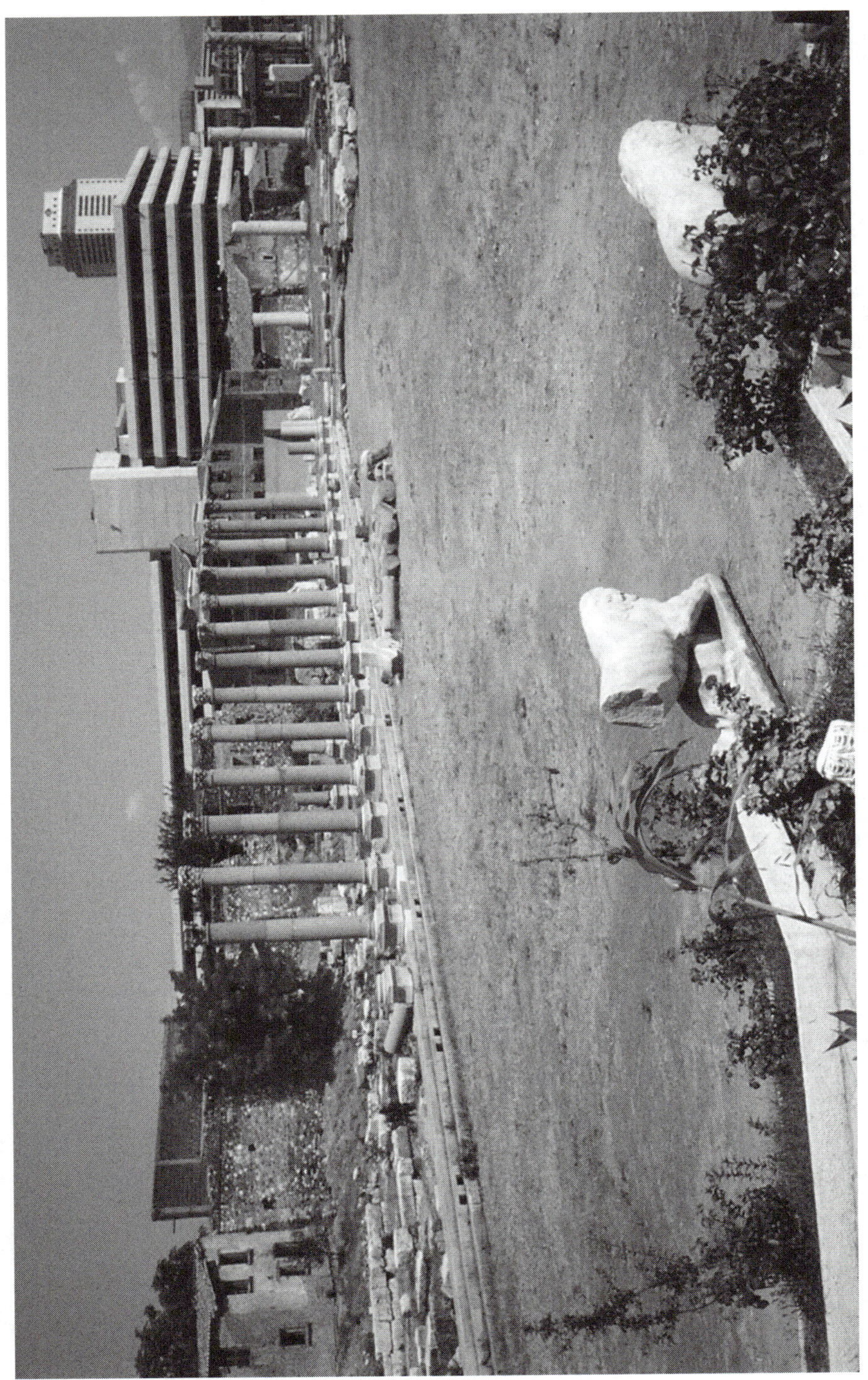

Figure 15.1: The agora with colonnade and the stone lions in Smyrna

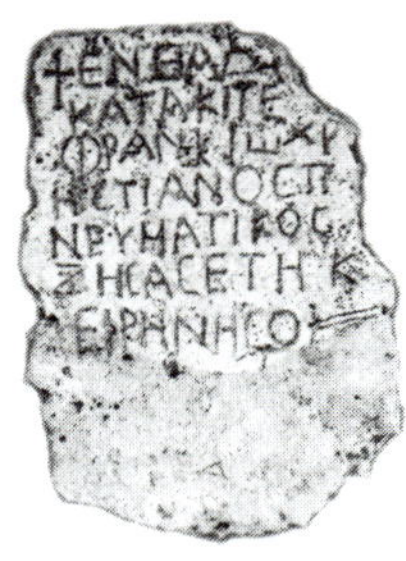

Chapter 15

Smyrna, Ionia, ca. 212/13 C.E.

An anonymous writer establishes three criteria for genuine prophecy

The man likes walking along the beach. It isn't much of a beach, as there is only a little sand; pebbles mostly and large rocks, but the sound of the waves lapping against the shore is soothing. He also likes the scent of the water. When the occasional strong wave breaks on one of the rocky outcroppings, it sends a huge spray in his direction. He lets the water mist his face. Little droplets drizzle down his cheeks onto his dark moustache and beard, and he can taste the salt on his lips.[1]

As he walks he feels the first rays of the morning sun on his back—not yet strong enough to warm him but, nonetheless, very pleasant. The sun also throws beams of light through the few clouds in the sky onto the bay, creating interesting patches where the water seems green rather than blue. On the horizon, where the waters of the Internum Mare, the Mediterranean Sea, meet the waters of the Smyrnaeus Sinus, the Bay of Smyrna, the man can see six trading vessels all in a row, slowly making their way toward the port—which is second in importance only to the port of Ephesus.

The man turns left, his face toward the sun, which is now a little higher in the sky, and walks up the hill to the city. He passes through the agora with its beautiful colonnade. As he always does, the man gently touches the heads of the pair of stone lions that ceremoniously guard the steps to the civic basilica. He knows that, for a Christian, touching the lions is an odd gesture but he cannot help himself. The lions remind him of so many of his fellow Christians who have been martyred by being thrown to the beasts. Doing so also reminds him of the story of Thecla who, if the story is to be believed, was befriended by the very lion who was supposed to devour her. Touching the lions is, for him, both a private acknowledgment of his willingness to become a martyr should it ever come to that and a silent act of defiance. Lions are not the ultimate victors, Christians who suffer for the true faith are.

That the true faith prevails is all that matters to the man. The true faith, however, is threatened not only by persecution from outside the church but also by antichrists within the church. The man has been reading the epistles written by a presbyter named John to Christian communities in his part of the province of

Asia. That presbyter, more than a century ago, warned that there are antichrists everywhere preparing the way for the ultimate Antichrist yet to come. In one of his epistles the presbyter expressly demanded that, with respect to prophets, Christian leaders should test the spirits to see if they are of God. But testing the spirits that energize prophets and prophetesses is more difficult than appears, at first sight, to be the case. One of the reasons the man is taking an early morning walk is to figure out criteria by which to test the spirits of the New Prophecy—a movement troubling the church at Smyrna.

This particular morning the man finally works out a way to commence his treatise against the New Prophecy. A statement written about antichrists by John, which the man read just before his walk, provided the key:

> They went out from us, but they did not belong to us; for if they had belonged to us, they would have remained with us. But by going out they made it plain that none of them belongs to us.[2]

Back at his desk, everything is now very clear to the man. Within the holy church of God spiritual gifts such as prophecy do exist, at least for as long as God deems charismata to be necessary. But the most important insight the presbyter John provides is that genuine charismata only exist *within* the church, not outside of it. Therefore, the man realizes, the claim made by the adherents of the New Prophecy—that the prophecies of Montanus, Maximilla, Priscilla, and other prophets and prophetesses of their movement are genuine—is *in fact* completely spurious. Because the New Prophecy movement established its own "churches" and left the true church, whatever passes for prophecy in those *pseudo*-Christian communities is not prophecy but *pseudo*-prophecy. If for no other reason, the so-called New Prophecy's "prophecy" is not prophecy because the term prophecy is restricted by definition to a spiritual gift that occurs *within* the true church—never outside of it. Even if members of the New Prophecy movement want to argue that their founders were members of the same catholic church when they uttered their oracles, the man can reply, on the authority of John, that in leaving the true church, Montanus, Maximilla, and Priscilla proved that they never really belonged there in the first place! The primary criterion for testing the validity of the New Prophecy, the man writes in his treatise, is whether its prophetic charismata occur *within* the church.

The man quickly moves to a second, related criterion. Unlike some of his contemporaries, the man doesn't really believe that charismata such as prophecy continue in the church at the present time. Instead, he believes that genuine prophecy ceased, by God's will, at the end of the apostolic era. When the last of those whom the apostles had approved as prophets and prophetesses died so, in his view, did genuine prophecy. Prophecy is no longer needed. The man's second criterion for testing the validity of the New Prophecy, which he writes down next in his treatise, is simply whether its prophetic charismata occurred *before* the time when genuine prophecy ceased.

The man knows that no matter how liberally one extends the time period of the apostolic age, it cannot be stretched long enough to encompass the years when Montanus, Maximilla, and Priscilla first began to prophesy. The man believes that this impales the contemporary leadership of the New Prophecy movement on the horns of a double dilemma. They have to prove either that genuine prophecy actually continues beyond the apostolic age or that, if it does not, how what Montanus, Maximilla, and Priscilla uttered can really be called prophecy. The man uses Maximilla's own words against her and against the whole movement. Maximilla, he reminds his readers, declared: "After me, a prophet shall no longer exist—only the end!"[3] If Maximilla was part of a continuous line of prophetic succession from apostolic times onward, the line should have continued beyond Maximilla but, according to the man, not even Maximilla herself believed that there would be prophets or prophetesses after her.

The man, writing his treatise in Smyrna rather than in Pepouza or Carthage, is unaware that adherents of the New Prophecy in those places have second- and third-generation prophets and prophetesses. The members of the New Prophecy movement who are the man's contemporaries have decided that Maximilla's statement is linked to "the very end," the *sunteleia,* the completion of all things, including prophecy. Until that time arrives, for the followers of Montanus, Maximilla, and Priscilla prophecy remains a legitimate and necessary phenomenon. The man in Smyrna challenges adherents of the New Prophecy "demonstrate that there are prophets after Maximilla."[4] His contemporaries in Pepouza or Carthage will be able to meet his challenge—if they ever get to read his treatise.

Now that he has finally started writing, the man in Smyrna has no difficulty continuing. He marvels at how rapidly the words are flowing from his pen onto the pages, which are mounting up into a neat little pile on his desk. Maximilla's *logion* about "the end" provides a third way for him to test not only oracles of the New Prophecy but all alleged prophecies. This third criterion is whether or not what is predicted in a particular prophecy actually comes true. Taking exactly the opposite approach to the *logion* than that taken by contemporary followers of Maximilla, who conclude that, because the end had not yet come prophecy has not yet been done away with, the man argues that because the end predicted by Maximilla has not come, the alleged prophecy is not genuine prophecy at all.

Sources:

Act. Paul. 33; 1 John 2:18–19; Anti-Phrygian, *Fr., ap.* Epiphanius, *Pan.* 48.1.4–48.13.8; Maximilla, *Log., ap.* Anti-Phrygian, *Fr., ap.* Epiphanius, *Pan.* 48.2.4.

Carthage, Africa Proconsularis, ca. 212/13 C.E.

Tertullian on ecstasy

Tertullian wonders whether there will ever be an end to revising his treatises. After the troublesome revisions and additions to *Adversus Marcionem,* he finds himself at it again. Not that he has to produce yet another edition of the *Adversus Marcionem;* fortunately, the third edition of that work can stand as it is. But he has just read a treatise against the New Prophecy movement by a man named Apollonius, written somewhere in the province of Asia.[5]

It has taken a few years for a copy of Apollonius' work to reach Africa Proconsularis. Tertullian wishes the treatise had arrived a few years ago when he himself was writing a treatise devoted totally to defending the New Prophecy. That work, the *De ecstasi* ("On Ecstasy"), could have taken into account Apollonius' false charges against the prophets and prophetesses of the New Prophecy movement. Tertullian sighs one of those long sighs his wife hates to hear, then characteristically pulls back his shoulders as a sign of both resignation and determination. He will simply have to revise the six books of the *De ecstasi* he has already written and then add a seventh to deal specifically with Apollonius' false allegations.

Before he begins revising, Tertullian, after reading Apollonius' treatise a second time, admits to himself that not everything Apollonius says is completely false—nor is it completely true. Tertullian takes up his pen and writes: "We differ in this alone, that we do not permit second marriages nor reject Montanus' prophecy concerning the impending judgment."[6] The note will be helpful to him later, when he points out that while Montanus did not, as Apollonius accuses, dissolve the institution of marriage altogether, the Paraclete's discipline does not permit remarriage. Apollonius' charge, therefore, contains a little bit of truth in that the adherents of the New Prophecy differ from other Christians with respect to marriage practices, but not in the way Apollonius alleges. With respect to the impending judgment that will come at the end of time and the New Jerusalem's descent near Pepouza, Apollonius' accusations are more accurate. Adherents of the New Prophecy and other Christians certainly differ on those issues. But, as Tertullian intends to spell out in more detail in the seventh book of the revised *De ecstasi,* the differences between those influenced in their Christian practice by the revelations of the Paraclete via the New Prophets and the *psychici* are merely in these two areas. In all other respects, the two groups of Christian beliefs and practices are identical.

No sooner has Tertullian formulated, in his mind, what he will write about marriage and the impending judgment than he realizes he may be about to overstate his case. Even if *he* doesn't perceive any major differences other than Montanus' teaching on marriage and eschatology, the *psychici,* whether in Carthage or elsewhere, certainly *imagine* other differences, such as the way the prophets and prophetesses of the New Prophecy movement prophesy. Tertullian wonders whether, in the revised version of the treatise, he should perhaps include some of the additional arguments supporting the necessity of ecstasy for genuine prophecy that he had used in *De anima* ("On the Soul"), his most recently completed treatise.

Tertullian thinks about the way he used the example of Adam in *De anima* to argue that the soul has the capacity to continue certain activities while the body is asleep or at rest. This capacity of the soul, Tertullian explained to his readers, is called "ecstasy"—something any literate person would have known from reading the Greek text of the story of Adam in the book of Genesis, since the word ἔκστασις (*ekstasis*) is used there for Adam's "deep sleep." There were, however, only a few literate persons in the Christian community in Carthage and not all of those could read Greek. Therefore, Tertullian had written:

> This power we call *ecstasy*, in which the sensuous soul stands out of itself, in a way that even resembles madness. Thus in the very beginning sleep was inaugurated by ecstasy: "And God sent an ecstasy upon Adam, and he slept." The sleep came on his body to cause it rest, but the ecstasy fell on his soul to remove rest: from that very circumstance it still happens ordinarily . . . that sleep is combined with ecstasy.[7]

Tertullian ponders whether he should say something like that in the revised version of *De ecstasi*.

Normally, of course, the ecstasy of sleep is expressed in dreams and fantasies, but for those who have received the charism of prophesying it is the means by which prophecy is granted. Adam was the first person who received this gift, Tertullian argued in *De anima*, when he prophesied about the relationship between Christ and the church, not just between husband and wife, by uttering the words "This now is bone of my bones and flesh of my flesh; therefore a man leaves his father and mother and clings to his wife, and the two become one flesh."[8] Adam's capacity to prophesy *in ecstasis* was the result of the Holy Spirit's gift, enabling him to enter into a state of *amentia*. But being "out of one's natural senses," Tertullian pointed out, should not be taken as madness or insanity. The capacity to recall one's dreams upon waking from sleep proves that one is not mad while dreaming. In the same way, the ability of prophets and prophetesses to recall and relate the revelations they receive while in ecstatic trances proves they are neither insane nor fake prophets, as the opponents of the New Prophecy movement allege. He must, Tertullian decides, definitely say something like that again in the new part of *De estasi*. As he picks up his pen again, Tertullian also decides to call the additional seventh book *Adversus Apollonium*.

Sources:

Tertullian, *Fr. ecst., ap.* Praedestinatus, *Haer.* 1.26; Apollonius, *Fr. ap.* Eusebius, *Hist. eccl.* 5.18.2; Tertullian, *Marc.*, esp. 4.22.5, 5.8.12; *An.*, esp. 9.4, 11.4, 21.2, 45.3–6.

Notes

1. Unfortunately, the identity of the man who is the subject of the first section of this chapter is unknown. As noted in Chapter 1, Nasrallah (2003, 4, 167) refers to the man as the "Anti-Phrygian," in that he characteristically speaks of the Montanists against whom he is writing as "Phrygians." Scholarly attempts to equate the "Anti-Phrygian" with persons known to have written against the New Prophecy, such as "Brother Miltiades" (e.g., Lipsius 1865, 225–27; on this Miltiades, see Chapter 4), Apollonius (e.g., Hilgenfeld 1884, 557), or Hippolytus (e.g., Bonwetsch 1881, 36–38; on Hippolytus, see Chapter 16), but whose anti-Montanist works have been (at least partially) lost, are unconvincing. Stewart-Sykes' theory (2002, 39) that the Anti-Phrygian belonged to the "same circle" which, later, produced the *Vita Polycarpi* ("Life of Polycarp"), is probably correct and has been adopted here as the geographic context. It is, however, possible that the Anti-Phrygian wrote his treatise elsewhere (although *not* in Phrygia itself).

2. 1 John 2:19, cf. Anti-Phrygian, *Fr., ap.* Epiphanius, *Pan.* 48.1.6. The Anti-Phrygian seems to have written his treatise in opposition to a published collection of Montanist *logia*,

many of which he quotes—and then uses to denounce the New Prophecy. Fortunately an extensive portion of the Anti-Phrygian's treatise has been preserved by being quoted by Epiphanius in his *Panarion* (48.1.4b–48.13.8), with occasional editorial insertions (e.g., 48.2.6b–48.2.7a). The Anti-Phrygian's treatise, as quoted by Epiphanius, preserves the single largest group of the *logia* of Montanus, Maximilla, and Priscilla. For further details, see Nasrallah 2003, 167–96 and Tabbernee 2007, 50–53.

3. Maximilla, *Log., ap.* Anti-Phrygian, *Fr., ap.* Epiphanius, *Pan.* 48.2.4.

4. Anti-Phrygian, *Fr., ap.* Epiphanius, *Pan.* 48.2.3.

5. On Apollonius and his anti-Montanist treatise, see Chapter 9.

6. Tertullian, *Fr. ecst., ap.* Praedestinatus, *Haer.* 1.26. Only this sentence from the *De estasi* has survived by virtue of having been preserved by an anonymous fifth-century author referred to by scholars as the Praedestinatus, on whom, see Tabbernee 2007, 272–73. From Jerome we know that "Tertullian added to the six volumes which he wrote against the church, concerning ecstasy, a seventh, exclusively against Apollonius, in which he attempts to defend all that which Apollonius asserts" (*Vir. ill.* 40). On Tertullian's defense of ecstasy, see Nasrallah 2003, esp. 129–54 and Tabbernee 2007, 133–38.

7. Tertullian, *An.* 45.3 [*ANF* 3:223], quoting the Septuagint version of Gen 2:21.

8. Tertullian, *An.* 11.4; cf. *An.* 21.2 and Gen 2:23–24, Eph 5:32.

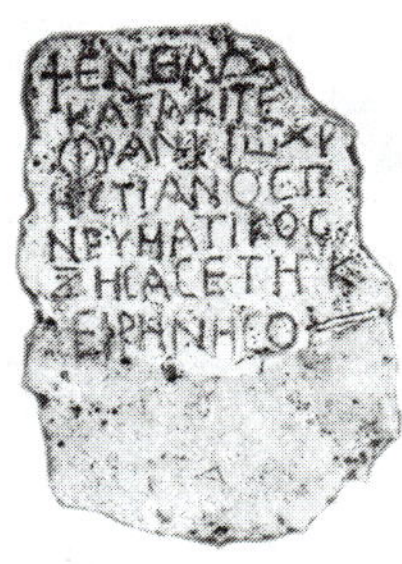

Chapter 16

Rome, Italia, ca. 223 C.E.

Hippolytus finds his inspiration

Hippolytus is so excited he can hardly contain himself. He has bought a statue. Not just any old statue but a true-to-life-sized marble statue of a woman seated in a chair. Both the chair and the woman are exquisitely carved. The sides of the chair consist of two flat side panels. The top of each panel is cut away and the remainder is shaped into a beautiful curve, the lower part forming the arms of the chair. As Hippolytus stands facing the chair, he notices that at the front of each arm there is a lion's head. The diameter of the side panels below the lions' heads is wider than he had expected, giving the chair a very sturdy appearance. The front of each panel, below the lion's head, is carved to resemble a leg with a lion's foot; the toes of each foot are clearly defined. Hippolytus is amazed at the master sculptor's attention to detail. Decorative scrolls are carved into the arms of the chair at the side of the lion heads and at the top of the chair.

The side panels themselves are slightly recessed, perfectly flat and—more importantly—completely blank. It was these flat blank panels that, as much as the seated figure herself, attracted Hippolytus to the statue from the moment he first saw it a few days ago. Hippolytus was on his way home and, as usual, took the most direct route through the Roman Forum, passing through the central arch of the triple-arched monument built exactly twenty years earlier in honor of Septimius Severus and his sons, Caracalla and Geta.[1] Hippolytus remembers how, as a newly arrived immigrant from Asia, he had stood at the edge of the crowd two decades ago on the day when Septimius rode through the arch on a chariot drawn by four splendid white stallions. The emperor was followed by his sons and what appeared to Hippolytus to be an endless procession of Roman soldiers. The emperor had been preceded by wagon loads of booty captured by Septimius and his armies during their most recent campaign. That campaign against the Parthians, concluded just three years earlier, was commemorated by the triumphal arch. The stonemasons had carved, at eye level, on the front of each of the four main columns of the arch, sculpted reliefs of Roman soldiers with their Parthian prisoners still wearing the distinctive Parthian caps.

How humiliating it must have been for the actual Parthians in Rome that day, to be at the very end of the procession, escorted by their captors in plain

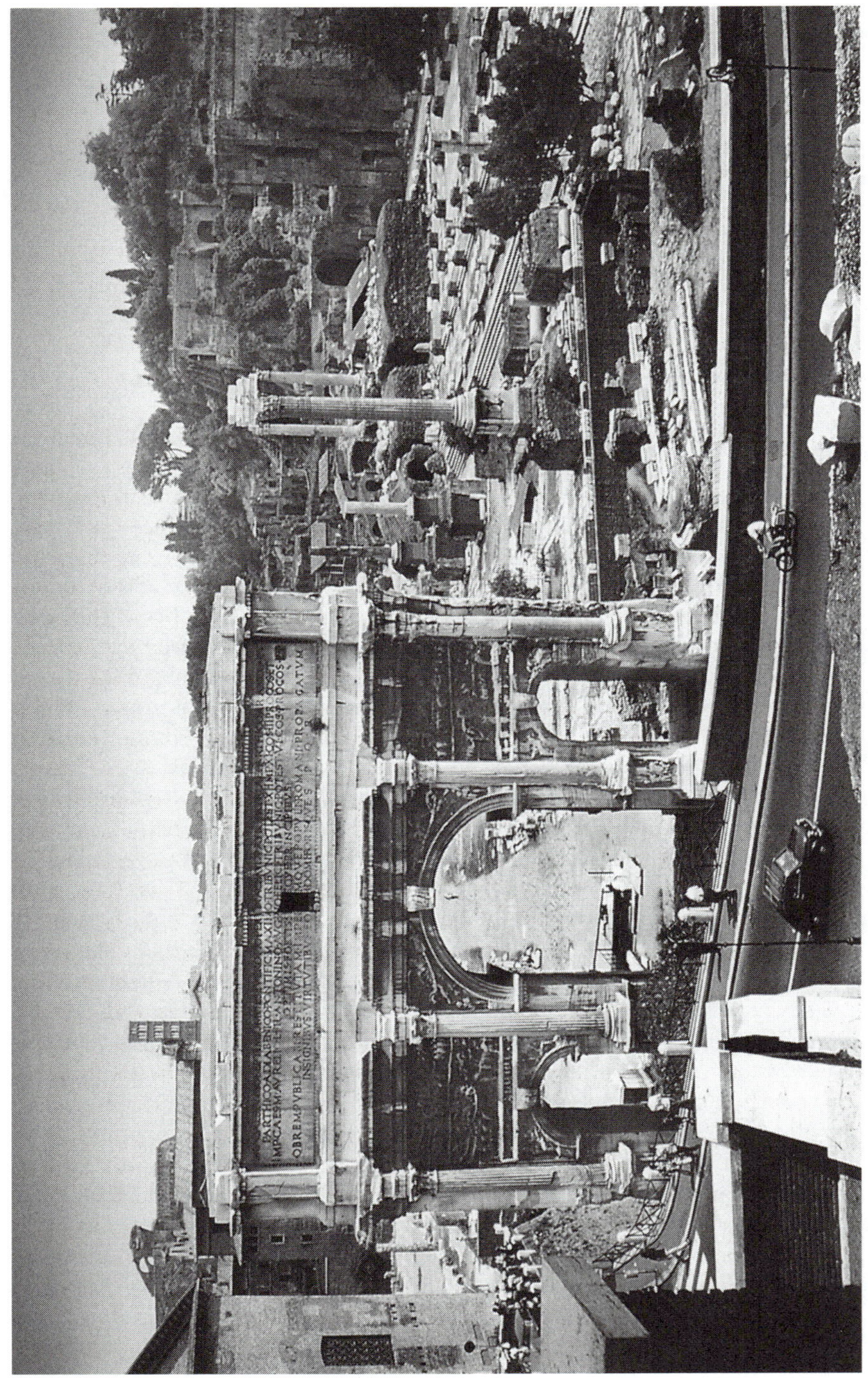

Figure 16.1: The Arch of Septimius Severus in Rome

sight of everyone, and led through the very arch that permanently records their plight. Hippolytus thought about this when he witnessed the procession with his own eyes. He thought about it again a few days ago, when he had stopped to look, once more, at the Parthians in their caps carved so realistically on the columns. Glancing also at the gilded bronze letters on the fascia at the top of the monument, Hippolytus had been reminded, however, that not everything carved in stone, or inserted into stone with dowels, remains a permanent record. When the old emperor Septimius died, his sons inherited the throne, but in less than a year Caracalla had murdered his brother Geta. *Damnatio memoriae,* the "damning of the memory," followed and every public record with Geta's name on it was removed or erased. The original gilded letters of the inscription, following Caracalla's own name, read: ET P. SEPTIMIO L. FIL. GETAE NOBILISS. CAESARI ("and Publius Septimius, son of Lucius [Septimius Severus], Geta, the most noble Caesar"). These were words Hippolytus had seen, again with his own eyes, for almost a decade. The inscription now only referred to Septimius Severus and Caracalla, the original reference to Geta having been replaced by new dowel-inserted letters reading: OPTIMIS FORTISSIMISQUE PRINCIPIBUS ("excellent and most powerful rulers").

Feeling just a little sad at the fate of the Parthians and of Geta but marveling at the skills of stonemasons, Hippolytus had, on the spur of the moment, decided to stop by a stonemason's workshop only a few streets from the forum. He likes going there, not only on business but for pleasure. As a presbyter, Hippolytus has the responsibility of caring for a number of house-churches, which he and his predecessors have welded into a Christian church-school community. He is also in charge of one of Rome's catacombs where the members of his community are buried. Callistus, the bishop who died only last year and whom Hippolytus didn't really like very much, had similar duties before he became bishop of Rome. Hippolytus has often gone to the workshop to commission a slab with an inscription to cover the body of one of his parishioners buried in the catacomb. Last week, however, when Hippolytus stopped by he simply wanted to see what new items there were in the courtyard of the stonemason's workshop. The new statue he came across—the one of the woman seated in the beautifully carved chair with its blank side panels—both surprised and delighted him. He couldn't get it out of his mind and went back three times before finally deciding today to buy it. He has plans for those panels—and for the statue as a whole.

The master stonemason had told Hippolytus that the woman the statue depicts was Themista of Lampsacus, a famous teacher-philosopher. Looking at the female figure now, Hippolytus can see that clearly. She is not only seated, the traditional position for teaching, but she holds a codex in her left hand. Her right arm is held demurely across her breasts, and she is draped in a most beautiful dress, with frills at the bottom of the skirt. Although the stonemason refers to the statue as Themista, Hippolytus thinks of her as Sophia, "Wisdom." He knows exactly what he will do with her and gives the stonemason explicit instructions about what to inscribe on each of the panels.

In the library of the house-church-school community Hippolytus oversees there are numerous books, many of them written by the more learned members of the community. Hippolytus likes reading these works. They not only enlighten him about a whole range of subjects but they inspire him to write his own books. He has also edited and updated some of the works written by his predecessors, such as the *Traditio apostolica,* a manual containing the Apostolic Tradition regarding the Eucharist and baptism as well as other matters.

Today Hippolytus is reading a long work consisting of ten books. It was written by the presbyter who was Hippolytus' immediate predecessor as superintendent of the house-church-school community. The work is titled *Refutatio omnium haeresium* ("Refutation of All Heresies"), although the author himself refers to the first four books as the *Philosophoumena* ("Exposition of Philosophical Tenets"). The author's purpose is to show that some heretics have more in common with pagan philosophers than with the truths of the Christian message, and that other heretics simply leave behind any semblance of critical reasoning and substitute nonsense for truth.

Hippolytus is particularly intrigued by a passage in Book Eight of the *Refutatio.* It deals with a group of people his predecessor considered even more heretical than the Quartodecimans. The house-church-school community Hippolytus now oversees had developed a unique Easter calendar that, for this community at least, overcomes the problems inherent in the Quartodeciman practice of always concluding the Lenten fast on the fourteenth day of Nisan irrespective of the day of the week this falls on. It also overcomes problems inherent in the way the other church communities in Rome calculate Easter Sunday. The system employed by Hippolytus' group is somewhat cumbersome and requires complicated tables of dates but, by breaking off their fasts on Sundays, Easter is always celebrated on a Sunday while keeping as close as possible to the exact anniversaries of Christ's death and resurrection. The Quartodecimans in Rome, however, remained vehemently opposed to what they considered to be an unacceptable compromise solution. Hippolytus' predecessor had countered by calling the Quartodecimans "heretics." What intrigues Hippolytus in particular is that his predecessor considered adherents of the New Prophecy to be even *greater* heretics.[2]

As Hippolytus reads on, he notices that his predecessor describes the followers of Montanus, Maximilla, and Priscilla as "Phrygians by race."[3] Hippolytus knows this is true with respect to the earliest adherents of the New Prophecy, including some later followers who emigrated from Phrygia to Rome. But he also knows that not all members of the movement are Phrygians. The movement has captured the minds and hearts of numerous non-Phrygian people in Rome as well as elsewhere. Before he has time to think about this, his predecessor's words cause him to correct himself. The *minds* of the followers of Montanus, Maximilla, and Priscilla haven't so much been captured as bypassed. As his predecessor points out, instead of applying critical reasoning to the so-called oracles of the prophets and prophetesses of the movement, or instead of heeding the warnings of those competent to judge the validity of the New Prophecy, the movement's supporters simply allow themselves to be deceived and swept along by an unreasonable faith in imposters.

The author of the *Refutatio* says that "the Phrygians" have a countless number of books containing the teachings of the founders of the New Prophecy movement and they have more regard for these than they have for the teachings of Christ and the apostles. Hippolytus wonders whether his predecessor actually saw any of these books or if he only heard or read about such books. If there are any copies here in Rome, he'd certainly like to see them for himself. The author of the *Refutatio* certainly seems very well informed about the practices of the members of the New Prophecy movement. He explains that they have novel fasts as well as feasts. Hippolytus has heard rumors that, in the house-churches belonging to the New Prophecy movement, they hold wineless Eucharists, but he is not sure if his predecessor is referring to such strange Eucharists in his comment about novel feasts.[4] There is however no lack of clarity about the author's reference to new fasts. He describes them as meals consisting of dry foods and cabbages—totally unappetizing and hard on the digestive system.

The author of the *Refutatio* admits that most of the followers of Montanus, Maximilla, and Priscilla hold the same beliefs as members of the orthodox Christian communities in Rome about God, the creator of the universe, and about Jesus Christ. Some however are "Modalists" and share the views of Noetus. Noetus of Smyrna, as Hippolytus knows, held views similar to those Praxeas brought to Rome from Asia during the time of Victor.

Hippolytus has been doing his own research on Noetus, the New Prophecy, and other heresies. For the earlier sects and heresies he is using materials produced by Irenaeus of Lugdunum, and, as he reads the *Refutatio,* he is taking copious notes. The reference by his predecessor to Noetus causes Hippolytus to decide that he will follow in his predecessor's footsteps and write a new, up-to-date heresiology concluding with the Noetians but starting with the Dositheans. Dositheus, according to the research Hippolytus had undertaken, was first the teacher and then the disciple of Simon Magus—Simon the Magician—the arch-heretic from whom all subsequent heresies are derived, just as all truth has one single source: Jesus the Christ himself.

After consulting his notes and determining how many heresies to include, Hippolytus jots down the provisional title of his new work: *Collected Writings Against Thirty-two Heresies Treated Individually Beginning with the Dositheans and Continuing up to the Time of Noetus and the Noetians.* What a mouthful, Hippolytus thinks, as he looks at his proposed title. He quickly writes down *Adversus omnes haereses* ("Against all Heresies") as the better alternative. Even though the shorter title is very similar to that of the book of heresies written by his predecessor, Hippolytus decides that it will have to do. Economy of words is preferred even over complete accuracy. Hippolytus has no intention of writing against *all* heresies—thirty-two is already too many, but he does intend to include the New Prophecy in his list. He has already alluded briefly to the New Prophecy in his *Commentarium in Danielem* ("Commentary on Daniel") and his *De antichristo* ("On the Antichrist"); his proposed heresiology will give him the opportunity to refute the troublesome New Prophets and their followers in more detail.

Hippolytus' daydreaming about his new writing project is interrupted by the noise of a cart being wheeled into the courtyard of the house that is is home to Hippolytus' house-church-school community. He walks to the window and sees, tied to the tray of the cart, the statue he has purchased. The master stonemason has come along in person to ensure the safe delivery of the seated woman teacher-philosopher, and, as Hippolytus hurries to the front door, the man is shouting instructions to his two co-workers.

Hippolytus' heart is in his throat as the men clumsily manage to get the statue off the cart and positioned in its place of honor in the center of the courtyard. Hippolytus relaxes as he walks all the way around the statue, inspecting it carefully for any damage. Satisfied that nothing has been broken or chipped, Hippolytus goes first to the right-hand panel and is delighted to see that the stonecutter has carved accurately what Hippolytus instructed him to carve there: the tables by which anyone who has access to them can compute the date of Easter according to the system devised by Hippolytus' community. What a joy to see these tables there so well set out in clear easy-to-read columns—and what a useful instrument for generations to come.

Hippolytus next looks carefully at the left-hand panel and sees that the stonecutter has done an equally fine job with that panel as well. The words are also in columns, but they are not the columns of Easter tables. They are a list of some of the books written by members of Hippolytus' house-church-school community, including his predecessor, another member who wrote a *Commentarius in Psalmos* ("Commentary on the Psalms"), and himself. Hippolytus wishes there were room for even more book titles on the panel but is content to know that the panel contains the community's most important works—all of which, and more, are available in the library next door.

Hippolytus thanks the stonemason and his helpers profusely, paying them what he still owes. After they have gone, he stands quietly for a while in the presence of Sophia—the new iconic expression of the spirit and ethos of the house-church-school community of which he is so proud to be the leader. Sophia, he believes, is the perfect symbol to adorn and give visible expression to all he still wants to achieve. Sophia, true Wisdom, is the very opposite of the false spirit that pervades the New Prophecy and other heresies. Looking again at the list of works on the left panel, Hippolytus is glad that each of the three authors, including himself, has written against the New Prophecy. As he walks back inside the house to begin his latest book against the false prophecy and against other heresies, he feels very inspired by Sophia.[5]

Sources:

EG 4:535–45 (No. 3); *Trad. ap.;* Author of the *Refutatio, Ref.* 8.19.1–3, cf. 10.25–26; Hippolytus, *Noet.* 9.2–3; *Comm. Dan.* 3.20, 4.7.1, 4.13.1, 4.18.7, 4.19.3; Author of *On the Psalms, Fr. Ps.* 1; Eusebius, *Hist. eccl.* 6.20.1–3, 6.22.1–2; Jerome, *Vir. ill.* 61; Photius, *Cod.* 121, 232; Irenaeus, *Haer.*

Notes

1. On the Arch of Septimius Severus, which was constructed in 203, see Claridge 1998, 75–76.

2. See Chapter 6 for the Quartodeciman Controversy and Modalism.

3. Author of the *Refutatio, Ref.* 8.19.1.

4. For a helpful discussion of the possible Montanist practice of wineless Eucharists, see McGowan 1999, 167 n. 77, 168, 173–74, 262–63.

5. Scholarly opinions regarding Hippolytus (ca. 170–ca. 236/7) range from him having been the first "anti-pope" at Rome (Döllinger 1876, esp. xv, 92–96) to him being a bishop in western Asia Minor somewhere around Laodikeia (Cerrato 2002). A close analysis of all the relevant data, however, indicates that Hippolytus was not a bishop at all but an increasingly prominent and influential presbyter who came to Rome from Asia Minor ca. 200 (Lampe 2003, 350). When, during the sixteenth century, the statue described in this chapter was rediscovered, it was headless. On the mistaken assumption that all the works listed on the left-hand panel of the chair were written by Hippolytus, the statue was restored with a man's head and assumed to have been a statue of Hippolytus. The restored statue is now in the Vatican Museum. On the statue, the identity of the person originally portrayed, and its function as the icon of Hippolytus' house-church-school community, see Brent 1995, esp. 3–8, 52–60, 109–14, 398–457, and 539. For the argument that the works listed on the chair are the writings of at least three authors belonging to the "Hippolytan school," see Brent 1995, esp. 115, 184, 203, 206, 301–6, and 367; and Tabbernee 2007, 70–78.

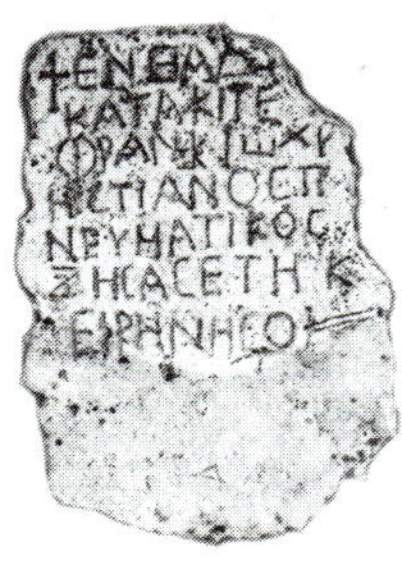

Chapter 17

Thyateira, Lydia, ca. 223 C.E.

Aurelius Gaius grieves the death of his wife

The sun is high in the Lydian sky as Aurelius Gaius enters the city of Thyateira on Lydia's border with Mysia. As usual, Aurelius Gaius arose early in his own village of Chorianos. On this day however, instead of tending to his chores, he decided he needed to get away for a while. His grief was simply too great to face mending the wooden fence around the yard behind his house. The fence fell down two weeks ago, but he didn't have the energy to cut down a tree for the new posts and rails needed to fix it. The garden has become overgrown, but he is incapable of pulling a single weed. He should wash his dishes and his clothes but simply eats off a dirty plate and wears the same shirt day after day—even though, unlike some of the other men in the village, he owns more than one. He has managed to cook some meals, but his heart isn't in it and he ate without any appetite. His beloved wife, Aurelia Stratoneikiane, is no longer there to share the meal with him. In everything he does around the house, he can still see Aurelia Stratoneikiane as close to him as she ever was, although he buried her almost three months ago.

The burial was a beautiful but heartbreaking affair. Aurelius Gaius commissioned a white marble sarcophagus. The inscription of the lid is a bold declaration of his Christian faith and that of his wife. The stonemason gave the Greek form of his name, carving the whole inscription, which concludes with a warning to anyone daring to utilize the sarcophagus inappropriately, in carefully crafted letters:

> Aurelios Gaios son of Apphianos, a Christian, prepared this sarcophagus for himself and for Aurelia Stratoneikiane his wife, being herself a Christian. No one else has the authority to place the body of another here; but if anyone were to put in another corpse, that one shall pay 1,000 *denarii* to the community of the Chorianonians.[1]

As he lovingly placed the body of his wife in the sarcophagus, Aurelius Gaius fervently prayed that no one would ever be fined for being brazen enough to place anyone else in the empty niche beside Aurelia. That place is reserved for him—and for him alone!

The decision to profess publicly on the lid of the sarcophagus that both he and Aurelia Stratoneikiane were Christians was not made lightly by Aurelius Gaius.

Christianity is not an officially sanctioned religion, but neither is it prohibited. Aurelius Gaius knows that, in the past, there have been periodic outbreaks of local hostility against Christians and that, in the future, Christians such as himself might risk persecution. Their Christian faith, however, has been so important to them during their life together that Aurelius Gaius felt that for him to refrain from public declaration of this fact would be to hide the essence of their being.

As he enters Thyateira, Aurelius Gaius is sure he made the right decision about the public confession of Christianity on his wife's and his own future final resting place. The potential risk is worth being honest about his Christian identity—something most of his neighbors back in Chorianos know anyway.

Aurelius Gaius has been to Thyateira on many occasions. Although Chorianos is within the territory of Hierokaisareia, not within that of Thyateira, Thyateira is the more important city in the neighborhood and about the same distance from Chorianos. Thyateira rose to prominence primarily as a garrison town on the imperial post-road from Pergamon to the east. Thyateira is the first city where couriers taking the northern route rest and change horses before going on to Sardis, Philadelphia, Laodikeia, and beyond. Riders taking the southern route from Pergamon stop first at Smyrna, then Ephesus, and also rest at Laodikeia on their way to the eastern provinces. Aurelius Gaius has heard on more than one occasion that the seven churches in the seven cities that are part of the northern and southern imperial postal routes in the Roman province of Asia were chosen to be the recipients of the seven letters from the risen Christ recorded in the book of Revelation because of their strategic locations. Aurelius Gaius has no doubt the tradition is accurate. Just as in the imperial system, mail for the surrounding cities and villages is dropped off at each of the "Seven Cities of Asia" by imperial messengers and then taken by other couriers to neighboring settlements, so the seven letters in the book of Revelation were able to be copied and distributed to nearby Christian communities using the local Christian "postal system."[2]

Aurelius Gaius wonders who brought a copy of the letter written to the church at Thyateira to the church at Chorianos. Whoever it was, that person's name has been lost to posterity—just as he suspects will happen to his own name. Aurelius Gaius, however, feels honored to be one of the anonymous Christian courier's successors. The official reason for his own trip to Thyateira today is to meet with the leaders of the Christian community here and carry back to Chorianos not only the latest news but also any mail to his co-religionists back home. Aurelius Gaius is glad that, on the spur of the moment, he made the decision to go today so he would be preoccupied with something other than his overwhelming grief.

The long journey has certainly helped and he is actually looking forward to meeting with the bishop, the presbyters, and deacons at Thyateira. As he passes the synagogue, Aurelius Gaius thinks back to Lydia, the "seller of purple," the "God-fearer" from Thyateira who, according to the tradition in the Acts of the Apostles, which he has read, was the first convert made by the apostle Paul outside of Asia.[3]

Aurelius Gaius passes the temple erected in honor of Helios Tyrimnaios Pythios Apollo, the sun-god who is the titular deity of Thyateira. He remembers a fresco he has seen of Jesus portrayed as Christos-Helios, the ultimate sun-god whose birthday is now being celebrated on December 25, just after the winter solstice—the period for the traditional festival of pagan sun-gods. Aurelius Gaius is relieved that, at least among his closest friends and relatives, Christ, rather than Helios-Apollo, is now worshiped.

Aurelius Gaius next walks past a large rectangular building. It is the civic basilica made of huge blocks of stone. It also was once a pagan temple but is now the place that, ever since the emperor Caracalla a few years ago made Thyateira the center of a new conventus, or judicial assembly, functions as the location of the court of justice whenever the proconsul visits the city. Aurelius Gaius finds himself wondering whether Christian communities in cities as large as Thyateira might ever be large enough or safe enough and wealthy enough to own basilicas in which to worship. He quickly dismisses the thought as ridiculous and fanciful.

Clustered around the civic basilica are a number of buildings that are the meeting places for the various guilds, such as that of "the purple sellers" to which Lydia presumably once belonged. Aurelius Gaius has heard that the prophetess referred to in the book of Revelation simply as "Jezebel," the name of the treacherous wife of the Jewish king Ahab, condoned Christian participation in the cultic activities associated with the professional guilds. Aurelius Gaius finds this difficult to believe. Surely a prophetess would not teach her followers to compromise themselves and the Christian faith in such a way. Certainly all the other prophetesses with whom Aurelius Gaius is familiar, such as Ammia of Philadelphia and Maximilla and Priscilla of Pepouza, would not have promoted a lenient attitude toward cultic participation.

Aurelius Gaius is fascinated by prophets and prophetesses but is not quite sure what to make of them. What he has learned about the New Prophecy, a movement now with numerous followers not only in Phrygia where it began but also in Lydia, his own region of Asia, intrigues him. In his grief, he can certainly understand the New Prophecy's strong teaching against re-marriage after the death of one's spouse. All he wants is his Aurelia Stratoneikiane back, no one else—ever. He is not so sure, however, about the strange manner of prophesying, which he has been told, was the means by which the oracles of the New Prophets were uttered. Ecstatic trances and frothing at the mouth sound too much like pagan practices.

With mixed feelings and thoughts about the New Prophecy still occupying him, Aurelius Gaius finally reaches the home of the Christian bishop of Thyateira. He is shown into the atrium where he is soon joined by his host and the presbyters and deacons of Thyateira. Aurelius Gaius is surprised and a little shocked to learn from the Christian clergy of Thyateira that, since his last visit, the whole Christian community in Thyateira has completely embraced the New Prophecy.

Sources:

IMont 13; Rev 2:18–28; Acts 14:14–15; 1 Kgs 16:31, 21:5–25; Epiphanius, *Pan.* 51.33.4.

Notes

1. *IMont* 13. Although the inscription on the lid which covered the sarcophagus which once held the body of Aurelia Stratoneikiane (and later, presumably, that of Aurelius Gaius) is dated, the part of the lid which contained the year is now broken away. The year, however, falls most likely between 212 C.E. (when the use of the *quasi-praenomina* Aurelia/us became popular) and 248 C.E. (after which, given the "Decian Persecution," open profession of Christianity on public monuments such as sarcophagi would have been extremely problematic); see Tabbernee 1997b, 100–103. The year given here for the events described (ca. 223 C.E.) falls within the most likely range of dates for the inscription and is also the most likely date for the year in which the Christian community at Thyateira (Akhisar) became completely Montanist; see Tabbernee 1978, 766; 1997b, 136–37. According to Epiphanius, the church at Thyateira remained totally Montanist for a period of 112 years (*Pan.* 51.33.4).

2. For the theory that each of the "Seven Cities of Asia," referred to in the book of Revelation was the center of a Christian, as well as imperial, "postal district," see Ramsay 1904, 191–92, 196.

3. Acts 14:14–15.

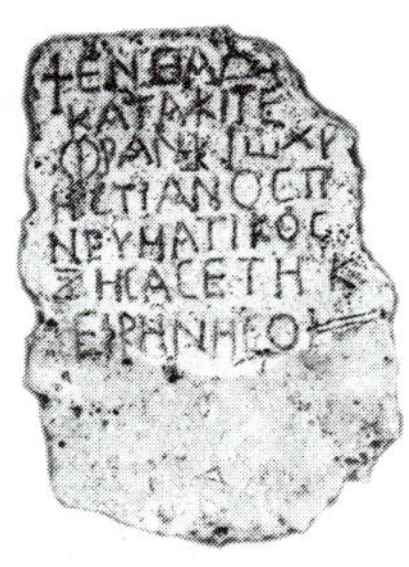

Chapter 18

Ikonion, Phrygian Galatia, ca. 233 C.E.

The New Prophecy is condemned on two counts

Firmilian has never seen so many Christian leaders in one place at one time. Although he is a bishop himself, having recently been appointed bishop of Caesarea in Cappadocia, he is not quite sure how to behave in the company of so many venerable men. Should he go up to some of them and introduce himself and perhaps be deemed too rash, or should he wait for others to come to him and perhaps be deemed too reticent—or even stand-offish?

Like his fellow-bishops, Firmilian has traveled from his home town to Ikonion, a city in originally Phrygian territory but now part of the province of Galatia. Firmilian is excited to be in Ikonion—a city evangelized by St. Paul himself. On the way, Firmilian stopped at Derbe and Lystra, two other south Galatian cities visited by St. Paul on each of his three missionary journeys. But nothing he saw at Derbe and Lystra had prepared Firmilian for Ikonion. Derbe and Lystra are small, unimpressive towns built on large mounds rising out of the surrounding landscape like artificial mountains created out of the ruins of preceding settlements. Ikonion, on the other hand, is a large city, built on a vast level plain, well laid out with broad streets. As he entered the city via the main gate, he was greeted by the happy sounds of street vendors hawking their wares and by the delicious aroma of the fruits and vegetables sold in the produce stands. Everyone seemed to be bustling around, busily engaged in the day's activities. After getting directions, he had finally reached his destination, the home of Paulinus, a layperson—but one who is a gifted orator and who was allowed by the former bishop of Ikonion, a man named Celsus, even to preach to the congregation.

Paulinus is also a good conversationalist, and on his first night in Ikonion Firmilian was regaled with many stories about the history of the church in Ikonion. Firmilian was fascinated by Paulinus' account of St. Paul and Thecla, a young woman who heard Paul preach in Ikonion. Thecla was so persuaded by St. Paul's message that, although she was betrothed to a prominent man in the city, she broke off her engagement, cut her hair, disguised herself as a man, and, having become a disciple of St. Paul, was commissioned by him to preach the gospel.

Firmilian had never heard of, or read about, Thecla, but Paulinus showed him a codex containing the *Acts of Paul and Thecla*. Drinking some of the wonderful

Cappadocian wine Firmilian brought with him, the two men had stayed up late into the night reading the codex. Firmilian particularly liked the part where Thecla befriended the lion who was supposed to kill her in the amphitheater, although the young Cappadocian bishop was not quite sure he believed that detail of the lengthy account of Thecla's life and ministry. After he went to bed, Firmilian wondered how much—if any—of the story of Paul and Thecla was really true.

That was last night. Now Firmilian is standing in the midst of the large group of fellow-bishops, wishing he knew whether or not to introduce himself. Fortunately, his dilemma is solved by an elderly man who approaches him. With a broad smile, the elderly bishop introduces himself and some of his colleagues—all bishops from Cilicia, the large province to the south of Phrygia, Galatia, and Cappadocia along the coast of the Internum Mare, the Mediterranean Sea. Soon they are joined by bishops from Galatia and Phrygia. Before long, Firmilian feels at ease. The elderly bishop who has taken a fatherly interest in him points out some other bishops he knows from even further afield. This, Firmilian realizes for the first time, is a very significant church council. He is simultaneously humbled and proud to be a participant.[1]

Following the mandatory opening speeches, the presiding bishop explains the main reason why the council has been convened. Each of the regions represented by the bishops present at the council is facing a pastoral problem that is, at the same time, a theological and a liturgical problem. Former adherents of the New Prophecy wish to become members of the Christian communities where those assembled at Ikonion are bishops. Consistent policies and procedures are needed, as ad hoc decisions are being made by the various bishops in their own local communities. Some bishops welcome the former followers of Montanus, Maximilla, and Priscilla with open arms, making no demands on them; others treat them like pagans or, at best, as catechumens, requiring them to be baptized as new Christians—even if they have already been baptized by clergy belonging to the New Prophecy movement. The main questions to be resolved, the presiding bishop points out, are whether adherents of the New Prophecy should be considered Christians or heretics and whether, in either case, the baptism performed by their clergy can be deemed valid.

Almost immediately the room where the assembled bishops are seated erupts with the sound of heated arguments. Some bishops argue passionately that as the followers of Montanus, Maximilla, and Priscilla believe in the same God all Christians do and as they teach the same as orthodox Christians do about Jesus Christ, there is no reason to reject the validity of their baptism. Other bishops, equally vehemently, argue that the issue is not so simple. Even if the adherents of the New Prophecy are orthodox with respect to God the Father and God the Son, their erroneous view of the Holy Spirit makes their whole Trinitarian theology questionable.

After the spontaneous hubbub settles down slightly, one of the bishops rises to his feet and declares: "Those who do not possess the true Lord the Father cannot possess, either, the truth on the Son or on the Holy Spirit."[2] All the bishops present concur with this statement. It is clear that those who hold heretical views about God the Father cannot possess the truth about the other members of the Trinity. They all agree that a basic principle has been clarified—a principle that works beginning with any member of the Trinity. Those who hold erroneous views about Christ cannot possess the truth about God the Father or about the Holy Spirit; those who are in error about the Holy Spirit must also be in error about the Father and the Son.

A hushed silence pervades the room. The assembled bishops have the answer to the first question posed to them by the presiding bishop. The presiding bishop summarizes what they have been saying about the adherents of the New Prophecy, whom he refers to as "Cataphrygians":

> Those called Cataphrygians, who try to claim they have new prophecies, can possess neither the Father nor the Son, because they do not possess the Holy Spirit. For if we ask them what Christ they preach, they will reply that they preach the one who sent the spirit that spoke through Montanus and Prisca. But since we perceive that there was no spirit of truth but only of error, we draw the conclusion that those who defend their false prophecy against the faith of Christ cannot possess Christ himself.[3]

The silence is broken by loud acclamations of assent. All the bishops agree: the adherents of the New Prophecy *are* heretics. Despite what they teach about God the Father and about Christ, their view of the Paraclete is in error and therefore they do not belong to Christ and Christ certainly does not belong to them.

The answer to the second question put before the council is also becoming crystal clear. Although the Cataphrygians have been baptized "in the name of the Father, Son, and Holy Spirit," they have not been baptized in the name of the *true* Holy Spirit. Therefore, they have not been baptized in the name of the *true* Father or the *true* Son—invalidating the whole ritual. Before the assembled bishops can vote on the matter, one of the bishops points out that baptism by Cataphrygians is invalid not only because of their erroneous view of the Holy Spirit but also because it is performed outside the context of the true Church. Like all heretics and schismatics, the Cataphrygians, having separated themselves from the Church of God, do not possess true charismata. Therefore, not having the spiritual authority to baptize, baptism by Cataphrygians is nothing but an empty ritual devoid of power and grace. Again, all the other bishops, including Firmilian, agree.

The formal vote is a foregone conclusion. While at the beginning of the council the bishops had been divided over the issue of whether adherents of the New Prophecy should be baptized if they want to join the catholic church, now there is complete unanimity on the matter. The followers of Montanus, Maximilla, and Priscilla have to be *baptized* if they desire membership in the one and only true Church. The former adherents of the New Prophecy may have undergone a ritual performed by heretical "clergy," but this ritual is not baptism. The so-called clergy may have used the same liturgical formula as catholic clergy but, while the words are identical, the content behind the words is not. The erroneous teaching about the Holy Spirit by the Cataphrygians perverts the meaning of the whole formula. Moreover, as schismatics as well as heretics, Cataphrygian clergy are pseudo-clergy who have neither the ecclesial authority to baptize nor the spiritual power to mediate the divine grace that makes true baptisms efficacious. Only *within the true Church* and only when performed by *real* clergy is baptism *baptism.*[4]

The next day, Firmilian says goodbye to Paulinus, his host, and begins the long journey home to Caesarea in Cappadocia. He is glad he came to the council. Not only has he met and made good friends in his fellow bishops, but he has learned exactly what to do when former members of heretical or schismatic groups, such as the adherents of the New Prophecy, want to be admitted to his own congregation. Just outside of Ikonion Firmilian stops, looks back over the city, then turns around and walks briskly down the road that will eventually take him to Caesarea. As he does he wonders how, in specific ways, he will put into practice what he has learned in Ikonion.

Sources:

Firmilian, *Ep., ap.* Cyprian, *Ep.* 75.7.1–4, 75.19.4; Acts 14:1–26, 16:6, 18:23; Eusebius, *Hist. eccl.* 6.19.18; *Act. Paul.* 33; *Act. Paul. et Thecl.*

Caesarea, Cappadocia, ca. 235/6 C.E.
Firmilian deals with a troublesome prophetess

Firmilian has been back home in Caesarea for almost two years now, but he often still thinks about the Council of Ikonion he attended. Not until this spring, however, did he have the opportunity to put into practice what he learned at the council. No former Cataphrygians have asked him if they can join his church. But now there is a woman in their midst, a prophetess, whom he suspects may, at the very least, have been influenced by the New Prophecy.

One day, in a state of ecstasy like that of the original New Prophets, the woman announced herself as a prophetess filled by the Holy Spirit, convincing many that she is a genuine prophetess. She backed up her claim with a number of seemingly miraculous acts. Last winter, which was a very harsh one, she claimed the Holy Spirit told her to walk barefoot in the snow. She did so, for all to see. Amazingly, she appeared to be completely unhurt by her walk. When some of the women examined her feet, there were no signs whatsoever of frostbite or even blisters! Firmilian wonders, however, whether the woman had been up to some kind of trickery—perhaps she had covered her feet with special ointment. More likely, her feet were spared by an evil spirit rather than by the Paraclete. Firmilian cannot imagine why the Holy Spirit would order the woman to walk barefooted in the snow, but an *evil* spirit might just pull such a stunt.

The woman also claimed that the Holy Spirit's powers through her were so great that she could cause the ground to tremble—and, sure enough, soon the area around Caesarea experienced earthquakes. Such earthquakes, however, occurred not only in Caesarea but throughout the whole of Cappadocia and in the neighboring province of Bithynia-Pontus. The earthquakes were so severe that whole cities were swallowed up by huge chasms, and they were so frequent that, as in other times of natural disasters Christians were blamed for causing them. The general population believed that the gods were angry because Christians refused to worship any deity other than their own. A fierce backlash against Christians had resulted in Cappadocia; the governor, Serenianus, proving himself to be a relentless persecutor.

Many of Firmilian's parishioners fled Caesarea because of the persecution, escaping to neighboring provinces where there were neither earthquakes nor local persecutions. How the new, self-proclaimed, prophetess in their midst could attribute the earthquakes to the Holy Spirit and why some people saw the earthquakes as evidence of her power is beyond Firmilian's comprehension. If anything, the woman or, more likely, the *evil* spirit that possesses her, is an opportunist. Knowing that earthquakes in the region come in series, she predicted seismic activity, as any informed person could have done, so she simply could pretend to have genuine prophetic powers.[5]

That the woman is one of the dreaded Cataphrygians seems plausible to Firmilian not only because of her ecstatic manner of prophesying and her claims to be filled by the Holy Spirit, but because she repeatedly says that she is on her way to Jerusalem. Some of those who hear her say this think she means Jerusalem in Syria Palaestina and that she also came from there. Firmilian, on the other hand, suspects that she may be referring to Pepouza in Phrygia—the place which Montanus named Jerusalem in reference to the New Jerusalem mentioned in the book of Revelation. Firmilian regrets that, when he was at Ikonion in Phrygian Galatia he didn't travel the extra distance to visit Pepouza personally. Despite the risk of being contaminated by evil spirits, he would have liked to see with his own two eyes the city that is still the hotbed of the Cataphrygian heresy.[6]

Firmilian looks out the window of his tablinum and notices a large gray cat stepping carefully around the few flowers that have blossomed in the crocus and lily beds in his small garden. The cat, moving noiselessly and purposefully, has her eye on a small bird trying to pull a worm out of the moist ground. Firmilian is relieved when the bird, just in the nick of time, flies out of the reach of his neighbor's cat. And he is glad for the signs of spring he has just witnessed. At least the prophetess won't be walking in the snow for a while—although he secretly wishes she would walk to Pepouza in Phrygia, to Jerusalem in Syria Palaestina, or to anywhere else outside his pastoral jurisdiction.

Firmilian also wishes he had learned about the presence of the woman earlier. She arrived on the scene, however, not in Caesarea itself but in one of the nearby parishes administered by a presbyter who functioned as a *chorepiskopos* or "country bishop." The woman so duped this rustic presbyter and a deacon that they united with her. Firmilian has heard rumors about the physical extent of the "uniting" but is prepared to leave these alone as simply rumors.[7] The most troublesome aspect of the cooperation between the presbyter, deacon, and prophetess, for Firmilian, is that the former has allowed the latter to celebrate the Eucharist and perform baptisms.

Firmilian is astounded that the woman uses the proper liturgical formula for both her celebration of the Eucharist and her performance of baptisms. Perhaps the rustic presbyter taught her these formulae. In this way, both sacraments administered by the prophetess appear to be in accordance with proper ecclesiastical norms. From what he learned at Ikonion, however, Firmilian knows how to counter the woman's claims and activities: the proper formulae, by themselves, are no guarantee of orthodoxy nor of the validity of a sacrament. Fortunately, an exorcist has just confronted the spirit possessing the woman and demonstrated that that spirit, previously deemed to be the Holy Spirit is, in fact, an evil spirit. Applying the principle agreed on at Ikonion, Firmilian himself can now also demonstrate that because the false prophetess is controlled by an evil spirit, which she erroneously claims is the Holy Spirit, she is a heretic and that the Trinitarian formulae she uses in the administration of the sacraments are not in accordance with ecclesiastical rule. Consequently, the rituals she performs are not truly sacramental.

Always an optimist, Firmilian hopes the woman will see the error of her ways, repent, and ask to be baptized into the true Church. But somehow Firmilian doubts this will be the outcome of the conversation he is about to have with the troublesome prophetess.

Sources:

Firmilian, *Ep., ap.* Cyprian, *Ep.* 75.10.1–5, 75.11.1.

Notes

1. The only extant account of the Council of Ikonion (Konya), which was held somewhere between 230 and 235 C.E., is contained in a letter from Firmilian, the bishop of Caesarea (Kayseri) in Cappadocia (ca. 230–268), written to Cyprian, bishop of Carthage (ca. 249–258) in 256 (*Ep., ap.* Cyprian, *Ep.* 75). The translations of quotations from Firmilian's letter are taken from Clarke 1989, 82–83, 90. Firmilian attended the council personally, but whether he stayed with Paulinus, while possible, is conjecture. Who presided over the council is unknown. Presumably it was the bishop of Ikonion, who may still have been Celsus, although the extant data regarding Paulinus, the lay preacher, and Celsus, the bishop who allowed him to preach (Eusebius, *Hist. eccl.* 6.19.18), predate the date of the council.

2. See Firmilian, *Ep., ap.* Cyprian, *Ep.* 75.7.3.

3. See Firmilian, *Ep., ap.* Cyprian, *Ep.* 75.7.3.

4. The decision made at the Council of Ikonion regarding the necessity of former Montanists to be (re)baptized if they wanted to (re)join the 'catholic church' is consistent with later canonical decisions (e.g., Council of Laodikeia [between ca. 343 and 381], *Can.* 8; First Council of Constantinople [381], *Ps.-can.* 7; Basil of Caesarea, *Ep.* 188.1) and, therefore, may have served as a precedent for such later conciliar and episcopal decisions.

5. Firmilian's account of the unnamed prophetess in his region, like his account of the Council of Ikonion (see above), is preserved because his letter containing these accounts is preserved within the corpus of the extant correspondence of Cyprian of Carthage. The events described in connection with the Montanist, or Montanist-like, prophetess occurred, according to Firmilian, about twenty-two years before he wrote his letter to Cyprian, soon after the reign of Alexander Severus (*Ep., ap.* Cyprian, *Ep.* 75.10.1). As Alexander, who became emperor in 222, was murdered in March 235, Firmilian is probably referring to the spring of that year, in which case the episode of the woman walking bare-

footed in the snow must have taken place during early 235—perhaps even in Alexander's time. It is also possible that the intended period extended into 236.

6. The Montanist identity of the prophetess, while likely and often claimed or taken for granted by scholars (e.g., Aland 1960, 116–17; Elm 1989, 221–22; Trevett 1996, 97–98, 168, 171 [= Quintilla?], 188–89, 192), is by no means certain and may not be accurate (see de Labriolle 1913a, 483–87; A. Jensen 1996, 186–87). As Jensen (187) points out, Firmilian himself never calls the prophetess a Cataphrygian, although he is obviously familiar with this designation for Montanists (*Ep., ap.* Cyprian, *Ep.* 75.7.3), nor does he link 'Jerusalem' with 'Pepouza' in the letter itself (*Ep., ap.* Cyprian, *Ep.* 75.10.3). Whether Firmilian privately had suspicions about the possible Montanist connections of his troublesome prophetess is speculation on my part.

7. Numerous scholars have presumed a sexual involvement of the unnamed prophetess with the rustic presbyter and with the deacon (e.g., most recently Heine 1989b, 103), but this reads too much into the word *commiscerentur* (*ap.* Cyprian, *Ep.* 75.10.4). Firmillian does not take action against the three people concerned for sexual misconduct. The alleged sexual connotations normally blamed on women rather than on men, appear to comprise nothing but a stereotypical trope. The view that the name of the presbyter was "Rusticus" (e.g., Heine 1989b, 103) is, in my opinion, far less likely than the view that the presbyter was a *chorepiskopos. Chorepiskopoi,* "country bishops" (i.e., presbyters with the [*quasi*] status of a bishop), were numerous throughout Cappadocia during the third and fourth centuries; see S. Mitchell 1993, 2:70–72.

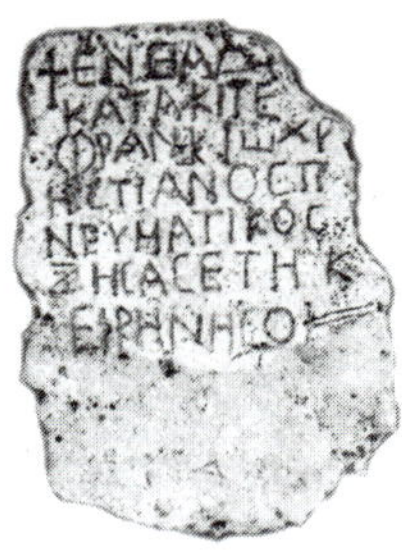

Chapter 19

Colonia Prima Flavia Augusta Caesarea, Syria Palaestina, ca. 240 C.E.

Firmilian and Origen discuss the New Prophecy

Origen is leaning against the railing of the main pier that encloses the Herodian harbor. It is a long pier, and it feels as if he is on a boat rather than on a finger-like protrusion into the Internum Mare. The wooden planks he is standing on are rocking slightly, giving him the distinct feeling of traveling on water. It is a hot day. Thankfully, the sea breeze blowing gently on his face is cooling him down. To his right, he can see two large boats, one after the other, entering the narrow opening into the huge rectangular harbor. The second boat is sailing far too fast for the comfort of the captain of the first boat, and Origen hears angry shouts telling the master of the second boat to slow his pace. Almost immediately, by the expert use of ropes, the wind is taken out of the sails of the encroaching vessel and a potential accident is averted.

Watching the progress of both boats from the outer harbor into the inner harbor toward their respective berths near the shore, Origen has a good view of the city built by Herod the Great. He can also see Herod's magnificent palace jutting out from the coast, built on a promontory. Origen presumes that Herod, like himself, enjoyed that spectacular seascape. Herod had certainly known what he was doing when he took over the originally Phoenician naval base named Turris Stratonis, Strato's Tower, after the round stone fort built at this part of the coast by King Strato I of Sidon. The site was perfectly located to become not only the premier port of this region of Syria Palaestina but also the capital of the province. With favorable winds, it takes only ten days to sail from here at Caesarea Maritima, as the city is called by the locals, to Rome. The harbor itself is the size of Piraeus, the port of Athens, and the population of the city, as Origen knows from first-hand experience, is still growing rapidly through the arrival of permanent immigrants. From where he is standing, Origen can see newly built houses on the slopes of the hills beyond the Herodian wall. Fortunately the city's two aqueducts, the longer one coming all the way from Mount Carmel seven miles away, provide ample supplies of clean, fresh water for old and new residents alike.

Origen turns around to look out over the sea again. The sun is no longer directly overhead, so he can tell exactly which way is west. Not that he can see that far, but about two hundred and fifty miles away in a more or less westerly direction is Alexandria, the city where he was born and where, until a decade ago, he had lived all his life. Origen finds himself reminiscing about his childhood in the city founded by and named after Alexander the Great. Even as a young boy, he used to do what he is doing now—go out on the pier of one or another of Alexandria's harbors, and stare out to sea, past the Pharos Lighthouse—one of the Seven Wonders of the World. He remembers having to jostle the crowds on the way to the harbors. Not even Alexandria's exceptionally broad streets were wide enough to cope with a population of almost half a million people.

As a young man, he also used to love to go to Alexandria's library, the largest collection of books in a single place in the whole world. It was said that the library contained five hundred thousand books—as many as every man, woman, and child in Alexandria. He is sure his love of reading and writing originated in those early visits to the library. Origen smiles to himself as he reflects on his own immense literary output: he is doing his own part in producing more books for people, especially Christians, to read. He is in the process of writing commentaries on every book considered by Christians to be sacred and, among others, has already written works on prayer, martyrdom, and on first principles.

Origen is particularly pleased with his *De principiis* ("On First Principles") which he had based on the notes of his early lectures to catechumens—people being instructed in the Christian faith as part of their preparation for baptism. Origen remembers vividly, as if it occurred only yesterday, when Demetrius, the bishop of Alexandria, came to him and asked him to take charge of the catechetical instruction for the whole Christian community in Alexandria. What an honor that was, and Origen still feels the glow of pride he felt as he eagerly accepted the appointment. He was so young! Not even quite out of his teens—but he had been a brilliant student under Clement, his predecessor as head of the catechetical school. Demetrius obviously, at least *at that time,* had great confidence in his capabilities and potential.

Origen smiles again to himself, while the wind from the Internum Mare continues to play with his beard. This time, the smile is provoked by some slight embarrassment. He is sure Demetrius was probably also influenced in choosing him to be chief catechist because of the zeal for martyrdom he had demonstrated.

Those were difficult times. A fierce local persecution had broken out. Some, including Clement, left Alexandria for safer provinces. Others, including Origen's own father Leonides, were imprisoned and subsequently put to death—Leonides by being decapitated. Origen remembers the desire for martyrdom rushing through his own veins at the time. He wanted to rush forward recklessly to join his father. Wisely, his family prevented him from doing so, but he is glad that he had at least sent his father a letter in prison entreating him not to submit to the officials' demands out of concern for his family. Origen assured Leonides that he would look after his mother and his six younger brothers. "Take care not to change your mind because of us," he had written,[1] exhorting his father to receive the crown of martyrdom which, for the time being, was denied him personally.

The embarrassment that was evoking his wry smile now wasn't so much about his youthful abortive attempt at provoking his own martyrdom. He had learned long since then that one should wait patiently for God to reveal through the circumstances of unprovoked arrest or through a special sign such as a dream or vision whether one is chosen to be a martyr. His embarrassment is due to another youthful zealous act he carried out after he had taken over Clement's earlier duties. One day, he had been stunned by the words of Jesus he was reading in one of the Gospels:

> For there are eunuchs who have been so from birth, and there are eunuchs who have been made eunuchs by others, and there are eunuchs who have made themselves eunuchs for the sake of the kingdom of heaven. Let anyone accept this who can.[2]

Origen remembers the excitement these words had evoked in him. If he could not literally carry out the command of Jesus to take up the cross and follow him to die a martyr's death, he could certainly carry out the command to become a eunuch literally. Not everyone was able to accept this command, Jesus had said, but some could, and Origen determined that, whatever it took, he would deny himself for the sake of being a faithful follower of Jesus. What was a little pain compared to the pain Jesus had suffered—or to what his father had suffered as a martyr?

The gruesome act required numerous attempts to accomplish. At first, despite his resolve, he couldn't make his hand grip the knife he had sharpened and honed for hours beforehand. He was still shaking when he made the first cut along the outside of his right testicle. He had screamed out in pain and nearly fainted at the sight of all the blood. There was so much blood and so much pain. How he had remained conscious while he sliced through the skin of his other testicle and then, holding his scrotum, had forced both testicles out of their pouches and cut them off, is something that amazed Origen afterward and ever since. He vaguely remembers binding his privates with strips of cloth to stop the bleeding, but this had been a difficult task, as there was no easy way to secure the bandages that kept falling off. For days he felt like a baby in a diaper.

Origen had hoped to keep his act a secret—a secret between him and God. But the bloody bandages and the fever that racked him for days and nearly killed him revealed what he had done. News of his action spread throughout the Alexandrian Christian community. Demetrius, when he learned of it, had even visited Origen personally. Origen still remembers how the bishop praised him for his zeal and how he encouraged him to continue with his catechetical instruction, once he was completely healed. The act had certainly enhanced his reputation as a teacher who took the faith seriously.

Today, standing on the pier at Caesarea Maritima, Origen is no longer sure that his act had been a wise one. He now knows so much more about how to interpret scripture than he did then. Indeed, Origen finds his mind wandering to the system of interpreting sacred texts he developed and that many of his former students are now using. Not every text is meant to be taken literally or even historically. There are metaphorical, allegorical, and even typological aspects of the words of scripture that often point to a spiritual meaning far more significant than the literal. Origen is now convinced that Jesus, in the Gospel attributed to Matthew, was really talking about *voluntary celibacy* rather than *castration,* and, in some ways, he regrets his youthful impulsiveness. On the other hand, as he has always admired the ascetics of the church, Origen is glad he is one of them—even though it cost him dearly.

As Origen has been thinking about his childhood and his youth in Alexandria, the sun has shifted further west and is now much lower in the sky. Origen knows he needs to hurry home. He is expecting a house guest: Firmilian, bishop of Caesarea in Cappadocia. Origen is delighted that he is finally going to meet the bishop of the city across the Internum Mare that bears the same name as the city where he himself resides—both cities named after members of the imperial family. Firmilian's city, Origen knows, was named after Tiberius Caesar. Origen, however, is proud that *his* Caesarea is a Roman colony named after Augustus, the *first* Roman emperor.

Origen has only been home for a few minutes when there is a knock at the door. The man standing outside, however, is not Firmilian but Theoctistus, the bishop of Caesarea. A few steps behind him is Alexander, the bishop of Jerusalem. Origen and Alexander were fellow students of Clement in Alexandria. Paradoxically, although Christianity started in Jerusalem, Theoctistus, as bishop of Caesarea, the capital of Syria Palaestina, is the more senior bishop. Origen has invited both men to be present to welcome Firmilian. Alexander already knows Firmilian, but both Origen and Theoctistus have yet to meet him personally, although Origen has been corresponding with him for the past two years.

From inside, the three men, a few moments later, hear the distinct sounds of a horse-drawn carriage pull up outside the house. By the time they open the door, the driver is depositing two large bags next to Firmilian who has just stepped out of the carriage. Alexander greets Firmilian warmly but respectfully, and introduces him first to their host, Origen, and then to Theoctistus. Origen, carrying one of the bags, shows Firmilian to the room prepared for his guest by the housekeeper. One advantage of being a eunuch, Origen can't help thinking, is that no one dares spread rumors about his having a female housekeeper living with him. While Origen escorts Firmilian to his room, the housekeeper shows Theoctistus and Alexander to the triclinium. Before long, Origen and Firmilian join the others in the dining room.

Firmilian is hungry after his long journey and the men quickly commence their meal, speaking very little while they delight in the food set before them. All they learn during the meal is that Firmilian arrived, as Origen suspected, on the second of the two boats he had watched entering the harbor that afternoon. Alexander and Firmilian also catch up on news about friends they have in common in

Cappadocian Caesarea—where Alexander served for some time as bishop before coming to Jerusalem.[3]

When the meal itself is over, the four men retire to Origen's large tablinum, a comfortable room crowded with codices, half-finished manuscripts, a couch, and two chairs. Although the day has been a hot one, being so close to the sea means that the evening, as most evenings in Caesarea, is cool. A small but adequate fire has been lit and keeps the men warm.

Firmilian, having his energies restored by the wonderful meal, eagerly asks to hear the details of how Origen ended up in Caesarea Maritima and why he moved from Alexandria. Origen feels his blood pressure rise. He is still furious at the way he was treated in the end by Demetrius, who originally had been such a supporter and mentor to him—even many years after he was appointed head of the catechetical school in Alexandria. Origen tells Firmilian that Demetrius sent him on a number of ecclesiastical visits to other Christian communities, including Rome, where, among others, he met the venerable Hippolytus and spent some time at Hippolytus' school. Gradually, however, Origen informs Firmilian, Demetrius' attitude toward him changed.

Theoctistus interrupts and suggests that Demetrius had become jealous of his famous protogé. He tells Firmilian that Origen visited Caesarea Maritima on one occasion and was asked by him and Alexander to preach to their congregations at Jerusalem and Caesarea. Origen preached magnificent and instructive homilies that greatly enlightened the faithful. When Demetrius heard of it, however, Demetrius complained, stating that laymen should not preach *in ecclesia*. "The layman Paulinus was allowed to preach by Celsus in Ikonion as was Euelpis by Neon in Laranda and Theodorus by Atticus in Synnada—and, no doubt, the same has been allowed in other places,"[4] Alexander asserts, declaring Demetrius to be totally wrong about the matter. Firmilian concurs. He has stayed with Paulinus in Ikonion and knows that the example Alexander cites is certainly true with respect to Ikonion. He doesn't doubt at all the veracity of the other examples.

With a slightly wavering voice that betrays the emotion he still feels over the injustice he suffered, Origen tells Firmilian that the next time he came here and Alexander and Theoctistus asked him to preach again, they first ordained him as a presbyter so that he would no longer be a layman and offend Demetrius. But Demetrius was even more offended by the ordination, claiming that Theoctistus and Alexander had no right to lay hands on *his* Origen. Matters escalated greatly at that point. While Origen was away, Demetrius, in rapid succession, convened two synods that resulted in Origen's excommunication. Fortunately, Origen tells Firmilian while looking directly at Theoctistus and Alexander, his friends in Syria Palaestina did not abandon him. He gladly moved to Caesarea Maritima, along with Ambrose, his patron.

As by now Firmilian is again feeling the effects of his long journey, Origen promises to tell him the story of Ambrose tomorrow, and the Cappadocian bishop heads off to bed. Theoctistus and Alexander also say goodnight to their host. Alexander will stay the night with Theoctistus before leaving for Jerusalem but promises to return frequently while Firmilian is here.

The next morning Firmilian rises early to find Origen already at work in his study. He is making some notes for his *Commentary on Titus,* which is one of his current projects. Origen works on multiple writing projects concurrently. That way he doesn't get bored—but he finds that sometimes one project interferes with another. Therefore, he is in the habit of making notes that serve as aids to subsequent dictation. He has decided that, later in the morning, he will show Firmilian how he produces his manuscripts—but to do so will require a walk.

As Firmilian enters the room, Origen looks up from his notes and asks what Firmilian knows about the *Cataphryges,* that is, the adherents of the New Prophecy movement. Firmilian tells him that, in fact, he knows quite a lot. Indeed, when he stayed with the lay preacher Paulinus, who had been mentioned last evening, he was in Ikonion to attend a church council, whose main purpose was to deal with the pastoral problems presented by Cataphrygians wanting to join catholic Christianity. Firmilian explains that, although there had at first been disagreement over the issue among the bishops present, it was decided that the Cataphrygians were heretics, not merely schismatics, and that they had to be baptized instead of just being received into fellowship. Origen agrees wholeheartedly.

Firmilian also tells Origen the story of a prophetess who had caused lots of trouble for him a few years ago and whom he suspects was a Cataphrygian.[5] The two men engage in a long discussion about how one can tell a Cataphrygian prophet or prophetess from a genuine prophet or prophetess. They conclude that this is very difficult to do, especially when prophets or prophetesses such as those belonging to the New Prophecy movement make orthodox statements about the Trinity. Firmilian is adamant, however, that any hint of unorthodoxy about the Holy Spirit, as in the case of the Cataphrygians, is to be taken as a sign of heresy.

Origen walks over to Firmilian and shows him a piece of papyrus. Firmilian reads aloud the words written on the papyrus:

> You should not come near to me since I am clean; for I have not taken a wife, nor is my gullet an open tomb but I am a Nazarene of God; just like them, I do not imbibe wine.[6]

Origen learned his lesson about taking statements too literally and knows that the reference to the Nazarene of God is metaphorical, not actual. He tells Firmilian that he has heard this is a Cataphrygian oracle. Firmilian agrees that this is certainly the kind of thing a Cataphrygian prophet might say. Firmilian assumes that the saying is not one of the *logia* of Montanus himself but that it was uttered by a subsequent, later-generation Cataphrygian prophet. As Origen is very interested in exegesis, that is, the correct interpretation of texts, Firmilian explains that the Cataphrygian prophets and prophetesses often employ a free-flowing exegesis of sacred texts, especially the *logia* of Jesus of Nazareth himself, to stimulate their own *logia*. For example, Firmilian points out, this particular *logion* appears to be based, at least in part and very loosely, on Jesus' response to his disciples following his teaching against divorce recorded in the Gospel attributed to Matthew.

The disciples had protested against Jesus' anti-divorce stance and had responded, Firmilian reminds Origen, with the words: "If such is the case of a man with his wife, it is better not to marry."[7] To this Jesus replied: "Not everyone can accept this teaching, but only those to whom it is given."[8]

Origen feels the blood drain from his face. He is as white as a sheet. This is the very text that introduces, what he now understands is Jesus' *metaphorical statement* about making oneself a eunuch for the sake of the kingdom of heaven. How ironic that he, in his youthful enthusiasm to obey Jesus, had misunderstood Jesus' intention, but the Cataphrygian heretics comprehend that the whole "eunuch text" refers not to doing physical damage to oneself but to "not marrying." The same gospel passage that led him to castrate himself led Cataphrygians to refrain from marrying. The heretics, he confesses to Firmilian, had found the less painful alternative to taking the text seriously. Firmilian, nevertheless, points out to Origen that even the Cataphrygians took Jesus' words too literally. Jesus did not command that people not marry—only that they not divorce for frivolous causes. Jesus merely concurred with his disciples that if people didn't take marriage seriously, it would be better if they didn't marry at all.

Origen and Firmilian spend the next half hour debating whether all Cataphrygians remain unmarried. If so, surely the whole movement would have died out or, at least would die out soon. It is more likely, the two men conclude, that total celibacy is the exception rather than the rule even among the adherents of the New Prophecy, but the Cataphrygians as a whole are strictly against divorce and they do not remarry after their spouses die.[9]

When prandium, late breakfast, is over, Origen asks Firmilian if he would like to accompany him to the scriptorium. Firmilian readily agrees as he wants to see exactly how Origen produces so many books so quickly. Origen gathers up some of his notes and other materials, including manuscripts and the papyrus fragment with the Cataphrygian *logion*. He puts everything in a leather bag and places the strap of the bag on a comfortable spot on his shoulder—the walk is going to be longer than usual. Origen has a few surprises for Firmilian on the way.

Origen closes the door of the house behind him and, turning left, the two men walk quickly along the street. The street slopes gently downhill. They pass the hippodrome but do not enter it. Seen one, seen them all, they agree, even though, Origen tells Firmilian, Caesarea's hippodrome is one of the largest in the whole Roman Empire. Origen is eager, however, to show his friend Caesarea's theater, not only because it can seat four thousand spectators but because it has a magnificent view of the city and the harbor. Ten minutes after passing the hippodrome, the men are climbing up the steep steps inside the theater. Slightly out of breath, Origen and Firmilian, halfway to the top, sit down in the middle of one of the circular tiers. Pointing to the stage below them, Origen tells Firmilian that that is where Herod Agrippa used to sit, dressed like a god in silver robes, before he had been eaten by worms and died a few days later, struck down by an angel because of his blasphemy.

From where they are sitting, the men look straight out across the Internum Mare. Firmilian, despite being overjoyed at visiting Origen in Caesarea, feels a little homesick for his own Caesarea across the waters. But here, the two men have a magnificent view of the harbor. The water around the harbor itself is crystal clear. From this distance, they can easily make out the huge stone blocks Herod the Great had lowered into the sea to create the foundations for the harbor. Firmilian can see exactly where his boat had entered the harbor from the north. Even from here he can see the three enormous statues at the entrance he couldn't help but notice yesterday as the boat slipped passed them heading into the harbor.

Now that they have caught their breath, Origen persuades Firmilian to accompany him all the way to the top tier of seats. There, they have a perfect bird's-eye view of the city, the Herodian wall, and Herod the Great's palace. Origen points out the fresh-water swimming pool between the palace and the sea. He tells Firmilian that once, when he was invited to a special function at the palace, he saw in one of the rooms a most spectacular mosaic floor, designed just like a carpet. He had also been shown the room where, according to tradition, St. Paul was imprisoned while Felix was the governor of Judaea.

Firmilian asks Origen whether when Pontius Pilate was governor, Pilate had used Herod's palace as his own headquarters. Assuring Firmilian that the building they are looking at was indeed Pilate's praetorium, Origen can't help thinking how perceptive Firmilian is. Could Firmilian have guessed what Origen is about to show him as the best surprise kept till last?

Without telling him where they are headed, Origen leads Firmilian down the steps of the theater back into the street and, through the southern gate of the Herodian wall, into the city itself. Soon the men are standing in front of a small building. It is the Tiberieum, a temple built in honor of the emperor Tiberius. Inscribed on the wall of the temple, near the entrance, Firmilian reads the words line by line:

> For the people of Caesarea,
> a Tiberieum.
> Pontius Pilate,
> Prefect of Judaea,
> has dedicated.[10]

Firmilian feels the hairs of his neck stand upright and his palms begin to sweat. Seeing, with his two own eyes, in inscribed letters the name of the man who crucified Jesus is a strange experience.

Origen had not intended to upset Firmilian so he leads him away quickly. They are, after all, on their way to the scriptorium. The scriptorium is in a building not far from Theoctistus' house. The scriptorium also functions as the Christian community's library. As they walk, Origen tells Firmilian about his friend and patron Ambrose. Ambrose had once been a follower of the heretic Valentinus. Origen remembers vividly the long conversations it took to persuade Ambrose to "see the light" and to accept the catholic Rule of Faith. However, once convinced, Origen tells Firmilian, Ambrose, a very educated man, became passionately interested in helping him reach an audience as wide as possible by producing numerous books. Ambrose even suggested topics on which to write, including a rebuttal to the claims of the philosopher Celsus that Christianity is a religion fit only for the weak and feeble-minded. Origen promises to give Firmilian a copy of his *Contra Celsum* ("Against Celsus"), a work of which he is very proud and which, like so many others, he has dedicated to Ambrose.

Firmilian asks if Ambrose had followed Origen to Caesarea from Alexandria and Origen smiles knowingly. Without saying another word, they walk the remaining few steps to the scriptorium. Origen opens the door and there to greet them is Ambrose. Not only had Ambrose followed Origen to Caesarea, but he had, out of his own resources, replicated in Caesarea the "literary factory" he had originally established at Alexandria for Origen's benefit. Ambrose even extended the enterprise by employing additional scribes to copy books other than those written by Origen.

Firmilian cannot believe the hive of activity going on within the walls of the building that once was a private residence. Ambrose shows Firmilian around the various parts of the scriptorium. He begins with the library itself, a spacious room with ample shelves. On the shelves, carefully arranged in order, are the exemplars, or originals, of all Origen's works as well as copies of other books made either here or brought from other libraries where they were copied. Firmilian sees, hard at work, a number of scribes, copying in beautiful majuscule script some of the exemplars kept in this room.

From the room next door, Firmilian suddenly hears Origen's loud clear voice. At first Firmilian thinks Origen must be talking to someone but then realizes that Origen is engaged in a monologue, not a dialogue. Slightly puzzled, Firmilian goes to the door of the other room and sees Origen standing at a high narrow desk. On the desk, Firmilian sees the notes and papyrus scraps Origen had packed into his leather bag as they left his house earlier that morning. Barely glancing at his notes, Origen is dictating to some amanuenses, or secretaries, sitting at desks placed at a lower level in front of him. Firmilian is amazed at the speed Origen dictates and the amanuenses write. Ambrose whispers to him that Origen can keep up this kind of dictation for hours on end and that there are seven amanuenses altogether who relieve each other at intervals while Origen keeps dictating.

Ambrose then shows Firmilian another room where scribes are just receiving the first rough copies of this morning's dictation. Their job, Ambrose explains, is to make fair copies of the dictated material, spelling out in full the abbreviations utilized by the amanuenses. Firmilian asks whether these fair copies are then the exemplars such as those he saw in the library. To answer this question, Ambrose takes Firmilian into yet another room where a group of women skilled in calligraphy are working. Ambrose explains that Origen takes the fair copies made by the scribes to check them for errors and, where necessary, make emendations or additions. Sometimes Origen takes the manuscript pages home to work on them in his tablinum, Ambrose tells Firmilian. That explains why this morning Origen had to bring back some manuscripts in his leather bag, Firmilian surmises. Origen then chooses the best fair copy, and that one is turned into the exemplar by one of the women working in this room, Ambrose explains. Only one exemplar can exist for a book in order to reduce the risk of unauthorized versions of the same text. All copies made at the scriptorium derive from a single "original." What happens when a copy made here is recopied elsewhere is, of course, out of their control, Ambrose laments.

When Firmilian and Ambrose return to the room where Origen is dictating, Origen is holding the papyrus with the Cataphrygian *logion* in his hand. He is dictating the final words, which Firmilian read earlier that morning: "I am a Nazarene of God; just like them, I do not imbibe wine." Although, as Ambrose had proudly told Firmilian, Origen could go on dictating for hours, seeing his friends enter the room he decides to stop. After all, today is a special day.

Over the meal they consume hungrily, along with some fine red wine, at Theoctistus' house, Origen, Firmilian, Ambrose, and Theoctistus talk about the Cataphrygians' abstinence from wine. They wonder whether such abstinence is practiced only by those extreme adherents of the New Prophecy movement who also refrain from marrying, or whether abstinence from wine applies to all Cataphrygians. Perhaps other Cataphrygians only abstain from wine during special times of fasting, Firmilian opines. He has heard that the adherents of the New Prophecy engage in xerophagies, or special fasts, during which they are not permitted to drink wine. Origen has also heard this and that the xerophagies last for two weeks during Lent but do not include the Saturdays and Sundays. In that case, the Cataphrygians' Eucharist would not be affected, suggests Ambrose, as they would still be able to partake of the sacred wine on the Lord's Day. The reference to the celebration of the Eucharist among the Cataphrygians sparks a whole new round of discussion. Firmilian, on the basis of what he learned at the Council of Ikonion, easily convinces the others that, as the Cataphrygians are schismatics as well as heretics, any alleged sacrament performed by their clergy is merely an invalid and non-efficacious ritual.

The men talk long into the evening before Origen and Firmilian make their way back to Origen's house. They do so not only this night but almost every night Firmilian is in Caesarea. The two men become firm friends and learn much from one another. On the day Firmilian has to leave, Origen accompanies him to the harbor. Standing on the gangplank that provides the only access to the boat that will take Firmilian back to Cappadocia, Firmilian invites Origen to come and stay with him. As the two men embrace and say their farewells, Origen promises that he will try to find the time to visit Firmilian in the other Caesarea, but secretly he doubts he ever will.[11]

Sources:

Pliny the Elder, *Nat.* 5.14, 5.19; Josephus, *Ant.* 13.11.2, 13.12.2, 15.9.6, 18.3.1, 19.8.2; Tacitus, *Hist.* 2.78; Eusebius, *Hist. eccl.* 6.1–3, 6.6, 6.8, 6.14.10–11, 6.18, 6.19.16–19, 6.23, 6.26–28; Origen, *Comm. Matt.* 15.30; *Princ.; Fr. Tit., ap.* Pamphilus, *Prol. Apol. Orig.* 1; Origen, *Cels;* Firmilian, *Ep., ap.* Cyprian, *Ep.* 75.7.1–4, 75.19.4; Matt 19:3–12; Acts 12:20–23, 23:25; Finegan 1992, 138–39 no. 129 [Pontius Pilate inscription, altered (my translation)], 139–40 no. 130 [Floor Mosaic in Promontory Palace, Caesarea (and fresh-water swimming pool)]; Tertullian, *Jejun.* 15.1–7.

Notes

1. See Eusebius, *Hist. eccl.* 6.2.6.

2. Matt 19:12.

3. For the detail that Alexander of Jerusalem (d. 251) had, during the early third century, been bishop of Caesarea in Cappadocia, see Gregory of Nyssa, *Vit. Greg. Thaum.* [PG 46.905]; Harnack 1908, 2:194 and n. 1.

4. See Eusebius, *Hist. eccl.* 6.19.18.

5. See Chapter 18.

6. Origen, *Fr. Tit., ap.* Pamphilus, *Prol. Apol. Orig.* 1.

7. Matt 19:10.

8. Matt 19:11.

9. It is unlikely that there were any active Montanists either at Alexandria or at Caesarea Maritima during Origen's lifetime. What Origen knew about Montanism, he appears to have learned from written sources, from his own teacher Clement of Alexandria (ca. 140/50–ca. 220), and especially from Firmilian of Caesarea (in Cappadocia) during the latter's visit to Caesarea Maritima. The specific details of Origen's and Firmilian's conversations about Montanism described in this chapter are speculative, although it is impossible to believe that some such conversations did not occur.

10. Finegan 1992, 138–39 no. 129 (altered).

11. Origen (ca. 185–ca. 253) was head of the catechetical school in Alexandria from ca. 203 until ca. 230/31 when he moved permanently to Caesarea Maritima. On the size of the libraries at Alexandria and Caesarea, see Carriker 2003, 31–36. The site of the library at Caesarea Maritima has not (yet) been discovered, nor is it clear from the sources whether, in Origen's time, the library was under episcopal control, contained the Christian community's literary collection, or included a scriptorium; see Carriker 2003, 30–31. My assumption is that the library was housed in a building which was one other than that which was the residence of either Theoctistus or Origen, although it could have been the residence of Ambrose. I also assume that there was a scriptorium, staffed by persons hired by Ambrose; see also Gamble 1995, 158 and n. 41, but see the cautionary comments of Carriker (2003, 16–17) even for a scriptorium at Caesarea in the time of Eusebius (on which see Chapter 22). Firmilian invited Origen to pay him a visit in Cappadocia (Eusebius, *Hist. eccl.* 6.27) but there is no conclusive evidence to indicate that Origen ever did so; see McGuckin 2004, 19–20.

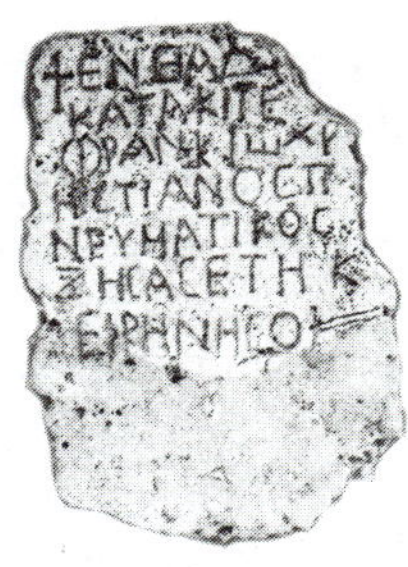

Chapter 20

Smyrna, Ionia, February 23, 250 C.E.

Polycarp remembered

Eutychian has looked forward to this day for weeks. It is a Saturday, but not just any Saturday—it is a special Saturday. It is a Great Sabbath, a high holiday celebrated by the Jewish community and by many Christians, particularly those of Jewish origin. But what makes this such a special day for Eutychian is not that it is a Great Sabbath but that it is the anniversary of the martyrdom of Polycarp.[1]

Polycarp, Smyrna's most famous and most revered bishop, had been burned alive in the stadium in front of a huge crowd. The martyrdom took place almost a hundred years ago but, to the Christians in Smyrna, it is as if Polycarp had been put to death only yesterday. The details of his heroic death are inscribed in the collective memory of the faithful by the annual reading of the graphic account of Polycarp's martyrdom.

Eutychian remembers the first time he heard the story of Polycarp's martyrdom read aloud. He was only a boy then, but the formal reading of the *Martyrdom of the Holy Polycarp*, as the document is called, made a profound impression on him. Eutychian had been sitting with his parents in an aula, a large hall, waiting with dozens of other Christian families for one of the presbyters to bring the exemplar from the church library. While they were waiting, his father told him that, soon after Polycarp died, the Christians at Philomelion, a city in Phrygia, asked for details about Polycarp's martyrdom. One of the presbyters of the time, a man named Evaristus, wrote the account Eutychian is about to hear. Evaristus had deposited the original, the exemplar, in the library of the Christian community at Smyrna, and a copy was sent to Philomelion with the request that the account be sent on to Christians further afield. Eutychian also remembers his father telling him that he heard that Bishop Irenaeus of Lugdunum, Polycarp's disciple, also owned a copy of the *Martyrdom of the Holy Polycarp* and that Irenaeus' copy had been copied many times by others.

Just then a presbyter carrying the exemplar came into the aula. All talking immediately ceased. Every eye in the room was on the beautifully bound original manuscript. The presbyter gave the exemplar to a lector, an officially appointed reader, who, with a deep resonant voice, read aloud the *Martyrdom* to the congregation.

Each person present, Eutychian remembers vividly, was on the edge of his or her seat, listening with rapt attention as the lector first of all read the account of the events leading up to Polycarp's arrest. Polycarp, Eutychian learned, was not the first martyr at that particular time in Smyrna. Polycarp was, in fact, the twelfth. Some of the earlier martyrs were whipped so mercilessly that all the flesh had been ripped off their bodies. The spectators could even see the brave Christians' exposed veins and arteries. Others were condemned and thrown to wild animals. The most famous of these was a young man named Germanicus. Eutychian couldn't believe his ears when the words the lector read from the exemplar described how Germanicus, rather than recanting his faith through fear of the beasts, pulled one of the beasts on top of him so that the reluctant animal might indeed devour him.

Not all of those condemned to the beasts were as brave as Germanicus. The lector had only just finished reading the story of Germanicus when Eutychian heard him read aloud an account of a Christian who turned out to be a coward. Eutychian, since that day, has heard the story of the coward so frequently that he can quote the passage effortlessly:

> Now a certain one named Quintus, a Phrygian having recently come from Phrygia, seeing the beasts, was afraid. But this was the very same person who had compelled both himself and several others to surrender voluntarily. The proconsul repeatedly entreating him earnestly, persuaded this man to swear an oath and to offer sacrifice.[2]

Eutychian remembers being shocked when he first heard these words. What a contrast to Germanicus this man Quintus was. What was so ironic, Eutychian can't help thinking, is that Quintus had *volunteered* for martyrdom by coming forward of his own accord before the governor, declaring himself a Christian. Surely he knew that he would be tortured in some way or thrown to the beasts.

Eutychian's father had told him later that Evaristus had purposely placed the stories of Germanicus and Quintus one after the other to stress the point that the Christian community in Smyrna does not condone reckless behavior in the face of persecution. If God chooses someone to be a martyr, this will be revealed by a dream or a vision or by unprovoked arrest. All faithful Christians may desire the martyr's crown and even pray that God will consider them worthy of martyrdom—but they must not answer their own prayers by recklessly seizing the martyr's crown for themselves by volunteering for martyrdom. Christians must never imitate Quintus. Instead, they should imitate Polycarp, who like Jesus, waited to be arrested. Polycarp's martyrdom was in accordance with the gospel—Quintus' abortive attempt at martyrdom was not.

While reminiscing about the first time he heard the *Martyrdom of the Holy Polycarp* read and about the discussions he had had with his father about the *Martyrdom,* Eutychian is walking along the narrow streets of Smyrna toward the stadium. He wants to see again, on this special day, the arena where Polycarp was martyred. That way, when he hears the story of the martyrdom read this evening, he'll have the image of the arena fresh in his mind.

As he walks, Eutychian wonders who today's lector might be. He himself hasn't been asked to read the *Martyrdom* to the congregation, but he hopes that whoever reads will have a beautiful, clear voice like the lector who read the *Martyrdom* when he himself was but a mere boy. Since that time, Eutychian's family had joined a Christian house-church in Smyrna that was part of the New Prophecy movement. Eutychian still bristles a little whenever he hears people refer to themselves as belonging to the "catholic church" and to him and his family as belonging to "the sect named after the Phrygians." Eutychian believes that they all belong to the same catholic church, even though there is disagreement between the adherents of the New Prophecy and the so-called catholics about the role of the Holy Spirit or Paraclete in using Montanus, Maximilla, and Priscilla as "mouthpieces" to convey new revelations about the way Christians are to live. Fortunately, Eutychian thinks, it is good that, on this day, all Christians in Smyrna celebrate the anniversary of Polycarp's martyrdom—even though they do so in separate communities. Eutychian is glad that his particular community has been able to secure its own copy of the *Martyrdom,* which will be read tonight to those who follow the teachings of Montanus, Maximilla, and Priscilla. Polycarp, after all, is as much *their* martyr as the most holy martyr of the so-called catholic church.

Eutychian enters the stadium and sits down on a seat near the far end. The stadium is totally empty except for him, but to Eutychian, it feels as if Polycarp is there along with the crowd that, on that fateful day so long ago, cried out: "Go and fetch Polycarp!"[3] Although Polycarp had originally decided to stay in Smyrna despite the danger, he had been persuaded by everyone to leave the city, staying some days with friends on an agricultural estate. As was his custom, he spent most of his time there in prayer. It was during one of his times of prayer that he fell into a dream-like trance and saw his pillow on fire. Polycarp, as Eutychian knew from the *Martyrdom,* took this as a sign that it was God's will that he be burned alive. He moved to another estate to make it more difficult for his pursuers to find him, but three days after the vision he was arrested and brought back to Smyrna in a carriage.

On the way back to the city, the eirenarch, or justice of the peace, tried to persuade Polycarp to offer publicly the required sacrifices and to say "Caesar is lord." "What harm is there in saying this, in order to save your life?" the eirenarch had asked Polycarp.[4] Polycarp refused, and he was taken directly to the stadium where the governor and a huge crowd were assembled.

Eutychian's mind must be playing tricks on him. It seems like he can hear the roar of the crowd that filled the stadium as Polycarp was brought into the arena. He can see the stage where the governor sat as he too tried to persuade Polycarp to recant. "Swear by the *tyche,* the 'genius,' of Caesar. Swear, curse Christ, and I will let you go," the governor, whose name was Lucius Statius Quadratus, says.[5] Polycarp replies: "Eighty-six years have I been Christ's servant and he has never wronged me. How can I then revile my king, the one who has saved me?"[6] The governor threatens to throw Polycarp to the wild beasts if he does not recant, and the crowd calls for a lion to be let loose on Polycarp, but Polycarp remains resolute and apparently without fear of the wild animals.

The images of Polycarp's arrest and trial in this very stadium are so real that Eutychian feels he is actually witnessing what transpired here so long ago. He shakes his head and brings himself back to the present. Polycarp, Statius Quadratus, and the crowd are not really in the stadium any longer—but they once were, right here. The written account of Polycarp's martyrdom, which Eutychian knows so well, reports that Statius Quadratus next threatened Polycarp with being burned alive, a punishment also called for by the crowd. This, of course, was exactly what had been revealed to Polycarp in his dream.

Eutychian looks at the very spot where, according to tradition, brushwood and logs had been placed around Polycarp who, with merely his hands bound behind his back, endured the flames without even flinching. Eutychian remembers from earlier readings of the *Martyrdom,* that Evaristus, who had personally witnessed the heroic event, described the flames as a sail in the wind, billowing around Polycarp and baking him, like bread baking in an oven—with a fragrance like that of incense or expensive perfume.

Eutychian wonders whether he himself would be brave enough to endure the flames, especially if he wasn't tied to the stake. He hopes and prays that he wouldn't be like the coward Quintus who had foolishly rushed forward to declare his Christian faith before the officials, only to recant at the first sight of the wild animals to which he was condemned. Eutychian wants to be an imitator of Polycarp, not Quintus, but part of him hopes it will never come to that.

Eutychian has barely closed the door of his house behind him when he hears the loud sound of a large fist pounding on the door. There is lots of shouting, ordering him to open the door. When Eutychian opens it, he sees Polemon, the neokoros, or temple verger, standing there with half a dozen soldiers. Before Eutychian can even ask what they want, one of the soldiers, a huge brute of a man, pushes past Polemon, grabs Eutychian literally by the throat and drags him out into the street. Two other soldiers pounce on Eutychian, turn him around and tie his hands behind his back with a piece of rope.

Still too shocked to speak, Eutychian notices that, off to the side, some other soldiers are guarding a man and a woman whose hands are also tied behind their backs. Eutychian recognizes the man. It is Limnos, one of the presbyters of the Christian community that hasn't adopted the teachings of Montanus, Maximilla, and Priscilla. Eutychian doesn't recognize the woman and, at first, assumes she must be Limnos' wife. Eutychian finally finds his voice and demands to know what is happening. Polemon responds by saying, "Surely you know of the emperor's edict, which commands you to offer incense to the gods!"[7] Eutychian indeed knows about Decius' edict—as does everyone else in Smyrna.

Gaius Messius Quintus Trajanus Decius became emperor less than six months ago, following his defeat of Philip the Arab in battle. Eutychian knew that Decius, wanting to ensure the favor of the gods and the loyalty of the populace, had decided that everyone should swear an oath of loyalty to him, as Caesar, and offer a pinch of incense to the gods. Hundreds of busts of Decius were produced very quickly in various workshops around the Empire so that people could take their oaths in front of the likeness of the emperor and then offer their sacrifices on an altar placed nearby. When they were finished, they received a certificate saying that they had performed the required duty. What Eutychian didn't know at the time was that, in cities such as Smyrna, special commissions had been set up to oversee the process mandated by Decius and that they were using the census rolls to make sure that no one slipped through the net.

Eutychian, Limnos, and the woman are taken by Polemon and the soldiers to the agora, stopping on the way to pick up more Christians. Decius' edict hasn't been promulgated in order to persecute Christians. Decius doesn't really care which god or gods people worship as long as they are prepared also to offer incense to the state gods and swear loyalty to him. When reports come to him about the Christians' refusal to do as he has commanded, he is both perplexed and furious. Decius cannot understand why Christians cannot, or will not, sacrifice and swear by his *tyche,* or genius, his animating spirit.

In order to please the emperor, the special commissioners in Smyrna redoubled their efforts to make sure that everyone, including anyone they know is a Christian, fulfills the requirements of Decius' edict. Polemon, as is fitting due to his position as neokoros, is in charge. He has decided that today, being a holiday, is a good day to round up as many Christians as possible.

When they enter the agora by means of the eastern stoa and its double gates, the agora is crowded with people. Polemon ascends the steps of the tribunal first and sits in the center chair in between the other special commissioners. Two scribes sit at little tables at one end of the tribunal. Next to each scribe is a wooden chest into which copies of the signed certificates of those who have already sacrificed are placed.

Eutychian, Limnos, the woman, and some others are ordered to stand before Polemon, who tells them that it will be wise for them to sacrifice so that they won't be punished. Starting with Limnos, Polemon asks, for the record, "What is your name?" "Limnos," the presbyter answers as the scribe writes it down. "Are you a Christian?" Polemon asks. "Yes, I am," replies Limnos. Then Polemon asks a question that Eutychian, listening to the interrogation, wasn't expecting: "To which church do you belong?" "The catholic one," Limnos responds. "Offer the sacrifice, Limnos," Polemon orders. "I am a Christian," Limnos answers. "At least make a sacrifice to the emperor," Polemon implores. "I do not sacrifice to men, for I am a Christian," are Limnos' last words as he is taken off to jail.

The woman is questioned next. "What is your name?" Polemon asks. Eutychian wonders how many times today alone Polemon has asked the same questions. He is interested, however, to learn this brave woman's name—a detail Polemon undoubtedly knows already but has to ask so that the scribe can write it down. "My name is Makedonia, from the village of Karine," the woman responds. No wonder I don't know her, thinks Eutychian. "Are you a Christian?" "Yes, I am," Makedonia replies. "To which church do you belong?" "The catholic one," is Makedonia's answer. She, too, refuses to sacrifice and is taken away to jail to await the proconsul's arrival for a more formal trial.[8]

The next person to be questioned is one of the men picked up by Polemon and the soldiers after they took Eutychian from his house. This man is also a stranger to Eutychian although the man, obviously, lives in Smyrna. To Eutychian's surprise, when asked about the church he belongs to, the man, whose name is Metrodoros, replies: "The Marcionite one."[9] Eutychian is stunned. He has been standing next to a heretic—a follower of Marcion of Sinope. Ironically, Metrodorus probably thinks that he is standing next to a heretic also. When it is Eutychian's turn to answer the same question, someone else shouts out that Eutychian belongs to "the sect named after the Phrygians."[10] Eutychian himself would have answered that he belongs to the catholic church but is a follower of Montanus, Maximilla, and Priscilla. But in the commotion that erupts Eutychian is not even given the chance to reply and he, like the others, is dragged off to jail to await the arrival of the governor. How long they will have to wait is anyone's guess.

Eutychian, Limnos, Makedonia, Metrodorus, and the other Christians arrested this morning are in the prison trying to figure out why Polemon questioned them about the particular group of Christians to which each one belongs. They did not even realize that officials such as Polemon would be able to distinguish one kind of Christian from another. Nor can they fathom what difference this makes to the special commissioners in charge of ensuring that all the inhabitants of Smyrna obey Decius' edict.

Just then, the outside doors open and a new group of prisoners is brought into the prison. Eutychian and Limnos recognize the newcomers: Pionius, a highly respected presbyter of the catholic church; Sabina, a very holy woman; and Asclepiades, a rather short man full of energy. Strangely, the three of them are wearing chains around their necks. Not chains put there by their captors, but chains, Pionus tells them, he himself made yesterday. Early this morning he placed the chains around his own neck and the necks of Sabrina and Asclepiades *before* their arrest. He did so to show those he was sure were coming to arrest them that he and his companions have no intention of sacrificing and that they may as well be taken to prison immediately. Polemon and the soldiers, of course, did not do this. They tried to make Pionius and the others sacrifice at the altar set up on the tribunal at the agora, just as they had done with Eutychian and his companions. But, as with those arrested earlier in the day, the attempt was an exercise in futility. Frustrated and angry, Polemon had Pionius and his two friends thrown into jail also.

Limnos greets his fellow catholics warmly and introduces Makedonia but doesn't quite know what to do about Eutychian and Metrodorus. As catholics, Limnos and the others shouldn't associate with heretics—but they do, after all, share the same cell, if not quite the same faith. There is an embarrassed silence, broken by Eutychian reminding them that this is the anniversary of Polycarp's death and that, whatever their other differences, they can at least celebrate that anniversary together—as they all hold Polycarp to be a great saint and venerate him as their forefather in the faith. Metrodorus is at first reluctant to participate. He has heard that Polycarp once called Marcion "the devil's firstborn."[11] However, Metrodorus is not sure the story is accurate and he agrees to participate.

Not one of the prisoners, of course, has a copy of the *Martyrdom of the Holy Polycarp*, but Eutychian and the others remember Evaristus' account well enough to be able to quote parts of it verbatim and to retell the rest of the story in their own words. They go to sleep, grateful that nothing, not even their imprisonment, has prevented them from commemorating Polycarp's martyrdom on its anniversary.

Sources:

Mart. Pol., including alternative ending; *Pass. Pion.* 1–11; Irenaeus, *Haer.* 3.3.4.

Smyrna, Ionia, February/March 250 C.E.

Sacrifice to the gods, or die

Eutychian is tired of being in prison. Every day new groups of Christians are brought inside, and every day members of the special commission and other officials come to try to persuade the Christians to recant and offer sacrifice to the state gods. No one as yet has been put to death, as the neokoros and the others do not have the power to execute those who fail to sacrifice, but the threat of execution hangs as heavily in the air as the putrid odor of the prison. Eutychian wishes the governor would come so they could get the official trial over with.

Instead of the governor who, understandably, wouldn't set foot inside the filthy prison, Polemon comes once more to the jail, this time with the commanding officer of the cavalry, a group of soldiers, and a large crowd of onlookers. Eutychian and the others are rounded up, and Polemon tells Pionius and his fellow catholics: "Look, the one who presides over you, Euctemon, has sacrificed; you should consent to do so also. Lepidus and Euctemon wish to interrogate you in the Temple of Nemesis."[12] Lepidus, they all know, is one of the special commissioners, and the Temple of Nemesis has become the main place where people sacrifice to satisfy the requirements of Decius' edict. Pionius, however, challenges Polemon's right to take them to the temple. "It is proper procedure for those who have been put in jail to wait for the arrival of the proconsul," Pionius exclaims.[13]

Polemon and those who came with him leave the prison but return quickly with even more soldiers and an even larger crowd. Theophilus, the commander of the cavalry, tells the prisoners: "The proconsul has sent a message saying that you are to be taken to Ephesus."[14] Pionius suspects deceit and says, "Let the one the proconsul sent with the message step forward and be the one who takes us there."[15] Theophilus is so furious at having been caught in a lie that he almost throttles Pionius to death with the scarf around his neck. Still holding Pionius by the neck, Theophilus pushes Pionius into the arms of one of the soldiers who takes him out of the prison and marches him off to the agora. Other soldiers take hold of the other prisoners and Eutychian suddenly finds himself being dragged along also.

At the agora, Pionius throws himself onto the ground in an act of passive resistance, not wanting to be taken to the Temple of Nemesis. It takes six soldiers to pick him up, and they carry him head down to the temple, dumping him unceremoniously in front of the altar. When Pionius looks up, he sees Euctemon standing piously beside the altar.

Eutychian also sees Euctemon and suddenly realizes why the commissioners have been asking him and the others about the particular branch of Christianity to which they belong. It is a strategy to try to convince them to sacrifice by showing them that people, including leaders of their own group, have already done so. Eutychian wonders whether Euctemon's apostasy will have any effect on Pionius and the other catholics. It does not! Pionius and those arrested with him stand their ground; they refuse to sacrifice. Pionius even chides the officials for their actions. "You punish us as disobedient ones but you yourselves are disobedient. You were commanded to punish us, not to force us to sacrifice against our wills," he shouts at them.[16] Lepidus tells Pionius not to shout. "Then do not force me," Pionius responds. "Light a fire and we will climb onto it by ourselves."[17]

The two men stare at each other, but the battle of wills is over. Pionius has called Lepidus' bluff. After a few more futile questions all the prisoners, including Eutychian, are taken back to the jail.[18]

Source:

Pass. Pion. 12–23.

Smyrna, Ionia, March 12, 250 C.E.
Eutychian's fate is resolved

Gaius Julius Proculus Quintillianus, proconsul of the Roman province of Asia, finally arrives in Smyrna. He wastes no time in dealing with the prisoners. In rapid succession, Pionius, Makedonia, Limnos, Sabina, Eutychian, Metrodorus, and the others are questioned, once again, about the cult or sect to which they belong and then ordered to sacrifice. Scribes record their answers, and when the Christians refuse to comply the governor threatens them with various kinds of punishment.

Eutychian watches and listens as Quintillianus condemns Pionius to be burned alive in the stadium. He secretly hopes that he himself will receive the same sentence. Although it is no longer the day of the Great Sabbath, the day on which Polycarp of blessed memory suffered the same fate in the same stadium, Eutychian feels that he is now ready to follow not only Jesus, who died on a cross, but Polycarp who died in the flames lit for him by one of Quintillianus' predecessors. Eutychian decides that, in imitation of Polycarp, he will insist that merely his hands be tied behind his back. Eutychian is so deep in thought about the details of his own impending martyrdom that he almost doesn't hear his name called out by one of the special commissioners. Belatedly, Eutychian responds by walking up to the tribunal to stand before the governor.[19]

Source:

Pass. Pion. 19–23.

Notes

1. The most likely date on which Polycarp, bishop of Smyrna, was martyred is Saturday, February 23, 155; see Tabbernee 2007, 228 and n. 87. See Musurillo 1972, 2–21, 136–167 respectively for the Greek text and an English translation of the *Martyrium Polycarpi* and the *Passio Pionii*. The translation of the passages from these two *acta martyrum* quoted in both sections of this chapter are, however, my own.

2. *Mart. Pol.* 4. Because Quintus is described as "a Phrygian" in *Mart. Pol.* 4, he is considered by some scholars to have been a Montanist, or, at least, a "proto-Montanist." However, both the early date of the reference to Quintus and the late date when the term "Phrygian" became synonymous, in orthodox Christian circles, with "a member of the Phrygian heresy" argue against Quintus being anything other than a person who, like some (but not all) later Montanists, volunteered for martyrdom. For a full discussion of the issues, see Tabbernee 2007, 226–30.

3. *Mart. Pol.* 3.2.

4. *Mart. Pol.* 8.2.

5. *Mart. Pol.* 9.2.

6. *Mart. Pol.* 9.3.

7. *Pass. Pion.* 3.2.

8. For the kind of questions asked of the Christians by Polemon, see *Pass. Pion.* 8.1–9.9.

9. See *Pass. Pion.* 21.5.

10. That there was a Montanist community in Smyrna at least by the time of the Decian Persecution (ca. 249–251) is assured by the reference to Eutychian in *Pass. Pion.* 11.2. Additional evidence for such a community at Smyrna in the latter part of the third century C.E. may come from the *Vita Polycarpi;* see Stewart-Sykes 2000, 21–33; 2002, 3–47, 86; Tabbernee 2007, 49–50.

11. Irenaeus, *Haer.* 3.3.4.

12. *Pass. Pion.* 15.2.

13. *Pass. Pion.* 15.3.

14. *Pass. Pion.* 15.4.

15. *Pass. Pion.* 15.5.

16. *Pass. Pion.* 16.6.

17. *Pass. Pion.* 18.2.

18. For a brief summary of the Decian Persecution, see Frend 1984, 318–24—although Frend overestimates the extent to which Decius (249–251) specifically targeted Christians in his legislation. Frend (321) also considers Euctemon to have been the catholic *bishop* of Smyrna, whereas Euctemon may merely have been a presbyter responsible for the oversight of one or more house-churches. The phrase describing Euctemon, ὁ προεστὼς ὑμῶν (*ho proestōs humōn*) (15.2), "the one having superintended you (plural)," employs the same word (προεστώς [*proestōs*]), as, for example, Eusebius (*Hist eccl.* 6.20.2b) does to describe Hippolytus who was not a bishop but a "superintendent" in charge of a house-church-school community in Rome; see Chapter 16 and Tabbernee 2007, 70–71.

19. There is no need to doubt the accuracy of the date provided by *Pass. Pion.* 19.1; 23 for the martyrs' final trial before the governor Julius Proculus Quintillianus and the execution of Pionius, Metrodorus, and, presumably, Eutychian. Both events occurred on the fourth day before the Ides of March when Decius was consul for the second time and his co-consul was Vettius Gratus, that is, March 12, 250; see Barnes 1968, 529–31 and Musurillo 1972, 167 n. 55.

Figure 21.1: Boxing trophies in the mosaic floor of the gymnasium at Akmonia

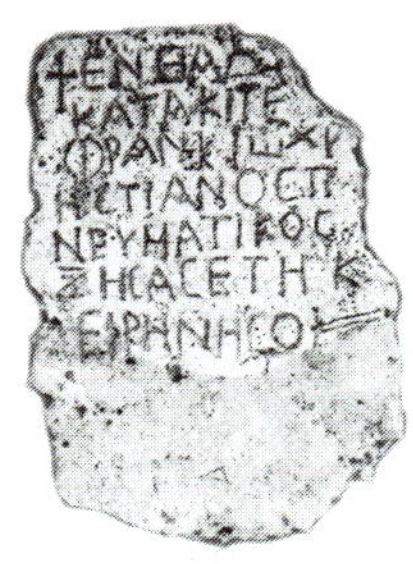

Chapter 21

Akmonia, Phrygia, 253/4 C.E.

The cost of a precious gift

Aristeas not only loves going to the gymnasium, it has become a daily necessity for him. The walk from the lower part of the city to the acropolis, the long narrow ridge where the public buildings, including the gymnasium, are situated, is always invigorating—especially early in the day when the air is still crisp and cool. This morning, however, Aristeas finds himself more distracted than usual. His bishop's most recent request occupies his thoughts so completely that he doesn't notice, as he typically would, the light from the rising sun tingeing the bluish mountain tops across the valley from the acropolis.

Yesterday the bishop asked him to donate some land for a *koimētērion*, a cemetery, at Akmonia for the Christian community. Aristeas wants to do this and knows which piece of property he should give. The thought of relinquishing that particular plot, however, is excruciatingly painful: the plot is where Aurelia, his wife, is buried. Oh, how he misses her. He loves her still. Each morning he wakes up, expecting to see her there next to him in bed. When he opens his eyes, the emptiness is unbearable. One reason he goes to the gymnasium each day is to substitute physical pain for his emotional pain. Paradoxically, Aristeas has discovered, aching muscles soothe an aching heart. He is sure that his heart will break completely if he gives away the very plot of land that is the only remaining physical connection he has to the woman who for so many years was his wife—no, much more than merely his wife. She was the one and only love of his life.

As he reaches the entrance to the gymnasium, Aristeas is feeling a little more confident that exercising will, as always, not only help him cope momentarily with his deep grief but also clear his mind to allow him to focus on the present rather than on the past. He used to be able to make decisions so easily, he remembers. Now even the decision to get out of bed each morning is a difficult one. Once at the gymnasium, however, everything seems more manageable. He quickens his stride and prays that during his workout, Aurelia will help him make the right decision.

The main building of the gymnasium is a large hall built in the shape of a civic basilica with an apse at the far end. The whole floor is covered with thousands of tesserae, the tiny square tiles that together make a huge mosaic. Where he enters, the tesserae are all the same color: brownish-gray. Aristeas knows, though, that the plainness of the mosaic at the entrance is a clever artistic ploy to make what the eye will see later have an even more dramatic impact on the visitor to the gymnasium than would otherwise be the case. As with all sensory pleasures, delayed gratification intensifies the experience.

Although he knows what is ahead, Aristeas' heart beats a little faster in anticipation as he walks toward the apse. Once there, Aristeas marvels, as if for the first time, at the exquisite beauty of the mosaic that fills the floor of the apse—the part where no sweaty athletes' feet may tread during their exercises. The area is reserved for the washed feet of gymnasium officials and victorious champions who there receive the prizes that are the well deserved rewards of their athletic achievements.

The floor mosaic closest to the semicircular end wall is in an arched panel that follows the shape of the apse. In the panel, Aristeas sees a rectangular table, skillfully created with yellow-brown tesserae to resemble wood. The table has four legs, each one having a lion's foot. Just above the feet, horizontal struts connect the legs, giving the table the appearance of stability as well as beauty. The stability is needed because on the table itself are three gray bags tied up neatly with red ribbon. The bag on the left is the largest and contains the most gold coins. It is the first prize. The winners of the second and third prizes will receive, respectively, the bags in the middle and on the right-hand side of the table. The work of the artisans who made the mosaic table and the bags of gold is so perfect that Aristeas feels like, if he bent down, he'd be able to pick up one or more of the bags. Even the smallest of the three bags would contain enough gold for him to buy some other land to give to the church for its cemetery rather than give the land with his wife's grave. If only the bag of gold were real and he could use it this way, Aristeas thinks, his problem would be solved.

Next to the mosaic table on the floor is a discus. Next to the discus is a pair of boxing gloves. At both sides of the table is a large vase containing palm fronds. Palm fronds, the symbol of victory, are given to the winners of athletic competitions. In Christian circles, palm fronds are also beginning to appear in artwork representing victorious martyrs. Aristeas remembers seeing a painting of St. Thecla with a palm frond in her hand, even though she hadn't actually died for the faith. Aristeas is sure that, despite the reluctance of some Christians to paint portraits or have "graven images," there will soon be artwork depicting the most recent martyrs who died under the persecution initiated by the emperor Decius. For a brief moment, Aristeas gives into the thought that he wishes he had been martyred for the faith, that way he'd be with his beloved Aurelia now.

Looking at the boxing gloves and the naked athletes depicted on a panel containing the table below the discus, Aristeas imagines himself winning one of the athletic competitions held regularly at the gymnasium. Ever since Aurelia died, he has had an almost uncontrollable urge to punch someone in the nose. He is not sure at whom he is angry, perhaps it is God—but putting on some boxing gloves and punching someone—anyone—right now sounds like a great idea, especially if it would enable him to receive, legitimately, an actual bag of gold that he could give to the bishop instead of land.

As his eyes stray to the side panels of the mosaic triptych, Aristeas notices some details he hadn't really seen before. Each of the panels has a triple border, the inner border having the egg-and-dart design that is so popular on monumental buildings and that often surrounds inscriptions on stone. In this case, the egg-and-dart design borders, in the end panels, surround inscriptions cleverly made from tesserae. The inscription on the right is above a female figure wearing a crown and holding a staff of authority in her hand. Aristeas reads the word ΓΥΜΝΑΣΙΑΡΧΙΑ (*Gymnasiarchia:* "Office of the Gymnasiarch"). The inscription on the left is over a similarly crowned, staff-bearing beautiful woman. Aristeas there reads ΑΓΩΝΟΘΕΣΙΑ (*Agōnothesia:* "Office of the President of the Games"). Aristeas wonders when the Gymnasiarch will instruct this year's President of the Games to schedule the next competitions.

When his workout is over, Aristeas feels better and he is able to think more clearly. Despite his prayer upon entering the gymnasium, he still hasn't decided what to do about the bishop's request—but he *has* decided that the only way he can make a decision is to ask Aurelia herself.[1]

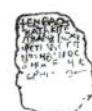  

Dressed again in his toga, Aristeas walks out of the gymnasium and down the hill. Just before reaching the street that would take him to his house, he turns right and descends further into the valley. Halfway down toward the stream there is a grassy plateau: the piece of land the bishop wants for the Christian *koimētērion.*

There are already three gravestones on the plot of land, and Aristeas pauses at the first one. It is a simple white marble funerary altar. On the upper moulding is a simple inscription: Ἡδῖα Χρειστειανή (*Hedia Chreistianē:* "Hedia, a Christian").[2] Aristeas remembers Hedia with fondness. She was an old woman of great faith and wisdom. He is glad that he had invited her family to bury her on his land.

As is his custom, he makes the sign of the cross at the graveside before walking the few steps to the second gravestone. It, too, is a bomos, a funerary altar made of white marble. In this case, however, the moulding doesn't have the name of the deceased. Instead, there is a date inscribed on it: this year's date. The left side of the altar's shaft is decorated with an open book-scroll with a stylus, symbolizing that the deceased was a literate person. The right side is blank. Aristeas wonders why no symbol was carved there. Typically, if the deceased husband's attributes were represented artistically by a symbol, so were the wife's. Perhaps, as the wife is the dedicator, she had prudently decided not to spend the extra money on decorating the stone with a symbol relating to her, even though the stone will one day become her gravestone as well. Aristeas makes a mental note to ask her about this at some opportune moment, then thinks how in-opportune it would really be to ask such a question.

Although he knows the text of the inscription that is carved on the front face of the shaft, he reads it again:

Figure 21.2: "Office of the Gymnasiarch" in the mosaic floor in the gymnasium at Akmonia

> I, Aurelia Julia, commissioned this tomb for my father Julianos, and for my mother Beroneikiane, and for my sweetest child Severos and for my daughter-in-law Moundane, in memory. Christians.[3]

This Aurelia is not *his* Aurelia. All free inhabitants of the provinces were given Roman citizenship by the emperor Caracalla forty years earlier. Caracalla's full, official name was Marcus Aurelius Antoninus Bassianus. Caracalla's father, the emperor Septimius Severus, claimed familial descent from the great Marcus Aurelius and had renamed his oldest son accordingly when he made Caracalla co-emperor. After having received Roman citizenship due to the generosity of Caracalla, most new citizens also adopted, as a *quasi-gentilicium*, the name of the *gens*, or "extended family," of the emperor as their own *praenomen*, or "first name." Aristeas had done so himself. His full name is Aurelius Aristeas. The Aurelia who had commissioned the tombstone he is now looking at normally went by her second name, Julia, derived from the name of her father, Julianos. His own beloved wife, however, liked the name Aurelia so much that it became the only name by which she was ever known.

What a tragedy Julia had experienced. That she had lost her father and mother was, for a woman of about fifty, to be expected. Aristeas knows almost no one that age who still has living parents. For Julia, however, also to have lost first her husband and now her sweetest son Severos and Severos' wife, Julia's daughter-in-law, is very sad. When earlier that year Aristeas had gladly given Julia the right to bury Severos and Moundane on his land and to place there a tombstone that also commemorated Julia's deceased parents, he had no idea that, so soon afterwards, he would experience his own excruciating grief. Now he understands Julia's grief more and is comforted by the knowledge that other people, like Julia, also understand his despair.

Aristeas, remembering the young couple, thinks that Severos was probably named after Caracalla's immediate family, the Severans. Julia, after all, was pregnant with Severos at the time when Caracalla, with one stroke of his pen, granted her and thousands of others citizenship. Still, standing there in front of the gravestone, Aristeas puzzles over the origin of the name of Severos' wife. Moundane is an unusual name. Perhaps the master stonemason in the workshop in Akmonia has spelled phonetically a name that is really Muntana or Montane. Try as he might, he cannot recall how the young woman's name was pronounced. After first seeing the spelling Moundane when the tombstone was erected on his property, Aristeas intended to ask Julia—but it hadn't seemed important at the time. Now something has happened that suddenly makes the question relevant. An itinerant preacher from Pepouza has come to Akmonia, promoting, once again, the oracles of Montanus, one of the founders of the New Prophecy movement. What if Severos' wife had been named after Montanus, the original prophet from Pepouza? Perhaps the family of Moundane/Montane had been early members of the New Prophecy. As adherents of the movement tended to stick together, Aurelia Julia and her husband had perhaps also been followers of Montanus. Aristeas, however, is simply not sure. He has never heard any member of Julia's family speak about the New Prophecy. This, thinks Aristeas, is a pity. The little he knows about the New Prophecy movement fascinates him, particularly its teaching that one should not remarry after the death of one's spouse.

Aristeas crosses himself once more and walks around the gravestone. At the back of the bomos he sees a stylized wreath. He remembers seeing similar wreaths on similar tombstones in the workshop when only a few weeks earlier he was there purchasing a stone for Aurelia's grave. His eyes had been so full of tears that he could hardly distinguish one pre-carved symbol from another. He wishes now that he had spent more time looking, but he was in no condition to do so. He just wanted to get the purchase over with. Aristeas, though, is satisfied with his choice—like the other gravestones already on his land, it is a simple marble bomos.

Having spent more time at the other tombstones than he intended, Aristeas heads for the center of the field where Aurelia's grave is located, sheltered by the shade of a gnarled old olive tree. Before he gets there, he stops one more time. Between the grave of Severos and Moundane is a huge rose bush. It has the most beautiful flowers Aristeas has ever seen. They are the color of claret wine. The bush is so tall that some of the roses are growing almost as high as his chest. Careful not to hurt himself, he carefully grabs hold of one of the long prickly stems and pulls the rose closer, almost burying his nose in it as he drinks in the perfume. The fragrance is intoxicating as he remembers how he and Aurelia had often stood there, side by side, excitedly testing rose after rose to decide which one was the most beautiful, the most fragrant of all. He can still hear her laughing out loud with delight as she, rather than he, found the most perfect rose each time. Aristeas sees something more and his heart skips a beat. For a long moment he is certain that Aurelia is there, again by his side, holding out today's most perfect rose for him. Suddenly she is gone. A pesky bee lands on the rose Aurelia has been holding, but Aristeas quickly chases it away with a flick of his right hand. Aristeas then bends down to touch the still swaying rose where she touched it. He lingers over the fragrance and marvels at the way perfume can evoke so many memories: wonderful memories.

At that very instant he knows what he must do about the bishop's request. Aurelia, his beloved Aurelia who loved roses, has indeed helped him decide. He takes a small knife out of his pocket and cuts off a dozen flawless roses. Holding them in his hands he carries them to Aurelia's grave. He puts the roses down, picking them up again one by one. Slowly and tenderly, with his heart overflowing with joy rather than grief, Aristeas takes each rose and pulls off the petals, lovingly strewing them over the grave. As the petals form a claret-red quilt on the mound of earth containing Aurelia's beautiful body, Aristeas thanks her for providing the perfect solution. He will give the Christian community the land on which already some Christians, including his Aurelia, are buried—but he will tell the bishop that there is a condition attached to the gift. The condition is that, from now on, every year on the anniversary of Aurelia's death, rose petals are to be strewn on her grave—even when he himself is no longer alive to perform personally this act of love.[4]

Sources:

CB 455–457; *IMont* 21–22.

Notes

1. The gymnasium at Akmonia (Ahat) was discovered in 2000 when I saw (and photographed) *in situ* the building and its magnificent mosaic. Unfortunately, later that same year, the mosaic was cut out of the floor of the building and sold on the black antiquities market. The culprits have been caught and the mosaic is currently in İstanbul as evidence for the impending court case.

2. *IMont* 22.

3. *IMont* 21. The date 253/4 for the year in which Aurelia Julia commissioned the tombstone for her family members is secure (Tabbernee 1997b, 173). For the view that Moundane's name was actually "Muntana," see Noy 2000, 175.

4. Hedia's epitaph, on which this chapter is based, is the only one of the three extant inscriptions actually discovered in Ahat itself. The inscriptions commissioned by Aurelius Aristeas and Aurelia Julia (*IMont* 21) were, respectively, discovered at Susuz and Kızılcasöğüt, nearby Turkish villages on the territory of Akmonia. All three inscriptions, however, appear to have been produced in the same workshop in Akmonia. The name of Julia's father is no longer extant on *IMont* 22 but may be restored on the basis of her own name. The substitution of *delta* for *tau,* as in *IMont* 21, is common in Phrygia; see Tabbernee 1997b, 151. The tombstone commissioned by Aristeas is inscribed on three sides. A record of the gift of land and the condition of an annual *rosalia* is inscribed on sides B and C, undoubtedly added later than the inscription on side A, which contains a partially extant date which numerically falls within the range 215–295 C.E.

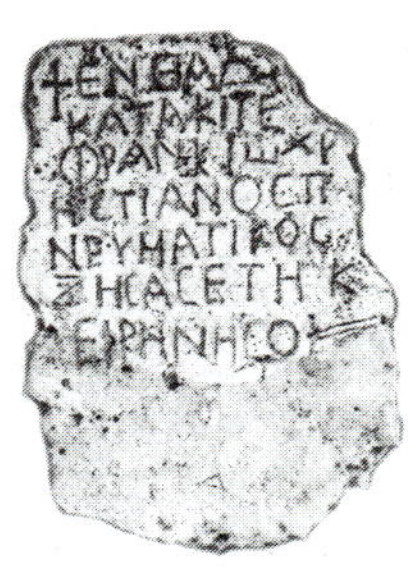

Chapter 22

Colonia Prima Flavia Augusta Caesarea, Palaestina, February 24, 303 C.E.

Eusebius writes a history of the church

Eusebius is extremely grateful for the Bibliotheca Origenis et Pamphili, the Library of Origen and Pamphilus, as the Christian library at Caesarea has come to be known. He spends almost all day, every day at the library systematically working through the collection, gathering material to include in the manuscript of his *Historia ecclesiastica*, his "History of the Church." As far as Eusebius knows, no one has ever attempted to write a comprehensive account of Christianity from its beginnings up to the present time.

The idea of writing a church history came to Eusebius while he was working on another project—a chronicle consisting of annotated tables covering the history of the world beginning with the birth of Abraham. In compiling his tables for more recent times, he gathered so much data about the church all over the world that he knows he has more than enough information to tell the story of how Christianity spread throughout the Roman Empire and beyond.

Eusebius is sitting at a wooden table in the library. A list of bishops who were prominent leaders of the churches in the time of the emperor Aurelian is on the table. Eusebius made the list some time ago, and he quickly scans the first two names: Firmilian of Caesarea in Cappadocia and Gregory, known as Thaumaturgus, "the Wonderworker," bishop of Neocaesarea in Pontus. Aurelian had been emperor a little more than a quarter of a century ago when Eusebius was a little boy. The first two bishops on the list, however, were already old men by then. How wonderful that both were connected with Origen here in Caesarea Maritima and that they had both been inside this very library—Firmilian as Origen's guest and Gregory as one of Origen's students.

Eusebius finds himself wishing, once again, that he had been born a couple of decades earlier so he could have been one of Origen's students himself—but by the time he was born Origen had already died from the severe tortures he had undergone during the persecution of Christians following the issue of Decius' edict. Eusebius is glad however that his own teacher, Pamphilus, was an ardent admirer of Origen. While himself also too young to have been a student of Origen,

Pamphilus came to Caesarea about two decades ago to establish a school like Origen's and to continue the kind of education Origen had provided. Pamphilus was ordained a presbyter by Bishop Agapius and spent a lot of his own money to enlarge the library by expanding its collection.

Eusebius remembers vividly how, when he went to Pamphilus with his idea of writing a history of the church, Pamphilus was so enthusiastic about the idea that he had even employed some additional research assistants to help Eusebius gather together all the relevant material in the library.

Eusebius and Pamphilus talked long into the night about how to organize the *Historia ecclesiastica*. Eusebius remembers telling Pamphilus that he didn't want merely to reproduce lists of bishops and major events. He had done that already in his *Chronicon*. He wanted instead to use the data at his disposal to show how the church had triumphed over all attempts to destroy it. He is getting close to finishing his manuscript. He only has to cover the last twenty-five years or so to bring his history up to the present age. Eusebius is more convinced than ever that his original concept had been right. In telling the story of Christianity, he has clearly demonstrated that the devil has attacked the church by two main methods: persecution and heresy. Neither had worked. Christians, on the whole, had faced their persecutors bravely as the many stories of the martyrs, which he included in the seven books of the history written thus far, reveal irrefutably. Heresies were equally futile weapons of the devil because, even though they were more insidious in that they attacked the church from *within*, their falsehood was eventually exposed by godly bishops.

Eusebius can't help thinking back to the time almost a year ago now when one of his research assistants brought him a whole set of manuscripts related to Montanus, Maximilla, Priscilla, and other leaders of the so-called New Prophecy movement. It hadn't taken him long to see that these people were not genuine prophets but pawns of the devil. Faithful bishops, such as Apolinarius of Hierapolis, Avircius Marcellus of Hieropolis, Julian of Apameia, Zotikos of Konana, Serapion of Antioch, and many others, such as Apollonius, had opposed the movement, excommunicated its leaders, and even tried to exorcize Maximilla and Priscilla. Eusebius felt very fortunate to have, in this very library, some of the earliest treatises written against the New Prophecy and some of the conciliar documents denouncing this dangerous sect. He is glad that by reading the *Historia ecclesiastica* everyone will be able to learn how, what he has decided to call "the Phrygian heresy," is nothing but a false prophetic movement inspired not by the Holy Spirit but by an evil spirit.

As Eusebius sits in the library at Caesarea, he has no idea that the publication of his "History of the Church" will be delayed by a whole decade, owing to an event occurring on this very day in far away Nikomedia, the capital of the Eastern Roman Empire.[1]

Sources:

Jerome, *Ep.* 34.1; *Vir. ill.* 75, 113; Eusebius, *Hist. eccl.* 1.1.1–7.30.22a (esp. 4.27, 5.3.4, 5.16.1–5.19.4, 6.30, 7.28.1), 7.32.25.

Gaza, Palaestina, May 21, 304 C.E.
The Great Persecution begins

It has been a horrible year. Diocletian's first edict was shocking. Not since Aurelian's reign had an edict been directed specifically at Christians. The ink, however, had barely dried on Aurelian's edict when divine justice intervened and Aurelian lay dead, his intended persecution halted before it could be carried out by provincial governors. That had been long ago, and most Christians like Thecla had assumed that there would never again be an anti-Christian edict or, if there were, that God would again intervene to protect the church.

Thecla is sitting in a courtyard outside the residence which Urbanus, the governor of Palaestina, uses whenever he visits Gaza. He is inside the house now but will soon come to the makeshift tribunal where Thecla and the other Christians brought here this morning are to be tried. While anxiously waiting for the proceedings to begin, Thecla cannot help thinking about how wrong she had been when she first learned of Diocletian's edict. Last year, in early March, when news of the edict promulgated in Nikomedia on February 24 reached Gaza, Thecla had been sure something terrible would befall Diocletian and his junior co-emperor Galerius to put a swift end to their attempts to eradicate Christianity. But God had not intervened. There had been no thunderbolt from the sky striking down the evil emperors. No worms had entered their intestines to kill them from the inside. Nothing. No sign of God anywhere!

Initially Thecla and her friends had not been too worried about the delay in God's intervention. Diocletian's first edict was, after all, not too devastating. Christians who held high office in the civil service and in the army were deprived of their rank and privileges. Caesariani, servants in the imperial households, if they were Christians, were threatened with slavery if they did not recant their faith. Christians in ordinary life were no longer protected in civil suits, as the edict prevented them from being plaintiffs while still allowing non-Christians to bring all kinds of charges against Christians. The worst part of Diocletian's first edict was that it had ordered church buildings to be razed to the ground and Christian scriptures to be burned.

The emperor had begun the destruction of Christian property in Nikomedia itself. Thecla had heard that the Christian basilica in Nikomedia was in a prominent part of the city, situated on a small hill, and visible from the imperial palace. Diocletian had sent soldiers to the basilica at dawn on February 23. They had forced open the doors, found the sacred writings and burned them, smashing everything else in sight. Diocletian and Galerius had watched everything from a tower built on top of the palace walls, debating whether to set the basilica on fire. In the end, Diocletian had decided not to give the order to do so, afraid that the whole section of Nikomedia where the basilica was located might erupt in flames. Instead he had sent in the Praetorian Guards with battle-axes and other implements. Within hours, Thecla had been told, the elite Roman soldiers had leveled the tall building to the ground.

Since then, Thecla knew from personal experience that many church buildings, including some at Caesarea Maritima, had been destroyed. She hoped that the great Christian library at Caesarea she visited last year was still safe and that the copies of the Christian scriptures and other books she had seen there had survived the onslaught. Fortunately, the library was housed in a building that was separate from the other church buildings and so may have escaped notice.

Thecla looks around at the other Christians. She recognizes Timothy, a leading member of the catholic church, but her closest companions are some of the other men in the courtyard. One of them is called Agapius and he is keeping a protective eye on her. These men belong to the New Prophecy movement or, as their detractors prefer to say, the sect named after the Phrygians. Thecla remembers how surprised and delighted she had been after arriving from Bizya in Thrace many years ago to find fellow followers of Montanus, Maximilla, and Priscilla in Gaza. She did not expect that. They all became very good friends. Her new friends asked her—as almost everyone invariably did—how she received her name. She told them, as they had undoubtedly guessed, that her Christian parents named her after Saint Thecla, the heroic companion of St. Paul.

Still waiting for the governor, Thecla's mind jumps to Eusebius, the great scholar in Caesarea she had met in the library when she visited it last year. After she had been introduced to him, Eusebius dubbed her "the Thecla of our own times."[2] She remembers that she liked that very much. She also liked the forthright way Eusebius had answered her questions, treating her like an equal. When, in talking about the persecutions, she had wondered aloud where God was in all of this, Eusebius gave a helpful response. He explained that, in his view, the persecution they were experiencing was the result of the chastening hand of God on a church that, during the preceding decades, had become increasingly arrogant, lax, divisive, hypocritical, and—at times—even sinful. With a twinkle in his eye, Eusebius couldn't resist telling Thecla that some of the unworthy bishops who were guardians of their day were now guardians, bishops, of the emperors' horses and camels! Eusebius was adamant, however, that it was not God who was the persecutor. Persecution was started by and conducted by the emperors who bear the sole responsibility for the pain and suffering the Christians underwent. All God did was to withdraw, temporarily, the restraining hand usually in place to prevent persecution. God's hand was still around, as was God's grace—despite appearances to the contrary. God was in the persecution in a positive sense by continuing to come to the aid of the individual Christians caught in the persecution, giving them the courage not to deny the faith and the strength to bear the suffering they were called to endure.

There is some activity at the door of the residence, suggesting that Urbanus is about to appear. Thecla hopes that Eusebius is right about God giving martyrs courage and strength. She is going to need both very soon. The commotion at the door of the house however is a false alarm. Thecla and the others have to wait a little longer.

Despite her predicament, time seems to be standing still for Thecla. She finds herself thinking about the most recent edict against Christians issued by Diocletian. It is the fourth edict in the span of little more than a year. After the first edict targeted Christian property and rank, two further edicts targeted the clergy—

imprisoning bishops and other leaders, torturing them into sacrificing to the state gods. Now the fourth edict decreed that all Christians, not just the clergy, have to swear allegiance to the emperors and sacrifice to the state gods. That's why she is here, caught in the largest net ever cast to catch Christians.

Urbanus finally makes his appearance. He is an arrogant man, very business-like in carrying out his duties. If the emperors decree that everyone must offer libations, then by the gods, everyone will—including the Christians. He, Urbanus, will ensure that they do. Urbanus strides purposefully up to the tribunal and sits down. Next, two officials sit down, one on each side of the governor, and Urbanus is ready to begin.

The first person brought before the governor is Timothy. Thecla watches as the governor orders him to sacrifice to the state gods. When Timothy refuses, Urbanus orders that he be roasted alive. Urbanus tells the soldiers who take Timothy away to make sure the fire is a moderate one that will burn slowly. Thecla, once more, prays hard for the courage and strength Eusebius had promised would be hers when the time came.[3]

Sources:

Lactantius, *Mort.* 11.1–13.1; Eusebius, *Hist. eccl.* 7.30.19–21; 8.1.7–9; 8.2.4–5; 9.18.15; *Mart. Pal.* (*L*) (*S*) 3.1; 11–12; (*L*) 3.2.

Colonia Prima Flavia Augusta Caesarea, Palaestina, March 21–24, 305 C.E.

Thecla prays that a promise comes true

Thecla and Agapius have been incarcerated for exactly ten months now. On the day of their trial in Gaza, Urbanus condemned them both to become food for wild animals. Thecla remembers that she was almost beside herself with fear—not so much fear of the beasts, but fear that she wouldn't be strong enough to stand her ground when they charged at her.

As Timothy had been executed on the same day as his trial, Thecla and Agapius assumed they too would be thrown to the wild beasts that day—but that had not been the case. Thecla thinks it would have been better to have died as a martyr back then. At least the whole ordeal would be over. Instead, for ten long months each morning had brought renewed hope and self-doubt. Each morning, as she awoke she hoped that she might not be thrown to the wild animals—and each morning she also prayed that if she were, she'd have the courage and strength to bear what the animals would do to her. After the first few weeks of emotional agony, she found some of the peace of mind Eusebius had promised. God is with her in the midst of the persecution after all. God is making her a stronger person, she is sure of it.

After a few months in the jail in Gaza, Thecla, Agapius, and some of the other followers of Montanus, Maximilla, and Priscilla had been brought here to Caesarea Maritima and locked up in the jail attached to the governor's residence.

Thecla has been told that it is the same building Herod the Great, the wicked ruler who tried to kill Jesus when he was but a baby, constructed as his palace on the shore of the Internum Mare. It is the same palace occupied by Pontius Pilate—the governor of Judaea who tried to wash his hands of the fate of Jesus but who had ultimately had Jesus crucified. Urbanus is in good company, Thecla thinks ironically. She, however, has reassured herself on more than one occasion that she is in far better company. Not only does she have her beloved friends with her in prison but the very rooms where they are being held had once held St. Paul himself. Thecla can almost feel his presence, and she has never been as proud of her name as she is now. Like the other Thecla, she knows she is St. Paul's companion—if not in life, then certainly in death.

Occasionally, when she and the others are briefly taken outside under heavy guard, Thecla can see both the theater nearby and the amphitheater in the distance. It is rumored that within a few days, as the annual pagan festival with its traditional bloody spectacles is about to be celebrated, she and all the others who have been condemned to the beasts will be taken to one or other of the venues to satisfy the non-Christian population's thirst for blood. Finally, thinks Thecla, the wait will soon be over.

Urbanus is about to make a speech, officially declaring the public games open when, to his own astonishment and all those in attendance, six young men rush up to the podium. Urbanus' bodyguards move to intercept the men but soon realize that the youths present no physical threat to the governor. Each of them has his hands already bound—amazingly, they have bound their own hands. They tell the surprised Urbanus that they, too, are Christians and wish to die with Agapius, Thecla, and the others.

Rarely speechless, Urbanus is temporarily at a loss for words. Composing himself, he asks the young men their names and their places of origin. One by one they come forward: Timolaus from Pontus, Dionysius from Phoenicia, Paesis and Alexander from Egypt, another Alexander from Gaza, and Romulus from Diospolis, the city once known as Lydda and, like Gaza, within Urbanus' own jurisdiction. How dare these men interrupt his opening of the games! If they want to die, so be it—but he is not going to give them the death they want right here and now. He will take his time thinking about their means of execution; in the meantime, let them cool their ardor in jail for a while.

Thecla and Agapius recognize Alexander from Gaza immediately as he and the other young men are thrown into the dungeon where they have already spent months. Alexander is pleased to see Agapius and Thecla, and he tells them what he and the others have done rather recklessly but courageously. Because of the young men's courage, Agapius and Thecla do not have the heart to tell them that their action is against the teaching of the church—volunteering for martyrdom has long been frowned upon. It is God who chooses martyrs. Martyrs do not choose themselves.[4]

A few days later two other men are also thrown into jail. The first is, coincidentally, also named Agapius. He, unlike the six young men, is not a volunteer for martyrdom but a tried and tested confessor who kept the faith despite horrendous tortures. The second man is yet another Dionysius—known already to Thecla and the long-time prisoners because he is one of the Christians from here in Caesarea Maritima who had come regularly to the prison on behalf of the Christian congregation to bring food and other necessities to Thecla, the first Agapius, and the others. His care of the prisoners has made him a visible target for a vengeful governor.

The next day the eight most recent inmates of Urbanus' jail are brought before the governor. He has decided on their sentence. They will each be beheaded in the prison. No fighting with wild beasts before blood-thirsty crowds for them. They will die today, quietly, quickly—ingloriously. The beasts are reserved for the first Agapius, his original male companions, and for Thecla. As the governor's decision is relayed to Thecla, she can hear the roar of the crowd in the distance and she prays yet one more time for the courage and strength promised by Eusebius.[5]

Sources:

Eusebius, *Mart. Pal.* (*L*) (*S*) 3.1–4.

Notes

1. Books 1–7 (till 7.30.22a) of the *Historia ecclesiastica* were written by Eusebius in the early years of the fourth century C.E. The work on the *Hist. eccl.* appears to have been interrupted by the outbreak of the so-called "Great Persecution" in February 303. At that stage, Eusebius had covered the history of the church up to and including the reign of Aurelian (270–275); see Tabbernee 1997a, 319–34, esp. 319–26, 333–34. Consequently, Eusebius had not yet described the events which had occurred during the last quarter of a century before he was writing, when his work was interrupted. The draft appears not to have been "published" (that is, finished, made into an exemplar, and copies made for circulation) until after the Great Persecution was over. The first actual edition, consisting of the revised draft, the completion of Book 7, and the addition of Books 8–9 seems to have been published in 313/14; see Tabbernee 1997a, 326; cf. Burgess 1997, 483–86. By the time his early work on the *Historia ecclesiastica* was interrupted, Eusebius, however, had dealt with all that he knew about the New Prophecy and the opposition to the movement. There is no hint of subsequent editing of the passages in Books 1–7 concerning Montanism at the time of the publication of the first actual edition of the *Historia ecclesiastica;* see Tabbernee 2007, 81–82. On the library at Caesarea Maritima during Eusebius' time, see Gamble 1995, 155–60 and Carriker 2003.

2. Eusebius, *Mart. Pal.* (*L*) (*S*) 3.1.

3. On Diocletian and the Great Persecution (ca. 303–313), see Frend 1984, 439–63. That Thecla was a Montanist is clear from the reference in the long recension (*L*) of *Mart. Pal.* 3.2 that she and some of her companions were "Phrygians." As Thecla came from Bizia, that is Bizya, in Thrace, the reference cannot be geographic but must refer to adherents of "the sect named after the Phrygians"; see Barnes 1981, 151 and Tabbernee 1997b, 217; 2007, 197–98, 235. Agapius was most probably, but not absolutely certainly, also a Montanist.

Whether Eusebius and Thecla ever met personally is unknown but not impossible. Eusebius certainly called her "the Thecla of our day(s)" (*Mart. Pal.* [*L*] [*S*] 3.1). Similarly, whether the library at Caesarea sustained any damage during the Great Persecution is not recorded in any extant source, but, if so, the damage may have been slight. Some years later, the emperor Constantine I (306–337) asked Eusebius to produce for him fifty codex copies of the sacred scriptures (Eusebius, *Vit. Const.* 4.36–37). This presupposes that the exemplars at Caesarea had remained intact. For a more detailed exposition of Eusebius' "theology of persecution," at the time described in this chapter, see Tabbernee 1997a, 326–29.

4. The young men's request of Urbanus that they might suffer the same fate as Agapius and Thecla by being thrown to the wild animals should not be taken to suggest that they were also Montanists and certainly not that Montanists were invariably voluntary martyrs; see Tabbernee 2007, 235.

5. Whether Thecla died in the arena at Caesarea in March 304 is unclear from Eusebius' account. Presumably, she and (the first) Agapius were taken to the theater during the games of that time to be thrown to the beasts. In *Mart. Pal.* 6.3, however, Eusebius reveals that Agapius was finally martyred on November 20, 306—two years and eight months after the time described in this chapter. According to Eusebius, Agapius had, on more than three previous occasions, been brought from the prison to the arena to be thrown to the beasts but, for a variety of reasons, had not actually been sent onto the field, his execution deferred until a future occasion. To claim either that Thecla (but not Agapius) was thrown to the beasts in March 304 and died on that date or that (like Agapius) she was returned to prison then and died on another occasion is to argue from Eusebius' silence. From Eusebius' account, it is clear that even Agapius did not ultimately die by being *eaten* by wild beasts. He, apparently, after having been mauled by a bear in Caesarea's theater remained alive for yet one more day. He was taken back to the jail where he and Thecla had spent so many months, if not years, together. The next day, heavy stones were tied to his feet and, presumably just outside of the governor's palace, he was thrown into the Internum Mare where he drowned; see Eusebius, *Mart. Pal.* 6.7.

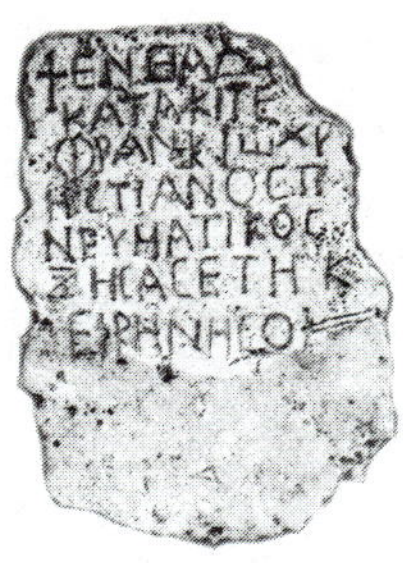

Chapter 23

Pepouza, Phrygia, ca. 305 C.E.
Quintilla's vision

Quintilla is absolutely certain. It is Christ who is coming toward her. She can recognize Christ anywhere, anytime—even in her sleep. As the figure dressed in a bright robe comes closer, Quintilla notices something unusual. Christ is a woman, not a man. The female Christ says nothing but lies down and sleeps beside her. Quintilla is overcome with emotion but remains silent, not daring to speak. Sometime during the night, she feels a warm glow and senses that supernatural insight has been imparted to her.

Quintilla is now fully awake. She looks around her carefully. The light of the morning sun rising over the mountains to the east of Pepouza illuminates even the darkest crevices of the room. There is no one else here. The female Christ has gone. Quintilla, the New Prophecy's latest Phrygian prophetess, quickly dresses and hurries from the house, not even pausing to eat anything.

Most of the followers of Montanus, Maximilla, and Priscilla are already up and preparing to undertake the day's chores. As Quintilla rushes into the house of the nearest family, she is barely coherent as she excitedly tries to tell them what has happened. The word spreads rapidly that an extraordinary event has occurred. The small community gathers quickly in the small basilica that is their regular meeting place, and expectantly waits for Quintilla to recover her composure so she can address them.

After only minutes, but what seems to Quintilla's followers like a very long time, Quintilla finally speaks. "In the form of a woman, dressed in a bright robe, Christ came to me," she says, "and put wisdom in me and revealed to me this place to be holy and Jerusalem to descend here from heaven."[1] One could hear a pin drop. A first no one speaks, but then, all at once, there is the cacophony of a multitude of voices, everyone speaking at the same time.

An old man who has been a member of the New Prophecy movement in Pepouza for many years tells the others that here, at last, is confirmation of what Montanus taught about the New Jerusalem. Almost simultaneously, an old woman, who has also been an adherent for decades, tells the gathered community that she had heard that Priscilla had once said something like Quintilla has just told them.[2] Someone else disagrees and reminds everyone that it was Maximilla who

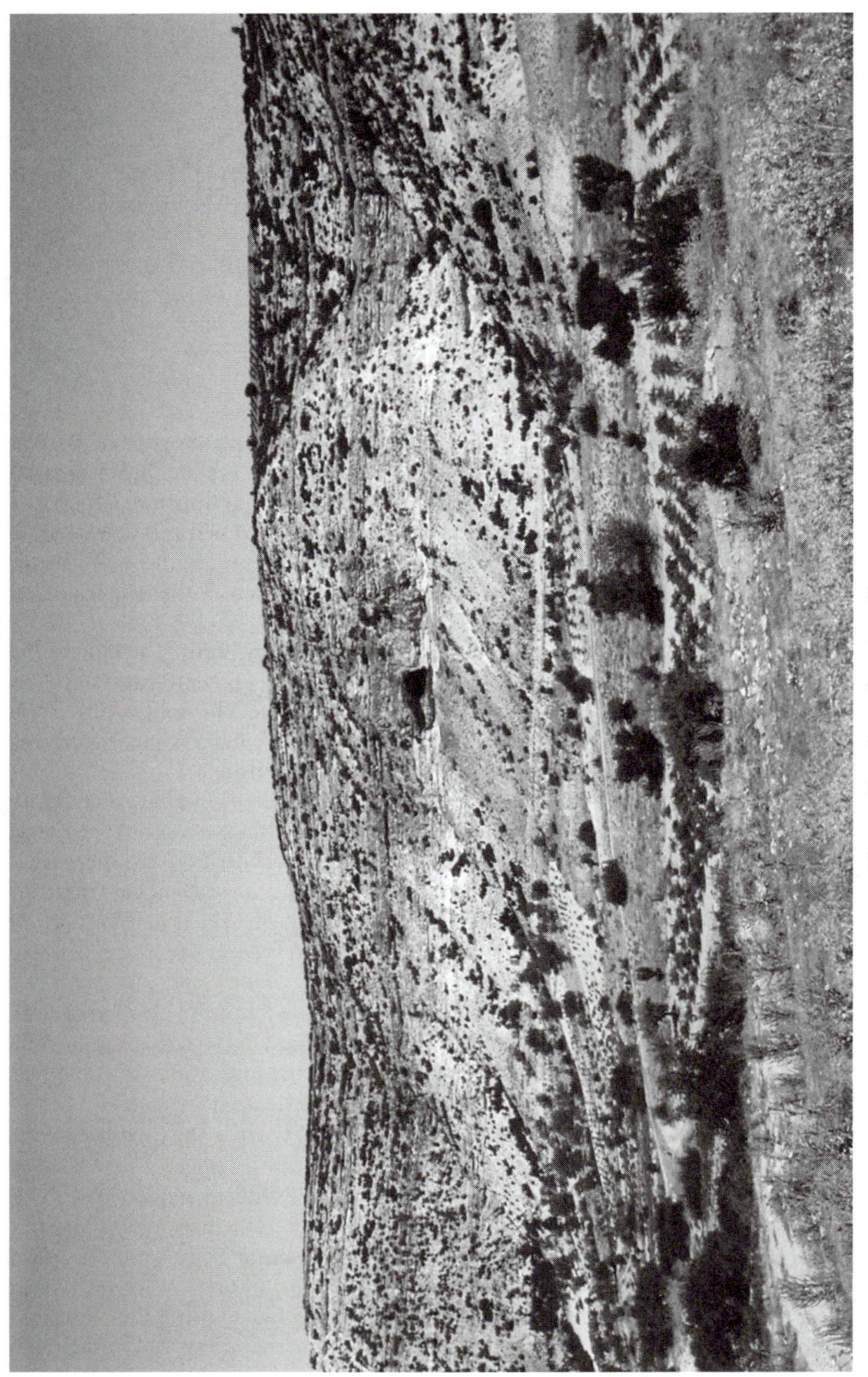

Figure 23.1: Site of ancient Pepouza

predicted the end of time. A voice from the back of the church calls out that it was Montanus himself who told the gravediggers to bury him fifty cubits deep because fire would come to consume all the face of the earth.[3] A woman who has been listening, as they all have, to the heated exchange is sure that the New Jerusalem will descend out of heaven *before* the destruction of the world by fire and that the descent of the New Jerusalem will delay the impending judgment.

From the row of seats in the apse, one of the elders speaks up. The prophecy about the New Jerusalem is not to be taken literally, he says. The New Jerusalem is not going to descend literally out of heaven. It is already here. All who believe the New Prophecy already experience the presence of God through the new revelations from the Paraclete given by Montanus, Maximilla, and Priscilla, of blessed memory. Practicing the ethical principles they have been taught by the New Prophecy means already living in God's new city here in Pepouza. If the *physical* New Jerusalem were really going to descend here literally, it would have done so long ago.

The presbyter's words spark a new round of heated debate, which goes on for hours. Not even the hunger pangs gnawing at their stomachs around noon nor the pressing chores of the day slows down the animated discussion that continues well into the afternoon. By that time, two factions of adherents of the New Prophecy have defined themselves at Pepouza. Henceforth, some will be known as Quintillians.[4]

Sources:

Quintilla, *Log., ap.* Epiphanius, *Pan.* 49.1.2–3; Maximilla, *Log., ap.* Anti-Phrygian, *Fr., ap.* Epiphanius, *Pan.* 48.2.4; *IMont* 2.

Pepouza, Phrygia, ca. 310 C.E.
The Montanist virgins prophesy

It is dark—very dark—outside. Inside the basilica it is also dark. The only light comes from the two rows of small oil lamps affixed to each of the long walls of the basilica. Despite the darkness, the basilica is full of people. The older ones are seated on small benches toward the front of the church near the altar, men on one side, women on the other.

Some of the old women are widows, "real widows," as they are called in scripture to indicate that these are widows enrolled in the "Order of Widows." They are women who, while not ordained, play an important role in the life and ministry of the congregation. They pray without ceasing; they visit the sick; they assist in the baptism of women; they provide hospitality on behalf of the congregation to those in need. In return for their ministry the congregation supports the widows' own needs. The widows are special people and, rightly so, they have their own special seats in the basilica—places of honor at the side of the altar.

Everyone else is standing, being careful to leave a wide aisle in the middle of the basilica. When the people first entered the dimly lit basilica, there had been

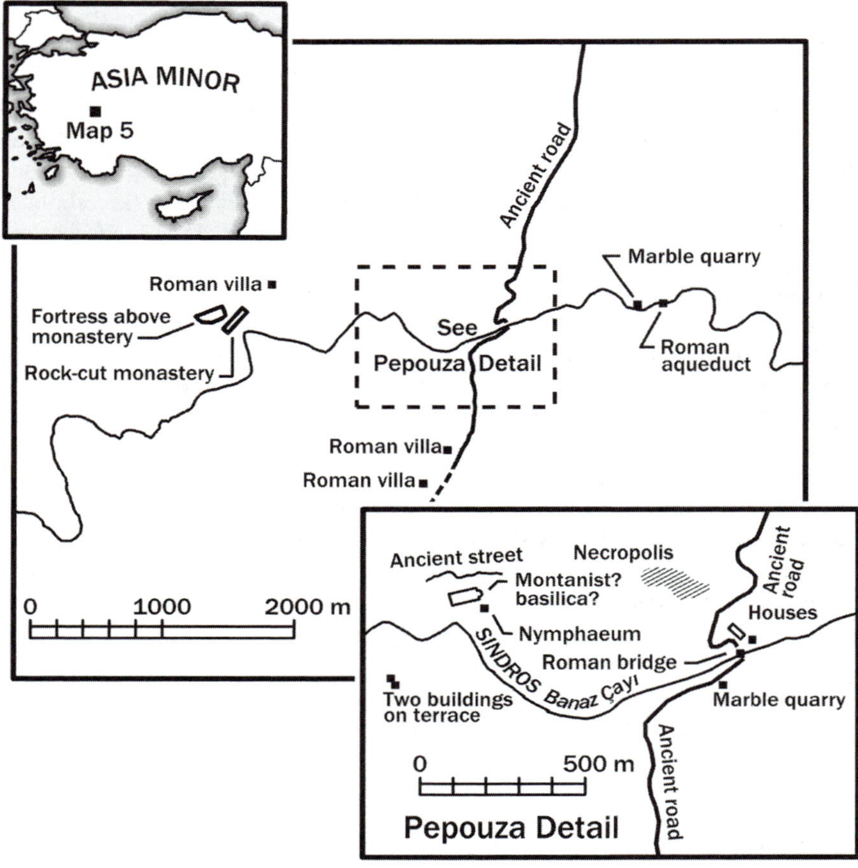

Map 5: Pepouza (detail)

some talking as neighbors and friends greeted one another and spoke about their favorite topics. How fortunate they are to be followers not only of Christ but also of Quintilla, their prophetess. She has taught them so much about the way the Paraclete first came via Montanus, Maximilla, and Priscilla to reveal how true Christians are to live in today's day and age. And wasn't it amazing that Christ came to Quintilla to confirm that Pepouza, *their* city, was indeed to be the site of the descent of the New Jerusalem? Five years had passed since that particular revelation, but they are still talking about it. Some of their leaders have figured out exactly where the New Jerusalem will descend. It will come to rest on the vast level plain that stretches north from the rim of the canyon where Pepouza itself is situated. The land is flat enough and large enough to accommodate the city as described in the book of Revelation—just as Montanus himself had once surmised. No doubt the New Jerusalem will reach as far as Tymion, the small settlement to the north of Pepouza.

While one group of worshipers is talking about the New Jerusalem, another group is discussing the remarkable fact that Christ had appeared to Quintilla in the form of a woman. Surely this is the ultimate confirmation of the words of the Apostle Paul that "in Christ Jesus," "there is neither male nor female."[5] Within their congregation, women as well as men can take leadership roles—whether as prophets, presbyters, or even bishops. At Pepouza they haven't had a woman bishop yet but, some speculate, it won't be long.

Almost as if by a pre-ordained signal, the talking suddenly stops. The silence is palpable. The older people seated in the front of the basilica rise to their feet and, along with those already standing, turn their whole bodies toward the rear of the church where the entrance is. People hardly breathe lest the sound of inhaling break the silence. One of the worshipers, an old man, has the urge to cough but he clenches his teeth and holds his breath in an effort to suppress the urge. Two ushers ceremoniously open the double doors leading into the basilica. Although the worshipers know what to expect, there is a collective gasp as they catch their first glimpse of the seven virgins standing, one behind the other, at the entrance.

Each virgin wears a pure white robe and carries a torch. The torches are lit and radiate a great deal of light above and around the virgins. Dressed in white, the virgins look like angels, brave angels who have overcome the darkness with light. The congregation is still absolutely silent as the lamp-bearing virgins process into the basilica down the central aisle. Suddenly the basilica is bathed with brilliant light. The darkness is completely banished as the virgins place their torches in the holders mounted strategically around the church.

After placing their torches in their predetermined places, the virgins—almost dancing—move to the front of the church near the altar. Every eye follows them and every ear listens expectantly to hear what they have to say today, as they prophesy to the people.[6]

Sources:

1 Tim 5:3, 6–10; Quintilla, *Log., ap.* Epiphanius, *Pan.* 49.1.2–3; Gal 3:28; Rev 3:12, 21:1–22:5; Epiphanius, *Pan.* 49.2.3–5.

Notes

1. Quintilla, *Log., ap.* Epiphanius, *Pan.* 49.1.3.

2. Epiphanius could not determine whether the *logion* quoted in this section of this chapter was uttered by Priscilla, one of the original Montanist prophetesses, or by Quintilla, a much later Montanist prophetess. His source for this particular *logion* was not the "Anti-Phrygian" (on whom see Chapter 1); Tabbernee 2007, 117–18. As little would have been gained by attributing a *logion* from an earlier prophetess to a later one, it seems best to assume that the *logion* was uttered by Quintilla and that it was she who claimed to have had the dream/vision in which a feminine Christ came to her, confirming Pepouza to be the site of the descent of the New Jerusalem. Presumably, by the time Epiphanius came to write his *Panarion*, the dream/vision and *logion* had been attributed, by some adherents of the New Prophecy movement, to Priscilla herself in order to give the *logion* greater authority.

3. *IMont* 2 (Tabbernee 1997b, 38).

4. Nothing definitive is known about Quintilla. One branch, at least, of the New Prophecy movement appears to have been named after her, but it is also possible that, in some fourth-century circles, the whole movement at Pepouza was known by her name. Theories that Quintilla was the prophetess described by Firmilian (see Chapter 18) or that she was the fourth person whose bones were interred in the shrine at Pepouza which also contained the bones of Montanus, Maximilla, and Priscilla (see Chapters 3, 34, and 38) are unconvincing; Tabbernee 1997b, 34; 2007, 118. That Quintilla flourished at Pepouza ca. 305 is speculative. Theoretically speaking, she may have been operative anytime after the original New Prophets and before Epiphanius wrote—that is, between ca. 178 and ca. 376. I have chosen 305, as it is after the time when Eusebius (who and whose sources appear not to have known about Quintilla) completed the unpublished draft of his *Historia ecclesiastica* (see Chapter 22). The date 305 also gives around seventy years for the double tradition about who actually uttered the *logion* to develop.

5. Gal 3:28.

6. Within Montanist congregations as well as in mainstream Christianity, there existed an "Order of Virgins" which paralleled and, in some cases overlapped with, the "Order of Widows"; see Tabbernee 1997b, 521–22. Mainstream Christianity also made use, at least occasionally of "lamp-bearing virgins" (e.g., see Gregory of Nyssa, *Ep.* 6.10). The unique aspect of the group of "lamp-bearing virgins" among the Quintillians at Pepouza—and Montanists elsewhere (e.g., Ankyra; see Chapter 36) is that they, according to Epiphanius, not only prophesied but exhibited "a kind of enthusiasm to the people present, working a deception to make everyone weep; they pour forth tears, as though, in compassion, they are evoking repentance and by their demeanor are lamenting human existence" (*Pan.* 49.2.4). Epiphanius is undoubtedly representative of other mainstream bishops in his denunciation of Montanism for allowing women to conduct penitential rites and being involved in other activities reserved in non-Montanist Christianity to *male* bishops, presbyters, and deacons. See also Tabbernee 1997b, 523–24.

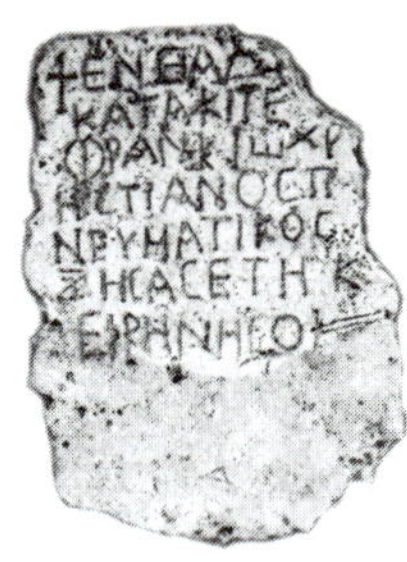

Chapter 24

Ankyra, Galatia, ca. 312 C.E.

The chalice of repose

The sun is still an hour away from rising, but Theodotus is already bustling around in his shop. Two small candles provide the only light. He is arranging his wares. He has learned just where to place his most attractive items so that the customers will see them and want to buy them. Today he is especially pleased with a silver chalice he acquired on the journey from which he only returned to Ankyra yesterday. He polishes the chalice until it gleams brightly in the candlelight, and he places it on a little table near the front door on a red silk cloth. Theodotus finds a rectangular piece of wood in the back of the shop, drapes some more red silk cloth over it, and fixes the silk-covered board vertically to one end of the table. Theodotus stands back to admire his handiwork. The red backdrop sets off the silver chalice beautifully. Perfect, he thinks to himself: no one with the means to buy the chalice will be able to resist it.

As he continues to arrange his wares, Theodotus can't help smiling. His recent journey to Malos, a village about two-days' walk from the city and situated on the beautiful Halys River, was very successful. Not only did he pick up, at bargain prices, many little treasures such as the silver chalice, but he also obtained the remains of the martyr Valens. Valens' body had been thrown into the Halys. Now, because of his journey to Malos, the martyr's bones are preserved for posterity and will be placed in a suitable reliquary.

Together with one of the presbyters of Malos, a man named Fronto, Theodotus had explored a large part of the Halys and found a site on the banks of the river that he believed would be the perfect place for a martyrium—not for Valens' remains but for those of some future martyr. Who that martyr would be he did not yet know, but he had told the surprised Fronto that God would supply the relics in due time.

The tiny bell on the shop's door suddenly rings as Theodotus' first potential customer enters. Theodotus knows the customer well. He is a man named Victor. Victor's eyes are drawn immediately to the gleaming silver chalice, displayed so artfully among the folds of red silk. He would love to own such a beautiful chalice, but, as Theodotus also knows, he will never be able to afford it. In any case, Victor is not here today to buy anything. He is here to tell Theodotus all that has been happening in Ankyra while he was away in Malos.

Theodotus is not surprised when Victor tells him that Theotecnus, the governor, has been relentlessly seeking out Christians, including Christians from their own community of adherents to the New Prophecy. Some have already been arrested, and Victor has no doubt that he himself will be arrested soon. Among those arrested, Theodotus learns from Victor, are their community's seven virgins. Theodotus is horrified. The seven virgins provide an important component of the community's liturgy. They carry torches and prophesy to the people at evening worship services. Someone must have betrayed them to the authorities for all of them to have been arrested on the same day.

Victor describes in graphic detail what had befallen Tecusa, Alexandria, Phaeine, Claudia, Euphrasia, Matrona, and Julitta. Theotecnus, the governor, was so angry when they refused to sacrifice at the altar of the imperial cult that he condemned them to a brothel. Fortunately, Victor tells Theodotus, God protected them and they escaped the ordeal unscathed, their virginity still intact. Today, however, they are to be taken to the lake just outside Ankyra where the governor has ordered them to play the role of pagan priestesses by washing the statues of Diana and Minerva.

Theodotus is very afraid for the women, especially for Tecusa—the most aged of them. She has been like a mother to him and instructed him in the faith and in the teachings of the New Prophecy. He and Victor pray fervently that the women will not succumb to the pressure to do as they are commanded. They all know that the statues are not real goddesses and that, in fact, there *are* no goddesses. Washing the statues, therefore, is not *really* venerating goddesses—but doing so will give the appearance to the pagan population that the seven women are no longer Christian virgins but priestesses of Diana and Minerva.

Theodotus need not have worried. By the time he and Victor get to the lake, the whole episode is over. Tecusa and the others, having refused to wash the statues or to sacrifice, have been drowned in the lake. The heavy stones tied to their bodies not only ensured their death but make it virtually impossible for the Christians to recover the bodies to give the women a Christian burial. Theotecnus has even stationed guards around the lake, just in case any foolish Christian tries to recover the bodies despite the danger. Victor and Theodotus leave grieving and frustrated—each to his own home and, eventually, to bed.

Theodotus wakes up in a sweat. His hair is dripping wet and his hands are shaking. For a moment he doesn't know where he is. The dream seemed so real. Tecusa called out to him from her watery grave. She scolded him for leaving her body and that of the others in the lake. While she was talking, she was floating underwater, her white robe billowing behind her. Theodotus suddenly shudders as he remembers seeing horrible fish with huge teeth swimming all around the virgins, ready to devour them. It was a nightmare rather than a dream. Tecusa implored him not to let the fish eat their bodies. Fully awake now, Theodotus determines that, come what may, he will recover the bodies of the seven virgins.

Miracles don't often happen, but Theodotus thanks God that they sometimes do. As he and Polychronius, Tecusa's nephew, arrive at the lake later that day, there is no sign of the soldiers. Their absence alone is a miracle. The greater miracle however is that within minutes there is a huge storm so strong that all the water in the lake is pushed to one side, leaving the other side almost totally dry. It is as if God were parting the Red Sea a second time. Theodotus and Polychronius run to the spot where they see the bodies of the virgins lying untouched by the fish. One by one, they carry the women's bodies out of the lake before the water returns. With the help of the other Christians who came with them, Theodotus and Polychronius take the bodies of the seven virgins to the Church of the Patriarchs and bury them in the hallowed ground nearby.

The following day, the whole city is in an uproar. Theotecnus is furious that the bodies of the seven virgins have been stolen from under the very noses of his soldiers. He demands to know who is responsible. Theodotus is so excited by what has happened that he is ready to volunteer that he himself is the culprit, and proud of it. Wisely, some of his friends talk him out of committing such a rash act.

Later the same day, Polychronius is arrested. Tortured mercilessly, Tecusa's nephew cracks under pressure and can't help revealing that Theodotus is the main person behind the recovery and burial of his aunt's body and those of the other aged virgins. When Theodotus hears of this, he is not perturbed. He has no doubt that he is to be a martyr also.

Once again it is early morning and, once again, Theodotus is bustling around in his shop. With everything that has been happening, no customers have bought any of his wares. Not that anyone is ever going to buy from him again, Theodotus thinks to himself. He picks up the silver chalice and, absent-mindedly, polishes it, as he had done only two days earlier so that, once more, it gleams brightly in the candlelight. Theodotus wonders who will own this beautiful object one day.

Victor and some other friends come in to say their farewells, knowing that Theodotus will soon be arrested. They are amazed at how calm he is. Theodotus puts the silver chalice on the silk-draped table and looks directly at his friends. He implores them not to interfere when the soldiers come. Reluctantly, Victor and the others agree to his request. Theodotus tells them that after his death, a presbyter from Malos, a man named Fronto, will come to Ankyra and asks his friends for one more favor. They are to ensure that Fronto will be given Theodotus' remains.

Before Theodotus' puzzled friends can respond to the strange request, there is the unmistakable sound of heavy military boots on the pavement outside the shop. The door is thrown open and two soldiers in full uniform enter. In no time, they arrest Theodotus and take him into custody. They march Theodotus to the tribunal where Theotecnus is already seated. Theotecnus, knowing that Theodotus is the leader of his particular group of Christians, has decided to see if he can persuade Theodotus to change religions. To the surprise of everyone, instead of condemning Theodotus to death for recovering the bodies of the seven virgins, Theotecnus offers Theodotus the prestigious position of priest of Apollo at Ankyra. How ironic, thinks Theodotus, that Montanus converted *to* Christianity from being a priest of Apollo and now he is being asked to convert *from* Christianity by becoming a priest of Apollo. Theotecnus, obviously, doesn't realize what he is asking. Theodotus, in no uncertain terms, declines the governor's offer.

Theodotus' corpse is supposed to have been burned, but God has intervened by sending a huge thunderstorm, soaking the wood of the pyre. The soldiers, guarding Theodotus' not-yet-burned body late at night, are bored. An old man leading a donkey pulling a cart comes by and, curious, the guards stop him. They ask what is in the cart and the man tells them it is wine, not just any old wine but the vintage wine for which his village is famous. When asked the name of the village, the old man tells them it is Malos. The guards have heard of the wine from Malos and are eager to try some. The old man whose name, the guards learn, is Fronto, offers to let them sample some of the wine. He even has with him a gleaming silver chalice into which he pours the wine before giving it to the soldiers. It is the most delicious wine they have ever tasted. It is also the most potent. As *sampling* wine is not in the guards' nature, they each gulp down large quantities of the wine in record time, soon falling down drunk on the ground.

Fronto unloads some of the jars of wine, making room on the cart for Theodotus' body. Once the body is carefully hidden among the remaining jars along with the chalice, Fronto climbs onto the cart himself and orders the donkey to go home. Unguided by human hands, the donkey begins the long journey back to Malos. The donkey pulls the cart all through the night, all through the next day, and all through the next night.

Fronto has been dozing, but when he wakes up he finds that the donkey has stopped at the very spot on the banks of the Halys River near Malos that Theodotus had identified as the site of the future martyrium of a then as-yet-unknown martyr. Looking at the body of Theodotus beside him in the cart, Fronto thinks how prophetic Theodotus was when he told him that God would supply the relics for this martyrium in due time. He tenderly unloads Theodotus' body, places it on the ground next to the silver chalice, and begins collecting stones to construct the martyrium.[1]

Source:

Pass. Theod.

Notes

1. That Theodotus (d. ca. 312) was a Montanist and perhaps even a Montanist bishop is highly likely although not absolutely certain; see Tabbernee 1997b, 526–33; 2007, 238–40. In this narrative, I (following Grégoire and Orgels 1951 and S. Mitchell 1982) assume that Theodotus and the seven virgins did indeed belong to a Montanist community in Ankyra. On groups of lamp-bearing virgins in Montanist circles, see Chapters 23 and 36. On the Martyrium of Theodotus at Malos (Kalecik), see Chapter 36. The silver chalice is not mentioned in the *Passio Theodoti Ancyrani*.

Figure 25.1: Marcus Julius Eugenius' sarcophagus

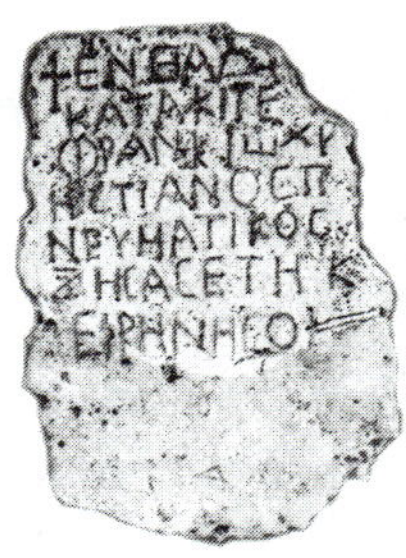

Chapter 25

Laodikeia Katakekaumene, Lycaonia, 337 C.E.

Constantine is dead

Bad news travels faster than good news. The courier's horse is trembling and snorting as the young man dismounts in a hurry. The strong odor of the horse's sweat clings to him as he rushes up to Marcus Julius Eugenius, who is coming down the steps of the basilica to meet the messenger. Eugenius is not an old man, he has yet to reach fifty years, but he moves rather slowly. The injuries he sustained while being tortured during the persecution under Maximin Daia took a toll, especially on his legs—Eugenius moves like an old man.

The courier reaches Eugenius before Eugenius is halfway down the steps and, without saying a word, thrusts a letter into the bishop's hands. Eugenius opens the letter and sees that it is from Eusebius of Nikomedia, the venerable bishop of Constantinople. Eugenius quickly scans the letter and gasps at the bad news: Constantine is dead. The only good news in the letter is that Eusebius baptized Constantine on the emperor's death bed just before he died.

Three deacons also come out of the basilica at the sound of the horse's hooves galloping on the large stone slabs that pave the road leading to the basilica's entrance porch. Eugenius asks one of the deacons to take the courier around the back of the church to the hostel reserved for visitors. He asks another deacon to ensure that the courier's horse is rubbed down with straw and given some hay to eat. He warns the deacon, unnecessarily, not to let the horse drink any water until the horse has cooled down.

Eugenius and the third deacon, the archdeacon in charge of all the other deacons, walk slowly up the steps back toward the entrance porch. The porch is a magnificent structure made of marble. Passing through the entrance, the two men hurry across the courtyard past the water fountain, rather than going the long way through the covered cloisters. Not until they reach Eugenius' study and sit down do the two men speak. The archdeacon respectfully asks the bishop how he thinks Constantine's death will affect their Christian community. Constantine, after all, was the world's first Christian emperor—even if he wasn't baptized until he was on his death bed as they have just learned.

Eugenius at first appears not to have heard the archdeacon. He sits silently in deep thought for a few minutes. Then he leans forward in his chair and tells

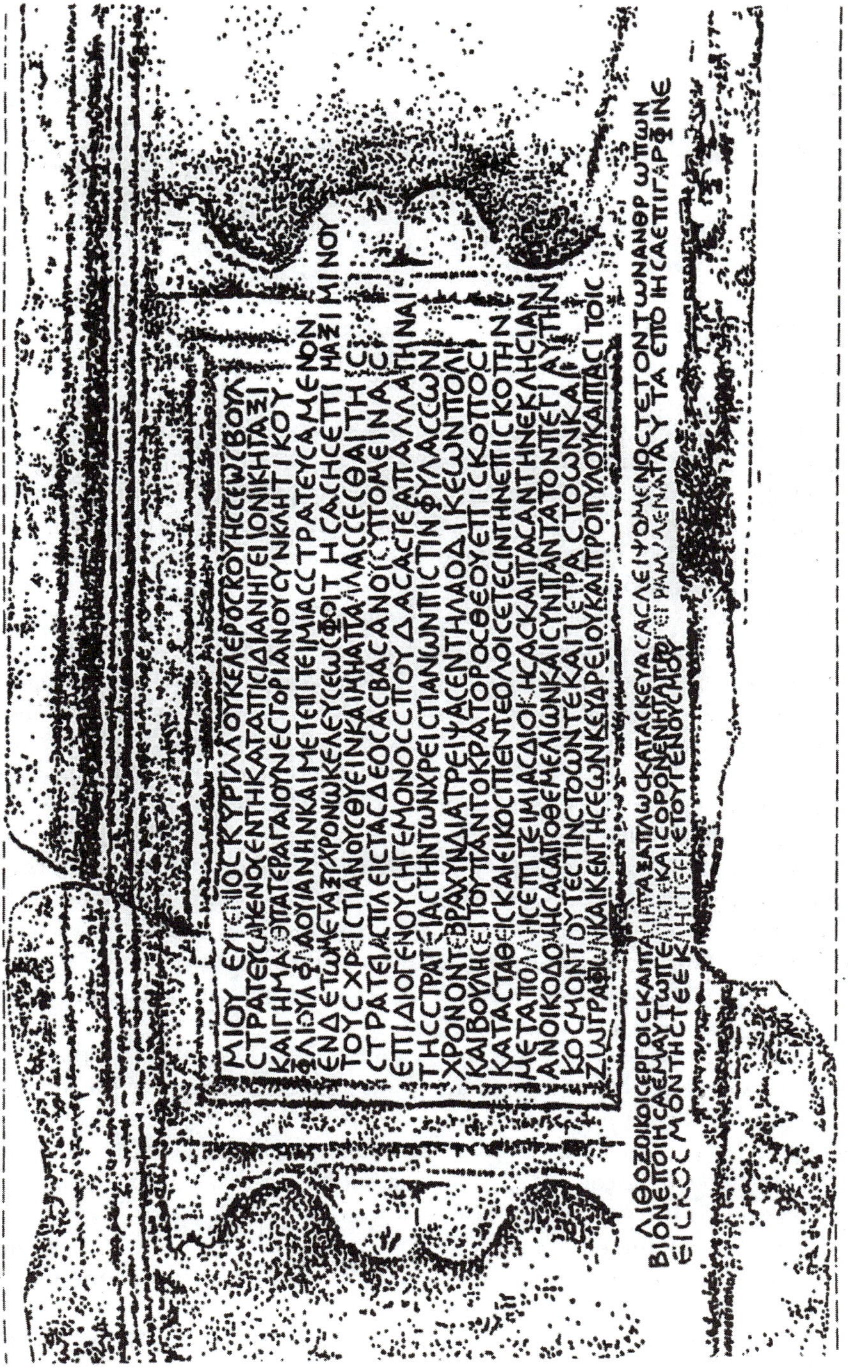

Figure 25.2: Marcus Julius Eugenius' epitaph

the archdeacon, a man in his late twenties, what it was like for Christians before Constantine became emperor. "I was stationed as a soldier at the headquarters of the governor of Pisidia,"[1] Eugenius tells the archdeacon. The archdeacon assumes rightly that Eugenius had not been an ordinary soldier but a junior officer—a rank befitting his status as the son of Cyrillus Celerus, a member of the town council of Laodikeia, and the son-in-law of Gaius Julius Nestorianus, a Roman senator no less. A tour of duty in the army, attached to the office of Valerius Diogenes, the governor, was the ideal way to begin the *cursus honorum*, the career path of sequentially more important offices for public officials, and ensure his rapid promotion to high civil office.

Eugenius finds his mind wandering back to the first months he was stationed at Antioch, the capital of Pisidia. The city was more beautiful than any he had ever seen. The entrance gate had fountains attached to it, creating a memorable impression on all who enter the city. The city's wide streets, theater, public baths, and aqueduct were sights to behold and, even though as a Christian he didn't like to admit it, the huge temple dedicated to Augustus was incredibly impressive. Much more interesting to him than any of the public buildings or pagan temples, Eugenius remembers, was the synagogue in Antioch. Still standing after all those years, it was the very synagogue, he had been told, where St. Paul preached about Jesus and converted a large number of people to Christianity. Eugenius had also been told that St. Paul came to Antioch from Cyprus because L. Sergius Paullus, the governor of Cyprus, gave St. Paul letters of introduction to his relatives, who had large land holdings near Antioch. Eugenius does not doubt the accuracy of the story. He has even seen the tombstones of some of the leading members of the Sergii Paulli family in Antioch itself.[2]

His first months in Antioch had been exciting and unproblematic for him—even as a Christian in the army. But all of that changed rapidly. While Eugenius was doing his very best to serve with distinction in the imperial militia, the emperor, Maximin Daia, took action against Christians in the army. Eugenius tells the archdeacon: "An order had been issued during the time of Maximinus that the Christians were to sacrifice and were not to be released from military service."[3]

Again Eugenius pauses as he replays in his mind the painful scenes of what happened next. Grossly understating his suffering, he continues his account: "Having endured, repeatedly, very many tortures when Diogenes was governor, I hastened to leave the service, keeping the faith of the Christians."[4] The archdeacon, who has been reading the Acts of the Apostles, can't help making the connection between what Eugenius has just said and what St. Paul told the very first Christians at Antioch. "Keep the faith," Paul had instructed them—no matter how much persecution and opposition you face.[5] The archdeacon, who had not previously heard Eugenius' personal story, now has even more respect for his bishop. Eugenius is a living martyr—a confessor. No wonder he was made bishop so soon after arriving back in Laodikeia—although the archdeacon assumes that Eugenius' family connections were not completely irrelevant in the appointment. The archdeacon also suspects that Eugenius' family connections helped him secure discharge from the army—even though Maximinus' edict decreed that Christian soldiers were not to be released.

Just then Flavia Julia Flaviana, Marcus Julius Eugenius' wife, comes into the study. She asks her husband if it is true that Constantine is dead. She has heard the news from one of the servants. Eugenius, a thoughtful, considerate man apologizes to Flaviana for not informing her of the news himself—but he is still trying to come to terms with what the news means for them and for all Christians. He doubts, Eugenius tells Flaviana and the archdeacon, that there will be a return to general anti-Christian persecution such as that under Maximinus. Constantine's sons, after all, are also Christians. But, Eugenius confides to the two other people in his study, Constantine's successors may not give Christians like themselves the protection they enjoyed under Constantine himself.

Their congregation is comprised of followers of Novatian *and* followers of Montanus, Maximilla, and Priscilla. The merger had been one of necessity for the adherents of the New Prophecy movement. Constantine, after first including both Novatianists and Cataphrygians in an edict condemning non-Catholic sects, later changed his mind about the Novatianists. The Novatianists, but not the Cataphrygians, were once more allowed to have their own church buildings and cemeteries.[6]

Eugenius remembers well the discussions that took place between himself and the leaders of the New Prophecy movement in Laodikeia. That had been fifteen years ago. Eugenius had been bishop of the Novatianist congregation for a decade then, and he knew the history of his church intimately. Novatian, a presbyter at Rome during the time of the persecution under Decius, had taken a strong stand against allowing apostates back into the church without completing an extended period of penance. The church is the "Bride of Christ" and, as such, she needs to remain absolutely pure. She cannot be tainted by the sin of those who deny the faith at the first sign of trouble. The so-called catholics were, according to Novatian, far too lax in taking the sinners back too easily. Eugenius is glad that, because of the split that occurred over the issue long ago in Rome, he now, many years later, is the bishop of a congregation that, following Novatian's teachings, has remained pure.

Eugenius, on the other hand, had had to learn a lot about the Cataphrygians, but he had learned quickly. One of the things he liked about the followers of Montanus, Maximilla, and Priscilla was their emphasis on ethical purity. The Cataphrygians, like the Novatianists, took sin very seriously and didn't let sinners such as apostates off easily. They also took a hard line against divorce and against remarriage after the death of one's spouse. They fasted longer and more frequently than Catholics and stood firm in the face of martyrdom. The Cataphrygians were his kind of people. He had welcomed them with open arms, and from then on the Novatianist and Cataphrygian congregations in Laodikeia merged to become one church under his leadership. The Cataphrygians, who would have lost their basilica and had had their sacred books burned as a result of Constantine's first edict, now, as "Novatianists," had enjoyed Constantine's protection.[7]

Sitting with Flaviana and the archdeacon, Eugenius hopes and prays that Constantine's sons will continue Constantine's policies. If they don't, not only the Cataphrygians but also the Novatianists will be in great peril.

Sources:

IMont 69; Eusebius, *Vit. Const.* 3.64–66, 4.61–64; Acts 13:4–52, 14:21–23; *CIL* 6.253, 6.31545.

Notes

1. *IMont* 69, *l.*2. The main details of the life and ministry of Marcus Julius Eugenius (d. ca. 340) are inscribed on the double sarcophagus which Eugenius had prepared for himself and for his family toward the end of his life (*IMont* 69, *ll.*18–19). The sarcophagus had been seen and the inscription copied during the eighteenth century and rediscovered in June 1908 by William Calder; see Calder 1908, 385–408. The sarcophagus, at that stage, was partially buried in a field south of the cemetery at Lâdik, the Turkish village also known as Halıcı, now occupying the site of Laodikeia. The sarcophagus was subsequently completely covered and lost until workmen, digging foundations for a house in 1997, found it again. It was seen in that year by Thomas Drew-Bear. The mayor of Lâdik/Halıcı, in preparation for the visit to the village of a team which I led in July 2000 and which included Professors Drew-Bear and Lampe, had the sarcophagus moved to the village and made the centerpiece of a small open air epigraphic museum. The text on the sarcophagus is beautifully inscribed. A related inscription (*IMont* 70) also refers to Eugenius along with his episcopal predecessor at Laodikeia, a man named Severus. That inscription, a memorial dedication, is carved on a plaque, now in the Konya Archaeological Museum. The plaque honoring both Severus and Eugenius appears originally to have been mounted on the wall of a memorial chapel in the basilica at Laodikeia where the sarcophagus of Severus stood next to the sarcophagus of Eugenius and Flaviana; see Tabbernee 1997b, 440–41.

2. See S. Mitchell 1993, 2:6–7 on the tombstones of members of the Sergii Paulli family.

3. *IMont* 69, *ll.*5–7.

4. *IMont* 69, *ll.*7–9.

5. Acts 14:22 [NRSV altered].

6. Constantine's edict, against the Novatianists, Cataphrygians, and other non-Catholic sects (Eusebius, *Vit. Const.* 3.66) has not survived, but a letter by Constantine summarizing the edict's content has been preserved by Eusebius (*Vit. Const.* 3.64–65). The edict, which included the demand that all property belonging to the sectarian groups was to be handed over to the Catholic church and that all heretical books were to be sought out and burned, was issued between the close of the First Council of Nicaea (August 25, 325) and the issuing of another edict on September 25, 326. The second edict is the one which once more allowed Novatianists to possess "their own buildings and places suitable for burial" (*Cod. theod.* 16.5.2); see Tabbernee 1997b, 343–44.

7. On the merger of Novatianist and Montanist churches, see Tabbernee 1997b, 347–48, 442–44. See Tabbernee 2007, 308–12 for a more detailed discussion of Constantine's anti-heretical/anti-Montanist legislation.

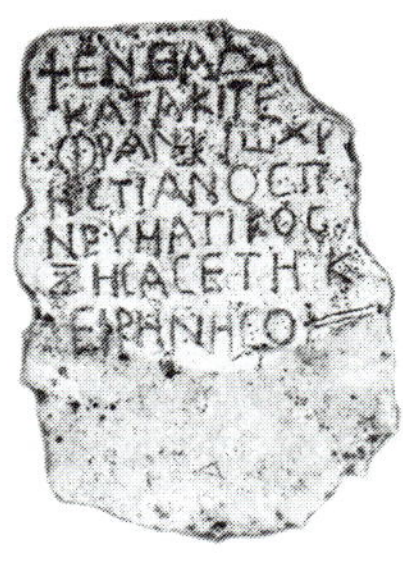

Chapter 26

Jerusalem, Palaestina, Holy Week, 348 C.E.

Cyril's lecture against the Montanists

Cyril loves his position as chief catechist of the Christian community in Jerusalem. Already a senior presbyter, he hopes that one day he will be bishop of Jerusalem—for him the most holy city of Christianity. For now, however, he is content to ensure that catechumens, those preparing for baptism and church membership, are well educated in the faith and in the ethical requirements of being a Christian.

Cyril enjoys teaching and is, so he has been told by others, an exceptional lecturer. He knows just how to put into simple words complicated aspects of the faith, making concepts such as the Trinity understandable even to persons not schooled in philosophy.

As a great teacher, Cyril organizes his catechetical lectures carefully. There are eighteen of them, not counting the introductory session, each based on a text of scripture. The first three lectures emphasize the importance of taking the process of catechesis seriously, the significance of repentance and remission of sins, and the relationship between baptism and salvation. Cyril is particularly pleased with the fourth lecture. It summarizes ten points of Christian doctrine, each one explained in subsequent lectures on the creed. In this way, even before the catechumens hear the creed for the very first time and commit it to memory, they can begin thinking about the issues involved.

Walking briskly through the labyrinth of narrow streets on his way to the Church of the Holy Sepulchre, where he has already given fifteen of his eighteen lectures, Cyril is delighted that his lectures thus far have gone very well indeed, especially the last three. No doubt the holy places within the new Church of the Holy Sepulchre, built by Constantine, helped reinforce the points he was trying to make concerning Christ's death and resurrection. Within the basilica is not only Golgotha, the place of the skull where Jesus was crucified, but also the tomb where he arose from the dead. What a setting for explaining the christological articles of the creed!

Cyril smiles as he remembers that the catechumens had listened with rapt attention to every sentence he uttered. Some wept silently as he told them in lecture thirteen:

> Christ stretched out his hands on the cross, that he might embrace the ends of the world; for this Golgotha is the very center of the earth. . . . He, who by his spiritual hands had established the heavens, stretched forth human hands; and they were fastened with nails, that his humanity, which bore the sins of humankind, having been nailed to the tree, and having died, would enable sin to die with it—so that we might rise again in righteousness.[1]

During lecture fourteen, Cyril noticed that his listeners were amazed at his own firsthand knowledge of the tomb of Jesus. The elaborate marble decorations now embellishing the tomb's entrance obscure the fact that there was once an outer cave in the rock leading to the sepulchre. Cyril remembers vividly seeing this second cave as a young man and he had watched as Constantine's workmen cut away the outer cave to make room for the decorations. The important thing, of course, is not what the tomb looked like originally but that Jesus rose from the very tomb now preserved forever as a holy shrine within the church to which he is hurrying to be on time for his next lecture—the sixteenth in the series.

The Church of the Holy Sepulchre is already crowded with catechumens as Cyril enters and walks to the lectern. As everyone already knows, this lecture and the next will be about the article in the creed that relates to the Holy Spirit. Cyril had recited the creed for the first time to the catechumens at the end of his fifth lecture. He had told them that even those who could write were not to write down the words of the creed used in Jerusalem. All of the catechumens were to learn the words by heart.

The Jerusalem Creed is not the same as the Nicene Creed although, Cyril likes to think, it influenced the wording of the Nicene Creed. For teaching the faith, Cyril and Maximus, the bishop of Jerusalem, prefer the Jerusalem Creed over the one ratified at Nicaea. The Jerusalem Creed does not have the troublesome word ὁμοούσιος (*homoousios:* "consubstantial"), adopted at Nicaea to explain the relationship between God the Father and God the Son. It also retains a longer, more detailed formulation of the article on the Holy Spirit. Instead of merely saying "We believe . . . in the Holy Spirit," as do those reciting the Nicene Creed,[2] those who recite the Jerusalem Creed say, "We believe . . . in one Holy Spirit, the Paraclete who spoke in the prophets."[3]

As Cyril reaches the podium, the noise of the catechumens practicing the article of the creed on the Holy Spirit dies down. The text for today's lecture is 1 Corinthians 12:1, 4: "Now concerning spiritual gifts, brothers and sisters, I do not want you to be uninformed. . . . Now there are varieties of gifts, but the same Spirit. . . ."

When he finishes the reading Cyril pauses, looks at his audience, and tells them solemnly that, in the Gospels, Christ warned that "whoever speaks against the Holy Spirit will not be forgiven, either in this age or the age to come."[4] Shock waves ripple through the catechumens before Cyril reassures them that they, unlike the heretics, need not be afraid. As long as he, as catechist, and they, as catechumens, speak about the Holy Spirit solely in scriptural terms, concentrating on what is written—not on what is *not* written—they have nothing to fear.

The heretics, on the other hand, have everything to fear because they have, serpent-like, sharpened their tongue against the Holy Spirit and dare to blaspheme the Holy Spirit. Cyril informs the catechumens that he is going to tell them about the blasphemous errors concerning the Holy Spirit promulgated by the various heretics so that they themselves, out of ignorance, will not fall into the same heretical errors. He assures them that they are not in any danger because quoting, for the sake of education, the statements of heretics will cause those statements to recoil on the heads of the heretics—not on their own heads.

In quick succession Cyril describes the errors of Simon Magus, the Valentinians, Manichaeans, and the Marcionites with respect to the Holy Spirit. Cyril's special scorn, however, is directed at the Cataphrygians, to whom he also refers as Montanists. The Cataphrygians, their leader Montanus, and his two so-called prophetesses Maximilla and Priscilla, are to be abhorred, Cyril exhorts the catechumens, for this crazy man Montanus had the audacity to equate himself with the Holy Spirit.

Cyril pauses for affect, lowers his voice, and calls Montanus a horrible man, full of impurity and immorality. Cyril, out of regard for the women in his audience, only hints at the precise nature of Montanus' immorality. But the minds of the women catechumens—working overtime—conjure up more wickedness than anything Cyril himself has heard or read about Montanus' alleged immorality.

Cyril *is* prepared to pass on to them one charge of wickedness his sources level against the Montanists: the charge of infanticide. Cyril accuses Montanus of *personally* "slaughtering and cutting into pieces women's wretched little children for unlawful food on the pretext of their so-called sacred rites."[5] Once again shock waves ripple through the audience; this time shock waves not of fear but of horror and revulsion. What a monster Montanus must have been! Images of a tall, strong, bearded man with a long knife slitting the throats of babies and infants, chopping them into pieces, fill the collective imagination of the catechumens sitting on long benches in the church. Every one can visualize Montanus handing out pieces of the flesh of slaughtered children as if they were pieces of eucharistic bread to be eaten cannibalistically.

The images of mad, blood-thirsty Montanus are so graphic that almost no one hears Cyril say that, because *Montanists* were erroneously known as Christians, *true* Christians were brought up on charges of infanticide and cannibalism in times of persecution. Nor do many hear Cyril say that Montanus also falsely named Pepouza as the New Jerusalem and dared to call himself the Holy Spirit. The alleged fate of wretched little children torn from their mothers' arms to be chopped up into Montanist communion food is the enduring image the catechumens take away from Cyril's lecture that day. That night in Jerusalem very few, if any, catechumens sleep.[6]

Sources:

Cyril of Jerusalem, *Catech.*, esp. 13.28, 14.9, 16.2–8; Matt 12:32; 1 Cor 12:1, 4; Kelly 1972, 183–84 [Creed of Jerusalem], 215–16 [Creed of Nicaea].

Notes

1. Cyril of Jerusalem, *Catech.* 13.28. Cyril, bishop of Jerusalem ca. 348/9–386/7, appears to have grown up in Jerusalem where he was made a deacon ca. 326 and a presbyter ca. 343. By 348 he was the most senior presbyter in Jerusalem and during Lent of that year gave the Catechetical Lectures referred to in this chapter. The translation of *Catech.* 13.28 is taken from *Nicene and Post-Nicene Fathers,* Series 2 7:89 (altered).

2. Kelly 1972, 183–84.

3. Kelly 1972, 215–16.

4. Matt 12:32.

5. Cyril of Jerusalem, *Catech.* 16.8.

6. Cyril's main source for his explanation of Montanism (*Catech.* 16.8) appears to have been Eusebius of Caesarea's *Historia ecclesiastica* (esp. 5.16–18). From Eusebius, or more specifically from Apollonius quoted by Eusebius (*ap. Hist. eccl.* 5.18), Cyril learned that Montanus called Pepouza "Jerusalem" and that Montanus (and other Montanist leaders) were allegedly involved in activities (such as the dissolution of marriages and gambling) deemed improper if not immoral. Cyril probably also had, either directly or indirectly, access to a collection of Montanist *logia.* In such a collection, Montanus, presumably, was recorded as utilizing at least one introductory formula containing a reference to the Holy Spirit/Paraclete speaking in the first person—leading to the charge that Montanus equated himself with the Holy Spirit; on which see Chapter 28.

It is not clear whether Cyril himself was the originator of the story of Montanus' alleged infanticide and cannibalism. The Praedestinatus (*Haer.* 1.26) mistakenly reports that Tertullian defended the charge of infanticide leveled on the early Montanist prophets. The Praedestinatus presumably assumed that Tertullian's explanation that Christians did not indulge in such practices (*Apol.* 9) was an exclusively Montanist (rather than 'catholic') apologetic. Perhaps Cyril, a century earlier than the Praedestinatus, had similarly misread Tertullian. Alternatively, the author of a no-longer-extant source read by Cyril may have come to such a conclusion. For the (very speculative) view that Apolinarius of Hierapolis was the first to level the charge of infanticide against the Montanists as a means of diverting the impact of such charges against 'catholic' Christians, see Rives 1996, 120–22. Rives also suggests that the work to which the Praedestinatus referred is Tertullian's lost *De ecstasi* and that this contained a defense of the specifically anti-Montanist charge of infanticide (Rives 1996, 118–19).

Cyril is the only author who specifically ascribes the horrific acts of infanticide and cannibalism to Montanus himself. All later extant sources see in Cyril's "Montanus" a euphemism for "Montanism." Most later Fathers are very skeptical about the veracity of the charges even when applied to "Montanism" rather than to "Montanus." Augustine of Hippo (354–430), for example, introduces his account with the words "They are said to have." He writes:

> *They are said to have* by-death-polluted sacraments, for *they are said to prepare* their supposed Eucharist from the blood of a one-year-old infant which they extort from its entire body through minute puncture wounds, mixing it with flour and hence making bread. (*Haer.* 1.26)

Similarly, Jerome states:

> I pass over polluted sacraments *which are said to involve* a suckling child. . . . I prefer not to believe such impropriety; everything reported about blood may well be made up. (*Ep*. 41.4)

Even the Praedestinatus adds qualifying statements to his account:

> I pass over things which are reported as though they are not firmly established. We make known that they [the Montanists] obtain the blood of infants merely so that we do not appear to be ignorant of all *that is said of them*. (*Haer*. 1.26)

For a full discussion of the issues involved, including a possible connection of the charge of infanticide with pre-baptismal tattooing, see Tabbernee 2007, 350–58.

Figure 27.1: Nanas' tombstone

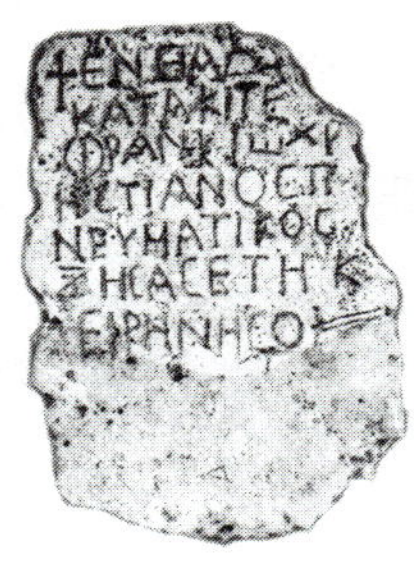

Chapter 27

The Phrygian Highlands, Phrygia, ca. 350 C.E.
The sleeping place

Hermogenes loves horses. His village is situated on the western edge of a large upland plain in the Phrygian highlands. The plain is high above sea level and receives plenty of rain. The soil is ideal for growing tall grass, which, in turn, is ideal for raising horses. Even in winter, the horses have more than sufficient food as some of the grass is mown to make hay to feed them when snow covers the ground.[1]

The only problem with the tall grass is that in the springtime it harbors a multitude of ticks. Hermogenes learned painful lessons as a young boy when, after running through the grass with his friends from the village,[2] he would come home infested with ticks embedded in his flesh. He would be scolded by his father for being so careless, but his mother would carefully remove the ticks, endeavoring to leave no head, leg, or other part of the tick behind. That, however, was not always easy and on more than one occasion his arms, legs, or even more private parts, had become infected.

Now, like his father before him, Hermogenes prefers to ride through the grass on one of the larger horses—making sure he wears long boots to cover his feet, ankles, and calves. Hermogenes' father is long dead and Hermogenes himself has run the family business for many years. He raises horses to sell to Roman cavalry officers and to anyone else who can afford the high prices he charges for the beautiful, strong animals with their shiny coats and muscular bodies.

Hermogenes is on his way back home from a trip to Kotiaeion, the largest city in the area. He left his village four days ago. It took him two days to lead the horses he was selling down the steep mountain road to the valley below, allowing the horses plenty of time to rest and eat so they would maintain their excellent condition on the way. He camped on the banks of the Tembris River the first night, hobbling the horses so they wouldn't stray while he slept. Early the next morning he rounded up the horses, crossed the river with them, and took them into the city itself. At dawn on the third day, he groomed the horses and took them to the marketplace. Within hours, all the horses were sold: six of them to the cavalry and two to the procurator of the large imperial estate that comprises most of the Upper Tembris Valley. He had received his expected price and more.

In addition to his own favorite riding horse, Hermogenes kept one of his other horses, a sturdy pack horse—stronger than a mule. With some of the money he received for the other horses, Hermogenes bought essential supplies at the market and the many shops that crowd the narrow streets of Kotiaieon. As it was only mid-afternoon, Hermogenes decided to head back home early rather than spend another night in the city as he had planned. His own mount and pack horse, carrying the goods Hermogenes bought, apparently also wanted to get back to familiar territory as soon as possible, and he made good time. By nightfall, they were in the foothills of the highlands.

Now on the fourth day, ahead of schedule, Hermogenes decides to treat himself to a detour and visit Midas City. Normally, he doesn't have the time to stop at the place where King Midas' tomb is located—but today he does have the time. He will still be home before dark.

Standing before the huge tomb carved into the side of a large natural stone wall and looking at the strange script of the Phrygian inscription which he cannot read, Hermogenes wonders if it is really true that everything the fabled Phrygian king touched turned into gold. Probably not, he admits to himself. Tying the pack horse to the limb of a tree near Midas' tomb, he climbs back onto his riding horse and slowly makes his way a little further down the rocky path. The path winds between the tomb and a large rock formation into which numerous, much smaller tombs have been cut. Soon Hermogenes comes to the edge of the mountain ridge where Midas City is situated. The view from the ridge is spectacular. He can see for miles across the landscape far below him. The panorama that stretches out before him is worth this detour all by itself.

Hermogenes, however, has not come for the view. He wants to see with his own two eyes the long tunnels cut deep into the rock that lead to the graves of the ancient Phrygians. Fifty or so horse paces further, Hermogenes sees the first of the tunnels on his left. He dismounts and quickly walks to the entrance of the tunnel. He had no idea that the steps would be so steep! He decides that this tunnel is too dangerous to enter, and he makes his way to another one further down the path. The second tunnel's steps are more manageable, and he descends carefully. The steps seem to go on endlessly. No wonder people in days gone by thought they were entering Hades, the abode of the dead itself, Hermogenes can't help thinking. He is glad he is a Christian and not superstitious like his forebears were.

Two-thirds of the way down the steps, Hermogenes can see some light. The light becomes brighter the further he descends, and he notices that at the bottom of the steps there is a small chamber. No doubt there were once ancient sarcophagi in the chamber, but it is now empty. The ceiling of the chamber is very low, so he has to bend down as he enters the mausoleum. He notices that there is a large hole in the back wall of the chamber. Grave robbers have dug a shaft from the rear of the chamber and broken into it. The light he saw earlier had filtered into the tomb through this shaft.

Hermogenes finds the chamber both beautiful and eerie at the same time. The light casts ominous dark shadows as well as rainbow-colored shapes onto the walls. He is glad he came, but he is also eager to get out of the chamber as quickly as possible. He almost runs up the steps and stands at the top, panting slightly like a horse, as his own horse—not panting at all—comes up to him and gives his arm a familiar nudge. Hermogenes mounts the horse and returns to Midas' tomb where he grabs the rope around the neck of the pack horse and heads for home.

On the way back to his village, Hermogenes thinks with great sorrow about Nanas, his daughter. What a wonderful daughter Nanas had been and what a blessing to their group of followers of Montanus, Maximilla, and Priscilla.[3] Parents shouldn't outlive their children![4]

Nanas had an amazing range of spiritual gifts. He tried to list them all on her tombstone. "Here lies a prophetess," he had the stonecutter carve on the horizontal moulding at the top of the stone, "Nanas, daughter of Hermogenes."[5] The stonecutter didn't do a very good job of keeping the letters in a straight line, but that doesn't matter to Hermogenes. What matters is that everyone who sees the stone and can read the words knows that Nanas was a prophetess—like Maximilla and Priscilla before her.

The stonecutter had been more careful inscribing the rectangular field on the front face of the tombstone. It is there that Nanas' gifts are listed. The words are inscribed on Hermogenes' heart just as they are on the stone. As he and his horses trudge home, he repeats the words to himself:

> With prayers and intercessions
> she besought the praiseworthy master;
> with hymns and adulations
> she implored the immortal one;
> praying all day and night long,
> she possessed the fear of God
> from the beginning.
> Angelic visitations and speech she had
> in great measure:
> Nanas, the blessed one,
> whose "sleeping place" . . .[6]

Hermogenes chokes on the word *koimētērion*, "sleeping place," "cemetery," a word used exclusively by Christians to indicate that the dead are not really dead—merely sleeping while awaiting the resurrection of the body. Even though he believes in the resurrection, it still hurts to think of Nanas in the ground "sleeping." At least Nanas has company in her cemetery, her sleeping place. Sadly, her husband, who also died before his time, is buried with her.

The last part of the journey goes by quickly for Hermogenes. He hadn't realized that he made the horses gallop the last few miles across the grassy plain. He finds himself at the gate of the Christian cemetery in his own village. He dismounts, ties the horses to the gate post, walks to Nanas' tombstone, and with tears streaming down his old face reads the few phrases he composed in honor of his son-in-law:

> . . . a "sleeping-companion," a much-loved husband has gone together with her into the all-nourishing earth.[7]

How he misses both of them! He had hoped his son-in-law could take over from him the family business of raising horses, but now that will never happen.

The horses tied to the gate post are eager to get home. They neigh loudly and Hermogenes hears them. But before turning around he looks again at the final sentence—which refers to him and his wife:

> Those who long after Nanas, have honored her greatly by erecting this tombstone as a memorial.[8]

That sentence had been the stonecutter's idea, but Hermogenes is glad it was carved. It is certainly true that he and his wife honored Nanas by preparing such a beautiful tombstone with such an accurate description of her ministry of prayer and prophecy. The horses whinny again, impatiently stamping their feet, and Hermogenes leaves the grave. It is time to go home.

Source:

IMont 68.

Notes

1. In Roman and Byzantine times, the grassy plains of the Phrygian Highlands produced numerous sturdy horses. That Hermogenes himself was a horse breeder, however, is possible but by no means certain.

2. The ancient village where Hermogenes and his family, including Nanas and her husband, lived, has not yet been identified. The modern name of the village is Akoluk. On the Phrygian Highlands, the ancient sites in the area, and the archaeological and epigraphic remains of Christianity in the Highlands, see Haspels 1971.

3. Despite some doubts expressed by Trevett 1999, 259–77; cf. Lane Fox 1987, 747 n. 1), the consensus of scholarly opinion is that Nanas was indeed a Montanist prophetess; see Tabbernee 1997b, 424–25; 2007, 375–76; Poirier 2001, 151–59; Hirschmann 2004, 160–67. Hirschmann sees in the phrase ἀνγελικὴν ἐπισκοπὴν καὶ φωνήν (*angelikēn episkopēn kai phōnēn*) (*ll.*10–11) a reference not to "angelic visitations and speech" but to episcopal authority. If so, this would make Nanas not only a Montanist prophetess but also a Montanist bishop—the only such female bishop known to us by name. Epiphanius (*Pan.* 49.2.5) attests the existence of women bishops among the Cataphrygians; see also Chapter 9.

4. It is not absolutely certain that Hermogenes and his wife survived their daughter and their son-in-law. The section of Nanas' tombstone referring to the dedicators is badly worn, resulting in *lacunae* in the text. Presumably, the names of the persons who erected the memorial were inscribed there, and those names may have been those of Hermogenes and his wife. That parents sometimes outlived their adult children is illustrated by *IMont* 53, a tombstone from ancient Aizanoi (Çömlekçi köy) now in the Kütahya (ancient Kotiaeion) Museum. Perhaps, however, the dedicators of Nanas' tombstone were not her still living parents but her followers; see Haspels 1971, 1:216.

5. *IMont* 68, *ll.*1–2.

6. *IMont* 68, *ll.*3–13.

7. *IMont* 68, *ll.*14–17.

8. *IMont* 68, *ll.*20–22.

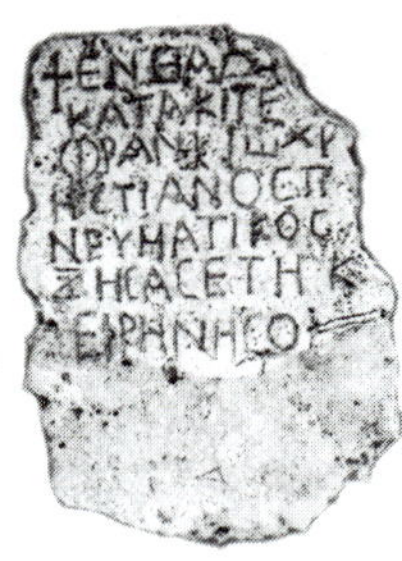

Chapter 28

Alexandria, Aegyptus, ca. 384 C.E.
A Montanist and an Orthodox tackle a divisive issue

Being blind has its advantages, Didymus finds himself thinking. Most of the time being blind is a nuisance. It takes him longer than most people to dress, to eat, and to do the simplest of tasks that sighted people undertake without giving them a second thought. But he has been blind for nearly seventy years—almost as long as most men live—and he has become used to the little inconveniences blindness causes. Didymus thanks God daily that his other faculties are still intact and that his blindness has even enhanced his other senses. In the absence of being able to see a manuscript with words on it, he has trained his mind to listen acutely and to memorize accurately everything he hears. People, he knows, are astounded by his memory and his prodigious knowledge of scripture, theology, and Christian tradition.

Didymus loves the responsibility of leading the catechetical school in Alexandria, a job originally given to him by Pope Athanasius of blessed memory. What an honor to hold the same position Clement and Origen each held more than a century ago. He is seated in his favorite blue chair, not that he can see its color. He knows the chair is blue only because one of his former students, the one who gave him the chair, told him it is blue. Didymus can visualize the color. He remembers what blue looks like from the time before he was blind. He was able to see until he was six years old and, even though that was a long time ago, he can still picture in his mind's eye the color of the sky on a clear, sunny day. How he wishes he could have seen the face of the student who gave him the blue chair—and the faces of his other students. What an inexpressible joy that would have been!

Didymus thinks back fondly to some of his favorite students who read to him over the years. He knows he shouldn't have favorites, but it is difficult not to like some students more than others. Jerome, Rufinus, and Palladius of Helenopolis had been among his brightest and best students. He wonders what they are doing now.

Suddenly there is a knock at the door, interrupting Didymus' thoughts. From the way the young man who enters the room sounds as he walks toward Didymus, Didymus not only recognizes him but knows that he is carrying the codex he asked the young man to fetch for him out of the church library. Yes, there are definitely advantages to being blind, Didymus thinks again to himself, and one of them is having his favorite students read to him.

The codex the young man has brought Didymus today is a copy of the *Dialogue between a Montanist and an Orthodox*. Didymus is not sure who wrote and published this dialogue,[1] nor whether the dialogue or debate actually occurred. He suspects not. After all, he himself has used the dialogue form as a literary device. Readers—or *hearers* such as he—like the dialogue format. It makes difficult topics so much more interesting and understandable when the various points at issue are portrayed as a real debate. Whether or not an actual Montanist and an actual Orthodox Christian had an actual debate that was later published word for word is irrelevant to Didymus. What he is about to hear read out loud to him are, no doubt, the kind of arguments a Montanist and an Orthodox would have made if there had been an actual debate.

The young man is a talented reader. He could have been an actor, Didymus thinks—although, given the pagan association of anything to do with the theater, he is glad the young man hasn't been tempted into that sinful profession. The young man changes the pitch of his voice to distinguish the two protagonists. He uses a high pitch for the Montanist and a low pitch for the Orthodox. This, as seems right to Didymus, makes the Orthodox sound more authoritative than the Montanist. The first part of the debate is more or less predictable. The Montanist claims that, through Montanus, the perfect revelation of the Holy Spirit, the Paraclete, has come. Didymus is a little surprised, however, that the Montanist states that "the complete," the *teleion*, came in fulfillment of what St. Paul prophesied in his First Letter to the Corinthians.[2] Didymus expected the Montanist to use the Gospel attributed to John to make this point. Didymus doesn't have to wait long, however, before allusions to the Fourth Gospel appear in the *Dialogue*.

Using the two "voices" assigned to the protagonists, Didymus' student reads the next section of the *Dialogue:*

Montanist: Why, then, do you not accept the holy Montanus?

Orthodox: Because he was a false prophet who did not speak a word of truth.

Montanist: Man, do not blaspheme the Paraclete.

Orthodox: I praise and glorify the Paraclete, the Spirit of truth, but I hold Montanus as the "desolating sacrilege."[3]

Didymus immediately recognizes the references to the "Paraclete" and the "Spirit of truth" as coming from the Fourth Gospel, as well as the reference from the Gospel attributed to Matthew regarding the "desolating sacrilege."[4] He can't help thinking how glad he is that Pope Athanasius, not long ago, finally sorted out which books are authoritative Christian scriptures and which are not. Because of this, the Orthodox can counter the Montanist's arguments with scripture.

Fortunately, as Didymus can think faster than his student can read out loud, Didymus misses none of the *Dialogue*. He hears his student enunciate clearly the Orthodox's response to the Montanist's question inquiring why the Orthodox considers Montanus to be the desolating sacrilege:

Orthodox: Firstly, because he says, "I am the Father, and I am the Son, and I am the Paraclete."

Montanist: But you say that the Father is one, the Son is another, and the Holy Spirit is another.

Orthodox: If it is we who say it, it is not worthy of faith, but if it is the Son who teaches that the Father is another and the Paraclete, the Holy Spirit, is another, it is essential to believe it.

Montanist: Show me where he teaches this.

Orthodox: It is where he said, "I will ask the Father, and the Father will give you another Paraclete the Spirit of truth. . . ."[5]

Didymus finds his mind wandering a little as he tries to follow the argument. He focuses his attention again and hears his student read the last part of the Orthodox's response:

Orthodox: How in hearing another Paraclete spoken of, do you not understand that there was one, another, besides him who was speaking?

Montanist: If there is another and another and another, that makes three Gods.

Orthodox: By no means![6]

As he listens, something troubles Didymus. Is the debate really about whether *Montanus* said *about himself* "I am the Father, and I am the Son, and I am the Paraclete"? The way the argument is developing, it seems that the debate is more about whether Montanists claim that there are no distinctions whatsoever between Father, Son, and Holy Spirit. Didymus remembers hearing that some early Montanists, at least in Rome, were Modalistic Monarchians. Perhaps the debate was about Modalism, not whether *Montanus* was claiming to be the Father, the Son, and the Paraclete. Not that Montanus could not have made such a claim at the beginning of one of his prophetic utterances to authenticate it, Didymus thinks almost aloud—but perhaps that isn't the issue here.

Didymus asks his student to commence reading again. To his delight, Didymus learns from the next part of the *Dialogue* that his instinct about the thrust of the argument is accurate. The Montanist argues that there is but one God while the Orthodox argues that this is only so in terms of God's nature, not in terms of *hypostasis* or substance. There are three *hypostases,* the Orthodox argues: Father, Son, and Holy Spirit. But, argues the Montanist, why then does Jesus, the Son, say, "I am in the Father and the Father is in me"[7] and "the Father and I are one"?[8]

Didymus listens intently to the exact words of the debate as it continues:

Orthodox: He did not say "I am one," but "we are one" so that we might know the independent existence of the *hypostases.* But it surprises me that you remember the Gospels, although you do not walk straight along the path of truth.

Montanist: I believe in the Gospels.

Orthodox: Point out to me, then, where it is written in the Gospels, "I am both the Father and the Son, as well as the Spirit.

Montanist: Whoever has seen me has seen the Father.

Orthodox: But, "the Father." He didn't say that he *himself* was the Father. . . .[9]

Didymus is suddenly tired of the pedantic theological hairsplitting put into the mouths of the Montanist and the Orthodox by the author of the *Dialogue.* Once again he thanks his student for reading to him and asks him to stop. This time he also asks the student to find one of the *notarii,* the stenographers, to whom Didymus dictates his treatises. He is working on a treatise on the Trinity and wants to incorporate the most important new idea he has gleaned from today's reading session.

The notarius enters and stands at the tall writing desk in the corner of the room. When the notarius is ready to write down his exact words, Didymus dictates: "Montanus alleges that *Jesus* said: 'I am the Father and the Son and the Paraclete.'"[10]

Sources:

Dial., esp. 1.1, 2.5–3.14; Matt 24:15; John 10:30, 14:9–11, 16:7–15; 1 Cor 13:8–12; Didymus, *Trin.* 3.41.1.

Notes

1. Although de Labriolle (1913b, CVII–CVIII) argued that the anonymous *Dialogue between a Montanist and an Orthodox* was written by Didymus of Alexandria (ca. 310/13–ca. 398), also known as Didymus the Blind, it is more likely that, as presumed in this chapter, the *Dialogue* was written by someone else but used by Didymus as a source; see also Tabbernee 2007, 294–95.

2. *Dial.* 1.1.

3. *Dial.* 2.5–3.1a.

4. John 16:7, 13; Matt 24:15.

5. *Dial.* 3.1b–3.3a.

6. *Dial.* 3.3b–3.4.

7. *Dial.* 3.7a.

8. *Dial.* 3.13b.

9. *Dial.* 3.14.

10. Didymus, *Trin.* 3.41.1. Scholars have traditionally assumed that Montanus equated himself with the Paraclete, citing *Dial.* 3.1: "I am the Father and I am the Son and I am the Paraclete," and *Dial.* 4.8: "I am the Father and the Son and the Holy Spirit" as evidence. While the statements quoted in the *Dialogue* are the kind of statements which Montanus

may have made as introductory formulae, authenticating his oracles (cf. Theodore of Heracleia, *Fr. Mt.* 24.5, quoted in Chapter 1), the context of the statements and especially that of their slight variant in *Dial.* 3.14: "I am both [καί] the Father and [καί] the Son as well as [καί] the Spirit," indicates that the point of the argument was that Montanus said that *Jesus* (not Montanus) said "I am the Father and the Son and the Paraclete" (cf. Didymus, *Trin.* 3.41.1). That the historical *Montanus* would have said something like what the author of the *Dialogue* and Didymus assumed in the context of a discussion on Modalistic Monarchianism is, however, impossible as Modalistic Monarchianism (Modalism) did not become an issue until *after* Montanus' own time; see also Tabbernee 2001b, 106–9; 2007, 380–83. Basil of Caesarea in Cappadocia (ca. 329/30–379), also known as "Basil the Great," believed that Montanists equated Montanus and Priscilla with the Paraclete and even baptized converts "into the Father and the Son and Montanus or Priscilla" (*Ep.* 188.1). Support for this view is sometimes seen by scholars (e.g., Trevett 1996, 219) in the text of an inscription from Mascula (Kenchela) in ancient Numidia (Algeria): "Flavius Avus, *domesticus,* has fulfilled what he promised in the name of the Father and of the Son (and) of *dominus* Montanus" (*IMont* 71). The absence of the words "(and) of the Holy Spirit" after "and of the Son," however, may simply be due to weathering of the slab and these words may have been there originally. Moreover, the slab containing the vow (not *baptismal* formula) appears to have been an altar top in a martyrium commemorating not the founder of the New Prophecy but the North African martyr who died on May 23, 259 in Carthage (*Pass. Mont. et Luc.*); see Tabbernee 1997b, 445–52; 2001b, 113–14.

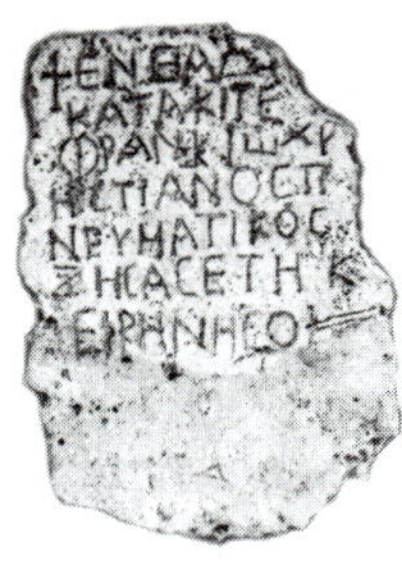

Chapter 29

Rome, Italia, 385 C.E.

Marcella receives a perturbing guest

Marcella makes it a habit never to go out in public unless accompanied by her mother Albina. Both women are widows. Marcella's father, the last in a long line of Roman consuls and praetorian prefects, died while Marcella was still a child. Marcella's own husband passed away less than seven months after their marriage. Beautiful, young, of noble birth, and very rich, Marcella had been pursued by eager suitors, including the consul Cerealis, who desired to marry her. Marcella, however, wanted nothing to do with them—even though Albina had, at first, aided and abetted the attempts of Cerealis and others to win over Marcella. Marcella had made up her mind: rather than remarrying she would dedicate herself to life-long chastity and become a virgin of Christ.

Marcella's decision to lead an ascetic life was not a popular one among her friends, especially the other women of noble birth within the Christian community at Rome. No one of Marcella's rank and social status had ever done anything so foolish. But Marcella could not be dissuaded. She gave away her beautiful clothes, wearing from then on merely plain black garments to keep out the cold. Not even a gold signet ring adorned her body, Marcella having decided to keep her wealth in the stomachs of the poor rather than on her person.

As Marcella and Albina cross the Pons Aemilius, following this morning's expedition to Transtiber to visit some Christian women who are ill and in need of food and medicine, Marcella can't help thinking that she made a wise decision to keep the house to which they are returning. The villa, some call it a palace, is a magnificent mansion in the aristocratic district on the top of Aventine Hill—the most southern of the seven hills of Rome. After her husband's death, Marcella considered selling the villa. Its location and magnificent views of the center of the city and across the Tiber would have fetched a handsome price and allowed her to give away even more money to the poor. Keeping the villa however enabled her to establish a monastic community in Rome, comprised of other virgin-widows like herself as well as never-married virgins such as her sister Asella. What a wonderful model for the other virgins Asella is, thinks Marcella, and how fitting that Asella is now the head of the monastic community in the house to which Marcella and Albina are headed. Marcella is glad that Athanasius, the great patriarch of

Alexandria, had himself, while in Rome, told her not only about Antony, the first Egyptian hermit, but also about the monasteries founded by Pachomius in the Thebaid—including some for virgins and widows. Fortunately, the villa she owns is ideally suited for a Roman community of ascetic women, and Marcella wasted no time in following Pachomius' example.

Albina and Marcella are about one-third of the way up Aventine Hill, and Albina needs to rest. She is feeling the effects of old age and sits down on one of the wooden benches along the way. Marcella joins her on the bench. Below the two women is the Circus Maximus and they can see some charioteers racing their chariots around the track, practicing, no doubt, for the *ludi Romani,* the Roman games held each September. The charioteers, chariots, and horses look very small from this distance—as do the guards on the walls of the Domus Augustana, the imperial palace on Palatine Hill overlooking the Circus Maximus. Marcella herself had once stood on those steep walls directly above the Circus Maximus and remembers feeling dizzy as she looked down on the activities below from the royal seats.

Having rested, Marcella and Albina continue their walk home up Aventine Hill. On the way they make just one more stop. Albina wants to pray at the new Basilica of Saint Prisca, constructed, so Albina and Marcella have been told, on the site of the home of Aquila and Priscilla—a home that served as a house-church for the earliest Christian community in Rome. Albina lights a candle in the church, crosses herself, prays for the soul of Marcella's deceased husband, and for that of her own long-dead spouse.

Thankfully, the road from St. Prisca's Church to Marcella's house winds in long zigzags up to the top of Aventine Hill. As the women approach the villa, set within a large wooded estate, Marcella is delighted that the grounds are well kept and the gardens still have some flowers in bloom. Marcella, Albina, Asella, and the other widows and virgins who live in the house reside in a serene, retreat-like setting, far from the noise and bustle of the city far below them.[1]

Upon entering the villa, Marcella is greeted by one of the virgins who tells her that she has a visitor. Visitors are no surprise. Marcella has a constant procession of them. Her favorite guest of late is Sophronius Eusebius Hieronymus, known to his friends simply as Jerome. Originally from Stridon in Dalmatia, Jerome studied in Rome a couple of decades ago—well before Marcella came to know him. He also spent a long time in the East, where he was ordained a presbyter in Antioch of Syria. At the request of Damasus, the bishop of Rome, Jerome had returned to Rome a few years ago to be Damasus' secretary. Because of his facility with languages, Damasus also asked Jerome to prepare a new complete Latin translation of the holy scriptures, a task that occupies much of Jerome's time—but not so much time that he can't visit Marcella frequently.

How Marcella looks forward to Jerome's visits! He is the most intelligent and most knowledgeable man Marcella has ever known. She loves his mind and his goodness. Insatiable in her own quest for knowledge about the scriptures, about the faith, and about the Desert Fathers and Mothers whom Jerome has met personally, Marcella not only plies him with numerous questions each time he visits but sends him letters full of questions in the days or weeks between visits.

Marcella smiles as she recollects how, at first, Jerome did not even want to see her. He had just arrived in Rome with Paulinus, bishop of Antioch in Syria, and Epiphanius, bishop of Salamis in Cyprus. The three men had traveled together from the East to Rome. What sights they must have seen and what conversations they must have had! How Marcella wishes she could have been on that journey, following, more or less, the footsteps of St. Paul and seeing some of the "Seven Cities of Asia" mentioned in the book of Revelation. She imagines all the questions she could have asked each of the three venerable clerics. After Paulinus and Epiphanius returned to their respective homelands, Marcella persisted in seeking access to Jerome's knowledge and wisdom. She, accompanied of course by Albina and some Roman male clergy, had even visited Jerome personally to persuade him to become her teacher. At last, reluctantly, Jerome agreed. He soon learned that Marcella was an exceptional student and his intellectual equal—never satisfied with superficial answers to her questions. She would frequently dispute Jerome's explanations, not because she doubted their veracity but because she wanted to see how he answered her objections so she could more fully comprehend the depths of his encyclopedic knowledge.

Assuming that her guest today is Jerome, Marcella hurries from the vestibule to the atrium—but is surprised to find a stranger waiting for her. She is so startled and disappointed that, although the man introduces himself she doesn't catch, or at least doesn't remember, his name. The man tells her he is a follower of Montanus, Maximilla, and Priscilla. For a moment Marcella thinks the man is talking about St. Prisca, also known as St. Priscilla—the familiar diminutive of the name Prisca. It soon becomes clear, however, that the Prisca/Priscilla whose church Marcella and Albina have just visited and the Prisca/Priscilla referred to by the stranger are by no means one and the same person.

By now a number of the other widows and virgins have joined Marcella, Albina, and the virgin who informed Marcella of her guest's presence. Marcella is glad the others are here, both for the sake of propriety and as witnesses to the discussion. Marcella has heard of Montanus and the Montanists. She knows that a Montanist community has existed in Transtiber for almost two centuries now, although she has never been to one of their house-churches. Perhaps she was in the vicinity of one that very morning without knowing it, she wonders to herself, while listening to her unexpected visitor.

The visitor, obviously intent on converting Marcella—or at least intent on getting her to become a patron and supporter of the movement bearing the name of Montanus—starts, as she expected him to do, with scripture. He reminds Marcella that there are a number of passages in the Fourth Gospel where Jesus tells his disciples that he will go to the Father and then send the Paraclete, the Spirit of truth, from the Father. Marcella knows the passages well and doesn't really need to be reminded of them. She is surprised, however, to hear the Montanist teacher say that the Paraclete had only come *fully* through the prophecies of Montanus, Maximilla, and Priscilla—not at Pentecost. The Montanist teacher explains that the full saving power of God did not come through Moses or even through the incarnate Christ but through the descent of the Paraclete, the Holy Spirit, upon Montanus, Maximilla, and Priscilla. Through the New Prophets, the Montanist teacher argues, the Paraclete has revealed the highest possible standards of ethical behavior—standards fit for an age of mature Christians.

Marcella is at once puzzled and intrigued. She has always believed that the Holy Spirit, promised by Christ, *did* come at Pentecost, but she is empathetic to what the Montanist teacher is saying about the importance of an ascetic lifestyle for mature Christians. He tells Marcella that Montanists fast frequently and that they do not condone remarriage after the death of one's spouse, equating remarriage with adultery. He also tells Marcella that Montanists take a dim view of the easy pardoning of serious sins. Marcella likes what she hears. Such strict views accord with her own, but she is still perturbed by what the Montanist teacher says about the Holy Spirit. After politely showing her unannounced guest to the door, Marcella goes to her study and writes Jerome a long letter.

The next morning there is a knock at Jerome's door. A courier stands there with a letter from Marcella. Jerome is not in the least surprised; lately Marcella's letters have become an almost daily occurrence. He thanks the bearer of the letter and takes it inside, wondering what today's questions might be. Recently Marcella asked him to explain why there are ten different names given to God in the scriptures of the old covenant and the exact meaning of various Hebrew words such as "Alleluia," transliterated rather than translated in the old Latin versions of scripture.

Jerome enjoys answering Marcella's questions. At times, they force him to do some additional research—or at least to give extra thought to issues he might otherwise treat superficially in his production of the *new* Latin version of the scriptures, the Vulgate. His correspondence with Marcella also allows him to let off steam occasionally, especially when other people criticize him or his work. Jerome takes criticism badly, particularly when he knows he is right—which, to the annoyance of both his opponents and, if truth be told, his friends, he almost always is.

Someone told Jerome recently that some slanderers were accusing him of "correcting" gospel passages, thereby going against the ancient texts and long-held understanding of these texts. His first inclination had been to ignore the accusation. Playing the lyre for asses is a futile exercise, he wrote to Marcella in the letter he finally composed in his own defense. The Lord's own words are, of course, not in need of correction, he told her. But the Latin manuscripts of the scriptures containing the Lord's words are so flawed by their many variations that he had decided, first of all, to restore the original Greek text from which, as even his opponents admitted, the earlier Latin versions are derived. Only then could he prepare a new Latin translation that is adequate. The asses who criticize him are so dumb that instead of playing a lyre or a lute for them, he should blow a trumpet in their ear—perhaps then they would understand.

Jerome laughs out loud at the image of his Roman opponents dressed in their fine clothes but looking like asses with long ears, into which he is trumpeting the truth about texts and translations. He wonders if Marcella too laughed out loud when she read his words. Perhaps she will tell him her reaction in the new letter he is holding in his hand.

Sitting at his desk, Jerome breaks open the seal on the letter. He cannot believe his eyes. The letter has nothing to do with the asses who are his opponents but with some other asses: the Montanists. He picks up his pen and begins to write his response.

The Acts of the Apostles, Jerome tells Marcella, reveals clearly the time Jesus had in mind for the coming of the Paraclete and the time when Jesus' promises, referred to by the follower of Montanus, were fulfilled. The passages from the Fourth Gospel were fulfilled at Pentecost: exactly ten days after the Ascension and fifty days after the Resurrection. This is confirmed by St. Peter's speech explaining to the puzzled bystanders that what they were witnessing as the Holy Spirit descended with tongues of fire on the disciples, who then themselves spoke in tongues, was what had been prophesied by the prophet Joel: the pouring out of God's Spirit would result in their sons and daughters prophesying, their young men seeing visions, and their old men dreaming dreams. If then, asks Jerome, the apostle Peter, upon whom the Lord founded the church, declared the fulfillment of both the prophecy and the Lord's promise at that particular time, how is it possible for us to lay claim to another time? The answer to Jerome's rhetorical question should be obvious to Marcella: it is *impossible* to hold, as the Montanists do, that the Holy Spirit, the Paraclete, came at a time other than at Pentecost. Ten days after Christ's ascension and fifty *days* after his resurrection is when the Paraclete came, not one hundred and thirty or so *years* afterward.

From Marcella's own letter, Jerome cannot tell whether the follower of Montanus who came to see her had argued for the continuance of revelation through prophetic succession. He explains to Marcella, nevertheless, that even should the Montanists try to make a case for the legitimacy of their "New Prophets" in this way, the point at issue is not prophecy itself but whether or not the utterances of the prophet are congruent with the authority of the scriptures, both old and new.

Jerome quickly dashes off a list of examples showing that the Montanist prophets and prophetesses fail the test. They differ from catholic Christians with respect to the Rule of Faith. Instead of believing that the Father, Son, and Holy Spirit are three distinct persons yet united in substance, the Montanists, according to Jerome, follow Sabellius, who confines the Trinity to a single person. While Montanists may seem to be faithful ascetics, their asceticism goes far beyond what is laid down in scripture. Scripture allows second marriages and desires the repentance of sinners—not their perpetual exclusion from the church. There is nothing in scripture that teaches that God, at first, tried to save the world through Moses, then through the Incarnation, and, having failed at both, finally did so through the Holy Spirit descending into Montanus, Maximilla, and Priscilla.

Now that the ink from Jerome's pen is flowing rapidly, the accusations against the Montanists fill a second page. Jerome describes Maximilla and Priscilla as demented and Montanus as *abscissum et semivirum*, a "chopped-off half man,"[2] alluding to the charge that Montanus, prior to his conversion to Christianity, had been a priest in the cult of Cybele.[3] If true, Montanus must have castrated himself as part of his initiation. Jerome passes over the allegation that Montanists have polluted sacraments, involving the blood letting of innocent infants. He hints, nonetheless, at the hypocrisy of the Montanists who, he claims, rigidly refuse to pardon others but commit grave sins themselves.

Jerome also accuses the Montanists of excessive fasting, claiming that they have three forty-day "Lents" a year, and of having an untraditional hierarchy of clergy: patriarchs in Pepouza; *koinōnoi*,[4] or regional bishops, in strategic locations; and bishops in each local church.

Jerome looks back over his letter and pens the conclusion. He assures Marcella that he knows that she is not really all that disturbed by the issues raised by the visit of the Montanist teacher but merely wants to know his views on these issues. Jerome seals the letter and goes in search of a courier who can take the letter to the mansion on Aventine Hill.

Sources:

Jerome, *Ep.* 24–27, 41, 127; Joel 2:28–32; Matt 16:18; John 14:28, 15:26; Acts 2:14–18; Rom 16:3–5a.

Notes

1. The exact location of Marcella's villa on Aventine Hill is now unknown. The house must, however, have been easy to find. In 393 Jerome, from his monastery in Bethlehem, wrote a letter to his friend Desiderius in Rome, telling Desiderius that if he wanted copies of his writings he could borrow them from Marcella at her house on Aventine Hill (*Ep.* 47.3; cf. 49.4 [to Pammachius, Marcella's cousin]).

2. Jerome, *Ep.* 41.4.

3. In Phrygia, there was a close connection between the cults of Apollo and of Cybele which makes it plausible that Montanus could have been a priest of Cybele *and* of Apollo (as claimed by *Dial.* 4.5–6); see Hirschmann 2005, 55–74. See also Chapter 1.

4. *Koinōnoi* ranked second in the Montanist hierarchy, below patriarchs but above bishops (Jerome, *Ep.* 41.3; cf. *Cod. justin.* 1.5.20.3). In my view, *koinōnoi* were regional bishops, responsible for a Montanist ecclesiastical district; see Tabbernee 1993; 1997b, 492, 512–13, 515 but contrast Buschmann 1995, 251–55.

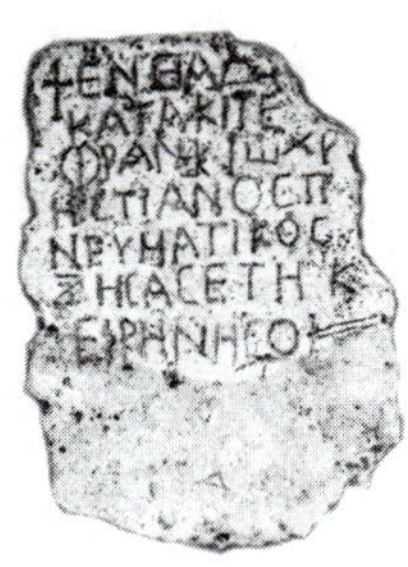

Chapter 30

Bethlehem, Palaestina, 387 C.E.

Jerome reflects on St. Paul and the "foolish" Galatians

Jerome has found the perfect place for his monastery. In fact, he cannot believe his good fortune. The place is underground, an ideal place to work, unaffected by the scorching heat of the summer sun in Palaestina. The caves in the grotto are spacious and, with minimal furniture installed, have become comfortable, albeit austere, living quarters, refectory, scriptorium, and chapel. Jerome's own cave is large enough to contain not only his bed but a writing desk and a cupboard for his works-in-progress and his completed manuscripts. The perfect location of Jerome's monastery however is not due to its spacious climate-controlled rooms but to its proximity to what is arguably Christianity's most holy site: the place where Jesus was born. Only the Church of the Holy Sepulchre in Jerusalem, having within its precincts the very places where Jesus died and rose from the grave, can rival the claim of the Church of the Nativity in Bethlehem.

It is just after dawn, a cool morning with, as usual, a spectacular sunrise. Jerome has already been outside to catch some fresh air and see the sun rise over the terraced slopes of Bethlehem. He is now back in the Church of the Nativity, saying his prayers. When he is finished, Jerome gets up from his knees at the back of the empty basilica and stands reverently, taking in the magnificence of the church built by Helena, the mother of Constantine. Forty huge red limestone columns capped with Corinthian columns, proudly showing off their intricately carved acathantus leaves and curved scrolls, stretch out before him in two double rows forming the nave and side aisles. He walks forward slowly, treading lightly on the mosaic floor. The mosaic, in a multiplicity of geometric designs made from thousands of earth-tone colored tesserae, looks like a rich carpet covering the whole floor of the basilica.

Jerome pauses at the front of the church, its east end, before ascending the steps to the octagonal platform there. The raised height is useful not only for making the clergy more visible during the liturgies conducted each Sunday and at other times during the week, but for those such as Jerome, those who are "in the know," it provides a great vantage point to see a special floor mosaic to the left of the raised platform. Turning so that he can see the mosaic more clearly, the labyrinth-like geometric design draws Jerome's eyes to the central panel—the

Figure 30.1: Plaque marking Jerome's monastic cell beneath the Church of the Nativity in Bethlehem

place where one would end up if walking an actual labyrinth. There, in the very center of the central panel, made out of black tesserae, is the word ΙΧΘΥΣ, "fish," the acrostic for "Jesus Christ, God's Son, Savior," marking the exact spot where, in a cave now beneath the floor of the church, Jesus was born.

Crossing himself, Jerome comes down from the octagonal platform and, being careful not to step on the word ΙΧΘΥΣ, which would be an inexcusable sacrilege, he makes his way down the steps next to the mosaic. The steps lead to the Grotto of the Nativity itself, marked by a silver star representing the star the Magi saw so long ago. Before he came to Bethlehem, Jerome was puzzled by the traditional story that the manger, in which Jesus was wrapped in swaddling clothes after his birth, was in a cave and that Jesus had actually been born in that cave. Seeing similar caves still being used today by the peasant farmers of Bethlehem to store their hay and to shelter their animals at night, convinced Jerome that the tradition is accurate. Saying a brief prayer at the Grotto of the Nativity beneath the great Constantinian basilica and crossing himself again, Jerome walks all the way around to the other side of the grotto into a passageway to the right. A few steps later he is back in his own room, thankful to God that he now lives and works immediately adjacent to the birthplace of the Christ whom he worships and serves.

It is time to get back to work. Jerome is glad that a few days ago he finished his commentary on St. Paul's Letter to Philemon. As every Christian knows, that letter is not a long one but it took him longer to finish the commentary than he expected. It is done now, and he has sent a copy, as is his usual practice, to Marcella in Rome. How he wishes that he could have persuaded her to come to the Holy Land to establish a monastic community here for women—just as she did in Rome. Despite his numerous entreaties, Marcella steadfastly determined to remain in Rome, where—he has learned—she has established a second monastic community in the suburbs outside the walls of the city. Fortunately, Paula, another of the great Christian noblewomen of Rome, and her daughter Eustochium *have* come to Bethlehem, supplying not only the funds for Jerome's monastery where he and his male companions live but also for the establishment of a convent for women they themselves lead.

Jerome misses Marcella and is thinking about the way she always used to ask him pertinent questions about the scriptures whenever she saw him, however briefly. He laughs out loud, shattering the silence of his monastic cell, as he remembers that Marcella didn't always like the answers he gave her. She tested everything. She was more like my judge than my disciple, Jerome muses.

Having procrastinated enough, Jerome reminds himself that it really is time to get to work. He has decided to tackle next a commentary on St. Paul's Letter to the Galatians—a much longer epistle than the one to Philemon, and much more complicated. Transitions are not easy for Jerome. Moving from one writing project to the next is always problematic, he reflects, but the only way out is in.

Jerome remembers well his journeys through Galatia: a rugged land with rugged people who still embody in their speech and habits their Celtic ancestors who had migrated to this area from the eastern Balkans as well as the influence of numerous subsequent immigrants. Just about every kind of perverse group can be found in Galatia, especially in its capital city, Ankyra, which he visited a dozen years ago. Jerome picks up his pen and writes:

> Whoever has seen Ancyra, the pre-eminent city of Galatia, knows, as do I, by how many schisms it is torn apart even now, by what a variety of dogmas it is raped. To say nothing of Cataphrygians, Ophites, Borborites, and Manichaeans—for these appellations of human disaster are already known. But who has heard of Passalorinchites, Ascodrogitans, Artotyrites, and other monstrosities more than by name in any other part of the Roman world. Traces of ancient foolishness remain to the present day.[1]

Jerome, writing in Latin, uses the Latin form of the name of the Galatian capital and alludes to St. Paul's comment calling the Galatians "foolish" for being so easily bewitched by false teaching.

Jerome is relieved that Marcella was never bewitched by the Cataphrygians who tried to convert her. He decides to write this commentary on Galatians for her. Almost as an afterthought, he also decides to write the commentary for Paula and Eustochium, his most recent patrons. He knows the three women have heard of the Cataphrygians, otherwise known as Montanists; the Ophites, strange serpent worshipers; the Borborites, people who allegedly use menstrual blood and semen in their Eucharists; and the Manichaeans, the followers of the Persian prophet Mani. Jerome is sure, however, that they have never heard of the Passalorinchites, the Ascodrogitans, and the Artotyrites. He himself had never heard of them until he visited Ankyra.

Jerome gets up from behind his desk and paces around the room, trying to remember exactly what Epiphanius told him about the Passalorinchites, Ascodrogitans, and Artotyrites when he, Epiphanius, and Paulinus of Antioch traveled across Galatian territory on their way to Rome five years ago. Epiphanius had already made a careful study of all the sects and heresies perverting orthodox Christianity and had published his *Panarion omnium haeresium,* his "Medicine Chest against All Heresies," only a few years before their trip together. Epiphanius was very knowledgeable about the various poisonous heretics against whom he prepared the antidotes in his "medicine chest," and Jerome had learned a lot from him—if only he could remember.

Stroking his long beard, which always helps him concentrate, Jerome finally remembers that Epiphanius equated the Passalorinchites with the Tascodrogitans. The Tascodrogitans received their name, according to Epiphanius, from Phrygian words meaning "peg" and "nose," because they placed their index finger, like a peg, against their nostrils as they prayed. Epiphanius thought the "nose-peggers" arose out of the Montanist movement, Jerome remembers, but Jerome is not sure this is correct.

Now that his brain cells are working again and his memory is coming back, Jerome also remembers that, on their long journey, Epiphanius argued that the Ascodrogitans and the Artotyrites were Cataphrygian sub-sects. Ascodrogitans, Epiphanius had said, received their name from their practice of dancing around a wineskin during the eucharistic liturgy. Jerome closes his eyes and tries to imagine the scene. A presbyter places a wineskin in the midst of the congregation. Men and women gather around the wineskin and start to gyrate slowly at first, then more quickly, until the whole congregation becomes a frenzied throng of humanity dancing faster and faster. The men begin to sweat profusely. The women's dresses become rearranged immodestly; their veils, if any, fall from their faces. Finally, the wineskin is picked up and passed around the crowd, each member drinking from the nipple-like teat at the end of the wineskin, while a priest chants: "The blood of Christ. The blood of Christ."

Jerome is almost in a trance himself and he shakes his head vigorously to dispel the blasphemous images. Surely nothing like what he has just imagined actually took place. Surely someone just made up an explanation for the name Ascodrogitans based on the similarity between the first part of the name and the Greek word ἀσκός (*askos:* "wineskin"). Perhaps, Jerome surmises, there were never any Ascodrogitans, nor dancing-around-wineskin Eucharists at all, the name Ascodrogitans simply being an alternative for the name Tascodrogitans, the initial letter *tau* having dropped away through local pronunciation.

More believable, though, is the explanation Jerome heard from Epiphanius concerning the name Artotyrites. Everyone who knows Greek knows that ἄρτος (*artos*) is the word for "bread" and that τυρός (*tyros*) is the word for "cheese." Thus Ἀρτοτυρίται (*Artotyritai*) are "bread-and-cheesers" and, according the Epiphanius, received their name from the practice of substituting cheese, that is curdled milk, for wine at their Eucharists. That there are people who do this is not surprising to Jerome. Perhaps, he thinks, they do so only at special times when, because of their strict fasts at those times, they are forbidden to drink wine even during the eucharistic liturgy. Jerome remembers that Epiphanius considered Artotyrites an alternative name for the Quintillians, a sub-sect of the Montanists, but he is not sure if Epiphanius' assumption is accurate.[2]

Having untangled—at least in his own mind—the intricate web of alleged Cataphrygian sub-sects, Jerome sits down again to write the next part of his commentary on Galatians. Suddenly, there is a loud knock on the door of his cell. Jerome is both surprised and annoyed. His brother monks know better than to disturb him in the mornings when he is writing. He opens the door and is about to reprimand the novice standing there when he notices the seal on the letter the young man is holding out to him. It is Marcella's seal. Without a word of thanks, or reprimand, Jerome takes the letter and closes the door.

Jerome's hands are trembling slightly as he sits on his bed with the letter held gently between his fingers. It has been weeks since he heard from Marcella. He hopes she is well. He hopes even more that she has changed her mind and is coming to him after all—well, of course not to *him* but to Bethlehem. What if she is not well? What if she is not coming to Bethlehem? What if . . . ? Minutes pass before he can bring himself to break the seal and open the letter. He gasps as he reads the unexpected and unwelcome news: Albina, Marcella's beloved mother, is dead.

Sources:

Luke 2:1–20; Matt 2:1–12; Justin Martyr, *Dial.* 78; *Protev. Jac.* 18.1, 19.2; Origen, *Cels.* 1.51; Finegan 1992, 34, no. 30 [Floor Mosaic with the word ΙΧΘΥΣ]; Jerome, *Ep.* 46, 47.3, 108.14, 127.8; *Comm. Phlm.; Comm. Gal.*, esp. praef. 1, 2.2; Gal 3:1–5; Irenaeus, *Haer.* 1.30.1–5; Epiphanius, *Pan.* 26.1.1–19.6, 37.1.1–9.4, 48.14.3–49.1.1; Filaster, *Haer.* 75.

Notes

1. Jerome, *Comm. Gal.* 2.2.

2. On the Tascodrogitans, Ascodrogitans, and Artotyrites, their alleged sacramental novelties and the imperial legislation against these supposed subsects of Montanism, see Tabbernee 2007, 331–34, 358–61.

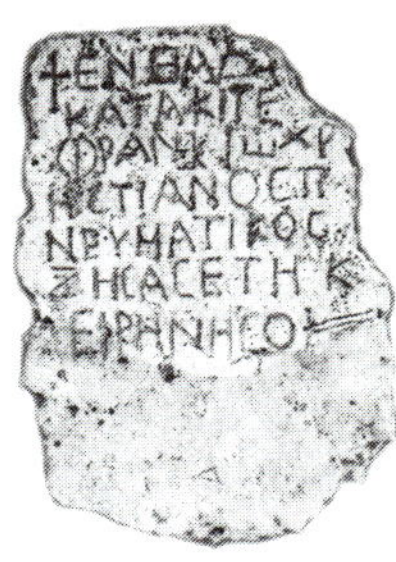

Chapter 31

Dorylaeion, Phrygia, ca. 390 C.E.

Epitaph of a pneumatikē

Loupinikos looks at the central, almost square, field on the face of the stone where the epitaph of his wife is carved. The stonecutter did a marvelous job—exactly as Loupinikos expected. The tombstone is a fitting memorial. The inscription reads:

> Loupinikos for Mountane, his wife, a Christian and a *pneumatikē*. In memory.[1]

Carved in the middle, above the inscription, is a Latin cross, reinforcing symbolically that Mountane was a Christian. On both sides of the cross the stonecutter had carved, at Loupikinos' request, the Greek letter *pi*. Why Loupikinos would want those letters in that particular place was puzzling to the stonecutter, but when Loupikinos came into the workshop a few days ago to commission the tombstone, the stonecutter did not question the customer's instructions. He learned long ago that the customer is always right.

Now that Loupikinos has come to collect the tombstone, the stonecutter's curiosity is about to be satisfied. Without even having been asked the question, Loupikinos tells him that the letters stand for Πνευματικὸς Πνευματικῄ, that is, "A *pneumatikos* to a *pneumatikē*."[2] The stonecutter has already carved the word *pneumatikē* in full next to the designation *Chreistianē* after Mountane's name but he still doesn't know what it means. Loupikinos explains to him that he and his family are Christians who belong to the New Prophecy movement started by Montanus, Maximilla, and Priscilla. Mountane's parents had even named her after Montanus, Loupikinos adds.

As followers not only of Christ but of the teachings from the Holy Spirit revealed to them through Montanus, Maximilla, Priscilla, and the more recent prophetesses of their movement, Loupikinos and Mountane had tried to live as *spiritual* Christians. The designation πνευματικοί (*pneumatikoi*) was commonly used among the members of the New Prophecy movement to distinguish themselves from other Christians who did not live up to the high ethical demands of the Holy Spirit.

The stonecutter who himself is a Christian thinks that Loupikinos' explanation contains a somewhat arrogant attitude toward other Christians, whom the members of Loupikinos' sect must look down on as being less spiritual than themselves. The stonecutter, however, does not say anything. After all, the customer is always right.

Source:

IMont 63.

Rome, Italia, ca. 393 C.E.

Octaviana honors martyrs and Montanists

Octaviana is walking along the Via Aurelia outside the Aurelian wall. She has just passed through the Aurelian Gate and is on her way to visit the Christian cemeteries, as she often does. Octaviana is especially interested in the tombs of the martyrs, the martyria. Most of these are constructed at ground level but some also have catacombs associated with them, where ordinary Christians are buried *ad martyras,* near the martyrs. Octaviana's first stop is the cemetery of St. Pancras. Pancras was a Phrygian by birth who, like many of the others from Asia Minor, emigrated to Rome and lived in the Asiatic sector of the city around the Via Aurelia. Pancras was martyred during the persecution of Diocletian, at the very spot where Octaviana is now standing. Octaviana has brought flowers and she lays three of the flowers in front of the monument marking St. Pancras' grave before moving on to the next cemetery a little further down the road.

Octaviana herself is an immigrant, but not from Asia Minor. She was born in Africa Proconsularis. Her husband Hesperius, an influential Roman, brought her to Rome as a young woman. She loves the city. It is so full of history, especially Christian history. Visiting the martyrs is her passion, and she indulges her passion almost every day. As she reaches the second cemetery, Octaviana strides purposely to her favorite tomb in this particular cemetery. It is not the tomb of a martyr, but that of a Christian named Ablabes. The slab covering the tomb is decorated with the carving of a dove holding an olive branch with its feet. Octaviana bends down to leave some of her flowers and reads:

> Here lies Ablabes, a Galatian from the district of Moulikos, son of Photinos, having lived thirty years, a *pneumatikos,* earth covers him. Peace to you.[3]

When Octaviana was a young woman still living in Africa Proconsularis, she had heard that the famous Christian teacher Tertullian used the word *spiritales,* "spiritual ones," to describe Christians who, unlike those he called *psychici,* "carnal ones," lived fully in accordance with the precepts of the Holy Spirit. Now, right at her feet, is the tombstone of a young man who, using the Greek rather than the Latin word, is designated as one of the spiritual ones: a *pneumatikos.*[4]

Octaviana's knowledge about Tertullian had come to her while she was still in North Africa through members of a group who called themselves Tertullianists.[5] Octaviana had kept in touch with them. In fact, she had done more than that. A broad smile crosses her face as she can't help expressing her pleasure at her latest act of patronage. She had paid for a Tertullianist presbyter to come from Africa Proconsularis and, through her husband's political connections, obtained permission for the presbyter to take over the care of the Martyrium of Saints Processus and Martinianus. Like Pancras, Processus and Martinianus were Phrygians who had been martyred at Rome. Their martyrium is the next one along the Via Aurelia. As Octaviana goes there to lay down the last of the flowers in her arms, she hopes that the Tertullianist presbyter will help many Christians living in Rome become *spiritales* or *pneumatikoi*.[6]

Sources:

IMont 72; Praedestinatus, *Haer.* 1.86.

Notes

1. *IMont* 63, *ll.*2–5. The name Mountane is a variant of the feminine form of the name Montanus. Taken together with the designation *pneumatikē* in *l.*4 of the epitaph and the most plausible interpretation of the puzzling abbreviations Π–Π provided in this chapter, there is little doubt that Mountane and her husband Loupikinos were Montanists; see Tabbernee 1997b, 401–6. If, as appears likely, that Mountane was born into a Montanist Christian family, there may already have been a Montanist community at Dorylaeion (Şarhüyük) during the first half of the fourth century.

2. *IMont* 63, *l.*1. The probable accurate designation of the formula Π(νευματικὸς) Π(νευματικῇ) ("a *pneumatikos* to a *pneumatikē*") as Montanist does not, however, mean that Phrygian epitaphs with the formula Χριστιανοὶ Χριστιανοῖς ("Christians for Christians") were specifically Montanist inscriptions; see Tabbernee 1997b, 146–51 and esp. 405–6.

3. *IMont* 72.

4. On the fourth-century Montanist community in Rome centered around the Via Aurelia, see Tabbernee 1997b, 456.

5. The relationship between Montanism and the "Tertullianists" is not absolutely clear. That there were (or, at least, had been) Tertullianists in Augustine's time is apparent from Augustine's statement that the Tertullianists in Carthage surrendered their basilica to the catholics (*Haer.* 86). Augustine assumed that the Tertullianists had been founded by Tertullian himself and that, therefore, Tertullian was a schismatic twice—once when he (in Augustine's view) left the "catholics" in Carthage to join the Montanists and the second time when he formed his own sect. Augustine, however, was wrong about Tertullian's first alleged schismatic action (see Tabbernee 2007, 129–32) and there is no reason to assume that Augustine was any better informed about the origins of the Tertullianists. The most likely explanation of the existence of "Tertullianists" is that they were people who admired Tertullian and his writings, including (and, perhaps, especially) those written after he became influenced by the New Prophecy movement. This need not mean, however, that "Tertullianism" is simply an alternative name for Montanism in North Africa; see Tabbernee 1997b, 475–76; 2007, 268–69.

6. The historical accuracy of the information about Octaviana derived from the Praedestinatus (1.86) is, like all of the Praedestinatus' data, somewhat suspect. That there were Tertullianists in Rome (as well as Montanists) in the late fourth and early fifth centuries C.E., however, need not be doubted; see Tabbernee 1997b, 455–56.

Chapter 32

Rome, Italia, 407 C.E.

The Montanists must flee

Frankios is only fifteen years old but he is already showing leadership qualities. The community of followers of Montanus, Maximilla, and Priscilla near the Via Aurelia in Rome is proud of the young man. For someone so young, Frankios is surprisingly mature—not just in ordinary matters but in spiritual ones as well.

Frankios fasts frequently and prays constantly. When he fasts his spirit goes to a deep place, far removed from the cares and concerns of his own every day life. Instead, he embraces the cares and concerns of the lives of other people. It is uncanny how he discerns what people are suffering and how his prayers help—even if the people for whom he prays don't know about his intercessions until much later, or ever. No wonder the community has already designated Frankios a *pneumatikos,* a "spiritual one."

Normally, the title *pneumatikos* is not bestowed by the Montanist community until later in a person's life—after they have themselves proven worthy of the designation. Frankios likes visiting the graves of two of the spiritual ones, a man named Ablabes ("Innocent"), and a man named Alexander. Frankios sees these *pneumatikoi* as role models.

The graves are in a hypogaeum, an underground tomb chamber, along the Via Aurelia between the cemeteries of St. Calepodius and St. Pancras. The chamber also holds the remains of other Montanists from their community, but Ablabes' tomb and that of Alexander are the most important. Ablabes' remains are covered by a simple rectangular slab, decorated with a dove. Frankios loves that dove. The dove is depicted flying very energetically, emanating a great deal of life and hope in the midst of despair and death. The dove is the symbol of peace—an olive branch held securely in its sturdy feet. The olive branch reinforces the last phrase of Ablabes' epitaph, which Frankios repeats aloud to himself: "Peace to you."[1]

Frankios moves a few feet to Alexander's tomb. The slab covering Alexander's remains is also carved beautifully. But instead of a dove, at the left side of the inscription there is a huge staurogram—a Latin cross with the top of its vertical arm curved around in a circle to represent the Greek letter *rho.* As a native Greek speaker, Frankios knows that the Greek word for cross is *stauros* and that a staurogram is a variation of the *chi-rho* christogram. The staurogram, like the *chi-rho,* represents Christ but emphasizes the death of Christ on the cross. The *chi-rho* christogram simply gives the first two letters of the word ΧΡΙΣΤΟΣ (Χριστός [*Christos*]), Christ. The staurogram, Frankios thinks, is a very fitting christogram for a tomb. It links the deceased with Christ in death and, just as Christ conquered death on the cross, it foreshadows resurrection.

Frankios notices, for the first time, that there is also a staurogram at the *end* of Alexander's inscription—although a much smaller one. Alexander's epitaph begins and ends with the symbol of hope and resurrection in the midst of death. As he did with Ablabes' epitaph, Frankios reads aloud the text on Alexander's tombstone:

> Here lies Alexander, a physician, a Christian and a *pneumatikos*.[2]

Alexander had not only been a respected member of the Montanist Christian community to which Frankios belongs, he had also been Frankios' family doctor.

When Frankios returns home after visiting the graves of Ablabes and Alexander, he finds his parents in a great state of despair. Frankios, however, is not completely surprised. All day long he has had the premonition that something is wrong but he didn't know exactly what it might be. Discerning the presence of an ominous threat and knowing the exact nature of that threat are not the same thing. Even before Frankios has the chance to sit down, his father tells him the bad news. They are going to have to leave Rome—the great bustling city they love and where Frankios and his parents have lived their whole lives.

The decision to leave Rome isn't being made lightly, nor is it a decision made of their own free will, Frankios' father tells him. The decision is forced on them by the action of Innocent, the bishop of Rome. Frankios' parents are bitter and complain that, unlike the aptness of Ablabes' Greek name, the Latin version *Innocens,* "Innocent," is a complete misnomer for the bishop: "Guilty" would be a more fitting name for him. Guilty of lack of compassion. Guilty of intolerance. Guilty of doing the emperor's dirty work. Guilty of exiling innocent people such as they.

For years now rumors that something like this might happen have been circulating among the Montanists in Rome—ever since they heard that Arcadius, the emperor of the now separate Byzantine Empire promulgated an edict in Constantinople prescribing extremely harsh penalties for Montanists. Montanists are no longer allowed to reside in Constantinople, the Byzantine capital. According to Arcadius, or, more likely, according to the so-called orthodox clergy who advise him, it is wrong for Montanists to live and work within earshot of the sacred liturgies of the orthodox church—as if Montanists aren't orthodox! Frankios' parents couldn't understand why Montanists couldn't visit and even attend eucharistic services at the Hagia Sophia, the basilica dedicated to the virtue of Holy Wisdom in Constantinople. They, of course, have never been to Constantinople and have never seen the Hagia Sophia built by Constantine, but they have heard about the beautiful basilica. Not that the Montanists in Constantinople would necessarily want to participate in the liturgies at the Hagia Sophia, but to be excluded from the church was bad enough. To be exiled from the city itself is incomprehensible! Did Arcadius and the orthodox clergy think that merely by being within the precinct of the city where the Hagia Sophia is located, the Montanists are polluting the liturgies conducted there?

As time went by, more news and more rumors arrived in Rome about Arcadius' action. Frankios' parents and the other members of the Montanist community in Rome became more and more worried. Not only did Arcadius order the expulsion of Montanists from Constantinople but also from all the cities in the East. Montanists could, presumably, live in the country—but even there they are not allowed to assemble together. If they did and were caught, Montanist clergy would be put to death. Any property they possessed was to be confiscated rather than left to their heirs. If the meetings were held on country estates, those estates were also to be confiscated and the manager of the estate involved was to be executed. All Montanist books were to be sought out and burned. Capital punishment would be the lot of anyone hiding such books or refusing to hand them over to the authorities.

Frankios had often overheard his father and some of the other leaders of the Montanist community in Rome speculate, late into the night, whether or not Arcadius' legislation could apply to them in Rome as well. After the death of the old emperor, Theodosius, there were now *two* empires ruled respectively by Theodosius' sons Arcadius, in Constantinople, and Honorius, in Rome. One of the Montanist leaders in Rome, however, knew that, despite the division of the Empire into two halves, all legislation was still technically enacted jointly by the two emperors—both names appearing on each law, regardless of whether the law was enacted in Constantinople or in Rome. What was unclear to everyone was whether legislation enacted in Constantinople would also be enforced in Rome and vice versa.

It has been almost ten years since Arcadius' anti-Montanist legislation was enacted, and until today no action has been taken against the Montanists in Rome, to the great relief of Frankios, his parents, and their fellow Montanists. But now, with two strokes of two different pens, everything is forever changed.

The news spreads like wildfire throughout the Montanist community in Rome. Honorius has issued a mandate to the Urban Prefect of Rome. The mandate also has Arcadius' name on it, but Honorius, unlike his brother, has not prescribed the death penalty for Montanist clergy, managers of estates, or people refusing to surrender Montanist books. At least that is a relief, Frankios thinks, when his father tells him of the details of the mandate as he himself heard them from others today. Honorius' mandate, though, is much more specific than the one issued by his brother almost a decade earlier. It makes it totally impossible for Montanists to continue to live in Rome.

Frankios' father tells him as many of the details of the mandate as he can remember. Membership in a Montanist group is now a public crime, making all Montanists in Rome very vulnerable. All that is needed is for someone to accuse them of being Montanists and they can be convicted as common criminals. If convicted they, according to this new mandate, will automatically have their property confiscated—unless they cede it to next of kin, but this is only possible if the next of kin is orthodox, not Montanist. Frankios can see the worry in his parents' eyes.

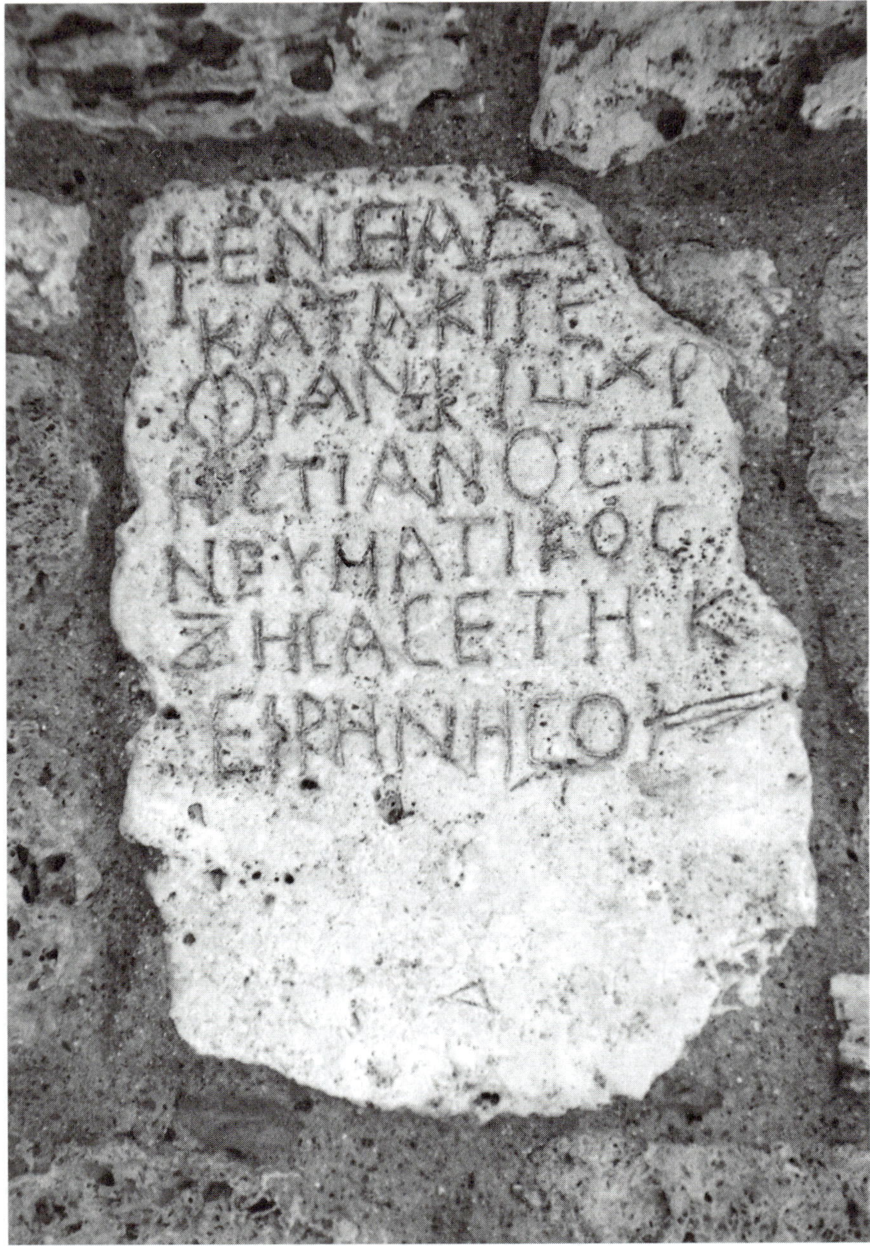

Figure 32.1: Frankios' tombstone

If they stay in Rome, they will lose their home. Frankios, a Montanist *pneumatikos*, cannot inherit the house nor can any of their relatives—they are all Montanists.

Honorius' mandate is very specific, Frankios' father informs his son. Montanists can no longer make valid wills nor enter into valid contracts to buy or sell property or even donate it. What is especially horrifying is that the inappropriately-named Innocent has been granted extra powers to use his ecclesiastical authority to ensure that the imperial mandate is carried out to the fullest extent. The stroke of the second pen is *Innocent*'s. Innocent has decreed that all Montanists residing in Rome must leave the city and either live communally in a monastery in the suburbs outside the Aurelian Walls or be exiled altogether to the countryside.

Despite his spiritual maturity, Frankios cannot stop tears from welling up in his eyes. He doesn't want to leave his home. He doesn't want to leave his friends. He doesn't want to live in a monastery in the suburbs. He doesn't want to live in the countryside far from Rome. He doesn't want Honorius' mandate to go into effect. He doesn't want Innocent's ecclesiastical legislation to be implemented. He doesn't. . . . He doesn't know what to do—other than to fast and pray.[3]

Sources:

IMont 72, 93; *Cod. theod.* 16.5.34, 16.5.40; *Lib. pont.* 57.1–2.

Clusium, Italia, ca. 412 C.E.
A life cut short

Frankios' father cannot believe that five years have passed since he, his wife, and Frankios had fled Rome. They had been fortunate. He sold their house—far too cheaply, of course—before Honorius' mandate and Innocent's ecclesiastical legislation had taken full effect. He and his family also sold most of their other possessions. At great personal risk, they kept some books containing the oracles of Montanus, Maximilla, and Priscilla. They also took with them some mementoes of their former life in Rome: a small black stone washed smooth by the waters of the Tiber; an oil lamp decorated with the Greek letters *chi* and *rho,* representing the first two letters of the name of Christ; and a signet ring with a fish engraved on it.

With some of the money they had received from the sale of their house and other possessions, Frankios' father had procured passage for them on a boat traveling north along the Tiber. He wasn't sure at the time exactly where they would end up. After three days, they disembarked at Clusium—about as far upstream from Rome as they could reach by boat. He had thought about traveling further on foot, but such a journey would have been difficult and, once in Clusium, he had felt safe enough—away from the influence of the anti-Montanist legislation. Clusium had been one of the twelve major cities of ancient Etruria and he could well understand why. The city itself is perfectly situated on a hill, the old Etruscan fortification still partly in place.

Now, five years later, standing on those same fortifications, he remembers how excited Frankios had been when they had first come to this very spot. They had looked at the magnificent panorama stretching out before them. He and Frankios had felt like birds—like the dove on Ablabes' tomb—with a bird's-eye view of the fertile fields far below them and the relief of being "free as birds," so far away from Rome. He had decided then and there to make Clusium his family's new home.

Soon some other Montanists from Rome came to join them and, even though Honorius' mandate specified that property used for Montanist assemblies was to be confiscated, no official ever bothered to enforce this legislation in Clusium. Frankios continued to be the kind of son that would make any Montanist father proud. He flourished in his new environment: a spiritual leader without equal in the small Montanist community in Clusium. At least, that is what he was and would have continued to be—if he had lived.

Frankios' father takes one more look at the spectacular scenery he had shared so often with his son. Turning around, he walks slowly, sadly, back to the edge of the hill where a narrow path winds its way down to the cemetery in a small grove of cypress trees. Having trodden the same path so many times in the last few months, he could find his way to his son's grave in the dark if he had to do so. But today there is still plenty of light even though the sun is setting. When he reaches the grave the sun hangs low in the western sky, but shines brightly on the tombstone. Wiping yet another tear from his eye, Frankios' father reads the words that are all too familiar:

> Here lies Frankios, a Christian and a *pneumatikos,* having lived twenty years. Peace to you.[4]

Source:

IMont 95.

Notes

1. *IMont* 72 *l*.4b.

2. *IMont* 93.

3. That Frankios and his family left Rome because of the persecution of Montanists under the emperor Honorius (395–423) and Bishop Innocent I of Rome (401–407) was first suggested by Ferrua (1955, 100) who also was the first to publish Frankios' epitaph (97–100). If so, as taken for granted in this chapter, they presumably belonged to a Montanist community centered around the Via Aurelia; on which, see Chapters 6 and 7 and Tabbernee 1997b, 455–56, 552. For the epitaphs of possible (but not certain) other members of this Montanist community at Rome, see *IMont* 73–74 and the discussion in Tabbernee 1997b, 457–62.

4. *IMont* 95.

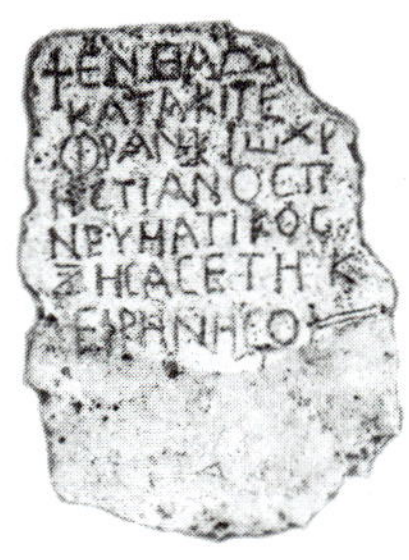

Chapter 33

Kyzikos, Mysia, ca. 425 C.E.

A Montanist goes on pilgrimage: to Pepouza via the "Seven Churches of Asia"

Neikandros feels slightly queasy. The small boat he is traveling on is having a rough time in the bad weather. Usually the sea between Constantinople and Kyzikos is very calm, and when he stands on deck at the bow of the boat he only feels a slight swell. Today, however, the boat is constantly battered by huge waves smashing against the bow as it climbs up what appear to him to be mountains of water only to plunge down heavily, seemingly to the bottom of the sea, once over the top of each oncoming wave. The boat has been struggling against an endless series of ferocious waves for over an hour now and making little headway.

Neikandros long ago abandoned his favorite vantage spot near the bow of the boat and is below decks, sheltering himself from the storm. More than the violent tossing of the boat is making him feel ill. Not having spent much time below deck before, he hadn't realized how rank it always is down here "in the hole." Oh how he wishes he were on deck, in calm weather, enjoying the sun, the fresh air, and the magnificent view of Kyzikos harbor as they approach the city. But that is impossible today, and all he hopes to do is survive the next couple of hours. He vows never to set foot on a boat again. Next time he needs to go to Constantinople, he will travel the long way around by land through Prusa, Nikomedia, and Chalcedon.

Trying to take his mind off his misery, Neikandros, ironically, finds himself thinking about another trip he is about to make. He had planned to take a boat from Kyzikos to Adramyttion for the first leg of his journey—but he will definitely not do that now. He'll go by foot, which, anyway, is a much more appropriate means of transportation for a pilgrimage.

Neikandros, bishop of the Montanist community at Kyzikos,[1] has been to Constantinople to encourage the few followers of Montanus, Maximilla, and Priscilla who are still there. A series of edicts by the emperors had tried to get rid of all Montanists, but, fortunately, those edicts have not been totally effective.[2] While some Montanists in Constantinople fled the capital to cities such as his own Kyzikos or to the countryside, a few faithful members remained in Constantinople—at great risk to themselves. Even in Kyzikos there is some risk of imperial agents taking action against the Montanists, but the risk is nowhere near as great as it is in the capital. Neikandros is glad he went to Constantinople to give his fellow Montanists some pastoral support. As the boat finally enters the harbor of Kyzikos, Neikandros is also glad the return trip from Constantinople is over.

Neikandros has always wanted to visit the "Seven Churches of Asia." There are, of course, now hundreds of churches in Asia, but ever since St. John wrote the book containing seven letters dictated by the risen Christ to seven of the earliest Christian communities in the Roman province called Asia, those seven churches have held special prominence: Ephesus, Smyrna, Pergamon, Thyateira, Sardis, Philadelphia, and Laodikeia. Of all the books in the Christian scriptures, Neikandros, as a Montanist bishop, likes the book of Revelation best. Not only does it contain the seven letters to the seven churches, it also describes the descent of the New Jerusalem from heaven. Neikandros has read the passages about the New Jerusalem countless times. He is convinced that the founders of the New Prophecy and Quintilla, the later Montanist prophetess, were right in believing that the New Jerusalem will descend somewhere between Pepouza and Tymion. Although the New Jerusalem hasn't come yet, it undoubtedly will when the time is right.

Time is puzzling to Neikandros. It is such a strange thing. When one looks forward expectantly to some event, like a feast day, that is still in the future, it seems as if time stands still and the day of the event takes forever to arrive. Then, when the day of the event *does* arrive, time no longer stands still but speeds up. The event seems to be over before it has even started. No wonder the second letter attributed to St. Peter says that, because with the Lord a day is like a thousand years and a thousand years a day, we should not reckon time with respect to Christ's second coming the same way we calculate ordinary time—which is a strange enough phenomenon all by itself. God's time is *God*'s time and in God's time, whenever that may be, the New Jerusalem *will* descend at or near Pepouza.

When Neikandros was in Constantinople, he finally decided to make a pilgrimage to Pepouza. Perhaps *this* is God's time and he will be privileged to be in Pepouza when the New Jerusalem arrives. But even if this isn't God's time it is still, Neikandros reflects, a good time for him to go to Pepouza. He isn't getting any younger, he reminds himself. Long journeys are not for old men. He has to make the most of his opportunities while he still can. Whether or not he will see the New Jerusalem is beside the point. He wants to see the place where the New Jerusalem will ultimately descend. He also wants to visit the basilica of the patriarch of Pepouza and worship there. Perhaps the patriarch will allow him to concelebrate the Eucharist, Neikandros finds himself hoping. But most of all, he wants to see the shrine containing the bones of Montanus, Maximilla, and Priscilla in the crypt underneath the basilica. How fortunate and blessed were the founders of the movement in which he is now a bishop, Neikandros says to himself, that they were the human instruments of the Holy Spirit, the Paraclete, when the Spirit provided new revelation about how Christians are to live as *spiritual* Christians, *pneumatikoi*. Neikandros hopes that when he dies, the word *pneumatikos* will appear on his tombstone. But the thought of dying is premature—he first has to make a pilgrimage. Next Sunday, after the Eucharist, he is going to leave Kyzikos for Pepouza, visiting each of the "Seven Churches of Asia" on the way. Neikandros prays that the four days until Sunday will fly by quickly. He cannot wait to get started—on foot, of course. He has already packed his boots.[3]

Sources:

IMont 1, 2, 86; *Cod. theod.* 16.5.34, 16.5.40, 16.5.65; Rev 2:1–3:22, 21:1–22:5; 2 Pet 3:8–13; Jerome, *Ep.* 41.3; *Cod. justin.* 1.5.20.3.

Pergamon, Mysia, ca. 425 C.E.
Healing at the Asklepeion

Neikandros has made good time. Traveling alone has its advantages. He has not been slowed down by the physical impediments of others. It took him four days of walking to get to Adramyttion, a beautiful harbor city like his own Kyzikos. He didn't stay to see the sights, however. Instead, he pushed on so that he could reach Pergamon by Saturday evening. In fact, he has made it by noon on Saturday.

Neikandros is standing at the end of a colonnaded street, the Via Tecta. He is at the entrance of the Asklepeion. Not that he has any intention of going inside that pagan place of alleged healing. But having arrived in the lower part of the city a little earlier than expected, he decided to take the slight detour, having been told that from the Asklepeion one has a magnificent view of Pergamon's acropolis. Neikandros agrees silently that his informants are absolute right. The view is spectacular.

The huge hill that forms the base of Pergamon's acropolis looms before Neikandros, like a huge fortress—which, in fact, it is. A series of protective walls ring the hill, interrupted occasionally by gates and watch towers. Neikandros sees a series of terrace houses built into the slope of the hill. He also sees the very steep rows of theater seats. The sun is directly overhead and shining on the Trajaneum at the very top of the acropolis. The temple was built as part of the imperial cult in honor of the emperor Trajan, Neikandros knows. Even from this distance, Neikandros can see that the Trajaneum is a beautiful temple, its Corinthian columns and triangular pediments glistening in the sunlight.

There are few clouds in the sky and despite his earlier resolve not to step one foot inside the precincts of the Asklepeion, the heat of the scorching sun and his curiosity get the better of him. No one is looking, so he considers it safe enough to take a peak at the complex of buildings that make up the healing center named after the god Asklepios. In the middle of the courtyard just inside the entrance, Neikandros notices a marble column. He stops to look at the reliefs carved around its base. He is not surprised to see that the reliefs portray pairs of snakes, the pagan symbols of healing. The snakes are drinking from round dishes. Neikandros can hear running water. The sound and the image before him remind him how thirsty he is—and against his will and better judgment he walks, past the Temple of Zeus Asklepios, toward the sound of the water.

When he gets closer, Neikandros sees that the sound is coming from a spring. He stoops to drink, scooping up the cool, crystal clear water with both hands. The

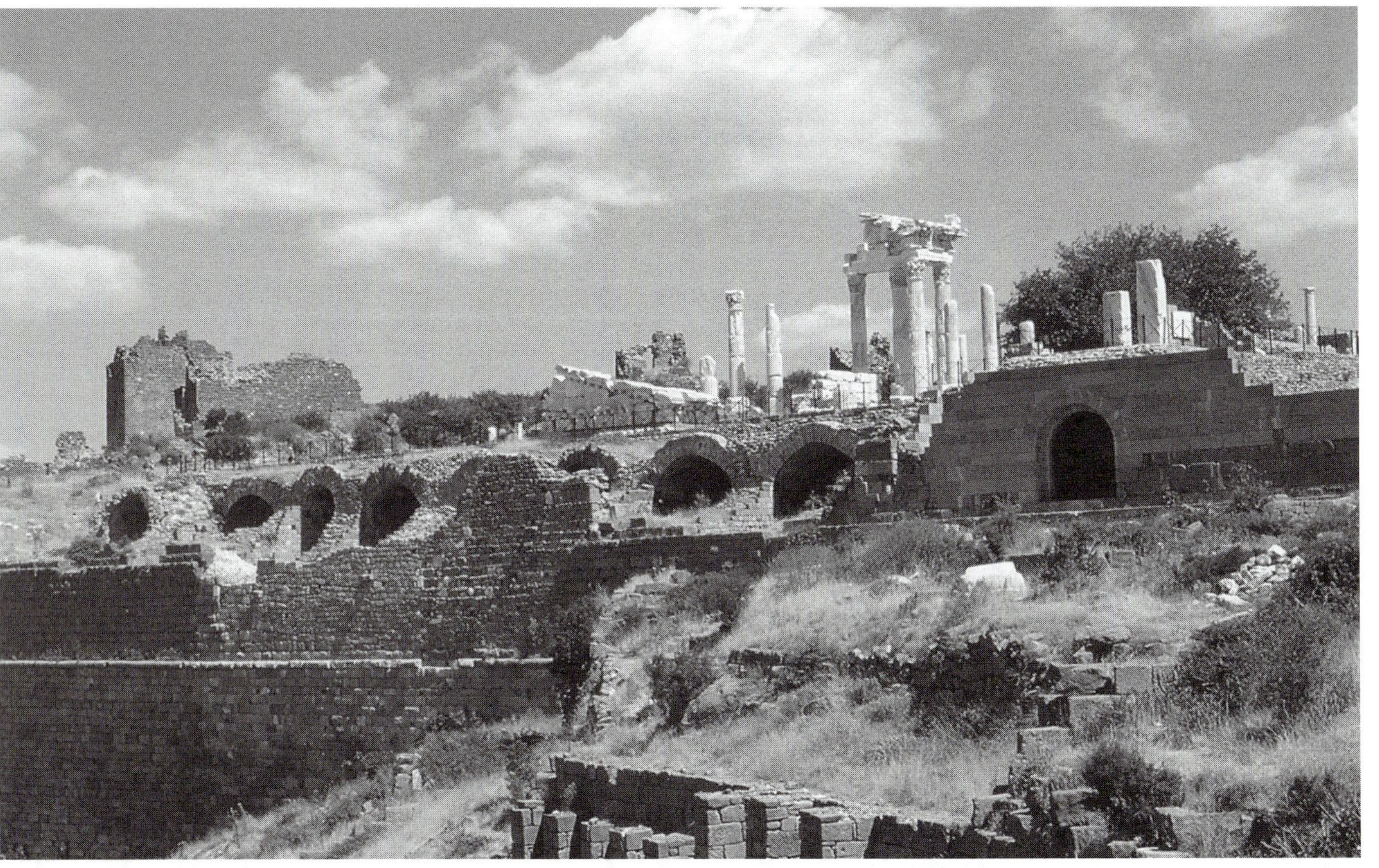

Figure 33.1: View of Pergamon's acropolis from the Asklepeion

water tastes of minerals, not exactly how he had expected it to taste. Suddenly, the sun is blocked out as a large man casts a shadow over Neikandros as he continues drinking. Shocked by the unexpected presence of the stranger, Neikandros quickly stands up. The man is dressed in the robes of a priest of Asklepios. To Neikandros' surprise, the priest has a kind face and a welcoming smile. No one who comes here is refused entry and no one who comes here ill leaves ill, the priest tells Neikandros. He also explains that the spring from which Neikandros has just drunk has curative powers. Presumably, the dishes from which the marble snakes in the courtyard are drinking must contain water from this spring.

As it would be rude to refuse the kind stranger's invitation to see some of the other buildings in the Asklepeion, Neikandros follows his guide to a large round building. They enter it through the cryptoporticus, a long, wide underground tunnel with an arched ceiling. Periodically there are round holes in the ceiling of the cryptoporticus. Through these holes Neikandros can hear very soothing music being played. The priest tells Neikandros that he must take off his shoes. Walking on the cool earth in his bare feet with the sound of the soothing music in his ears makes Neikandros relax. Immediately, the stress of the journey is released from his body. The pain from aching feet and calf muscles disappears. All the walking has given him a corn on the side of the big toe on his left foot. The priest tenderly puts a small pad with ointment on his toe. He feels so much better than when he arrived at the Asklepeion less than half an hour ago. Neikandros cannot believe that a pagan healing center could have any, let alone this good, effect on him.

The large round building is a hospice where patients stay and rest. It has comfortable beds and chairs. The Asklepeion also has a library and even a theater where dramatic plays are performed. Healing depends not only on curing one's physical ailments, the priest explains, the patient's mind and soul must also be healed. Once more surprised at how much he and the pagan priest are of one accord, Neikandros cannot disagree.

After having said farewell to his guide, Neikandros retraces his steps along the colonnaded street. He turns left and follows another street to the amphitheater where Agathonike, Papylos, and Karpos were martyred during the persecution under the emperor Decius. He wants to see the holy spot because, according to reports he has heard, Agathonike, Papylos, and Karpos were adherents of the New Prophecy movement. Neikandros is not sure how accurate these reports are, but he doesn't care whether they are true or not. Even if the three martyrs are non-Montanist martyrs, the amphitheater is a sacred place worthy of a visit on the first part of his pilgrimage.

The amphitheater is larger than any Neikandros has ever seen before. He enters the empty amphitheater in silence and sits in a seat on the fourth tier. From there he has a good view of the arena and wonders exactly where Agathonike, Papylos, and Karpos were put to death. Neikandros knows that Agathonike, Papylos, and Karpos were each nailed to stakes before being burned to death. He imagines that the stakes were probably erected in the middle of the arena so that, wherever the spectators were seated, they would have a good view as the flames licked at and finally consumed the bodies of the martyrs. Just as it doesn't really matter whether Agathonike, Papylos, and Karpos were Montanists, it doesn't matter exactly where in the amphitheater they died, Neikandros reminds himself, as he prays for their souls.[4]

Time, the enemy of protracted contemplation, flies by too quickly. Neikandros leaves the amphitheater, retracing his steps slightly until he reconnects with the Via Tecta. Walking toward Pergamon, the opposite direction from the Asklepeion, Neikandros soon reaches the forum of the lower city. Instead of taking the bridge that crosses the Selinus River at the edge of the forum, Neikandros enters a huge red brick basilica. The basilica, at the far end of the forum, is an architectural marvel, spanning the river itself. Originally constructed as a temple for Isis and Serapis, Egyptian deities, the basilica now serves as the main church building for the orthodox Christians of Pergamon. Not surprisingly, after it had been exorcised and remodeled, the Red Hall had been dedicated to St. John. Neikandros wants to see inside the basilica before sundown because tomorrow, when he will try to attend the eucharistic liturgy at the red brick church, he, as a Montanist, will probably not receive the kind of welcome he received today by the pagan priest of the Asklepeion.[5]

Sources:

Rev 2:12–17; *Mart. Carp.* (A), (B).

Thyateira, Lydia, ca. 425 C.E.
The pressure to conform

It has taken Neikandros two and a half days to walk from Pergamon to Thyateira and he is exhausted. Fortunately, his corn is completely healed. He is, however, a little disappointed about what he is seeing in Thyateira. The city is nothing like Pergamon. There is no acropolis, no amphitheater, not even a theater. Neikandros wonders how Thyateira can even be called a city, for it has little to recommend it other than its strategic location as a staging post on the main road from Pergamon to Sardis. Here, for those rich enough to afford it, horses can rest or be exchanged and coach travelers can stay overnight in cheap lodgings. While looking for his own lodgings for the night, Neikandros reminds himself that, because of its location, Thyateira is not only an important stopping place on the imperial post-road, but the center of a *Christian* "postal district."[6]

For Neikandros the Montanist, Thyateira, despite its unimpressive character as a city, is nevertheless a very important pilgrimage site. It is the only city among those whose Christian community received a letter from the risen Christ where the whole congregation later became Montanist. Thyateira's Christian community, Neikandros is told, adopted the New Prophecy in the time of the emperor Alexander Severus and remained totally Montanist for more than one hundred years. Papylos, one of the men martyred alongside Agathonike under Decius, was a deacon from Thyateira, Neikandros has learned. If by that time the church at Thyateira had been fully Montanist for more than a quarter of a century, Papylos must have been a *Montanist* deacon, Neikandros figures. Having seen Pergamon, the city where Papylos died, Neikandros is pleased to see the city where Papylos lived and served as a deacon in the Montanist community.

Neikandros has heard that Thyateira was forced back into the "catholic fold" by Constantine's anti-Montanist legislation. He can certainly believe that that is what happened. If the more recent imperial legislation is anything to go by, there would have been immense social pressure on the Christians at Thyateira to conform.[7] Neikandros is grateful that his own Montanist community at Kyzikos has not succumbed to the current imperial pressure—as did the Montanists in Thyateira during the time of Constantine.

Neikandros again passes the now orthodox Christian basilica. As in Pergamon, the huge rectangular red brick building was once a pagan temple. Unlike the Church of St. John in Pergamon, however, the basilica in Thyateira had functioned, for a while, as a civic building. Peeking inside, Neikandros sees the beautifully decorated apse at the eastern end of the sanctuary. He doesn't stay long but hurries out to find his lodgings, glad that tomorrow is not Sunday. He does not want to experience being rejected from the Eucharist again.

Sources:

Rev 2:18–28; Epiphanius, *Pan.* 51.33.4; *Mart. Carp.* (A) 24–27, (B) 1, 3.1–2.

Sardis, Lydia, ca. 425 C.E.

Sacred space

Although every one of the cities Neikandros has visited thus far, and still intends to visit on his pilgrimage, belongs to the Roman province of Asia, the character of each one is influenced by the particular region in which it is located. Sardis, where Neikandros is today, used to be the capital of the ancient kingdom of Lydia. Sardis is a rich, populous city, made prosperous in part by the gold discovered and refined in the area.

Neikandros can't believe that only a few steps away from the basilica he is visiting there is a gold refinery. He wonders whether the fabled King Croesus once owned this very refinery. From where he is standing, just outside the church, Neikandros can see the acropolis of Sardis, with its fortifications and many new buildings, high above the lower city.

This church is the second one Neikandros has visited in Sardis today. The first was a much larger basilica than this one. He was impressed by that basilica's imposing size, visible from a long way off as he approached the city. A little further along the road, Neikandros passed the gymnasium with its ornate façade and saw the Jewish synagogue, next to the gymnasium's palaestra, or exercise field.[8] He quickly walked past the row of Jewish shops, stopping only at the building at the end of the row—a public latrine.

Neikandros is now on the way to a third church in Sardis and, from what he has heard, the most interesting one. He can hear the sound of the waters of the

Figure 33.2: Byzantine church and Temple of Artemis at Sardis

Paktolos River on his right as he walks along the path that, more or less, follows the left bank of the river. Within minutes he turns a bend and sees the impressive remains of a temple—the Temple of Artemis, he has been told. Some of the columns of the temple have been removed, as have many of the stones, all used as building materials for some of the new buildings in Sardis, Neikandros presumes. In the far corner of the temple is what he came to see: a small jewel of a basilica, beautifully decorated with frescoes covering its plastered inside walls. Through the large window in the apse he can, once again, see the acropolis high above him.

Neikandros marvels that pagan sacred space can so readily be turned into Christian sacred space. On his way through the ruined temple to the little basilica, he saw numerous crosses and Christian graffiti scratched into the stones of the unused temple, evidence of the temple's exorcism and sanctification. If only Montanists and other Christians could learn to live side by side as easily as the former Artemis temple and the little Christian basilica do, Neikandros laments. After all, Melito, the bishop of Sardis at the time when Montanus, Maximilla, and Priscilla started the New Prophecy movement in neighboring Phrygia, was, like them, a prophet and an ascetic. Some people, Neikandros has heard, even thought Melito was sympathetic to the New Prophecy. Whether Melito was, indeed, favorably disposed toward Montanism, Neikandros doesn't know. He does find himself thinking, though, that contemporary orthodox Christians in Sardis would probably want to exorcise him and other Montanists, like they exorcised the Temple of Artemis, before they would be prepared to co-exist peacefully.[9]

Sources:

Rev 3:1–6; Eusebius, *Hist. eccl.* 4.26.1–14.

Smyrna, Ionia, ca. 425 C.E.
Where Polycarp and Eutychian were martyred

Neikandros is not sure whether there ever were Montanists in Sardis, but he is glad he went to see the city and its three Christian basilicas. Sardis was, after all, one of the "Seven Churches of Asia." Smyrna, however, the city to which he is now headed, definitely had a Montanist community for many years, perhaps—at least according to some—as early as the time of St. Polycarp of blessed memory.

Neikandros doubts there were Montanists in Smyrna as early as Polycarp's time but he knows for sure that a Montanist named Eutychian was martyred in Smyrna during the persecution under Decius. Just as he had seen the very place where Agathonike, Papylos, and Karpos were put to death in Pergamon, Neikandros is determined to see the stadium where, in successive centuries, Polycarp and Eutychian suffered death. His desire to see the stadium at Smyrna was the reason Neikandros had turned back toward the sea and gone to Smyrna rather than going from Sardis directly to Philadelphia. Whichever route he took, he would have had to do some backtracking to visit each of the "Seven Churches of Asia"

Figure 33.3: The Church of St. John (including Tomb of St. John) in Ephesus

and Pepouza. Neikandros had considered going to Philadelphia right after Sardis and then on to Pepouza, returning by way of Laodikeia, Ephesus, and Smyrna. But he had quickly rejected that possible itinerary. The whole purpose of his trip is to make a pilgrimage to Pepouza, visiting the "Seven Churches of Asia" on the way. Pepouza, therefore, should be the *final* destination—not a stop along the itinerary—and, in any case, he couldn't wait to see the stadium in Smyrna.

Nearing Smyrna, Neikandros picks up his pace as he thinks of the sites he will see in the city. All the walking he has done during the past few weeks has made him fit and strong. His leg and calf muscles no longer hurt, the corn on his left big toe is gone, and his belly no longer protrudes. He looks ten years younger than when he left Kyzikos less than a month ago.

Before he knows it, Neikandros finds himself at the top of Mt. Pagus, the fortified hill overlooking the lower city and the harbor. The view is spectacular and, although coming from a harbor city himself, Neikandros cannot help but be impressed with the number of ships docked in the harbor. No wonder this is the second-most-important harbor in Asia, supplanted only by Ephesus. To his left, slightly downhill, is the stadium. Neikandros almost runs the rest of the way, he is so eager to get there. As he had done in the amphitheater in Pergamon, Neikandros sits on a seat in the fourth tier of the stadium, imagining exactly where Polycarp and, later, Eutychian paid the ultimate price for being Christians. He crosses himself and prays for their souls, and for the souls of all the others—Montanists and non-Montanists alike—who were martyred in this very stadium. When he is finished, Neikandros makes his way down to the lower city. He has heard that there are still a few Montanists left in Smyrna, and he goes to the agora in search of someone who might be able to give him the information he needs to connect with any remaining followers of Montanus, Maximilla, and Priscilla.[10]

Sources:

Rev 2:8–11; *Mart. Pol.* 4, 13–18; *Pass. Pion.* 11.2, cf. 21.5.

Ephesus, Ionia, ca. 425 C.E.
The tomb of St. John the Divine

Neikandros has never seen a city as beautiful as Ephesus. No wonder it is the pre-eminent city of Asia.[11] He is especially impressed with the Library of Celsus and its ornate façade. Being on a Christian pilgrimage, however, Neikandros is not in Ephesus to see buildings erected by pagans—no matter how beautiful.

Neikandros walks from the Library of Celsus, along Marble Street, to the theater. Once again, almost out of habit now, he ascends the steps of the theater to the fourth row, sits down and imagines the spot where St. Paul was arrested. He also visits the place where, according to tradition, St. Paul was imprisoned. Strangely, he cannot sense the presence of St. Paul in the so-called prison and cannot help wondering whether what he is seeing is the actual site. In any case, as a Montanist pilgrim, he is far more interested in St. John.

From the theater, Neikandros walks along the street formerly known as Harbor Street, but which has recently been renamed the Arcadian Way, in honor of emperor Arcadius, the son of Theodosius the Great. Arcadius spent lots of money, Neikandros has been told, beautifying this street. It is only mid-morning but already very hot, and Neikandros is grateful to Arcadius for building a covered portico on both sides of the wide street. The shade provided by the porticoes is a great relief. The porticoes even contain shops, and Neikandros cannot resist buying a small, ring-shaped loaf of bread. The aroma of freshly baked bread is nothing less than heavenly.

Neikandros sees a number of lanterns set on poles, like candelabra, along the street. These, he presumes, light the Arcadian Way at night. After a quick look at the harbor, Neikandros turns right, passes the harbor baths, and is amazed by the size of the Olympieion, the Temple of Hadrian in the guise of Zeus Olympios. He continues alongside the stadium and the gymnasium before exiting the city by its north gate. Neikandros finds himself on the sacred way to the Artemision, the Temple of Artemis of the Ephesians, said to be one of the Seven Wonders of the World.

Not wanting to be contaminated by the huge statue of the fertility goddess, displaying her many breasts, or, as someone once told him, her "bulls' testicles," Neikandros averts his eyes as he hurries past the temple. His breathing is heavier now, not only because he almost ran past the Artemision but because he is climbing steadily. The last part of his journey, beyond the Artemision to the Church of St. John, is especially steep as the basilica is built almost at the top of a hill. Neikandros, nearly out of breath despite his new-found fitness, is glad the church is not all the way at the top of the hill.

Neikandros enters the church silently, noticing immediately that it is built in the shape of a cross. Reverently, he walks the length of the nave to the part of the church where the horizontal beam of a cross would intersect with the vertical stake. There Neikandros finds what he came to see: the tomb of St. John. Neikandros is moved to tears. The tomb, like the church itself, is in the shape of a cross. Neikandros is not sure whether to believe the story that John dug his own cross-shaped tomb and slept in it before his death, but he has no doubt that what he is seeing is John's actual tomb. He is thankful to the emperor Constantine for having built such a beautiful and architecturally appropriate church over the tomb of St. John, the man who, before he died, had a vision of the New Jerusalem descending out of heaven.[12]

Thinking about the New Jerusalem makes Neikandros almost wish he had made a different choice about his itinerary back in Sardis. If he had gone on to Philadelphia then, he would be at Pepouza by now and he could see Laodikeia, Ephesus, and Smyrna on the way home. What is it about human beings, Neikandros wonders, that makes us second guess even our best decisions? Of course he made the right choice in Sardis! Keeping Pepouza as the last place to visit on his pilgrimage was, and remains, the right thing to do.

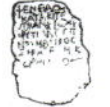  

Neikandros cannot believe his good fortune. One of the Christians he has just met in the Church of St. John has offered him a ride to Laodikeia in his carriage. The man travels frequently between Ephesus and Laodikeia on business and is leaving early tomorrow morning. Neikandros is welcome to come along. Given how his legs feel after climbing all the way to the Basilica of St. John today, Neikandros did not hesitate to accept the kind invitation. His only regret is that he would have liked to see the grave of one of Philip's daughters—the one not buried at Hierapolis—and to have tried to locate the exact place in Ephesus where Alexander, one of the New Prophecy's early leaders, had lived.[13] He shrugs his shoulders philosophically, reflecting that, even on a pilgrimage, there are always choices to be made.

Sources:

Rev 2:1–7, 21:1–22:5; Polycrates, *Ep.*, *ap.* Eusebius, *Hist. eccl.* 3.31.3, 5.24.2–3.

Laodikeia, Phrygia, ca. 425 C.E.
Neither hot nor cold but lukewarm

The horses pulling the carriage of his newly-found friend are young and strong. They made good time as they sped along the excellent road between Ephesus and Laodikeia. The whole journey has taken less than two days to this particular Laodikeia near the Lykos River, a tributary of the Meander.[14] The carriage driver slows the horses down to a walk as they enter the city, pass the gymnasium and the water tower that, his friend tells Neikandros, supplied hot and cold running water to the baths and some of the private houses of Laodikeia even before St. John wrote the book of Revelation. Suddenly the reference in the letter to the church at Laodikeia to hot and cold running water, alluding to Laodikeia's plentiful but sometimes lukewarm water supply, makes perfect sense to Neikandros.[15]

The carriage stops outside a large building. It was originally a nymphaeum, consisting of a huge rectangular pool with multiple fountains at both ends. At one time a statue of Isis stood at the edge of the pool, along with other life-sized statues. All of these have been removed, Neikandros learns from his friend, including the pool itself. The nymphaeum now, as Neikandros can see for himself, has been converted into an enclosed building, decorated with Christian symbols.

As they enter the building, Neikandros wonders whether this is where the Council of Laodikeia was held. He is interested to know because this council, which occurred about a hundred years ago, he has heard, reacted to Montanist practices by forbidding the ordination of women as presbyters and presidents, and legislating that even Montanist clergy wanting to become Catholics needed to be baptized by Catholic clergy. Neikandros' friend tells him, however, that while the long, rectangular building would, no doubt, have made an excellent venue

Figure 33.4: The Water Tower near the Roman Baths at Laodikeia

for the council, the renovations to the former nymphaeum were not done until recently—well after the time of the council. Neikandros' friend doesn't know for certain where the council met but presumes it was in the city's main basilica—a church, not surprisingly, dedicated to St. John.[16]

Both men stay overnight in the guest quarters of the former nymphaeum and the next morning, while his friend conducts the business that brought him to Laodikeia, Neikandros explores the city. Fascinated by the water tower and its symbolic significance, Neikandros retraces the last part of the route they took in the carriage and stands looking at the strange pyramidal rock-cut tower with its terra cotta pipes. Across the valley he can see the aqueduct that feeds the tower. A short distance from the water tower, in a natural depression, is Laodikeia's stadium. Neikandros heads for the fourth tier of seats but this time he has to walk down, rather than up, to reach that particular row. He finds himself wondering whether any Christians were ever martyred here.

Neikandros leaves the stadium, slowly climbing back up the steps and walks past the baths to the Church of St. John. The church is nowhere nearly as impressive as the one dedicated to the apostle in Ephesus, but Neikandros is happy to visit it—even if it is probably the site of *anti*-Montanist, rather than *pro*-Montanist, activities.

To his surprise Neikandros discovers that Laodikeia has two, not just one theater, as well as an odeon. Not wanting to spend time at each, Neikandros stops one of the citizens of Laodikeia in the street and asks his advice about which one to see. The man tells him that the smaller of the two theaters has a magnificent view of Hierapolis. As Hierapolis is where the other daughters of Philip are buried, Neikandros decides to go to see that theater. When he enters the theater, Neikandros, this time, does not stop at the fourth tier of seats but continues all the way to the top. From there he concurs that his informant is absolutely right. Across the valley, Neikandros can see the calcium-covered slope of the plateau on which Hierapolis is built. The sun shining on the pure white mineral deposits makes the city look like a castle made of cotton. Neikandros is delighted that he can see, even at a distance, the city where Philip's daughters, important figures in the line of prophetic succession to which Montanists lay claim, are buried along with their father. Although Hierapolis is not one of the "Seven Churches of Asia," Neikandros will pay a brief visit to Laodikeia's neighbor tomorrow. He wants to pray at the tomb of Philip's daughters.[17]

Source:

Rev 3:14–22.

Philadelphia, Lydia, ca. 425

Home of Ammia

While in Hierapolis, Neikandros was tempted to take the road leading directly north out of the city—the shortest route to Pepouza. Instead, he took the northwest road leading to Philadelphia.[18] It would be unforgivable, as close as he

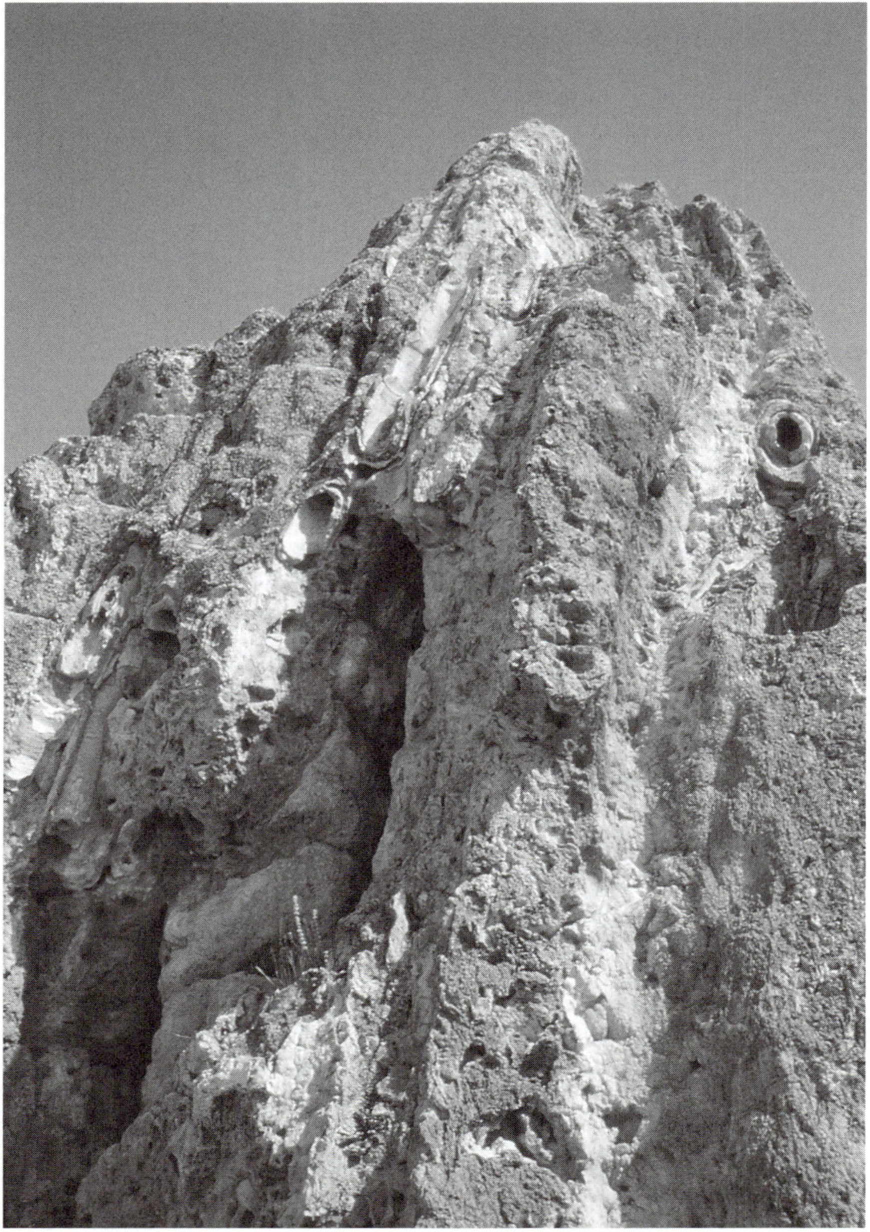

Figure 33.5: Detail of the Water Tower showing the pipes imbedded in it

is to the last of the "Seven Churches of Asia," not to visit that city. And, as a Montanist, he has two particular reasons to go to Philadelphia. First, Philadelphia is the city where Ammia, the famous prophetess, was based. Very few Montanists, Neikandros reflects, can say, as he will be able to say when he completes his pilgrimage, that they have seen each of the places where Philip's daughters, Ammia, Montanus, Maximilla, Priscilla, and later Montanist prophets and prophetesses, such as Quintilla, prophesied to those who were open to what the Holy Spirit had to reveal to them.

The second reason is that it is in the letter of the risen Christ to the church at Philadelphia that the descent of the New Jerusalem out of heaven is first mentioned. This important reference must have provided Montanus with his first clue regarding the location of the site where the New Jerusalem will descend—a place almost due east of Philadelphia. It is fitting, therefore, for Neikandros to finish his pilgrimage by walking east from Philadelphia to Pepouza, toward the rising sun.

Not as fortunate as he was on his journey from Ephesus to Laodikeia, Neikandros once again has to walk the whole distance from Hierapolis to Philadelphia, not ride in a carriage—but at least the road is in excellent repair. Now, two days after leaving Hierapolis and three days after leaving Laodikeia, Neikandros finds himself crossing a bridge over the Kogamos River into the thriving little city of Philadelphia. Located strategically on the imperial post road from Rome to the eastern provinces of the Empire, Philadelphia is an important commercial center. Neikandros almost has to fight off the overly persistent street vendors as he makes his way to yet another Basilica of St. John.

Too many years have passed since Ammia lived in Philadelphia. No one in the city knows anything about her. An old man remembers hearing a tradition about a prophet named Quadratus who, centuries before, also prophesied in the vicinity, but he knows nothing about Ammia. Neikandros is excited to hear about Quadratus, as Quadratus is also part of the Montanist line of prophetic succession, but he is more than a little disappointed that he will not be able to find Ammia's grave. At least he has seen the landscape Ammia saw each day of her life,[19] Neikandros observes ruefully to himself, as he decides to make his stay in Philadelphia a short one. He cannot wait to leave as early as possible tomorrow to go to Pepouza. The ultimate destination of his pilgrimage is only a three- or four-day walk away.

Sources:

Rev 3:7–13; Anonymous, *Fr., ap.* Eusebius, *Hist. eccl.* 5.17.3–4.

Notes

1. The bishop whose name is probably restored correctly as Neikandros (see Tabbernee 1997b, 517) and who is the main character in this chapter, was undoubtedly a Montanist. His tombstone reads: "Memorial tomb of [Neik]andros, *episkopos* (and) holy *pneumatikos*" (*IMont* 86, altered). For other examples of Montanist *pneumatikoi* ("spiritual ones"), see Chapters 31 and 32.

2. On the anti-Montanist legislation of the late fourth and early fifth centuries, see n. 16 (on Laodikeia) below and Tabbernee 2007, 301–2, 318–25.

3. There is no evidence that Neikandros undertook a pilgrimage from Kyzikos (Erdek, near Bandırma) to Pepouza (near Karayakuplu), but it is by no means impossible that he did so. Epiphanius (*Pan.* 48.14.1–2, 49.1.4) relates that, at least in his day (ca. 376), Montanists venerated Pepouza and gathered there to celebrate the Eucharist, to be baptized, and to await the appearance of Christ. It is also possible that, if Neikandros undertook a pilgrimage to Pepouza, he, as a Montanist, may have visited the "Seven Churches of Asia" on the way. All the sites described in this chapter, whether or not Neikandros himself saw them personally, are accurate for ca. 425 and could have been seen by any Montanist (or other) pilgrim or visitor at that time.

4. Unlike for Thyateira (see below), there is no direct evidence for a Montanist community in Pergamon (Bergama). It is possible (but not certain), however, that Agathonike and, at least, Papylos who, along with Karpos (the bishop of Julia Gordos [Gördes]), were martyred in the amphitheater at Pergamon during the Decian Persecution (ca. 250/1), were Montanists; see Tabbernee 1997b, 140–41; 2007, 224–26.

5. On the Asklepeion in Pergamon, see Hoffmann 1998 and on the "Red Hall" basilica, see Nohlen 1998.

6. For the view that Thyateira, like each of the seven cities whose Christian community is addressed in the book of Revelation, was the center of a Christian "postal district," see Ramsay 1904, 191–92, 196, 316.

7. The most likely time for Thyateira to have been exclusively Montanist for 112 years (Epiphanius, *Pan.* 51.33.4) is between ca. 223 and ca. 335; see Tabbernee 1997b, 136–38. If so, as already mentioned, Papylos, one of those martyred with Agathonike at Pergamon, ca. 250/1, would have been a Montanist. He is referred to as a deacon of Thyateira (*Mart. Carp.* [B] 1) and a citizen of that city (*Mart. Carp.* [B] 3.3; cf. [A] 32), which must mean that, if Epiphanius' information is accurate, Papylos was a deacon of the *Montanist* Christian community; see also Tabbernee 1997b, 140–41.

8. Sardis had a large Jewish community dating back to the fifth century B.C.E. A civic basilica next to the gymnasium at Sardis was turned into a synagogue ca. 150–ca. 250 and further renovated ca. 320–ca. 340. The synagogue and extensive remains of the row of shops still remain today, as do the gymnasium, gold refinery, the Temple of Artemis, and each of the churches described in this chapter.

9. Melito, bishop of Sardis (Sart), ca. 170, has been viewed by some scholars (e.g., Grant 1971, 162; 1988, 96–97) as an active opponent of Montanism. If so, there may have been Montanists at Sardis in Melito's time, but the evidence for Melito's anti-Montanist activity is not conclusive; see Tabbernee 2007, 25–27.

10. It is likely that there were Montanists at Smyrna in Neikandros' day. Montanists certainly existed in the city in the previous century, as the new preface written by a fourth-century editor of the third-century *Vita Polycarpi* ("Life of Polycarp") makes a direct reference to contemporary Montanist issues (*Vit. Pol.* 2); see Stewart-Sykes 2002, 7–22. On Eutychian and the Montanist community at Smyrna in the third century, see Chapter 20. The view that there were Montanists at Smyrna as early as the time of Polycarp's martyrdom is based on the reference to a man named Quintus, "a Phrygian recently arrived from Phrygia" in the *Martyrdom of Polycarp* (4). The various attempts to deal with the numerous chronological and other issues to be resolved in order for Quintus to be deemed with certainty a Montanist are unconvincing; see Tabbernee 2007, 226–30.

11. Ephesus (Efes), founded originally as a Greek settlement in ancient Ionia, ca. 1100 B.C.E., was the most important city in the Roman province of Asia—although Pergamon

and Smyrna vied for that honor. For the early (second-century) connection between Ephesus and Montanism, see Chapter 9.

12. The Basilica of St. John, able to be visited by Neikandros or any other pilgrim ca. 425, was the Constantinian basilica built in the fourth century over the grave assumed to be that of St. John the Apostle. A second tomb honoring a man named John at Ephesus also existed (Eusebius, *Hist. eccl.* 3.39.6; Dionysius of Alexandria, *Ep., ap.* Eusebius, *Hist. eccl.* 7.25.16; Jerome, *Vir. ill.* 9, 16). The second tomb was presumably that of "John the Presbyter"; see Schoedel 1993, 249–52. For the view that one of these was a Montanist shrine, see Grant 1968, 304.

13. On the tomb of one of the daughters of Philip at Ephesus, see Tabbernee 1997b, 504–6. On the utilization of tombs of prophets and prophetesses in orthodox/Montanist propaganda, see Tabbernee 1997c. On Alexander, see Chapter 9.

14. The Laodikeia (Eskihisar) referred to in the book of Revelation is not to be confused with Laodikeia Katekekaumene (Lâdik/Halıcı) in eastern Phrygia/Lycaonia—on which see Chapter 25. The Laodikeia of Revelation is "Laodicea on the Lycus" (*Laodicea ad Lycum*) in western Phrygia, strategically located at the intersection of roads providing access from the East to Lydia and Mysia and from the West to Phrygia, Caria, and to Pamphylia.

15. The exact date of the construction of the water tower at Laodikeia is uncertain. The tower could have been built in the early second, rather than the late first century, in which case any alleged connection with the reference to hot, cold, and lukewarm water in Rev 3:15–16 is a moot point. In either case, the tower, which still exists today, was in Laodikeia in the fifth century where a pilgrim, such as Neikandros, would have seen it.

16. The third-century *nymphaeum*, whose pools and fountains were fed by the water tower, had been made into a covered-in building and decorated with Christian symbols before ca. 425. A number of synods were held at Laodikeia, the most significant of which took place sometime between 343 and 381. According to a twelfth-century inscription from Bethlehem:

> The holy synod of the bishops in Laodikeia was convened because of Montanus and the other sectarians. It is they which the holy synod anathematized as heretics and as enemies of the truth. (*CIG* 4.8953)

Canon 8 of the synod itself reads:

> Concerning those who are converted from the sect of those named after the Phrygian: Even if they belong to their so-called clergy, or even if they are called the greatest (among them), such persons are to be instructed with all due care and baptized by the bishops and presbyters of the Church.

The greatest (*megistoi*) among the Montanist clergy referred to here are the patriarchs and *koinōnoi* (regional bishops), on which see n. 18 (on Philadelphia) below and Chapters 29, 35, and 37.

Canon 11 of the Council of Laodikeia prohibits the ordination of *presbytides* ("women presbyters") or of *prokathēmenai* ("women presidents"). This canon may have been promulgated to counter Montanist-influenced practices; see Tabbernee 1997b, 68–72.

17. On the tomb of Philip and his daughters at Hierapolis, see Chapter 35.

18. It is likely that there was a Montanist community in Philadelphia. There was at least one in the vicinity at Myloukome (Mendechora) as attested by the tombstone of a Montanist *koinōnos*, regional bishop (*IMont* 84), see Chapter 37. The epitaph of another Montanist *koinōnos* (*IMont* 85) has been found at Karakuyu, the site of an ancient

settlement on the territory of the ancient city of Bagis (Güre) in Lydia, 75 km N.E. of Philadelphia. Interestingly, that particular Montanist regional bishop is designated *Paulou hagiou Philadelphou koinōnou kata topon,* which should be translated as "the holy Paul, son of Philadelphos, *koinōnos* of the region." This epitaph, therefore, does not supply additional confirmation of Philadelphia being the center of a Montanist ecclesiastical region; see Tabbernee 1997b, 515. Attempts to identify Ardabau, the place were Montanus began his ecstatic prophesying (see Chapter 1) with sites near Philadelphia, either at Kallataba (Ramsay 1895–1897, 1,2: 573 n. 3; Calder 1922/3, 324) or at Adruta (Hemer 1986, 270–71 n. 74) are unconvincing (Tabbernee 1997b, 18).

19. On Ammia, the prophetess operative in Philadelphia ca. 140–ca. 160 and her contemporary Quadratus, see Tabbernee 2007, 138–40. Ammia and Quadratus were claimed by both mainstream Christians and Montanists as belonging to the authentic line of prophetic succession. Ammia and Quadratus, however, preceded the New Prophecy and were not part of the movement itself.

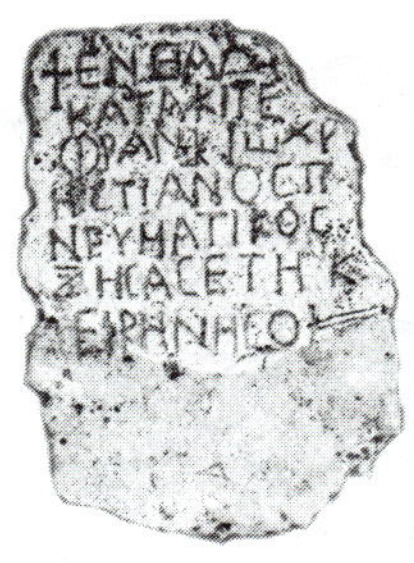

Chapter 34

Blaundos, Lydia, ca. 425 C.E.

Nearing the end

Neikandros has been traveling for six weeks now, but he is almost at his final destination. The road from Philadelphia to Blaundos, where he stayed last night, was in good repair, and he had traveled the distance in two days. Blaundos is an interesting little city set on a plateau high above steep canyon walls. The city is fortified, and he felt very secure as he slept soundly within its walls. The residents of Blaundos told him this morning that Pepouza lies about twelve miles east of Blaundos, in a fertile valley situated in the canyon. Following the canyon, however, Neikandros was told, would take him too long as it twists and turns repeatedly. He takes the advice of one of the older men of Blaundos and, passing through the city's ornate gate, takes the main road north out of the city, away from the canyon. Neikandros then turns right onto a minor road, one that cuts through a vast plain that seems to stretch out into the landscape forever.[1]

Pepouza, Phrygia, ca. 425 C.E.

The holy city

Without knowing it, Neikandros has crossed the border from Lydia into Phrygia, but these days borders don't mean anything. The old neighboring kingdoms of Lydia and Phrygia were long ago incorporated into the Roman province of Asia, and this remains the case under the Byzantine emperors who now rule the province from Constantinople. The huge plain Neikandros is walking across is, unbeknown to him, still controlled in part by procurators accountable to the imperial authorities.

Neikandros has been walking for more than four hours. In the far distance directly ahead of him he can see a chain of mountains. The mountains appear to be blue and very tall. He pauses to take in the magnificent landscape. Much closer to him and slightly to his right, Neikandros sees another, slightly smaller mountain. It is dome-shaped and dominates the plain. From the top of that mountain, Neikandros suspects, one can see all the way to the more distant chain of mountains that surround the plain. Neikandros is sure that the mountain at which he

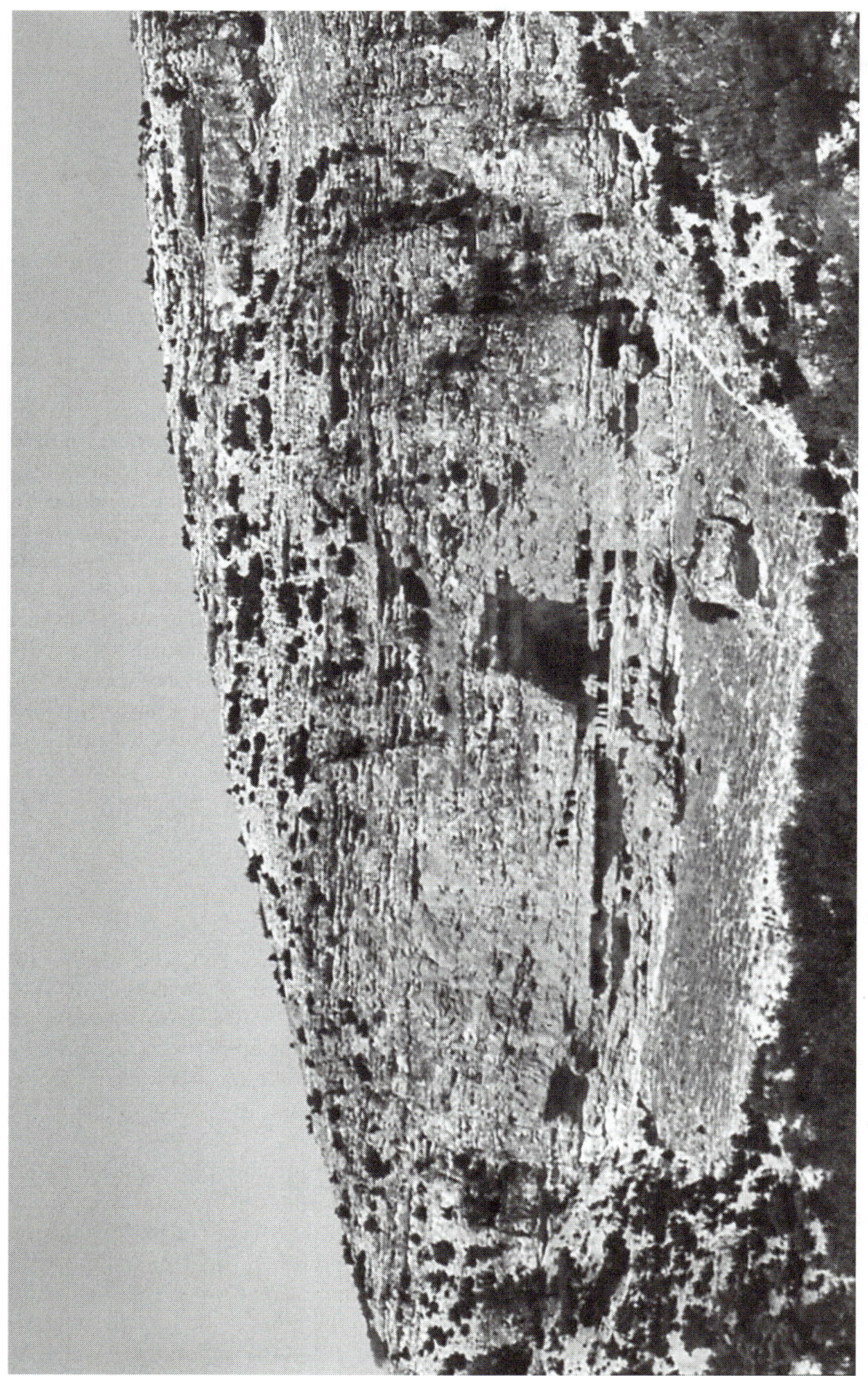

Figure 34.1 Remains of an ancient monastery near Pepouza

is looking is the one Montanus identified as the mountain from which, one day, the New Jerusalem will be be seen descending out of the sky. He is very excited, knowing that he must be getting extremely close to Pepouza.

Suddenly, the road he is on veers to the right and Neikandros finds himself walking parallel to the canyon. The canyon is the most beautiful he has ever seen, its rocky outcroppings vibrant with brilliant colors: reds, yellows, and pinks. He can hear the rushing waters of the Sindros River far below him. Excitedly curious, Neikandros leaves the road and walks to the edge of the canyon. Not thinking about any potential danger, he sits on a rocky ledge at a place where the canyon wall drops away vertically for what must be hundreds of feet. He can see clearly, at the bottom of the canyon, the river making its way westward. On the banks of the Sindros there are river flats, green with grass. A few cows are grazing. There are also some goats eating whatever they can find, the bells around their necks echoing loudly throughout the canyon.

Neikandros, unexpectedly, hears one man's voice and then another's. He turns his head and notices for the first time, far below him to his right, a large structure carved into the canyon wall. The two men are talking, no doubt not very loudly, but their voices are amplified by the hard surfaces of the canyon as they pull some ropes on a pulley. While Neikandros watches the tiny figures below him, he realizes that they are pulling large clay jars, filled with water from the Sindros, up the hill. The intricate pulley system seems to make the task virtually effortless.

An eagle is circling high overhead and then flies to its nest high above the rock-cut structure. Neikandros' eyes are adjusting to the way the sun casts shadows on the walls of the canyon, and he now sees what he couldn't see before. The structure must be a huge monastery or hostel.[2] He cannot determine exactly what it is, except that it is a place where many people live. The two men working with the pulleys look like monks, but perhaps they are simply members of the Montanist community working in a hostel for Montanist pilgrims such as he. Neikandros can see three levels of rooms. There must be at least a hundred rooms, Neikandros thinks to himself. He also sees what he assumes to be a chapel.

The men Neikandros has been watching are now climbing a wooden staircase that leads to a wooden verandah on the outside of the monastery or hostel. He can, occasionally, see other men on the verandah but most of the people who inhabit the rock-cut structure must be inside, staying in the cool rooms out of the sun. Neikandros looks for a way down to the monastery or hostel, but there are only a few goat paths, which appear very treacherous. Lots of very slippery rocks on which he slides dangerously convince Neikandros to return to the road he was on. He much prefers to continue on that road rather than risk his life scrambling down the almost perpendicular slopes of the canyon. Now that he is this close to the final destination of his pilgrimage, he doesn't want to break his neck and be lying helplessly on the rocks below for the eagle to fly out of its nest and consider his eyes delicacies to be fed to its young. A cold shiver runs up Neikandros' back as he walks back to the road—away from the edge of the precipice.

Neikandros passes a villa but keeps going. Who knows who lives there or how welcoming the residents might be? Less than five minutes later, the road again

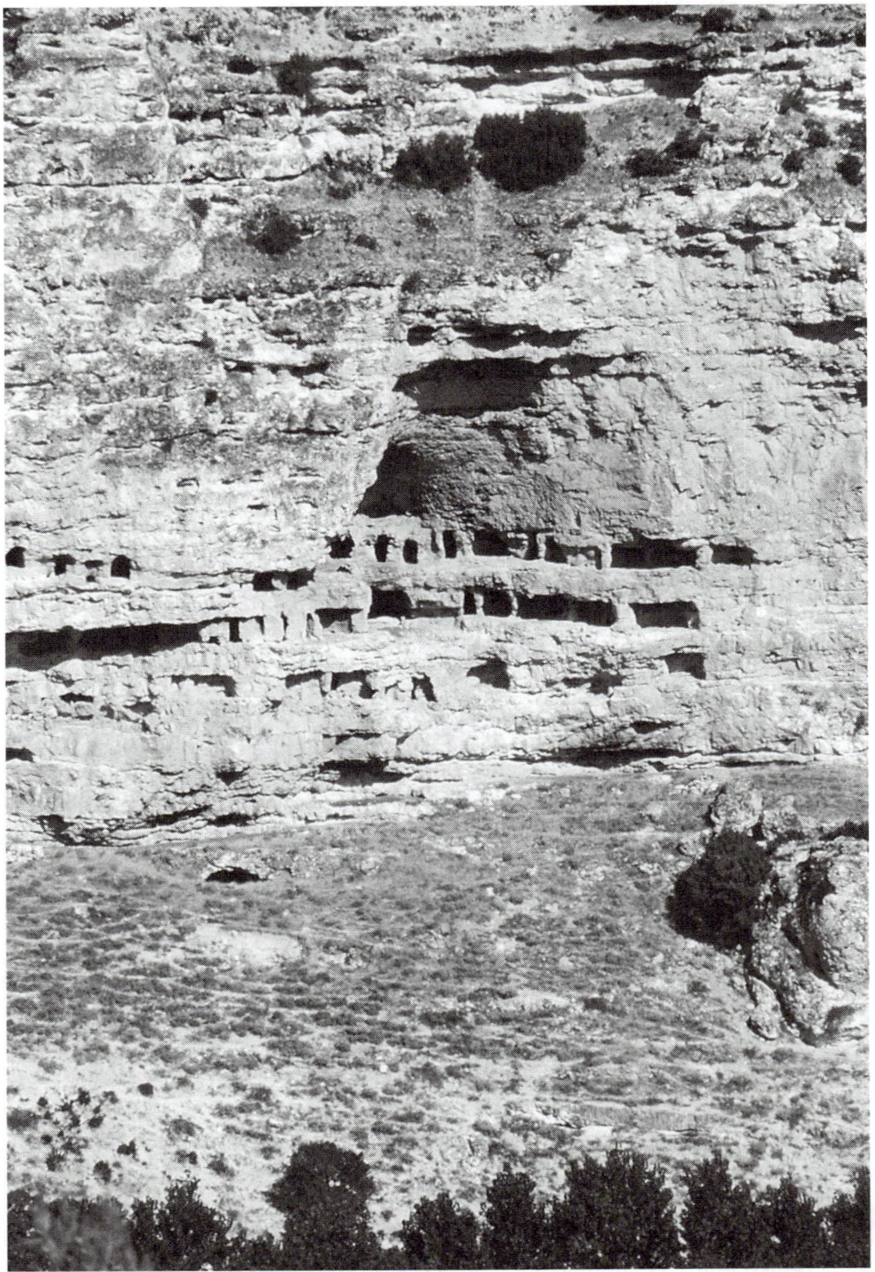

Figure 34.2 Remains of an ancient monastery near Pepouza

runs very close to the edge of the canyon. This time, Neikandros gets his first view of Pepouza. It is a bird's-eye view and, for a moment, Neikandros imagines he is an eagle who sees this view every day. The city is larger than he expected. He has heard that Pepouza was razed to the ground. Perhaps it was also damaged by earthquakes or other causes some time in the past, but if so, Neikandros thinks to himself, there has been a lot of rebuilding. The city itself is situated on a raised plateau in a large, oval-shaped valley at which he is now looking. On a narrow point of the plateau, close to but high above the river, Neikandros can see what must be a large basilica—although from this distance, it looks like a toy building. Neikandros can't help wondering if the basilica is that of the Montanist patriarch and whether the shrine containing the bones of Montanus, Maximilla, and Priscilla is in that building. Closer to him, on this side of the basilica, Neikandros sees what appears to be the agora, the marketplace. All around it are large buildings, perhaps shops and storehouses. Further away he sees the roofs of houses both on this side and on the other side of the Sindros.

There is still no way for Neikandros to get down to the city itself. After all, he is *not* an eagle nor a mountain goat. Soon, however, he comes to a junction in the road. While the road he is on continues straight ahead, an adjoining road swings back the opposite way at an angle. Neikandros takes the second road, which zigzags down the hill toward Pepouza. The canyon is on his left now instead of, as during his journey thus far, on his right. Before long he passes the necropolis of Pepouza and enters the city. By now it is nearly dark, but not so dark that he cannot find his way through the agora to the basilica he saw earlier from the top of the canyon.

From the agora, Neikandros walks to the atrium at the front of the basilica. He swings open the squeaky gate and crosses the threshold into the church. The interior is lit with countless candles. He pauses silently, trying not to disturb the old man with the white beard seated in the chancel. The man's chair is a cathedra, a bishop's chair so ornate that Neikandros knows immediately that the old man must indeed be none other than the patriarch.[3]

After what could not have been more than a few moments, the patriarch gets up out of his cathedra. While old in years, the patriarch's body is surprisingly young. He stands erect, no sign of any stooped shoulders, and quickly crosses to where Neikandros is standing. The patriarch, without being told, understands immediately that Neikandros is one of the New Prophecy movement's faithful bishops and he welcomes Neikandros to his church and to Pepouza. The patriarch knows why Neikandros is here. Without a further word, the patriarch takes a torch from the wall of the church. He beckons Neikandros to follow. The patriarch leads the way to some steps along the south wall of the basilica. Staying close on the heels of the patriarch, Neikandros descends the steps and follows the old man into the crypt underneath the church.

As Neikandros had hoped, in the middle of the crypt stands a large marble shrine. There are candles all around the shrine. By the light of the candles, Neikandros sees an enormous rectangular sarcophagus made of iron plates, sealed with lead. The patriarch steps to one side, making room for Neikandros to approach the

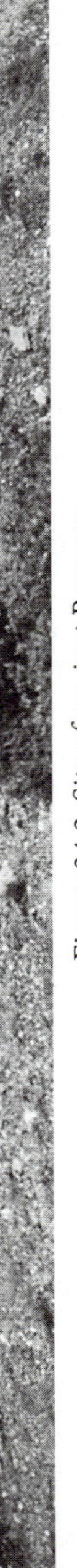

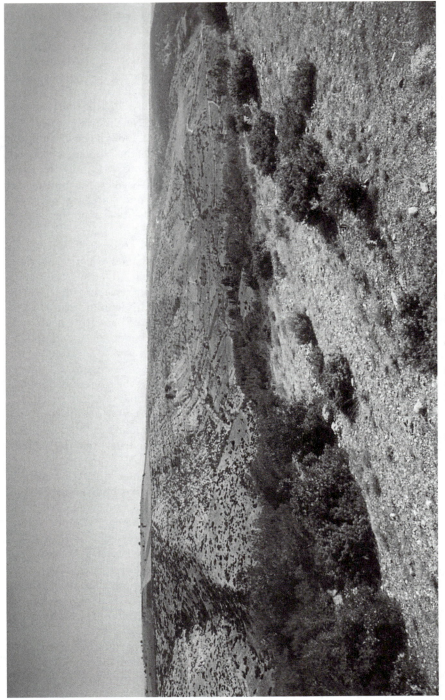

Figure 34.3: Site of ancient Pepouza

shrine. Neikandros takes a few more steps and reverently touches the inscription on the shrine. "Of Montanus and the women,"[4] the inscription reads. Tears stream down Neikandros' face. Here before him are the bones of Montanus, Maximilla, and Priscilla. His journey is over, his pilgrimage complete.

Sources:

IMont 1, 2, 86; Jerome, *Ep.* 41.3; *Cod. justin* 1.5.20.3.

Notes

1. As pointed out in Chapter 33, there is no specific evidence that Neikandros (if that was truly the name of the Montanist bishop from Kyzikos) went on a pilgrimage to Pepouza. A pilgrim to Pepouza from Philadelphia, however, would almost certainly have stayed overnight at Blaundos (Sülmenli), or at least passed through this fortified city, the ruins of which exist to this day.

2. For details of the site of Pepouza (including the basilica) and the rock-cut structure 1.2 km west of Pepouza itself, see Tabbernee 2003, 87–93 and Tabbernee and Lampe 2008. In late Byzantine times, the rock-cut structure definitely functioned as a monastery belonging to the "Orthodox Church" (see also the Epilogue). The earlier use of the structure is, however, still unclear. It may have been a monastery as early as the fourth century. Aetius of Antioch (ca. 313–ca. 365/7), for example, was exiled to Pepouza by Constantius II (337–361) in 360 (Philostorgius, *Hist. eccl.* 4.8). Earlier, Constantius had exiled both Hilary of Poitiers (ca. 315–ca. 367) and Paulinus of Trier (ca. 300–358) to Phrygia. Hilary, bishop of Poitiers (ancient Pictavi) from ca. 353, spent four years (356–359) in Phrygia. Paulinus, bishop of Trier (ancient Augusta Treverorum) from 249, was sent to Phrygia in 353 and died there in 358. Hilary's account of the evils perpetrated by Constantius included the complaint that he had forced Paulinus to be banished from all Christian society and to be polluted through contact with heretics from "the den of Montanus and Priscilla" (*In Constant.* 1.11). This *may* indicate that Paulinus, as well as Aetius, was exiled to Pepouza—perhaps to live in the monastery just outside the city. Hilary's comment that Paulinus was banished from all ("Orthodox") Christian society *may* also indicate that the monastery (if that is where Paulinus [and later Aetius?] stayed) was a Montanist rather than an "Orthodox" institution. Alternatively, the "monastery" may not yet have been a *monastery* but a Montanist hostel accommodating pilgrims *and exiles.*

3. On Montanist patriarchs at Pepouza and elsewhere, see Tabbernee 1993, 256–57; 1997b, 117–23, 497–502, 530 and Chapter 35.

4. *IMont* 2 (Tabbernee 1997b, 38).

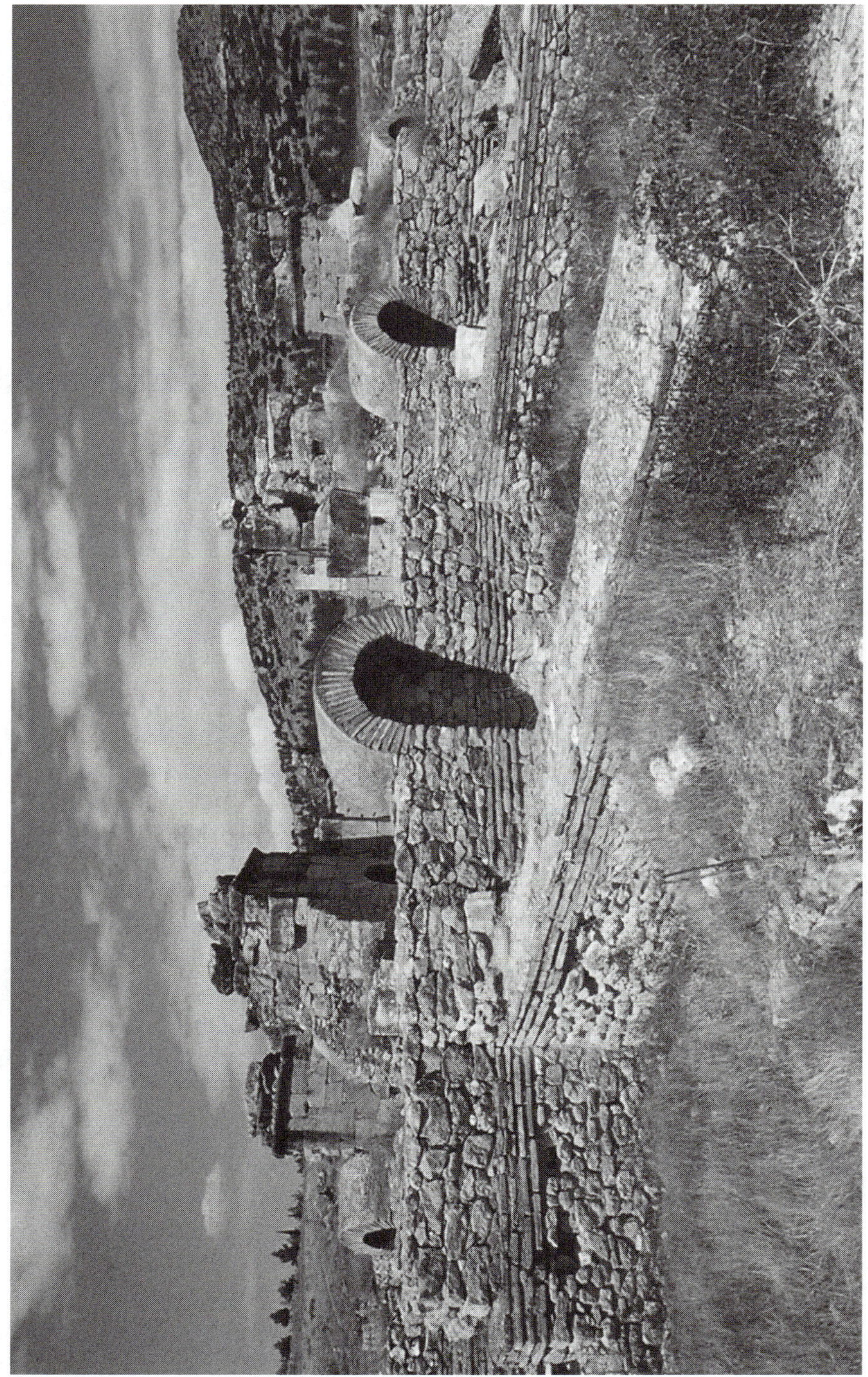

Figure 35.1 Martyrium of St. Philip in Hierapolis

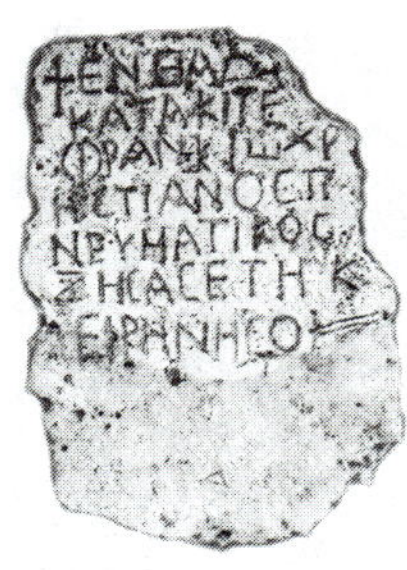

Chapter 35

Hierapolis, Phrygia, ca. 450 C.E.

Honoring the prophetic tradition of St. Philip and his daughters

Kyriakos has just left his house, where his wife is lovingly washing the vegetables she is preparing for dinner. A special guest is coming, so the dinner has to be just right and, knowing the culinary expertise of his wife, Kyriakos is more than confident that it will be. Among the vegetables his wife is preparing is eggplant—which Kyriakos loves. His mouth is already watering as he thinks about the taste of his favorite vegetable. He has never been able to figure out how something as ugly and purple on the outside and so stringy and leathery on the inside can become so incredibly tender and luscious when cooked properly. Thank God, his wife knows how to cook properly; the patriarch will be impressed.

But first Kyriakos has a few errands to run. The first errand takes him to the Martyrium of St. Philip, situated on a rise, two-thirds of the way up the large hill east of the city. The climb is a steep one. He walks past the theater to his right and then, already puffing slightly, he continues up the hill, turning left onto the path that leads to the martyrium. It is a beautiful building. Kyriakos, annoyed at himself for getting older and having to rest, pauses to catch his breath. From where he is standing, the martyrium looks like a large square building. But once inside, past the exterior rooms, some of which function as guest rooms for the countless pilgrims who visit the site each year, the martyrium itself is octagonal in shape.

The last few steps are very steep, but to Kyriakos' relief, he finally makes it. He enters the martyrium through one of its four centrally located entrances and goes up one more set of steps into the colonnaded, covered walkway leading into the martyrium. Turning right, he soon reaches the arched corridor surrounding the central octagonal chamber. The pillars of the corridor are big and solid enough to support the dome that covers the central octagon. Above the arch in each pillar is a slightly different Christian symbol. He particularly likes the one that intertwines the star of David with the cross of Christ, showing the continuity of faith and purpose of Jews and Christians. He also likes the staurogram with the *alpha* and the *omega*, respectively, in the left and right lower quadrants of this particular circle-enclosed symbol.

Normally when he visits the Martyrium of St. Philip and his daughters, Kyriakos walks very slowly, procession-like, in the octagonal corridor, reverently taking

Figure 35.2: Church of the Pillars in Hierapolis

in the serenity of the sacred nature of the space. Today, however, he is in a hurry. He makes his way quickly through the corridor, past the side chapels, to the shrine itself where the remains of Philip the apostle are buried. At times, Kyriakos has, privately, wondered whether some of the traditions about Philip the apostle and Philip the evangelist have become merged, but he has never publicly voiced his thoughts about the matter. How is one to know such things anyway?

As he knew he would, Kyriakos finds Eugenios at the shrine. Eugenios is the archdeacon in charge of the martyrium.[1] Eugenios is standing unobtrusively to the side of the shrine, ensuring that today's pilgrims do not damage the memorial to St. Philip or that of his daughters in the adjacent chapels. Eugenios has told Kyriakos numerous, almost unbelievable, stories about the inconsiderate behavior of pilgrims, especially those who seem intent on taking with them a small piece of the shrine itself. Fortunately, most pilgrims merely want to scratch their names on the martyrium walls near the shrine. Kyriakos fully understands the urge to immortalize one's name in stone. The second errand he is about to undertake has exactly that purpose, but he is glad, nevertheless, that Eugenios is here in the martyrium to discourage the devout—albeit inconsiderate—pilgrims from placing graffiti on the martyrium's walls.

Eugenios sees Kyriakos and comes over to him. The two men speak in hushed tones so as not to disturb the meditation and prayers of the pilgrims. Kyriakos, a presbyter of the Montanist community in Hierapolis, tells Eugenios, an archdeacon in the same community, that, as they had both hoped, Gennaios the Montanist patriarch is indeed coming to participate in tomorrow's celebrations. Eugenios is overcome with joy and wants to know all the details. The two men, whose excited voices have become louder despite their good intentions, move a little further away from the pilgrims at the shrine.

Gennaios is arriving from Pepouza later this afternoon, Kyriakos tells Eugenios, in time for dinner—a dinner to which he also invites Eugenios. Teasingly, Eugenios replies that he will only come if Kyriakos' wife serves eggplant.

Kyriakos, after saying goodbye to Eugenios, walks down from the Martyrium of St. Philip, glad that Eugenios can be present for the dinner with the patriarch. He will seat Eugenios beside the patriarch on one side while he sits on the other; they have so much to talk about. No doubt Gennaios will want to know all about the way the martyrium is fulfilling its role. As the Montanists trace their prophetic tradition to Philip's daughters and back even further to other prophets like Agabus, the martyrium plays a significant role in the life and witness of the New Prophecy in Hierapolis. Kyriakos knows that Apolinarius, one of the city's early bishops, tried to eradicate Montanism from Hierapolis. Fortunately, this attempt was unsuccessful and now, almost three hundred years later, Montanism not only still exists in the city but is thriving. Indeed, they have prospered so much that tomorrow the Montanist community is dedicating a new basilica—one to rival the two non-Montanist basilicas in the city.

Instead of retracing his earlier route, Kyriakos turns left onto a small road above the theater. From there, he has a magnificent view of the city. The buildings look like miniatures. They are far enough away from the edge of the steep plateau not to be in danger of falling off but, from here, it seems as though some buildings are dangerously close. Kyriakos understands, though, why these buildings have been built where they are—they are virtually on top of the brilliantly white calcium-covered hillside with its pools in the travertine formations. Living there must be like living simultaneously on the shores of the Internum Mare and at the top of a snow-covered mountain all year round. An added advantage is that, from where those buildings are situated, there is a great view across the vast plain to Laodikeia and beyond.

Going downhill is certainly easier than going uphill, Kyriakos reflects as he descends rapidly to the city below him. Taking the shorter route, through the agora at the south end of the city, Kyriakos arrives almost exactly at his destination. He stands at one end of the street he just entered and admires the beautiful new basilica he and his family have had built for the Montanist community at Hierapolis. It is a long, spacious church, buttressed by tall, rectangular pillars. He suspects that the building will be known as the Church of the Pillars for generations to come.

Kyriakos makes his way to one of the pillars near the entrance. His second errand this afternoon is to see, with his own eyes, that the dedicatory plaque has been inscribed correctly and mounted onto the pillar properly. Details, he thinks to himself, success is always in the details. Nothing must be left to chance. The white marble plaque glistens in the sun as he approaches it. The stonemason has indeed done an excellent job. The letters of the inscription are carved boldly and beautifully, and the plaque is mounted securely. Gennaios will be very happy when he sees the plaque tomorrow during the dedication ceremony.

Kyriakos is pleased with the words he composed for the text of the plaque:

> In the time of our most holy and most divinely beloved archbishop and patriarch Gennaios, I, the most pious presbyter Kyriakos, son of Eustochios, and my grandchildren Joanna and Kyriake, have borne as fruit the founding of the most holy church of Christ. . . . [2]

Bearing good fruit for God is what life is all about, Kyriakos thinks, as he stands up straight after bending down to read the plaque which is, as his hurting back indicates, perhaps mounted a little too low to the ground after all. Never mind, he thinks. Where the plaque is placed doesn't matter; what matters is that he has done good work for God by building this church.

Walking home to meet Gennaios, who should have arrived by now, Kyriakos is a little sad that the physical fruit he and his wife have born, their children, are no longer alive to see the new church—the other fruit of their labor for God. Joyfully, however, their grandchildren, Joanna and Kyriake, have not suffered untimely deaths. The grandchildren, one of whom, like himself, bears a name signifying that she belongs to Jesus, the *Kyrios,* "the Lord," are also waiting for him at home. How proud they will be tomorrow to see their names on the plaque as co-sponsors of the church.

As he approaches the house, Kyriakos' mouth begins to water again. What is it about eggplant?[3]

Sources:

IMont 82, 83.

Notes

1. *IMont* 83. It is most likely, but not absolutely certain, that Eugenios was a *Montanist* archdeacon in charge of the Martyrium of St. Philip; see Tabbernee 1997b, 502–8.

2. *IMont* 82. Although it is possible that Gennaios was the "orthodox" archbishop of Hierapolis and that his title "patriarch" is to be taken as a somewhat loose equivalent of "metropolitan," a strong case can be made for Gennaios being the *Montanist patriarch at Pepouza* during the time the "Church of the Pillars" was dedicated; see Tabbernee 1997b, 501–2.

3. That Kyriakos visited both the martyrium and the "Church of the Pillars" on the day before the dedication of the church is speculative—as is the detail that Kyriakos' wife cooked eggplant for dinner that day.

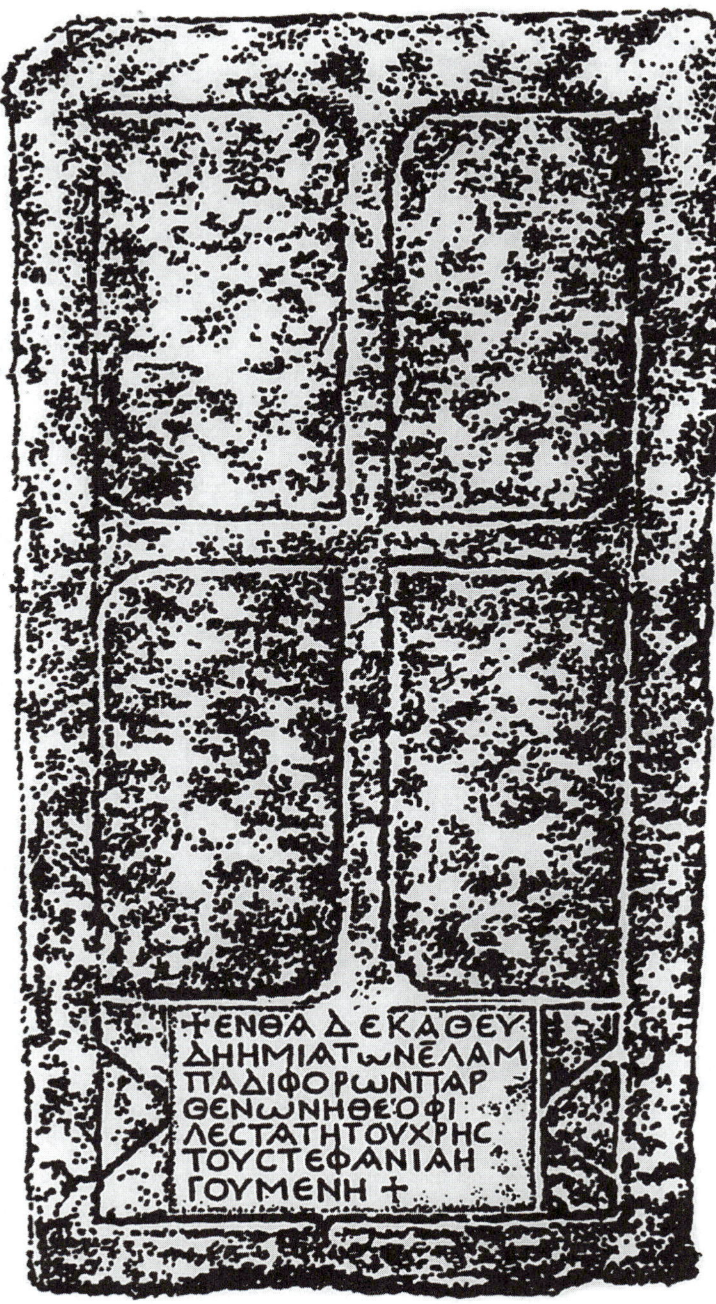

Figure 36.1: Stephania's tombstone

Chapter 36

Ankyra, Galatia, February 13–20, 510 C.E.

Trophimos, a Montanist apostle supports the faithful

Trophimos is proud of his title. It is "apostle," and he has worn the title with great joy ever since he was commissioned by the patriarch at Pepouza. Following the tradition started by Montanus himself, Trophimos, like generations of earlier apostles from Pepouza, has been sent out on numerous occasions from the spiritual and organizational center of the New Prophecy movement at Pepouza to other places. During his long apostleship, he has traveled many miles and met with numerous congregations, proclaiming what the Paraclete revealed through Montanus, Maximilla, and Priscilla.

Trophimos' most recent apostolic mission has brought him to Ankyra. The patriarch at Pepouza wants him to bring greetings to the community of adherents at Ankyra and to encourage them to live according to the high standards of the New Prophecy. Keeping the teachings of Montanus, Maximilla, and Priscilla is, at times, difficult, and the patriarch wisely decided that a visit from an apostle from Pepouza would be good for the adherents who live in the capital of Galatia. Not that the patriarch had any reason to worry, Trophimos thinks to himself, for he has always found the community in Ankyra to be faithful. But it never hurts to be reminded of one's duty, as Trophimos knows. On his second day in Ankyra, a Sunday, at the end of his sermon, Trophimos called each member of the community to continue to live a life of holiness.

Today, one of the leaders of the community has taken Trophimos to the Christian cemetery where he shows Trophimos a large gray tombstone. The tombstone is rectangular in shape, made of limestone. More than two-thirds of the face of the stone is dominated by the shape of a cross, incised to form four panels set within a border. The border continues downward to form a fifth panel, cut horizontally beneath the cross. Inside the horizontal panel a *tabula ansata,* a smaller rectangular panel with handles, has been carved. Inside the *tabula ansata,* Trophimos sees an inscription, beginning and ending with a cross. He reads:

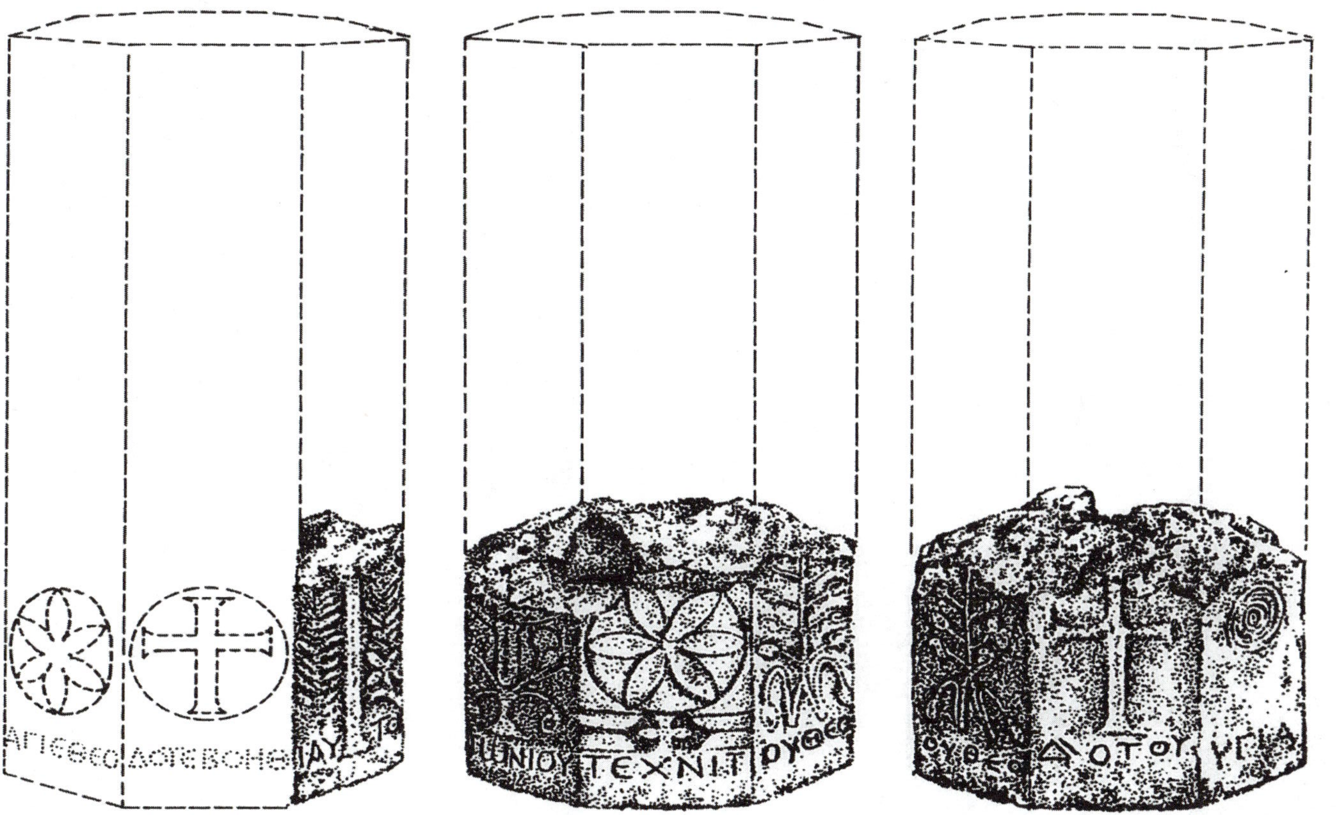

Figure 36.2: Column-bases of Martyrium of St. Theodotus

> Here sleeps one of the five lamp-bearing virgins, the most-divinely beloved one of Christ, Stephania, the *hēgoumenē*.[1]

The patriarch had asked him to pay his respects to the final resting place of Stephania, the well-known *hēgoumenē*, or leader, of the lamp-bearing virgins at Ankyra. Trophimos crosses himself and prays a prayer for Stephania's soul. He is a little surprised at the designation Η ΘΕΟΦΙΛΕΣΤΑΤΗ ΤΟΥ ΧΡΙΣΤΟΥ (ἡ Θεοφιλεστάτη τοῦ Χριστοῦ [*hē theophilestatē tou Christou*]), "the most-divinely beloved one of Christ." The term is often used for senior male clergy but almost never for women. Stephania must have been highly regarded for the title to be placed on her tombstone.

Trophimos is even more surprised to read that Stephania was the leader of *five* lamp-bearing virgins, not, as he had expected, *seven*. He is used to the seven lamp-bearing virgins at Pepouza and had assumed there would be seven such virgins at Ankyra also. He asks his guide about the unusual number. His companion explains patiently that the number is not strange at all. Hadn't Trophimos ever heard of the wise virgins who, in Jesus' story about the virgins awaiting the arrival of the bridegroom, carried additional oil with them just in case the bridegroom was delayed? They, not their foolish companions who did not have the forethought to anticipate a potential delay in the coming of the bridegroom, had the means to welcome the bridegroom when he finally arrived. They had sufficient oil in their lamps and with the light of their lamps escorted the bridegroom to the wedding feast. Of course Trophimos has heard of the *five* wise virgins. He immediately gets the point. Because Jesus, the bridegroom of the church, has been delayed in his coming, the number of lamp-bearing virgins at Ankyra has been changed from seven to five to symbolize the community's patience in waiting for the second coming of the Messiah—and their readiness to participate in the celebratory banquet, whenever it will be held.

The patriarch at Pepouza had given Trophimos one more task to accomplish while he is in Ankyra. He is to visit the Martyrium of Theodotus at Malos.[2] The patriarch had told him the story of Theodotus. Theodotus' heroism in recovering the bodies of the seven aged virgins during the persecution under Theotecnus had particularly enthralled Trophimos. That must have been a time before the New Prophecy movement in Ankyra changed the number of lamp-bearing virgins from seven to five, he realizes as he is traveling to Malos.

Trophimos wishes that, like Fronto almost two hundred years ago, he had a donkey and a cart to make the two-day journey from Ankyra to Malos. But he doesn't have a donkey or a cart. Fortunately, the journey is almost over. Coming toward him from the village of Malos is a man, whom he guesses correctly is his host Aglaomyris.

Aglaomyris is a wealthy landowner whose property adjoins the village. Aglaomyris welcomes Trophimos warmly and accompanies him the rest of the way to his large house. It is late in the day and, after a wonderful meal, Trophimos asks to be excused. He is not feeling well and needs to rest.

The night's sleep seems to do Trophimos a lot of good. He wakes early but finds that Aglaomyris is already up and about. As the weather is not too cold, the two men decide to leave straight away to walk to the martyrium, which is less than half a mile from Aglaomyris' house. Aglaomyris and Trophimos walk slightly downhill toward the river. They come to a grassy field where there are a few cedar and juniper trees that, during summer, provide shade for Aglaomyris' sheep, goats, and his prize possession—a cow. Aglaomyris tells Trophimos that it is a pity he isn't here a few months later, when the whole field will be covered with tall blue wildflowers that exude a delicate fragrance. Trophimos, however, is delighted to be here now. The air is filled with the sound of many birds singing their morning songs and calling to each other in a ritual Trophimos doesn't fully understand.

Trophimos looks back over his shoulder at the village and the mountain behind the village. The mountain rises from the plain like a large bowl turned upside down. There is almost no vegetation on the mountain, only huge rocks. Trophimos thinks the mountain's flat top could one day make an excellent site for a fortress.

Turning again toward the Halys River below them, Trophimos follows Aglaomyris a few more steps to the martyrium. It is a small but impressive building. In the middle of the building are four columns supporting a canopy. Beneath the canopy on a tall pillar is a reliquary that Aglaomyris says contains the bones of Theodotus. As he did in front of Stephania's grave, Trophimos crosses himself and prays for the soul of the departed.

When he looks up, Trophimos notices that the columns appear to be new and beautifully decorated at their base. He walks around the first of the hexagonal columns and sees, in turn, a rosette in a circle, a cross in a circle, and a cross with palm leaves on both sides of it. Palm leaves, Trophimos knows, symbolize martyrdom. Next there is a cross in a circle above a vine. Then another rosette in a circle above a small cross and yet another vine, or possibly a tree, Trophimos is not sure which it is. Aglaomyris has moved away to another part of the building, so Trophimos cannot ask him what that particular symbol is supposed to be. On the next to last face of the column is a fourth cross, this time without a circle, and on the last face, surprisingly, there is a serpentine circle. Reading the word inscribed beneath the stylized serpent, however, the symbol makes sense. The word is (ΥΓΙΑ/ὑγίᾳ [*hugia*]) "health." Walking around to the hexagonal column's first face, Trophimos reads the whole inscription: "Holy Theodotus: aid the health of Antonius, artisan, and of Theodotus."[3]

Trophimos joins Aglaomyris at the door that provides the only entry to and exit from the martyrium. There, he notices another inscription: "Aglaomyris adorned the entire shrine of the prize-winning martyr."[4] No wonder the columns and the whole martyrium look so new, Trophimos thinks to himself, his host paid for the reconstruction and beautification of the original martyrium built by Fronto. Trophimos asks Aglaomyris about the second Theodotus named on the inscription carved on the column. His host tells him that Antonius was the stonemason he had hired to do the reconstruction of the martyrium and that, by coincidence—or by the grace of God—Antonius' assistant had the same name as the saint whose shrine they were beautifying. Aglaomyris confides in Trophimos that he had been more than a little annoyed when Antonius took it upon himself to carve an inscription invoking Saint Theodotus to guarantee him and his assistant good health—but shrugging his shoulders, he admits that he can't really blame Antonius for doing it.

Trophimos' own health becomes worse as he travels back to Ankyra the next day. He arrives very late on Friday evening, thinking he should have scratched a graffito on one of the columns in the martyrium at Malos, imploring the aid of St. Theodotus for his own well being. He is glad, though, that he went to Malos to see the shrine and that he fulfilled all the tasks the patriarch at Pepouza had given him to do. Tomorrow he intends to write the patriarch a detailed report.[5]

Sources:

IMont 87–89; S. Mitchell 2005, 212 [Trophimos inscription]; Matt 25:1–13.

Notes

1. *IMont* 87.

2. On Theodotus, see also Chapter 24. Whether the cult of St. Theodotus at Malos was Montanist (or even exclusively Montanist) is debatable; see Tabbernee 1997b, 531–33; 2007, 238–40.

3. *IMont* 88.

4. *IMont* 89.

5. The four inscriptions on which this chapter is constructed are all to be dated to the fifth or sixth century. The most likely date for Trophimos' death is Saturday, February 20, 510 (S. Mitchell 2005, 213–14; Tabbernee 2007, 347). Whether Stephania's epitaph and the inscriptions at the Martyrium of St. Theodotus pre-date 510 is conjecture on my part as is the possibility that Trophimos visited both Stephania's tomb and the martyrium (let alone in one week). That Trophimos was a Montanist "apostle from Pepouza" and that he died and was buried in Ankyra (presumably in 510) is confirmed by the inscription recently discovered and published by S. Mitchell (2005).

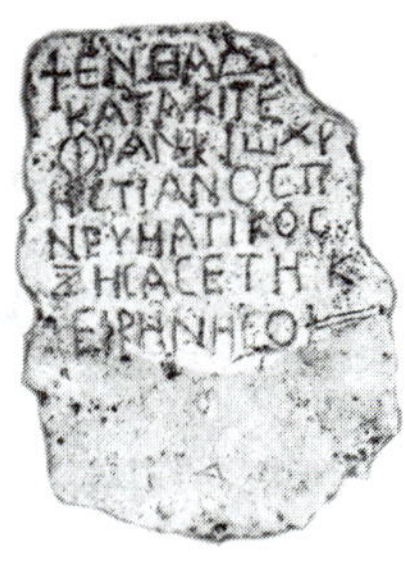

Chapter 37

Myloukome, Lydia, March 515 C.E.

Praÿlios convenes a synod

Praÿlios has convened a synod. As *koinōnos* of the region, it is his right and responsibility to do so. It is time for all the Montanist bishops of southeast Lydia to come together. Praÿlios would like to hold *annual* synods so that matters can be addressed quickly—or at least soon after they arise. Trying to get the other bishops to agree to such annual meetings is high on his list of priorities for the synod. He decides, however, that he will not bring up this matter until they near the end of this particular synod.

Being a *koinōnos,* a "regional bishop" responsible for more than his own congregation, is a difficult task. Before he, reluctantly, agreed to be consecrated as *koinōnos,* Praÿlios had no idea how obstinate his fellow bishops could be. Each one was used to being in charge. Some of the women bishops were as troublesome as the men. Praÿlios is glad, though, that there are women bishops in his region as he believes strongly that St. Paul's Letter to the Galatians should be taken as a direct command from God stressing that "in Christ," that is, "within the *Body of Christ*—the Church," the old division between male and female no longer exists. Just as there is neither "slave" nor "free person," "Gentile or Jew," in Christ, there is neither male nor female—all are one in Christ Jesus.[1] Even though in society women, like men, have specific roles, in church no role and no office is dependent on one's gender.

Praÿlios remembers the vitriolic exchanges he has had with some so-called orthodox bishops on the matter of women clergy. Not one of them could have read Galatians—even though all of them claim they are guided by the scriptures. Praÿlios remembers especially one old bishop who became so angry over the issue that the veins in his neck became extremely puffed up and swollen. The man pointed his finger at him and shouted at him. Praÿlios was afraid the veins on the man's neck would burst. The bishop shouted out that women could not be priests because priests represent Christ and Christ was a man, not a woman. Praÿlios couldn't quite follow the logic of the man's argument fully but came to understand, for the first time, the almost primeval irrationality that underlay the man's vehement attack on him. No wonder Montanists, like himself, are so feared and hated by the majority of Christian bishops. The Montanist practice of ordaining women as priests and as bishops threatens the very foundations of the patriarchal power of orthodox bishops: the superiority of maleness.

The alleged superiority of maleness over femaleness in the society in which both orthodox and Montanists live is difficult to relinquish, even for male *Montanist* bishops, Praÿlios recognizes. He thinks back to the first Montanist regional synod over which he had presided a few years ago. Among those gathered together were three women bishops—each of them a strong personality, well-versed in scripture and the Christian tradition, and very articulate. Praÿlios had been amazed and shocked that, at first, when one or other of these women bishops began to say something the Montanist male bishops, who should have known better, talked right over the women. It had taken all his skills as the chair of the synod to enable the women to have their say. He didn't want to be rude to the offending, insensitive male bishops, but at times he had to interrupt them and stop them from speaking so that the women bishops could complete what they had begun to say. Fortunately, the last synod was much better—some of the male bishops having learned to modify their behavior—and he hopes that at this synod they will be better still. They have a lot to discuss and to decide.

Sources:

Gal 3:28; *IMont* 84.

Myloukome, Lydia, March 8, 515 C.E.
The Easter controversy, again

All of the bishops, the *chorepiskopoi,* and the presbyters of the region have arrived safely in Myloukome. They have gathered in the basilica and are seated, in proper order, on wooden benches—the most senior bishops at the front of the church.

Praÿlios is seated in the cathedra, the bishop's chair, on the raised platform in the chancel facing those participating in the synod. It is Sunday, and the morning has been spent celebrating the Eucharist in this very space. After a simple but more than adequate lunch, it is time to do business. Praÿlios tells those present that the first item on their agenda is the date of Easter. A few of the bishops groan audibly. Not again. Hasn't the date of Easter been discussed enough? Haven't they been faithful to the tradition that dates back through luminaries such as Polycrates of Ephesus, Melito of Sardis, and Polycarp of Smyrna—even when all the non-Montanist bishops of Asia betrayed this tradition after the Council of Nicaea?

Praÿlios waits for the murmuring to settle down before proceeding. Praÿlios explains that the purpose of the tradition has always been to make Easter coincide as closely as possible with the Jewish Passover. That way, the Lenten fast, as they all know, can be concluded on the day Christ died. A strict adherence to this being the fourteenth day of the Jewish month of Nisan, however, results in the celebration of Easter sometimes falling on a day other than Sunday. Consequently, as they all also know, those who have betrayed the Quartodeciman tradition base their

Easter calendar on a system that makes Easter always fall on a Sunday. They do so, Praÿlios tells those seated before him, on the basis of a lunar calendar.

Praÿlios pauses for effect. After a few moments of expectant silence, he continues. There is a much better way to calculate the date of Easter, he informs his audience. Using a *solar* calendar rather than a lunar calendar solves the problem. By using the cycles of the sun rather than the cycles of the moon, one can figure out exactly which day in every year corresponds most closely to the day of Passover—the day on which Jesus actually died. All they need to do, then, is celebrate Easter, the day of resurrection, on the very next Sunday regardless of how many days intervene. One of the bishops wants to know what happens if the fourteenth of the month also falls on a Sunday in this new system. In that case, Praÿlios explains, Easter is still celebrated because the day of resurrection triumphs over the day of crucifixion.[2]

Suddenly the basilica is filled with the voices of all the bishops, *chorepiskopoi,* and presbyters seeming to speak all at once as they ask one another how the new system would work. Even if it *does* work mathematically, some bishops argue that it won't work in their church because it has never been done that way and it will be impossible to implement. Other bishops are very enthusiastic about the idea and see it as a great solution to a vexing problem. As they are talking excitedly about what Praÿlios has just told them, no one, at first, notices that Praÿlios has slumped sideways in his chair and his head has fallen backwards at a strange angle. A hush gradually falls over the assembled clergy as, one by one, they come to realize that Praÿlios, their *koinōnos,* is dead.

They take Praÿlios' body reverently from the church, wash it carefully, and anoint it tenderly. They bury Praÿlios before sundown.

Sources:

IMont 84; Eusebius, *Hist. eccl.* 5.23; Sozomen, *Hist. eccl.* 7.18.12–14; Pseudo-Chrysostom, *Serm. pasch.* 7; *Vit. Pol.* 2.

Myloukome, Monday, March 9, 515 C.E.

Epitaph of a holy man

The stonemason has worked feverishly all day long but is pleased with his work—as are the bishops who commissioned him just that morning to carve Praÿlios' tombstone. They gave the stonemason the text of the inscription, and he copied it onto the rectangular marble slab faithfully. He even decorated the stone with both a staurogram and a *chi-rho* christogram.

All the Montanist bishops, *chorepiskopoi,* and presbyters who had come to Myloukome for the synod are still here. They assemble, not in the church, but, as twenty-four hours ago, at Praÿlios' grave. The two most senior bishops, a man and a woman, accompany the stonemason to the head of the grave where he ceremoniously erects the stone for all to see. As each of the bishops, *chorepiskopoi,* and presbyters file past, they read:

The holy Praÿlios, the *koinōnos* of the region, was taken up into heaven on Sunday, the fifteenth day of the month Xanthikos in the year 545, during the eighth indiction,[3] at the time of the synod of the Myloukometians.[4]

Source:

IMont 84.

Notes

1. Gal 3:28.

2. On the Quartodeciman controversy, see Chapter 6. On the Montanist solar calendar, see Beckwith 2005, 97–102 and Tabbernee 2007, 367–69.

3. Indictions were fifteen-year tax cycles. The indiction number identifies the position of the designated year within the indiction cycle. The "eighth indiction," literally "indiction number eight," means that half of the tax cycle has already passed (and, consequently, half of the taxes liable for the period should already have been paid). Unfortunately, indiction cycles, unlike Olympiads (which use a comparable—but four-year—cycle to specify particular years), were not numbered. Correlating the data given in Praÿlios' inscription, however, with the Actian era (which commenced 31/30 B.C.E.) used in Lydia at the time, it is possible to determine that, because 15 Xanthikos in year 545 of the Lydian era fell on a Sunday during indiction 8, the date specified by Praÿlios' epitaph is March 8, 515 C.E.; see Tabbernee 1993, 275. Whether or not the tombstone commemorating Praÿlios was produced as early as the day after his death is speculative.

4. *IMont* 84. On the marble plaque commemorating Praÿlios, see Tabbernee 1997b, 509–13. Praÿlios was a Montanist *koinōnos* or regional bishop; see Chapter 29. For the epitaphs of other Montanist *koinōnoi*, see *IMont* 80, 85 and Chapter 33. The name Myloukome (modern Mendechora; 15 km N.W. of Philadelphia) has been restored on the inscription on the basis of *CIG* 2.3420 (*l.*10).

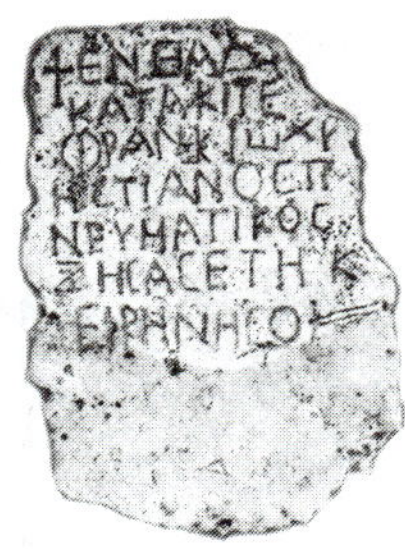

Chapter 38

Pepouza, Phrygia, 550 C.E.
Breaking the Montanists: the death blows

John of Amida[1] knows Asia like the back of his hand. Although he was born in Roman Mesopotamia and now officially lives just outside of Constantinople, he has for nearly two decades undertaken countless journeys across the length and breadth of the province of Asia. He is on an important mission for God, a mission given to him directly by the emperor Justinian eighteen years ago.

John is traveling along a narrow road that crosses a large fertile plain. Fortunately, he is riding in a carriage. He is accompanied by a contingent of soldiers, assigned to him by Justinian himself, to help him accomplish his critically important mission. The officers, dressed in their colorful uniforms, are on horseback slightly ahead of him, their red cloaks draping from their shoulders onto the rumps of their horses, their brass helmets gleaming in the sunlight. The enlisted and conscripted men are marching in military formation behind the carriage. The carriage is only going as fast as the soldiers can march, which John thinks is fine. He is in no hurry.

Out of the right window of the carriage, John looks absent-mindedly across the agricultural plain to the mountains in the distance. He is thinking about the monastery in Sycae, near Constantinople, where he is the abbot. He wonders if his fellow monks are well and how they are doing without him. Hopefully, they are "well enough." Being the emperor's, and God's, ambassador has its drawbacks. One good thing however is that he has been able to establish many new monasteries in Asia, mainly by confiscating pagan temples or buildings belonging to heretics and Jews, and putting these to proper Christian use. Perhaps he will be able to do the same in the little city of Pepouza, which one of the officers has reassured him is now only a few more minutes away.

The carriage lurches suddenly as one of its wheels hits a pothole. John finds himself thrown against the left window of the carriage. As he pushes himself back into the hard wooden seat, he notices a large dome-shaped mountain out of the window. The mountain dominates the landscape. John assumes that the mountain is the one people have been telling him about. If the stories he has been told are accurate, this is the mountain from which Montanists believe the New Jerusalem will one day be seen descending out of heaven. John has never heard

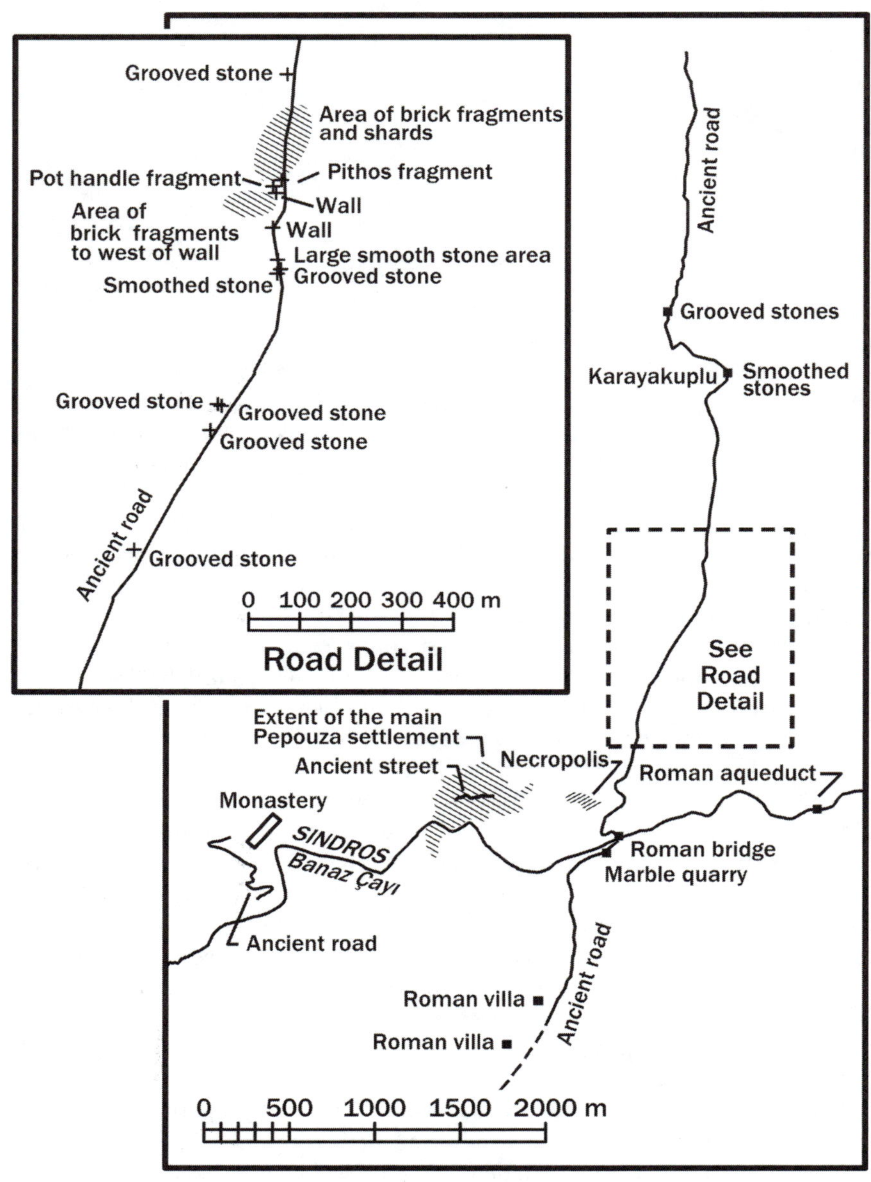

Map 6: Pepouza–ancient roads

such nonsense. It is a good thing he is almost at Pepouza to destroy, once and for all, the center of the Montanist heresy.

John remembers vividly how, through Justinian's wife, he had been introduced to Justinian. He had come to know Theodora soon after becoming abbot of the monastery at Sycae. Theodora, unlike Justinian, was very interested in theology, especially in christology. She wanted to know all about the divinity of Christ and how, as a human person, Jesus could be both human *and* divine. She had asked him very astute questions, John remembers, and expressed beliefs very similar to his own, namely, that Christ had only one nature, a divine nature, not two natures, as some claim. John is glad that, despite their difference in rank and status, their common theological views led to a kind of friendship and that this led Theodora to introduce him to Justinian.

Before long, the emperor had asked him to travel throughout Asia to ensure the emperor's new anti-heretical legislation is being implemented. His mission is to convert, by force if necessary, pagans, heretics, and Jews to Orthodox Christianity. No one had told him that the mission would last almost twenty years, and perhaps longer. Not that John has spent every moment of the past eighteen years traveling through Mysia, Lydia, Phrygia, and the other regions of the province of Asia, but he does so many months each year. At first it was fun—coming into a new city, finding the nearest temple, cutting off the head of the marble statue of whichever god was enshrined, rolling the head down the hill or into the nearest river, confiscating heretical basilicas and Jewish synagogues, exorcizing and baptizing—often reluctant—converts, installing orthodox clergy in new Byzantine churches, and establishing monasteries. But now all this has become routine, hard work.

The carriage lurches again as the road zigzags down the steep incline from the agricultural plain to the river valley where Pepouza is situated. High above him to the right is a rocky canyon wall protecting the city nestled between it and the river. It is still mid-morning and John has instructed the soldiers and the carriage driver to go directly to the large basilica in the city's center. That basilica, John has been told, is the seat of the Montanist patriarch and the place where the bones of Montanus and some of the Montanist prophetesses are buried.

The carriage passes through some narrow streets, the horses' feet echoing loudly on the paving stones, then enters a wider street next to the agora before stopping in front of the Montanist basilica. The mounted army officers are already at the door of the basilica, and the foot soldiers close ranks and follow John to the atrium. John crosses the atrium and stands at the threshold. In a loud voice, he proclaims that he is taking possession of the building in the name of the emperor.

One of the officers swings open the doors to the church and John enters the basilica. The church is totally empty. There is no sign of the patriarch or of any other Montanist. John wonders whether he has found the right church or whether the Montanists of the city may have taken refuge in one of their other churches in Pepouza. He hopes that, if so, they are not doing what he has heard some other Montanists elsewhere in Phrygia have done. Rather than being forced to convert, those Montanists, he has been told, gathered in their basilicas and set them on fire, burning the churches down on top of themselves—perishing along with their buildings.

Although John fully intends to use fire himself in connection with the Montanist churches in Pepouza, that Montanists would incinerate themselves is senseless and incomprehensible to him. He would rather they go into exile than commit suicide. He had noticed a number of large caves in the canyon walls as they were coming into the city and suspects that some of the Montanists may be hiding in them. The stone walls looked soft enough to carve, and John wonders whether there might be some rock-cut dwellings in the vicinity, perhaps a monastery or something that can be turned into a monastery.

A number of soldiers with torches have followed John into the basilica. One of them almost runs down a flight of steps and calls out to say that he has found something interesting. John and the others also go down the steps but more slowly and more carefully than the young soldier with the torch. There before them, in the crypt, is a large marble shrine. As they come closer, they can read the inscription: "The tomb of Montanus and the women."[2]

Suddenly all of John of Amida's weariness is gone. He is no longer tired, no longer going through the motions of his mission. Within grasp are the bones of one of the most notorious heretics of all time. John cannot believe his good fortune. He *is* in the right place. This is the basilica of the Montanist patriarch. Contrary to the reports he has heard, the bones of Montanus and his associates had not been burned in the time of Justin, the uncle and predecessor of his own emperor Justinian. He can't wait to burn the foul bones himself.

John orders the soldiers to break open the shrine. As they begin doing so, there are loud noises on the steps behind them. John looks around to see a crowd of people rush down the steps. The Montanists of Pepouza, apparently, have neither committed mass suicide nor gone into hiding. They say nothing but stand silently in the crypt. The only sound now is that of axes and hammers breaking open the shrine. Inside the shrine is a huge sarcophagus made with plates of iron, sealed with lead. The soldiers have great difficulty breaking the lead seals. Finally, they take the iron lid off the sarcophagus. It takes four men to lift the lid and place it on the mosaic floor of the crypt.

John and some of the Montanists approach the iron coffin. As he peers inside, John sees four mummified bodies. He had expected to find three bodies, not four. He wonders who the fourth person is. No doubt another Montanist prophet or prophetess, he surmises. The other three, he is certain, are Montanus, Maximilla, and Priscilla.

Each of the corpses has a thin oval-shaped disk of gold placed over its mouth. John has opened countless graves and seen dozens of corpses with gold disks, or gold coins, placed over their eyes. But he has never seen gold disks placed over the mouths of the deceased. He wonders whether it is common practice in this part of Phrygia for people to be buried with gold coins or disks on their mouths. The gold on the mouths of the corpses before him also makes him think of his namesake John, the archbishop of Constantinople. More than a century ago John was such a great orator that he was nicknamed Chrysostom, "Golden-mouthed." Perhaps the Montanists who buried their founding prophets and prophetesses considered the alleged mouthpieces of the Paraclete equally "golden-mouthed."

Most likely John will never know the answer to the puzzle of the golden disks, so he shrugs his shoulders and turns to the nearest Montanist and, pointing to the largest of the corpses, says:

> Are you not ashamed that you are going astray after this abomination, and you are calling him "Spirit" although a spirit does not have flesh and bones?[3]

One of the Montanists, an old man with a long beard, is at first puzzled by the question. Then the old Montanist realizes that the man in an abbot's cassock who had asked him the question must assume, as many of the opponents of the New Prophecy do, that Montanists equate Montanus with the Paraclete, the Holy Spirit. The old Montanist tells Abbot John firmly that he is not at all surprised to see the *bodies* of Montanus and the others. Montanus is not, and never has been, called Spirit, Holy Spirit, or Paraclete by adherents of the New Prophecy. Montanus, like Maximilla, Priscilla, Quintilla, and the other prophets and prophetesses of the movement, was merely one of the human instruments of the Spirit—not the Spirit itself.

John has little interest in the Montanist leader's explanation of the relationship between Montanus and the Holy Spirit. All John knows and cares about is that Montanus and those buried with him were heretics. He tells the nearest soldier with a torch to throw his torch into the sarcophagus. The room is still lit by the candles surrounding the shrine and by the torches carried by some of the other soldiers. For a moment, an eerie stillness hangs in the air. Then the soldier throws his torch and there is the sound of crackling, as a remnant of the centuries-old robe in which Montanus was buried catches fire. The flames spread to the other corpses in the coffin and the putrid odor of burning mummified bodies fills the overcrowded crypt. The Montanists in the room start to weep, at first silently, and then more and more audibly, until their high-pitched keening almost shatters John's old eardrums. Some of the Montanists are screaming out that the end of the world is about to come. The Montanists' grief, mourning, and apocalyptic predictions are so intense that John fears that if he doesn't get them out of the crypt, they will all willingly perish in the flames consuming the bodies of their founders.

It takes all the skill the soldiers in the crypt can muster to force the mourning and weeping Montanists up the steps. One soldier remains behind to ensure that the fire does its job—and nothing more. John does not want the fire to spread to the rest of the building.

Back inside the nave of the basilica, John sends the soldiers off to find Montanist books, which the emperor, by edict, has forbidden anyone to possess. Before long, the soldiers come back with a few codices and old papyrus rolls. John orders that the books be taken outside and thrown onto a pile of kindling wood. While the Montanists continue to watch and weep, John consigns all their precious books, including those containing the oracles of Montanus, Maximilla, and Priscilla, to the flames.

Only one task remains for John to do at this particular Montanist basilica. He walks back inside the church with four of the soldiers, each carrying a lit torch. John sends the four soldiers to the four corners of the church and asks them to apply their torches ceremoniously, but briefly, to those corners. Not sufficient to do any serious damage but to symbolize that the building is being purified by fire. John then stands in the middle of the chancel and pronounces the words of exorcism, casting out all evil spirits from the church. Next, he takes the censer he has brought with him and twists its brass cover to let in more oxygen so that the incense will flow freely. He walks around the chancel swinging the censer. Almost at a run, he walks the full length of the nave, filling the building with orthodox incense.

In confiscating their most important basilica, a church whose status—but not architectural splendor—rivals, at least for them, St. Peter's in Rome and the Hagia Sophia in Constantinople, John knows he is depriving the Montanists of their future. By burning their books, he is depriving them of their prophetic tradition. By burning the bones of their founders, he is depriving them of their physical link to the past. John is overjoyed with his threefold accomplishment. Montanism, the New Prophecy, will never survive the death blows he has dealt it today in Pepouza. The few remaining Montanists, whose weeping and mourning pierce the air outside the church, are the last Montanists to exist anywhere, and tomorrow he will begin to convert, instruct, and baptize them so they will be orthodox Christians. The New Prophecy is as dead as its founders and like them, after the burning of their bones, will leave almost no evidence that it ever existed.[4]

Sources:

John of Ephesus, *Hist. eccl.* 3.36–37; Procopius, *Hist. arc.* 11.13–23; *Cod. justin.* 1.5.18–21; *IMont* 1 = Pseudo-Dionysius of Tell Maḥrē, *Chron.* [entry for year 861 of Seleucid era, i.e., 550 C.E.]; *IMont* 2 = Michael the Syrian, *Chron.* 9.33 [entry not dated, but inserted between entries dated by the 27th and 29th year of Justinian I, i.e., between 554/5 and 556/7 C.E. = 555 C.E.].

Notes

1. Because in 558 he was consecrated as the Monophysite bishop of Ephesus, John of Amida (ca. 507–ca. 588), also referred to as John of Asia, is best known as John of Ephesus. In this chapter, however, he is still referred to as John of Amida because the events described occurred in 550, eight years before his consecration. Even after he became Monophysite bishop of Ephesus, John continued to live at Sycae, on the outskirts of Constantinople where, since 541, he had been abbot of the Monastery of Mar Mara (St. Mara).

2. *IMont* 2 (Tabbernee 1997b, 38).

3. *IMont* 2 (Tabbernee 1997b, 38).

4. John's mission to convert pagans, heretics, and Jews in Asia Minor did not stop at Pepouza. According to his own account, he devoted altogether thirty years of his life to his mission, converting seventy thousand people, building ninety-eight churches, turning seven synagogues into churches, and establishing twelve monasteries (John of Ephesus, *Hist. eccl.* 3.36–37). No doubt some of the churches and monasteries were confiscated,

purified, and re-consecrated buildings or structures, rather than new constructions. Such, at least, as appears to have been the case with respect to the Montanist cathedral in Pepouza and possibly with respect to another Montanist church and perhaps the monastery at Pepouza, On the archaeological remains of what may well have been the Montanist cathedral and its crypt and of the monastery at Pepouza, see Tabbernee and Lampe 2008, 209–30, 248–53. For a discussion of the anti-Montanist legislation of Justinian I (527–565), see Tabbernee 2007, 325–28. On the shrine at Pepouza containing the bones of Montanus, Maximilla, Priscilla, and a fourth Montanist dignitary, see Tabbernee 1997b, 28–47.

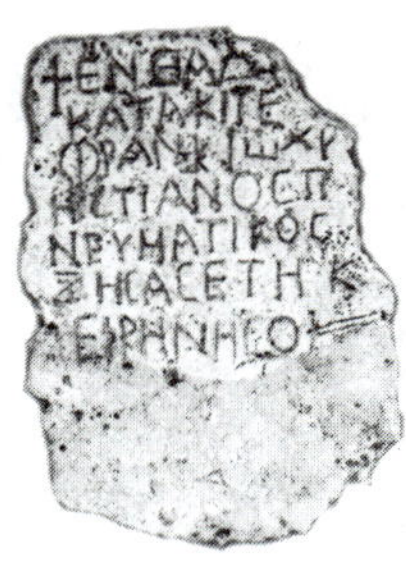

Epilogue

Pepouza, Phrygia, 787 C.E.

A people forgotten

The two middle-aged men are weary. It has been a long and tiring journey to Nicaea and back. They are glad they went but are also very glad to be almost home again.

Euthymius, the abbot of the monastery at Pepouza, and Theophylactus, senior member of the governing body of the monastery, are delighted that they were invited to participate in the Second Council of Nicaea—the first large council held at Nicaea since the one convened by the emperor Constantine many centuries ago. That council had produced the Nicene Creed, which Euthymius and Theophylactus recite each Sunday together with the other monks during the eucharistic liturgy. The council they have just attended didn't formulate a new creed, but it did produce a number of dogmatic decrees. Theophylactus remembers feeling very proud as he affixed his signature to those decrees. He wrote slowly and deliberately: *Theophylactus praeses Pepuzon.*[1] Euthymius was not at that particular session of the council, but earlier he too had signed his name and ecclesiastical title on the list of bishops and abbots attending the council: *Euthymius hegumenus Pepuzentium,*[2] he had written.

The journey back to Pepouza has been made more pleasant by the conversation the two men have had about the people they met at the council and the ideas they discussed. If only they could have such conversations at home in their rock-cut monastery located high above the Sindros River in the beautiful canyon near Pepouza. Most of their fellow monks are simple men, ignorant about the finer points of theology. Perhaps loving God, praying, and working hard are all that is really important, Euthymius confides to Theophylactus: *ora et labora,* prayer and work.

For the past few hours, they have been on a more or less level road, traversing the southern reaches of a vast agricultural plain. The two men have timed the last part of their journey well. They walk past the ancient necropolis, the cemetery of Pepouza, in the middle of the afternoon. Theophylactus, in particular, doesn't like being in the vicinity of the cemetery late in the day, when tall shadows give the allusion of ghost-like beings among the tombs. As they begin to walk down the dusty zigzagging road and descend into the river valley below, they see the dome-shaped mountain on the other side of the canyon disappear. Although they have lived here all of their adult lives, neither one knows anything about that mountain. It must have been important to someone or some group of people in days gone by as it dominates the landscape, but no one has ever told them who that someone or that group might have been.

Euthymius and Theophylactus turn right at the fork in the road, not taking the left one that leads past a row of tenement houses, to the bridge crossing the Sindros. The road veering to the right goes through the center of Pepouza and then follows the river to their monastery. They stop at the basilica. It is a beautiful building with a crypt below it. They have heard rumors that the crypt once housed a large marble shrine and that the shrine, likewise, contained a huge sarcophagus with the bones of some important people. Who those important people were neither Euthymius nor Theophylactus knows. The men have heard that the basilica once belonged to a heretical group of Christians—but they have no idea who those heretics were.[3]

Out of the corner of his eye, Euthymius spots something on the ground near the basilica. The item is covered with soil. As he picks it up, he sees that

Figure E.1: A bread stamp found at Pepouza

it is a baked clay bread stamp—an implement used in making small loaves of eucharistic bread. The bread stamp has a small handle that protrudes from the center of a circular disk. He turns the disk over and sees that it is divided into four quadrants, representing a *panis quadratus*—eucharistic bread, scored so it can be divided into four pieces. Each quadrant has a cross within it. They are interesting crosses, shaped like Latin crosses but with ball-like circles at the end of each of the arms. Examining the bread stamp more closely, Euthymius has a strange feeling that it may have been there for centuries, covered by soil and only recently dislodged by the feet of people such as he and Theophylactus. He wonders when and by whom the bread stamp was made. Could it have been used by the heretics who built and once occupied the basilica? If only he knew who they were.

Before setting out with Theophylactus for their monastery, located a little further along the same road, Euthymius replaces the bread stamp where he found it, carefully recovering it with soil. He has no need of it, and it seems more fitting to leave it in its involuntary hiding place—perhaps for a few more centuries.[4]

Sources:

Mansi 1761–1762, 13.153, 13.631C.

Notes

1. Mansi 1761–1762, 13.631C.

2. Mansi 1761–1762, 13.153. On Euthymius and Theophylactus and their monastery at Pepouza, see Tabbernee and Lampe 2008, 19–20, 209–30, 250–53.

3. The anti-Montanist activities of John of Amida/Ephesus at Pepouza in 550, described in Chapter 38, ended the New Prophecy movement in Phrygia—Montanism's last foothold within Christianity. A report that the Byzantine emperor Leo III (717–741) in 721/2 attempted to baptize Montanists by force but was foiled in the attempt by the Montanists incinerating themselves and their churches (Theophanes, *Chron.* AM 6214) is not only suspect because of its similarity to Procopius' account of what Montanists allegedly did in the time of Justinian's persecution of them (see Chapter 38) but also because the term "Montanists" here may have been a Byzantine nickname for a particular group of Jews who had some supposed similarities to or affinities with the earlier, but by then extinct, Montanists; see Sharf 1966, 37–46 and Tabbernee 2007, 398–99. Exactly how much Euthymius and Theophylactus knew about the earlier history of Pepouza and its importance as the center of Montanism is impossible to determine. Local tradition probably kept some information circulating in the area for the more than two centuries which separated the time of Euthymius and Theophylactus from the time when the last Montanists lived in Pepouza. Even today, twelve centuries later still, distorted oral traditions among the villagers of Karayakuplu, the Turkish village 1.2 km N.E. of the site of Pepouza, relate that the ancient city in the valley of the Banaz Çayı (Sindros) was the home of Christian holy men—and that Jesus and his apostles even visited it!

4. The bread stamp described in the Epilogue remained unnoticed, covered by dirt until September 2001 when it was discovered by one of the members of our team during the archaeological surface survey of Pepouza (Tabbernee and Lampe 2008, 188–89).

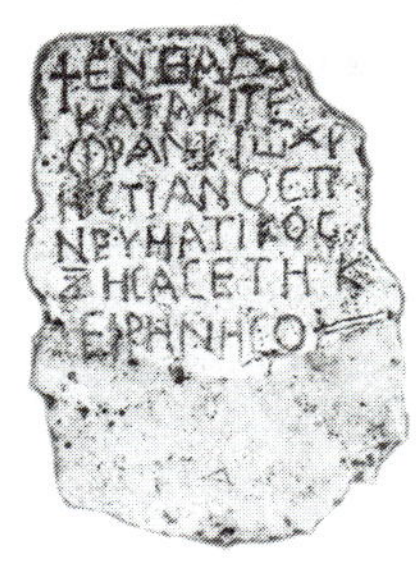

Bibliography

Aland, Kurt. 1955. "Der Montanismus und die kleinasiatische Theologie." *Zeitschrift für die neutestamentliche Wissenschaft und die Kunde der älteren Kirche* 46:109–16.

———. 1960. "Bemerkungen zum Montanismus und zur frühchristlichen Eschatologie." Pp. 105–48 in idem, *Kirchengeschichtliche Entwürfe: Alte Kirche, Reformation und Luthertum, Pietismus und Erweckungsbewegung*. Gütersloh: Mohn.

Amat, Jacqueline. 1996. *Passion de Perpétue et de Félicité suivi des Actes: Introduction, texte critique, traduction, commentaire et index*. Sources chrétiennes 417. Paris: Cerf.

Barnes, Timothy D. 1968. "Pre-Decian *acta martyrum*." *Journal of Theological Studies*, NS 19:509–31.

———. 1981. *Constantine and Eusebius*. Cambridge, Mass.: Harvard University Press.

———. 1985. *Tertullian: A Historical and Literary Study*. Re-issued [from the 1971 ed.] with corrections and a postscript. Oxford: Clarendon.

Basso, Michele. 1986. *Guide to the Vatican Necropolis*. Vatican City: Fabbrica di S. Pietro in Vaticano.

Bauer, Walter. 1971. *Orthodoxy and Heresy in Earliest Christianity*. Edited and translated by Robert A. Kraft, Gerhard Krodel et al. Philadelphia, Pa.: SCM.

Beckwith, Roger T. 2005. *Calendar, Chronology and Worship: Studies in Ancient Judaism and Early Christianity*. Ancient Judaism and Early Christianity 61. Leiden: Brill, 2005.

Berruto Martone, Anna Maria. 1999. *Dialogo tra un Montanista e un Ortodosso*. Bologna: Edizioni Dehoniane Bologna.

Boeckh, August. 1828–1877. *Corpus inscriptionum graecarum*. 4 vols. Berlin: Reimer. [Abbr.: *CIG*]

Bonwetsch, G. Nathanael. 1881. *Die Geschichte des Montanismus*. Erlangen: Deichert.

Braun, René. 1962. "*Deus Christianorum*": *Recherches sur le vocabulaire doctrinal de Tertullien*. Publications de la faculté des lettres et sciences humaines d'Alger 41. Paris: Presses Universaires de France.

———. 1974. "*Chronologica Tertullianae:* Le *De Carne Christi* et le *De Idolatria*." *Annales de la Faculté des Lettres et Sciences humaines de Nice* 231:271–81.

Brent, Allen. 1995. *Hippolytus and the Roman Church in the Third Century: Communities in Tension before the Emergence of a Monarch-Bishop.* Supplements to Vigiliae christianae 31. Leiden: Brill.

Bundy, David. 1989/90. "*The Life of Abercius:* Its Significance for Early Syriac Christianity." *The Second Century* 7:163–76.

Burgess, R. W. 1997. "The Dates and Editions of Eusebius' *Chronici canones* and *Historia ecclesiastica.*" *Journal of Theological Studies,* NS 48:471–504.

Buschmann, Gerd. 1995. "Χριστοῦ κοινωνός—(MartPol 6,2): Das Martyrium und der ungeklärte κοινωνός—Titel der Montanisten." *Zeitschrift für die neutestamentliche Wissenschaft und die Kunde der älteren Kirche* 86 (1995): 243–64.

Butler, Rex D. 2006. *The New Prophecy & "New Visions": Evidence of Montanism in* The Passion of Perpetua and Felicitas. North American Patristics Society. North American Patristic[s] Society Patristic Monograph Series 18. Washington, D.C.: Catholic University of America Press.

Calder, William M. 1908. "A Fourth Century Lycaonian Bishop." *Expositor,* 7th ser. 6:385–408.

———. 1922/3. "Philadelphia and Montanism," *Bulletin of the John Rylands University Library of Manchester* 7:309–53.

Carriker, Andrew J. 2003. *The Library of Eusebius of Caesarea.* Supplements to Vigiliae christianae 67. Leiden: Brill.

Carrington, Philip. 1957. *The Early Christian Church.* 2 vols. Cambridge: Cambridge University Press.

Cerrato, John A. 2002. *Hippolytus between East and West: The Commentaries and the Provenance of the Corpus.* Oxford Theological Monographs. Oxford: Oxford University Press.

Claridge, Amanda with Contributions by Judith Toms and Tony Cubberley. 1998. *Rome: An Archaeological Guide.* Oxford Archaeological Guides. Oxford: Oxford University Press.

Clarke, Graeme W. 1989. *The Letters of St. Cyprian of Carthage.* Vol. 4. Ancient Christian Writers 47. New York: Newman.

Davies, J. G. 1955. "Tertullian: *De Resurrectione Carnis LXIII:* A Note on the Origins of Montanism." *Journal of Theological Studies,* NS 6:90–94.

Delehaye, Hippolyte. 1921. "Martyr et confesseur." Analecta Bollandiana 39:20–49.

Döllinger, Johann J. I. von. 1876. *Hippolytus and Callistus.* Translated by Alfred Pummer. Edinburgh: T. & T. Clark.

Dunn, Geoffrey D. 2004. *Tertullian.* The Early Church Fathers. London: Routledge.

Ehrman, Bart D., ed. and trans. 2003. *The Apostolic Fathers.* 2 vols. Loeb Classical Library 24–25. Cambridge, Mass.: Harvard University Press.

Eisen, Ute E. 2000. *Women Officeholders in Early Christianity: Epigraphical and Literary Studies.* Translated by Linda M. Maloney. Collegeville, Minn.: Liturgical Press.

Elm, Susanna. 1989. "Perceptions of Jerusalem Pilgrimage as Reflected in Two Early Sources on Female Pilgrimage." Studia patristica 20:219–23.

———. 1994. "Montanist Oracles." Pp. 131–38 in *Searching the Scriptures: A Feminist Commentary*. Vol. 2. Edited by Elisabeth Schüssler Fiorenza. New York: Crossroad.

Ferrua, Antonio. 1955. "Una nuova iscrizione montanista." *Rivista di archeologia cristiana* 31:97–100.

Finegan, Jack. 1992. *The Archeology of the New Testament: The Life of Jesus and the Beginning of the Early Church*. Rev. ed. Princeton, N.J.: Princeton University Press.

Fishwick, Duncan. 1972. "The Temple of the Three Gauls." *Journal of Roman Studies* 62:46–52.

———. 1987–2005. *The Imperial Cult in the Latin West: Studies in the Ruler Cult of the Western Provinces of the Roman Empire*. 3 vols. Leiden: Brill.

Frend, William H. C. 1961. "The 'Seniores Laici' and the Origins of the Church in North Africa." *Journal of Theological Studies*, NS 12:280–84.

———. 1965. *Martyrdom and Persecution in the Early Church: A Study of a Conflict from the Maccabees to Donatus*. Oxford: Blackwell.

———. 1974. "Open Questions Concerning the Christians and the Roman Empire in the Age of the Severi." *Journal of Theological Studies*, NS 25:333–51.

———. 1984. *The Rise of Christianity*. London: Darton, Longman & Todd.

———. 2003. *From Dogma to History: How our Understanding of the Early Church Developed*. London: SCM.

Froehlich, Karlfried. 1973. "Montanism and Gnosis." Pages 91–111 in *The Heritage of the Early Church: Essays in Honor of the Very Reverend Georges Vasilievich Florovsky on the Occasion of his Eightieth Birthday*. Edited by David Neiman and Margaret Schatkin. Rome: Pontificia Institutum Studiorum Orientalium.

Gamble, Harry Y. 1995. *Books and Readers in the Early Church: A History of Early Christian Texts*. New Haven, Conn.: Yale University Press.

Grant, Robert M. 1968. "Church History in the Early Church." Pp. 287–306 in *Transitions in Biblical Scholarship*. Essays in Divinity 6. Edited by J. Coert Rylaarsdam. Chicago: Chicago University Press.

———. 1971. *From Augustus to Constantine: The Thrust of the Christian Movement into the Roman World*. London: Collins.

———. 1988. *Greek Apologists of the Second Century*. Philadelphia, Pa.: Westminster.

———. 2003. *Second-Century Christianity: A Collection of Fragments*. 2d ed. Louisville, Ky.: Westminster John Knox.

Grégoire, Henri and Paul Orgels. 1951. "La passion de S. Théodote d'Ancyre, oeuvre du pseudo-Nil, et son noyau montaniste." *Byzantinische Zeitschrift* 44:165–84.

Groh, Dennis E. 1985. "Utterance and Exegesis: Biblical Interpretation in the Montanist Crisis." Pp. 73–95 in *The Living Text: Essays in Honor of Ernest*

W. Saunders. Edited by Dennis E. Groh and Robert Jewett. Lanham Md.: University Press of America.

Guarducci, Margherita. 1967–1978. *Epigrafia greca*. 4 vols. Rome: Istituto poligrafico dello Stato, Libreria dello Stato. [Abbr.: *EG*]

Harnack, Adolf. 1908. *The Mission and Expansion of Christianity in the First Three Centuries*. 2 vols. Second enlarged and revised edition. Translated and edited by James Moffatt. Theological Translation Library 20. New York: Putnam's Sons.

———[von]. 1999. *Marcion: The Gospel of the Alien God*. Translated from the 2d. [German] ed. [1924]. Durham, N.C.: Labyrinth.

Haspels, Caroline H. E. 1971. *The Highlands of Phrygia: Sites and Monuments*. 2 vols. Princeton, N.J.: Princeton University Press.

Hauken, Tor, Cumhur Tanrıver, and Kazım Akbıyıkoğlu. 2003. "A New Inscription from Phrygia." *Epigraphica Anatolica* 36:33–43.

Head, Barclay V. 1887. *Historia numorum: A Manual of Greek Numismatics*. Oxford: Clarendon.

Heine, Ronald E. 1987. "The Role of the Gospel of John in the Montanist Controversy." *Second Century* 6:1–19.

———. 1989a. "The Gospel of John and the Montanist Debate in Rome." Studia patristica 21:95–100.

———. 1989b. *The Montanist Oracles and Testimonia*. North American Patristic[s] Society. North American Patristic[s] Society Patristic Monograph Series 14. Macon, Ga.: Mercer University Press/Washington, D.C.: Catholic University of America Press.

———. 1998. Review of William Tabbernee, *Montanist Inscriptions and Testimonia: Epigraphic Sources Illustrating the History of Montanism*. *Journal of Theological Studies*, NS 49:824–27.

Hemer, Colin J. 1986. *The Letters to the Seven Churches of Asia in Their Local Setting*. JSNTSup 11. Sheffield: JSOT Press.

Hilgenfeld, Adolf. 1884. *Die Ketzergeschichte des Urchristentums*. Leipzig: Fues.

Hirschmann, Vera-Elisabeth [Vera]. 2000. "Untersuchungen zur Grabschrift des Aberkios." *Zeitschrift für Papyrologie und Epigraphik* 129:109–16.

———. 2003. "Ungelöste Rätsel?: Nochmals zur Grabschrift des Aberkios." *Zeitschrift für Papyrologie und Epigraphik* 145:133–39.

———. 2004. "'Nach Art der Engel': Die phrygische Prophetin Nanas." *Epigraphica Anatolica* 37:160–67.

———. 2005. *Horrenda Secta: Untersuchungen zum frühchristlichen Montanismus und seinen Verbindungen zur paganen Religion Phrygiens*. Historia Einzelschriften 179. Stuttgart: Steiner.

Hoffmann, Adolf. 1998. "The Roman Remodeling of the Asklepeion." Pages 41–60 in *Pergamon: Citadel of the Gods*. Edited by Helmut Koester. Harvard Theological Studies 46. Harrisburg, Pa.: Trinity Press International.

Jensen, Anne. 1996. *God's Self-Confident Daughters: Early Christianity and the Liberation of Women*. Translated by O. C. Dean, Jr. Louisville, Ky.: Westminster John Knox.

Jensen, Robin M. 2000. *Understanding Early Christian Art*. London: Routledge.

———. (forthcoming). "'With Pomp, Apparatus, Novelty and Avarice': Alternative Baptismal Practices in Roman Africa." Studia patristica (forthcoming).

Kearsley, Rosalinde A. 1992. "The Epitaph of Aberkios: The Earliest Christian Inscription?" *NewDocs* 6:177–81.

Kelly, John N. D. 1972. *Early Christian Creeds.* 3d ed. New York: McKay.

Keresztes, Paul. 1970. "The *Constitutio Antoniniana* and the Persecutions under Caracalla." *American Journal of Philology* 91:446–59.

———. 1989. *Imperial Rome and the Christians.* 2 vols. Lanham, N.Y.: University Press of America.

King, Karen L. 2003. *What is Gnosticism?* Cambridge, Mass.: The Bellknap Press of Harvard University Press.

Kirschbaum, Engelbert. 1959. *The Tombs of St. Peter and St. Paul.* Translated by John Murray. London: Secker & Warburg.

Klijn, Albertus F. J. and Gerrit J. Reinink. 1973. *Patristic Evidence for Jewish Christian Sects.* NovTSup 36. Leiden: Brill.

Labriolle, Pierre de. 1913a. *La crise montaniste.* Paris: Leroux.

———. 1913b. *Les sources de l'histoire du montanisme: Textes grecs, latins, syriaques.* Paris: Leroux.

Lampe, Peter. 2003. *From Paul to Valentinus: Christians at Rome in the First Two Centuries.* Translated by Michael Steinhauser. Edited by Marshall D. Johnson. Minneapolis, Minn.: Fortress.

Lampe, Peter and William Tabbernee. 2004. "Das Reskript von Septimius Severus und Caracalla an die Kolonen der kaiserlichen Domäne von Tymion und Simoe." *Epigraphica Anatolica* 37:169–78.

Lane Fox, Robin. 1987. *Pagans and Christians.* New York: Knopf.

La Piana, George. 1925. "The Roman Church at the End of the Second Century." *Harvard Theological Review* 18:201–77.

———. 1927. "Foreign Groups in Rome during the First Centuries of the Empire." *Harvard Theological Review* 20:183–394.

Lipsius, Richard A. 1865. *Zur Quellenkritik des Epiphanios.* Vienna: Braumüller.

Madigan, Kevin and Carolyn Osiek, eds. and trans. 2005. *Ordained Women in the Early Church: A Documentary History.* Baltimore, Md.: Johns Hopkins University Press.

Mansi, Giovanni Domenico. 1761–1762. *Sacrorum conciliorum nova et amplissima collectio.* Florence: Expensis Antonii Zatta.

Manson, Thomas W. 1957. "Martyrs and Martyrdom." *Bulletin of the John Rylands University Library of Manchester* 39:463–84.

McGinn, Sheila E. 1997. "The 'Montanist' Oracles and Prophetic Theology." Studia patristica 31:128–35.

McGowan, Andrew. 1999. *Ascetic Eucharists: Food and Drink in Early Christian Ritual Meals.* Oxford: Clarendon.

———. 2006. "Tertullian and the 'Heretical' Origins of the 'Orthodox' Trinity." *Journal of Early Christian Studies* 14:437–57.

McGuckin, John A., ed. 2004. *The Westminster Handbook to Origen.* Louisville, Ky.: Westminster John Knox Press.

Merdinger, Jane E. 1997. *Rome and the African Church in the Time of Augustine.* New Haven, Conn.: Yale University Press.

Merkelbach, Reinhold. 1997. "Grabepigramm und Vita des Bishofs Aberkios von Hierapolis." *Epigraphica Anatolica* 28:125–39.

Mitchell, Margaret M. "Looking for Abercius: Reimagining Contexts of Interpretation of the 'Earliest Christian Inscription'." Pages 303–35 in *Commemorating the Dead.* Edited by Laura Brink and Deborah Green. Berlin: Walter de Gruyter.

Mitchell, Stephen. 1982. "The Life of Saint Theodotus of Ancyra." *Anatolian Studies* 32:93–113.

———. 1993. *Anatolia: Land, Men, and Gods in Asia Minor.* 2 vols. Oxford: Clarendon.

———. 2005. "An Apostle to Ankara from the New Jerusalem: Montanists and Jews in Late Roman Asia." *Scripta classica Israelica* 25:207–23.

Musurillo, Herbert, ed. and trans. 1972. *The Acts of the Christian Martyrs.* Oxford: Clarendon.

Nasrallah, Laura S. 2003. *"An Ecstasy of Folly": Prophecy and Authority in Early Christianity.* Harvard Theological Studies 52. Cambridge, Mass.: Cambridge University Press.

Nissen, Theodor. 1912. *S. Abercii vita.* Bibliotheca scriptorum graecorum et romanorum Teubneriana. Leipzig: Teubner.

Nohlen, Klaus. 1998. "The 'Red Hall' (Kızıl Avlu) in Pergamon." Pages 77–110 in *Pergamon: Citadel of the Gods.* Edited by Helmut Koester. Harvard Theological Studies 46. Harrisburg, Pa.: Trinity Press International.

Noy, David. 2000. Review of William Tabbernee, *Montanist Inscriptions and Testimonia: Epigraphic Sources Illustrating the History of Montanism. Classical Review* 50 (2000): 174–76.

Oliver, J. H. and Robert E. A. Palmer. 1955. "Minutes of an Act of the Roman Senate." *Hesperia* 24:320–49.

Osborn, Eric F. 1997. *Tertullian: First Theologian of the West.* Cambridge: Cambridge University Press.

Pearson, Birger. 1990. *Gnosticism, Judaism, and Egyptian Christianity.* Minneapolis, Minn.: Fortress.

Poirier, John C. 2001. "The Montanist Nature of the Nanas Inscription." *Epigraphica Anatolica* 37:151–59.

Ramsay, William M. 1883. "The Cities and Bishoprics of Phrygia." *Journal of Hellenic Studies* 4:370–436.

———. 1889. "Early Christian Monuments in Phrygia: A Study in the Early History of the Church, V." *Expositor,* 3d ser. 9:392–400.

———. 1895–1897. *The Cities and Bishoprics of Phrygia: Being an Essay of the Local History of Phrygia from the Earliest Times to the Turkish Conquest.* 1 vol. in two parts (cited as 1 and 1,2). Oxford: Clarendon. [Abbr.: *CB* (only when cited by inscription number)]

———. 1904. *The Letters to the Seven Churches of Asia.* London: Hodder & Stoughton.

Ritschl, Friedrich et al. 1862–. *Corpus inscriptionum latinarum*. Berlin: Reimer/Walter de Gruyter. [Abbr.: *CIL*]

Rives, James. 1996. "The Blood Libel against the Montanists." *Vigiliae christianae* 50:117–24.

Robeck, Cecil M. 1992. *Prophecy in Carthage: Perpetua, Tertullian, and Cyprian*. Cleveland, Ohio: Pilgrim.

Salisbury, Joyce E. 1997. *Perpetua's Passion: The Death and Memory of a Young Roman Woman*. New York: Routledge.

Schoedel, William R. 1993. "Papias." *ANRW* 2.27.1:235–70.

Sharf, Andrew. 1966. "The Jews, the Montanists and the Emperor Leo III." *Byzantinische Zeitschrift* 59:37–46.

Shaw, Brent D. 1982. "The Elders of Christian Africa." Pp. 207–26 in *Mélanges offerts en hommage au Révérend père Étienne Gareau*. Ottawa: Éditions de l'Université d'Ottawa.

Staccioli, Romolo A. 2006. *Villas of Ancient Rome*. Translated by Francesca Caruso. Rome: Azienda di Promozione Turistica di Roma.

Stewart-Sykes, Alistair. 2000. "*Vita Polycarpi*: An Ante-Nicene *Vita*." *Augustinianum* 40:21–33.

———. 2002. *The Life of Polycarp: An Anonymous Vita from Third-Century Smyrna*. Early Christian Studies 4. Sydney, Australia: St. Pauls.

Tabbernee, William. 1978. "The Opposition to Montanism from Church and State: A Study of the History and Theology of the Montanist Movement as Shown by the Writings and Legislation of the Orthodox Opponents of Montanism." PhD diss., University of Melbourne.

———. 1985. "Early Montanism and Voluntary Martyrdom." *Colloquium* 17:33–44.

———. 1993. "Montanist Regional Bishops: New Evidence from Ancient Inscriptions." *Journal of Early Christian Studies*: 249–80.

———. 1997a. "Eusebius' 'Theology of Persecution': As Seen in the Various Editions of His Church History." *Journal of Early Christian Studies* 5 (1997): 319–34.

———.1997b. *Montanist Inscriptions and Testimonia: Epigraphic Sources Illustrating the History of Montanism*. North American Patristic[s] Society. North American Patristic[s] Society Patristic Monograph Series 16. Macon, Ga.: Mercer University Press/Washington, D.C.: Catholic University of America Press. [Abbr.: *IMont* (only when cited by inscription number)]

———. 1997c. "'Our Trophies are Better than your Trophies': The Appeal to Tombs and Reliquaries in Montanist-Orthodox Relations." Studia patristica 33:206–17.

———. 2000a. "Noiseless Books and Pilfered Manuscripts: Early Christian Desk-Top Publishing in Carthage." Paper presented at the annual meeting of the North American Patristic[s] Society on May 27, 2000 at Chicago, Ill.

———. 2000b. "'A Species of Fornication': Tertullian's Polemic against Remarriage among Christians." Paper presented at the annual meeting of the American Academy of Religion/Society of Biblical Literature on November 20, 2000, at Nashville, Tenn.

———. 2001a. "To Pardon or Not to Pardon?: North African Montanism and the Forgiveness of Sins." Studia patristica 36:375–86.

———. 2001b. "'Will the Real Paraclete Please Speak Forth!': The Catholic Montanist Conflict over Pneumatology." Pp. 97–118 in *Advents of the Spirit: An Introduction to the Current Study of Pneumatology.* Edited by Bradford E. Hinze and D. Lyle Dabney. Milwaukee, Wisc.: Marquette University Press.

———. 2003. "Portals of the New Jerusalem: The Discovery of Pepouza and Tymion." *Journal of Early Christian Studies* 11:87–94.

———. 2005. "Perpetua, Montanism, and Christian Ministry in Carthage in *c.*203 C.E." *Perspectives in Religious Studies* 32:421–41.

———. 2006a. "Recognizing the Spirit: Second-generation Montanist Oracles." Studia patristica 40:521–26.

———. 2006b. Review of Hirschmann. *Horrenda Secta: Untersuchungen zum frühchristlichen Montanismus und seinen Verbindungen zur paganen Religion Phrygiens.* In *Journal of Early Christian Studies* 14:537–38.

———. 2007. *Fake Prophecy and Polluted Sacraments: Ecclesiastical and Imperial Reactions to Montanism.* Leiden: Brill.

Tabbernee, William and Peter Lampe. 2008. *Pepouza and Tymion: The Discovery and Archaeological Exploration of a Lost Ancient City and an Imperial Estate.* Berlin: Walter de Gruyter.

Temporini, Hildegard and Wolfgang Haase, eds. 1972–. *Aufstieg und Niedergang der romischen Welt: Geschichte und Kultur Roms in Spiegel der neueren Forschung.* Berlin: Walter de Gruyter. [Abbr.: *ANRW*]

Thurston, Bonnie B. 1989. *The Widows: A Women's Ministry in the Early Church.* Minneapolis, Minn.: Fortress.

Tilley, Maureen A. 1994. "The Passion of Perpetua and Felicity." Pp. 829–58 in *Searching the Scriptures: A Feminist Commentary.* Vol. 2. Edited by Elisabeth Schüssler Fiorenza. New York: Crossroad.

Trevett, Christine. 1996. *Montanism: Gender, Authority and the New Prophecy.* Cambridge: Cambridge University Press.

———. 1999. "'Angelic Visitations and Speech She Had': Nanas of Kotiaeion." Pp. 259–77 in *Prayer and Spirituality in the Early Church.* Vol. 2. Edited by Pauline Allen, Wendy Mayer, and Lawrence Cross. Everton Park, Queensland, Australia: Centre for Early Christian Studies.

Williams, Michael A. 1996. *Rethinking "Gnosticism": An Argument for Dismantling a Dubious Category.* Princeton, N.J.: Princeton University Press.

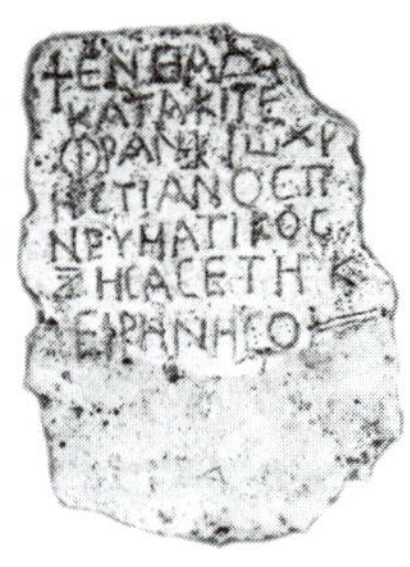

General Index

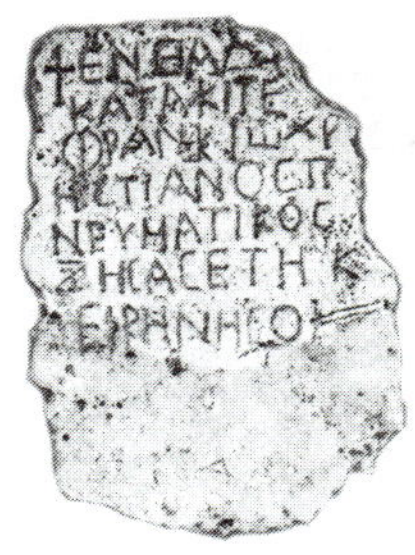

Index of Ancient Sources

Jewish, Greek, and Roman Texts

Legislation

ECCLESIASTICAL

IMPERIAL

Inscriptions